To Reb & family
With love
Betty Balsam.

The Crescent Moon

The Crescent Moon

Betty Balsam

Windsor House Publishing Group
Austin, Texas

The Crescent Moon

Written by Betty Balsam

Edited by Willa C. Gray

Printing History
First Edition March, 1998

ISBN: 1-881636-07-0
Library of Congress Card Number: 98-060399

Windsor House Publishing Group, Inc.
11901 Hobby Horse Court, Suite 1516
Austin, TX 78758

PRINTED IN THE UNITED STATES OF AMERICA
10 9 8 7 6 5 4 3 2 1

Dedication

To my husband and
son Edward

Chapter 1

A representative from the U.S. Embassy in Tehran was waiting for her in the V.I.P. lounge at Mehrabad airport. He said, "My name is Jim Talbot. I'm here on behalf of the American Embassy It's my duty to inform you that the moment you step on Iranian soil, which is when you leave this lounge, there is nothing we can do to help you if you run into trouble."

This was Andrea's first trip overseas. Her husband received a telephone call from Iran and ten days later she, Mani and their four-year-old daughter, Kelly, were on their way. She and Kelly hadn't taken an eight thousand mile journey and crossed an ocean to be separated from her husband and hear this. The child was heavy but her presence was comforting.

"Why not?"

"Since you're married to an Iranian, you are considered an Iranian citizen by the government of Iran. Your American passport will be seized and replaced with an Iranian passport. Once you have an Iranian passport, you are out of our jurisdiction. If you anticipate trouble, we can help you return home now. Not later."

The only trouble she'd anticipated was finding proper medical care. Kelly was prone to pneumonia because she was born with multiple birth defects. She was hard of hearing, had trouble focusing her eyes and could take few steps at a time. She was confined mostly to her bed or her wheelchair.

"How are we going to take care of Kelly?" she'd asked Mani on the plane.

"We have doctors in my country. Good doctors. Many trained in the best medical centers in the world. Where do you think you're going? To the interior of Africa?"

He didn't have to be so defensive. She hadn't intended for her remark to be a criticism. But then he'd been a bit touchy ever since they'd boarded. Wouldn't she have been the same way?

She looked from Kelly's peaceful face to the face of the emissary.

"I have a loving, caring husband who's also a great father to our daughter. I suspect we'll have some adjusting to do, but with my husband there to help us, it shouldn't be too difficult."

Jim Talbot smiled. "That's what they all say when we warn them. Only that's not how it works. Iranians are like chameleons who blend into their environment. They act totally westernized when they're in a western country but when they return home, they immediately revert to their roots. It's almost as if they never left."

Revert to their roots? What did he mean by that? Mani was not the only Iranian she knew. There was Mani's brother, Sayid, and other Iranians studying at the University of Washington. Mani and Sayid were dashing, handsome men, flashing smiles, intelligent. For a while, she had trouble deciding which brother she was more fond of.

Eventually Mani had won her heart. They'd been happily married for six years. He treated her like a queen. She wasn't worried about him reverting to his roots. Her concern was for Kelly's health and not knowing what the attitude of Iranians toward the handicapped was. She shifted the child's weight to her left shoulder, brushed some hair aside and let her go back to sleep.

"What could go wrong?"

"Women and female children have very few rights. I can't over emphasize the repercussions of that alone. Basically, you and your daughter will be at your husband's mercy. You need his written permission to travel, to take your daughter out of the country or just about anything else you might want to do. If he is like the rest, you'll notice the change almost immediately."

Of course Mani was not like that. He brought her fresh flowers every week, helped do the chores, opened the car door and made sure she was seated before he sat down. He'd never raised his voice or said an unkind word to her, or to anyone else. Kelly was forever catching colds. Whenever she had fever, Mani stayed up all night checking the child's breathing. Yet, he was rude to the flight attendant when he caused her to spill a few drops of Vodka on his pants, had barely talked to her throughout the flight and had left her to tend to Kelly alone after disembarking. Nonsense, she admonished herself. He's human after all. It was a long flight. He's tired, Kelly's tired and I'm tired. The anticipation of seeing his family after seven years, would make anybody nervous.

"I . . . I don't understand."

"Nor did many other American women who married Iranians. That's why we have chosen to warn all newcomers in advance."

His words had an ominous ring to them. The implications were clear. She'd be a virtual prisoner if her husband chose not to cooperate. But her husband was different. And for her, seeing how the rest of the world lived, was an impossible dream come true, a dream she nurtured since she was a child. There was no need for concern. Or was there? Supposing Jim

Talbot was right. Supposing she found herself deprived of rights she was born to and took for granted. What were her options?

This is ridiculous. Not a fair association at all. A gross generalization. A duty the emissary has to perform. There are always exceptions to any rule. There's no doubt in my mind that Mani is not like that. I have yet to meet a gentler, kinder person. Who but Mani would have dashed into a burning house with roaring flames to save the life of an old woman? A total stranger. Everyone who knows him, admires and respects him. Even if Mr. Talbot's claims are true, Mani won't change. He can't. He knows how committed I am to women's rights issues. How hard I fought since I was a teenager in the sixties to advance the cause. And in the seventies, he was by my side at every demonstration, every march, every meeting. Together, we might be able to do the same here. A man of his values and devotion to wife and child, could never become a chameleon. Mr. Talbot might know Iranians better than she did, but he did not know her husband.

"I appreciate your concern. Thank you for your time. Now if there is nothing more, I'd like to join my husband. He'll think we've abandoned him."

"Please. This is your only chance. Take a couple of minutes more and think about what I told you. I know you feel it can't happen to you. If we didn't feel strongly about it, I wouldn't be here talking to you at one in the morning."

It had been a long flight. She was tired. "Excuse me. I believe I've already heard you out. I'm sure my daughter is exhausted. I'd like to leave."

Her voice had been sharper than she'd intended. She smiled at the emissary and said more gently, "You've done your duty. I'm sure we'll be fine."

Jim Talbot had a look of despair on his face. But he said nothing more. He escorted her to the door.

She wasn't prepared for what she saw. There was a sea of people stretching their necks to get a glimpse of her. She scanned the reception room for Mani. He was nowhere to be seen. A large crowd was watching her every move but no one approached her. Then she spotted a familiar face. It was Sayid, her husband's younger brother, walking toward her, a little unsteady, looking older, but Sayid nonetheless.

"Hi there," she said, delighted to see a familiar face. "It's nice to see you."

"Hello. You're looking good."

"Thank you. I feel good. How have you been?"

"Great."

He looks jaundiced, Andrea thought. It must be the fluorescent lights.

Kelly's head slipped down to her chest. She placed the child's head back on her shoulder.

"Do you know where Mani is? I need Kelly's wheelchair. I can't carry her much longer. She's getting heavy."

"Mani left with his friend Farhad. He took the luggage. Was the wheel chair with the luggage?"

"Yes."

Sayid took Kelly from Andrea then directed her to a spot where his mother was waiting. Delighted, Andrea rushed over and embraced her. The mother stood still, staring at her blankly.

Andrea wondered if embracing her was the wrong thing to do or if her mother-in-law was just tired, disappointed or perhaps not feeling well.

"Follow me," Sayid said.

The crowd made way for them to pass.

Sayid pointed to a car parked in front of the exit under a no parking sign.

"What about your mother?" Andrea asked. "How will she get home?"

"You saw the crowd. Someone will give her a ride. I'm afraid this car does not have much of a back seat. Do you mind sitting up front?"

"Not at all. Thank you." It was the latest model convertible Mercedes coupe.

He opened the door for her, helped seat her, then placed Kelly in her lap. He got behind the wheel. His breath was smelling of whisky, his speech was slurred.

He drove like a maniac, his hand on the horn, ignoring traffic lights, oncoming cars, and one way streets. Andrea searched for a seat belt. There was none. She tightened her grip on Kelly.

He must have sensed her discomfort. "Don't be scared. This is the only way to drive here. You're lucky. It's past one in the morning. Traffic is light."

"You call this light?" Her voice shook.

"I hope traffic will be your only concern."

"I'm sorry. I didn't hear what you said."

"Never mind. Just relax. We'll be home soon."

When they arrived, she took a deep breath, relieved they'd made it safely.

The house was filled with relatives and friends.

"It's required by custom," Sayid explained. "Many have traveled hundreds of miles to witness the occasion and to show their respect."

Mani stood in the crowd, the center of attention, talking excitedly, gesturing. He looked completely relaxed. A woman stood near by. She whispered something in Mani's ear. Mani turned around, saw his wife waiting in the hallway. He made his way through the crowd, to his brother. "Could you have the servant take Kelly to her bed, please?" he asked.

Sayid didn' reply. He carried the child up the stairs, to a room immediately to the right of the stairs. Andrea tried to follow him. Mani stopped her. "I'd like you to meet my friends and family. Come with me."

"I'd love to darling. Could I tuck Kelly in bed first?"

"Kelly can wait. All these people have come to show their respect for us. It's not nice to keep them waiting."

"I'll only be a minute."

"Damn."

"Oh, Mani. I'm sure they'll understand a mother wanting to take care of her child, especially after such a long trip."

He gave her an icy glare and walked away.

She climbed the stairs to the room where she saw Sayid take Kelly. Sayid had placed Kelly on a twin bed. Kelly was asleep.

"This is it," he said, spreading his hands out in a circular manner, a half mocking grin on his face. "It's not the Waldorf but then nobody invited you. Did they?"

She didn't answer him. He was struggling to keep his balance. She knew he was drunk. She found it strange. She'd seen him at a number of parties at the University of Washington where he was a student for a year. He'd insisted on nonalcoholic drinks despite repeated urgings from his friends. She figured the excitement of seeing his brother after many years must be too much for him.

She dressed Kelly in her pajamas and tucked her in bed.

"Thanks for the ride and thank you for bringing Kelly up to the room. I have to go downstairs. Mani wants me to meet the guests." She hurried from the room.

Seeing his wife descend the stairs, Mani put on a charming smile. He took her by the arm, went around and introduced her to everyone. She was greeted by warm, curious looks, appraising her every move.

Few spoke English. The formalities over, the wife of a cousin of Mani's, an American, invited Andrea to join her in the living room. She said her name was Irene. She brought tea and assorted pastries for Andrea. "You'll need the energy," she said. "It will probably be morning before the guests leave and you can rest."

Andrea took the tea gratefully and drank it.

"Have you lived here long?" Andrea asked.

"Almost ten years."

"Do you like it?"

"I like it now. I didn't at first. There was too much adjusting to do."

"An emissary from our embassy was at the airport to warn me about that."

"They've had problems. Many find it impossible to adjust. It's not easy. But once you get to know the people, you'll like them. They're friendly, polite, generous. But they do things differently. Not the way you and I are used to doing."

"Irene!" Sayid's voice interrupted their conversation. "My dear Irene, I did not see you at the airport. When did you get here?"

"We were at the airport," Irene said without turning to look at him. "You were too busy at the bar to notice anyone."

"Oh, oh, you've got your claws sharpened again," Sayid laughed heartily at his own joke and walked away.

"I must say," Irene remarked, "for a man who never touched alcohol he sure is making up for lost time."

A couple were leaving. They approached Andrea. They shook hands, said goodbye and left. They spoke Farsi. Andrea answered in English. Irene translated. It bothered Andrea. She'd have to do something about it, soon. The resolve made her feel better.

As though reading her mind, Irene said, "If you plan to live here, do yourself a favor. Learn the language. You'll find it difficult but the people are most obliging. They feel privileged if they can help."

"I certainly will. I plan to enjoy every minute of my stay. Mani hasn't made up his mind yet. He's not sure he wants to settle here. We'll see."

"I'd be very surprised if he didn't. There are lots of opportunities for making money. The country is changing much too fast. There's demand for just about everything. New businesses and service industries mushroom practically overnight. He'd be foolish not to take advantage of an opportunity like this."

"I'm afraid Mani is not much of a businessman."

"Very few are, but they're making fortunes."

"Is that what your husband does? I mean business."

"No. He's a neurosurgeon. I'm a nurse. We met at Johns Hopkins."

"And he likes it here?"

"Sure. It's his country."

"I doubt Mani will. He's thoroughly Americanized."

"I wouldn't bet on it. You'll be amazed how quickly they revert to their roots. You'll have trouble recognizing the man you married."

"Revert to their roots." Andrea wanted to ask her if the change took place soon after boarding a plane bound for home. She said nothing, opting instead to listen and learn.

"We don't live far from here," Irene said. "I'll give you my phone number. Call me."

Andrea smiled gratefully, "Thanks. I'll do that."

"We have to leave. My husband has a full schedule in the morning."

Andrea saw Mani motioning for her to join him. He seemed like his old self again, full of life. A handsome man in his early thirties, with black hair and dark brown eyes stood nearby holding an empty glass. "This is Farhad," Mani said, "My oldest and best friend."

Farhad shook hands, smiled but said nothing.

Mani took Andrea by the arm directing her toward a couple who were getting ready to leave.

They said goodbye to the couple with two sleepy children.

"What time is it?" she asked.

"Three thirty five," he said casually.

"Mani, do you think it would be rude if I went to our room? I feel exhausted and sleepy."

"When we have a houseful of guests. Yes, I'd say it's rude."

"Do you think they'll be leaving soon?"

"Would you like me to open the door and throw them out?"

She stared at him. Irene was right. She already had trouble recognizing the man she'd married.

She sat on the sofa waiting patiently, occasionally startled by her eyelids refusal to stay open.

Another hour passed. Dawn broke. There were still many guests who seemed to be in no hurry to leave. The servants were busy in the kitchen preparing breakfast.

Andrea got up, walked to the foot of the stairs, stopped and said, "I hope everyone forgives me. I'm tired. I have to go to bed. Good night everybody."

As though on cue, a roomful of eyes watched her climb the stairs, an expression of disbelief registered on their faces.

Something, she didn't know what, made her turn and look back. Mani worked his way, through the crowd, toward the stairs. He looked furious.

She reached the room and closed the door.

It was reopened instantly. Mani stood in the doorway, a murderous look in his eyes. His lips twitched. "People have come from miles around just to see us. Is this how you show your appreciation?"

"You should have warned me. I would have prepared myself."

He stepped out and slammed the door shut.

Chapter 2

For the first time in days, the Abbassis did not have visitors. By early afternoon, the bright July sunshine had nudged the temperature into the eighties. The contrast reminded Andrea of home, of Seattle with its gray skies and drizzle. She felt restless, claustrophobic. Because her husband insisted on her presence when there were guests in the house, she did her best to oblige. Despite his cool, almost hostile attitude toward her since leaving the States, she was determined to do everything possible to please him.

She found him with his friend Farhad, in the dining room, having a discussion, their voices barely above a whisper.

"Hi," Andrea said, smiling broadly. "Isn't it a beautiful day?"

"It sure is," Farhad agreed.

Turning to Mani Andrea said, "Darling, Kelly is asleep. I'd like to go for a walk. Would you come with me?"

"I can't. I'm expecting friends."

"Do you need me?"

"No. We're going to discuss business."

"Then it's all right if I go?"

"Fine."

"Do you have a map?"

Farhad burst into laughter. "A map of this city? You must be kidding. Any map will be obsolete before it reaches the printers."

"Is that right?"

"Go see for yourself. The city is changing daily. The demand for housing is unprecedented. Beautiful old buildings are torn down and replaced with monstrous modern apartment complexes. There are new roads carved out to accommodate the landlords building anywhere they find space. The main streets are there, but the government keeps changing the names to honor the Pahlavi dynasty. What good would a map do?"

"I see."

"Stay in the neighborhood," Farhad said. "Don't worry. You won't get lost."

Andrea turned to Mani, "May I talk to you alone for a moment?"

"Anything you have to say to me you can do so in Farhad's presence."

His answer caught her off guard. "I wanted to know if it was all right to leave while Farhad was here. You did say I had to be present when there were guests in the house."

"Farhad is not a guest. He's staying with us for the time being."

"Oh, all right. I'll be back in an hour."

"Take your time." It was Farhad. For reasons she couldn't fathom, she sensed a subtle, controlled hostility in his voice whenever he talked to her.

When she stepped out into the street she realized what Farhad had said about the city changing daily was not an exaggeration, at least not in the immediate neighborhood.

Youssefabad, where the Abbassis had lived for the past thirty years, bustled with construction workers. Apartment buildings, at different stages of construction, could be seen next to shacks. Delivery trucks and cement mixers roared up and down the narrow street. She continued walking. The same pattern repeated itself all over the neighborhood.

Andrea concluded city planning was a luxury the Iranian government preferred to do without.

The noise from the trucks came to an end when the last truck drove away. The street was quiet again. Andrea neared the main street. It was heavily trafficked and noisy. She decided to explore it some other time. She headed down a narrow alley. Sounds of a child sobbing stopped her. She looked around. A little girl stood in a doorway, crying.

She walked over and hugged the child. "What's the matter?" she asked.

The child looked at her with big, tear filled eyes. She said something in Farsi then burst into tears again.

The frustration of not knowing the language irked Andrea. She looked around for a passerby who might be able to help. Several people stopped but no one spoke English. Meanwhile the child continued to cry. Andrea searched the street again in hopes of spotting someone who could help. Eventually, she saw a young man, carrying a stack of books, walking on the other side of the street. Andrea crossed the street and caught up with the young man.

"Excuse me. Do you speak English?"

"A little."

"Could you help me please," she beckoned. "There's a child across the street, crying. I don't know what's bothering her. Could you find out?"

"Yes, of course."

They walked over to the doorway and the young man talked to the girl.

"She says her little brother is lost. Her mother is not home. She was playing with her three year old brother when the five year old disappeared. She can't find him."

"Has she checked the apartment?"

"She says there are only two rooms. He's not in the apartment."

"Let's go look for him."

The young man talked to the child then explained to Andrea. "The three year old is in the house. She can't leave him alone and she does not have a key to get back in."

"Does she know where her mother is?"

"Sima, that's her name, says her mother had to go to a meeting. She teaches school."

"What's the name of the school?"

"Kourosh Elementary School."

"Does she have the number?"

"No."

"How can we get the number?"

The young man thought for a moment. "We can try the operator."

"Do you know where we can find a telephone?"

"We don't have a phone but our neighbors do. He's a general. I'm sure they won't mind."

"Let's give it a try. Please tell Sima to wait for us."

The young man obliged. They walked down the hill. Andrea heard a car start across the street. She saw a black Chevrolet with darkened windows. It looked identical to the car parked close to the Abbassi residence. Ordinarily, she wouldn't have paid much attention to it. But the tinted windows, unlike any other car on the block, caught her attention. The car cruised at minimum speed. Andrea had an eerie feeling. Because of the tinted windows, she couldn't see the driver. It looked as though the car was rolling down the hill on its own.

They reached the General's house. The young man rang the doorbell.

A soldier in uniform opened the door. He spoke to the young man in Farsi. He seemed satisfied with the explanation he was given and ushered them in.

The General's wife was a German woman in her forties.

She invited them to sit down. After hearing their request, she offered to call the operator herself. She spoke fluent Farsi and English.

"There are no telephone directories," she told Andrea. "Because we don't have enough phone lines, people pay exorbitant prices to buy phones on the black market. A directory would be useless. Let's hope the operator is helpful."

Upon being told who the caller was, the operator put the call through immediately. Sima's mother was called from her meeting to answer the phone. She told the General's wife she'd be on her way home immediately. She expected to arrive in less than ten minutes.

The young man turned to Andrea. "It's a good thing we came here, otherwise, we wouldn't have been able to manage on our own."

The General's wife smiled. "Yes, being in the military has its advantages. How about a cup of tea?"

"I better not," Andrea said. "Sima was very upset. I should go tell her that her mother is coming home."

"Only if you promise to stop by soon and have a cup of tea or coffee with me. Forgive me. I did not introduce myself. Everyone calls me the General's wife. I forget who I am sometimes. My name is Helga. I'd like to get to know you better."

Andrea was touched by her hospitality and charm. "I promise. Thank you both very much for your help."

She hurried up the street wondering what it took to make a person so generous and friendly and how Sima was faring.

Sima stood in the same spot holding her little brother's hand. Andrea tried to explain that her mother was on her way home. Sima looked at her with sad, drooping eyes but said nothing.

They waited together for a few minutes. Soon Andrea saw a woman dressed in black, her head covered with a black scarf, holding the hand of a boy who looked to be four or five years old, walking hurriedly in their direction.

"Mama, Mama," Sima yelled at the sight of her mother.

Andrea smiled and said hello.

"I'm terribly sorry to have caused you all this trouble," the young woman apologized in perfect English. "Here's my lost son. I found him wondering two blocks north of here. He was looking for me."

"That's wonderful," Andrea said truly relieved. "Sima was quite upset."

The mother rushed to the daughter, embraced and kissed her. "She's not used to it. She's not quite seven years old yet. I've never left them alone but I had no choice. I had to go to a meeting."

Andrea hesitated for a moment. She did not know what to say. "Well, I better go. I hope . . ."

"Oh, no, you mustn't," the mother insisted. "Please come in. I haven't even thanked you properly."

"There's no need for that. I'm glad you found your son. Sorry we had to interrupt your meeting."

"It was boring. I was glad I could leave. Do you have time? Perhaps you could join me for a cup of tea."

"That would be nice, thank you."

The apartment was on the ground floor. It consisted of two small rooms, a kitchen and a bathroom.

"It's not much, but it's all I can afford. By the way I'm Layla."

"I'm Andrea." They shook hands.

They settled around a small, round table in the kitchen next to a large window overlooking the street. Layla lit the samovar to brew tea.

"Do you live around here? I haven't seen you in the neighborhood before."

"We're about five minutes away. We arrived a week ago from the States. I'm American, my husband was born in Iran. This is my first time out."

"This is quite different from America, isn't it?"

"It's different. Maybe that's what's so nice about it."

"That's wonderful. I'm glad you like it."

"The people amaze me. They are . . . they are so friendly, trusting. It is unbelievable and refreshing."

Layla remained silent. She watched the children playing with blocks in the small room adjacent to the kitchen.

"What do you teach?" Andrea asked.

"I teach Farsi from first to sixth grade. Actually, I'm hoping I'll be able to."

"Why not? Are there too many applicants for the position?"

Layla smiled. "The job is mine. That's not the problem. I haven't been able to find someone to care for the children while I work. For Iranians help is very difficult to find nowadays. They prefer working for foreigners because foreigners pay them much more. I can't say I blame them."

Andrea guessed Layla couldn't be more than thirty years old.

"No day care centers I presume."

"No. No such thing."

"What are you going to do?"

Layla studied her guest. "Don't worry. I'll find a way."

Andrea perked up, cocked her head to one side. Her voice was full of excitement, "How would you like to make extra money?"

Layla pulled herself back in her chair seemingly captivated by Andrea's enthusiasm, "How?"

"Do you think you'll have time after school to take on private tutoring?"

"You mean teach Farsi to students? I have time, but where would I get the students? I have advertised in the newspapers to teach English. I have had no response so far. Not having a phone doesn't help matters much."

"I'll pay you whatever the going rate is to teach me Farsi. Except for my husband's brother, no one in his family speaks English. Everyone I've talked to has advised me to learn the language. I want to surprise my husband. How about it?"

Layla listened carefully. "Are you sure you didn't decide to learn the language just to help me?"

"Absolutely not. Can't you see, it will be perfect for both of us. You can use the money to hire a baby sitter and I'll learn the language and keep it a secret. If he asks me where I'm going, I'll say I'm going for a walk."

"You think he'll believe you."

"Sure he will. I went for walks every day at home."

The tea was ready. Layla got up, put two glass teacups on a tray, poured the tea and approached Andrea. She glanced out the window and froze on the spot. "Oh, no!" She dropped the tray. Trembling, she collapsed in a chair.

Astonished at Layla's sudden change of behavior, Andrea checked the street. She found nothing except cars parked mostly on the sidewalks. She rushed to Layla's side. "What is it? What happened?"

Layla covered her face with her hands and sobbed quietly.

"Please, let me help you. What has you so upset?"

"They're here again," Layla stammered through sobs.

"Who? There's no one out there. I just checked."

Layla dried her eyes and turned around slowly. "You see that black Chevrolet with the tinted windows parked across the street?"

Andrea had seen it. "What of it?"

"That's Savak. Oh, my God! What will happen to the children?"

"Layla, please calm down. Why would Savak want anything to do with you?"

"Oh, God, what am I going to do? They're here again."

Andrea hugged her gently. She felt frustrated and helpless. Why should a black Chevrolet send a perfectly sensible women into instant hysterics?

Then she recalled what she'd seen.

"Layla, there's something wrong with your assumption. A similar Chevrolet is parked about fifteen feet north of our house. It's there every time I look out the window. I saw the same type of car across from the General's house. I don't think they want anything to do with you. Maybe a Savak agent lives in the neighborhood. Who cares? Why are you so worried?"

Layla stopped crying and looked up. "A car like that means only one thing. Trouble. That same type of car took my husband away."

Andrea was stunned.

"They said he's a communist agitator," Layla continued. "It was three months ago. They put him in the 'frying pan.'"

"What's that?"

"A heated table Savak uses to extract confessions. Few ever make it off the table. He died three days later."

Tears rolled down Andrea's cheeks despite her best efforts to control herself.

"I'm so sorry." She wanted to hug Layla, comfort her. She couldn't. She did not trust herself.

The children, sensing their mother's troubled state, gathered around her, clinging to her.

Layla wiped her tears, pulled herself together and sat erect. "I promised myself, no matter what happens, I'll never let them crush me. And I won't." She reached and embraced the children, comforting them.

"At least I know who they are," Andrea mused. But she was troubled.

With genuine concern Layla reached for her friend's hand and gave it a gentle squeeze. "I'd find out why they're there if I were you. When did you say you arrived?"

"Last Friday. Why?"

"You said you live five minutes away from here. Where exactly is your house?"

"Up this street and to the left. It's the house with a fenced front yard."

"I know which house you mean. No Savak agent lives in this neighborhood. They're there for a reason. In all probability it's the same car. They are following you. Is your husband involved in politics?"

"No, of course not."

"That doesn't mean a thing, you know. Savak believes in punishing the innocent as well as the guilty - to keep the public in fear. Makes it easier for them to control dissent. I passed by your house last Thursday. The school janitor gave me the name of a woman who might be interested in taking care of the children. She lives two blocks north of you. I went to talk to her. There was no Savak car there. Believe me, I'd notice it if it was there."

Andrea stopped to think. Layla was well informed and what she said stood to reason. A thought nagged her. It had to have been the same car she saw rolling down the hill across from the General's house. It was parked there when she left. Only then, she'd been preoccupied with the little girl. It hadn't occurred to her to make the connection. Suddenly, it was like a revelation. There was no doubt in her mind it was the same car. Andrea made a game of remembering license numbers while driving or walking. It helped pass the time. The numbers matched.

She said, more to reassure herself than out of conviction, "If they're following me, they're wasting their time."

Layla stared into space reflectively. "No," she said in a low voice. "They're not wasting their time. Trust me. They know what they're doing. Their successes and their excesses are legendary. It's frightening and all too true."

"I realize that. But why would they be interested in me?" Andrea felt a sudden heat rush to her face.

Layla glanced at her sharply, then, in a voice tight with emotion said, "Make no mistake. This is not the States. I lived and studied there. I know. How long was your husband in the States?"

"Seven years."

"Was he a student?"

"Yes."

"There's your answer. They have files on all the students

studying abroad."

"Why all? I can understand their wanting to keep tab on those who are anti Shah but it seems to me it would be a monumental job to keep track of every student abroad."

"They have all the money and all the trained staff they need. Have you seen the Shah on television in the States?"

"Several times. Why?"

"Did you notice how the protesters always wore hoods?"

"Yes, of course."

"They wear hoods to protect their identity from Savak. In response, Savak considers everyone suspect until proven otherwise."

The information was not new to Andrea, only the extent. Was Layla exaggerating because of her own painful experience? When she talked, her eyes turned cold, full of sadness. There was no anger in her voice nor self pity in her words. Only resignation.

Andrea shuddered involuntarily. Could she possibly have the courage this strange woman had if faced with similar circumstances? She wasn't sure.

"So you think they'll be watching my husband to make sure he's not an agitator."

"Every student who returns to this country is kept under observation. Why should they make an exception of your husband?"

"I'll grant you that. But my husband is at home and they are following me. I mean really, what can they hope to achieve?"

A faint smile flitted across Layla's mouth. "Your questions don't surprise me. It's because you're not used to the convoluted Middle Eastern way of thinking. They work in pairs. One of them is following you while the other is watching your house. If, in the meantime, your husband decides to leave, they'll radio for another car to follow him. The house will be under twenty four hour surveillance for as long as they feel it's necessary."

Andrea shrugged. "Let them. I'm sure they'll soon get tired and leave."

"Meanwhile, be careful, please."

"I will. But if that's the case, maybe we should postpone my Farsi lessons for a while. My coming here might draw attention to you. I don't want to cause you problems."

"No. I told you. Despite what they did to us, I will not let them interfere in my life. I'm free all day until school starts. Is eleven in the morning all right?"

"Super. I'll be here. I've got to go. Thanks for your hospitality."

"Before you go, let me tell you how we can be sure if they're following you or it's me they want. If they leave, soon after you leave, then you'd better alert your husband to their presence."

"Will do. Take care."

Andrea walked out the door refraining from looking in the direction of the parked Chevrolet. She walked with brisk, determined steps. It took her four minutes to reach the Abbassi residence.

Layla was right. A shady looking character lurked a few feet away. He leaned against a lone, leafless tree, protruding through a small patch of earth in the sidewalk. Soon, the black Chevrolet came to a stop next to the man and the man got in.

Andrea opened the door of the house and went in. There was no sign of Mani or Farhad. Mrs. Abbassi senior was absorbed watching a show on television.

She'd been gone longer than she'd planned. She climbed the stairs quickly to check on Kelly.

Sayid stood at the top of the stairs with a saturnine face and blood shot eyes, staring haughtily at her.

Chapter 3

Sayid reached for Andrea's hand, stumbled, grabbed the railing and steadied himself. An area, exquisitely decorated by an interior designer, separated the two bedrooms. The family referred to it as the Persian room. There were two love seats made of Persian carpets in the form of large pillows, a round, hand carved silver tray which served as the coffee table, half a dozen pillows made of silk carpeting, and original etchings by Iranian artists covered the walls. Sayid made his way carefully to the love seat and sat down.

Andrea sat next to him. She scanned his face for a possible clue. He looked pale, his eyes were red, his expression blank.

"Sayid, are you all right?" She wondered if her question bordered on the ridiculous.

"All right?" He appeared to be racked by unbearable pain. "What do you mean, all right?" He didn't look at her. His breath reeked of alcohol.

"Would you like a cup of coffee?"

He turned bleary eyes on her. "No, I don't want coffee."

She hesitated. Her thoughts shifted to Kelly helpless, patient, undemanding. Kelly was always on her mind. Shortly after delivery, her obstetrician had come to her room. "Did you at any time in the first three months of your pregnancy have a rash?" he asked. She had. In the second month. She remembered it well. She and Mani had returned from a picnic when she discovered the rash. "It's nothing," Mani told her. "It will be gone in a day or two." It did. And she forgot all about it. "You must have had German Measles. Your daughter has severe physical and probably mental abnormalities," the doctor continued.

After that she heard nothing, saw nothing. For days she did not eat or sleep. Mani did not leave her bedside. Gradually, with his help, she overcame the anger, the depression, the resentment but not the pain. It gnawed at her every time she looked at the child or thought about her.

"I better check Kelly. She must be awake by now."

Kelly had an anxious look on her face. Andrea hugged her, ran her fingers through her daughter's curly black hair and whispered softly, "I love you." She picked Kelly up and returned to the Persian room. Sayid was where she'd left him. His head rested on the pillow, his eyes were closed. She seated Kelly on the other love seat then went to the kitchen to prepare Kelly's dinner.

When she returned Sayid was totally engrossed in making funny faces at Kelly. Kelly seemed delighted with the attention. She gurgled and smiled.

Andrea was touched. Sayid hadn't shown any interest until then. It was the first time anyone in the family was kind to the child. Everyone else avoided her, even mention of her. It was as though her handicap was contagious, a matter to be ashamed of. It was a painful realization which Andrea attributed partly to the culture and partly to her husband's detached attitude since their arrival. Mani always kissed his daughter good night. Since their arrival though, he acted as though she didn't exist. But they had so much company and he had so much on his mind.

"Thanks for entertaining her," Andrea said. "She loves attention. With some food in her stomach she'll be ready for the night. Maybe when Grandma is through watching Bonanza, she'll let Kelly watch cartoons." She turned to Kelly. "Would you like that?" She knew the child loved cartoons.

Andrea felt Sayid's eyes follow her as she fed Kelly. It seemed whatever had been bothering him was temporarily forgotten. When Andrea was through, she took Kelly to the living room to watch television. Naene glared at her but said nothing.

She returned to go to her room to change her clothes. Sayid lounged on the love seat. Only now he had a bottle of Scotch in his hand. "Want to join me?"

"No thanks."

Sayid got up, bent over the rails and called for the maid to bring ice, soda water and two glasses. Andrea went to her room to change. She parted the curtain and peeped out the window. The man she'd seen leaning against the tree was back, smoking, looking around aimlessly. The black Chevrolet was not there.

They must be taking turns having dinner, Andrea surmised.

She moved away quickly. The grubby appearance of the man had a disturbing effect on her. Layla's warnings gained new intensity as she pondered about the reasons prompting such drastic measures, its effects on its victims. Who was ultimately responsible for it? She decided to ask Sayid. Perhaps his explanation would be less emotionally tainted.

She walked from the room and motioned for Sayid to join her. He staggered to her doorway. She tiptoed to the window as though her footsteps would alert an outsider to her presence and parted the curtain cautiously.

"Sayid please come over here. Maybe you can tell me who that man is."

"I don't have to come over there. I know who he is."

"You do? Who is he? Why does he just stand there?"

"My dear, innocent sister-in-law, do not worry yourself with matters about which you can do nothing."

Andrea chuckled nervously. "That does not tell me who he is. Does it?"

"Supposing I told you he is the devil himself and he is waiting to get you. What could you do about it?"

Exasperated, Andrea said, "I went for a walk this afternoon. I met a woman who claims her husband was killed by the secret service. Something about a 'frying pan.' The reason the conversation came about was because she went into hysterics when she saw a black Chevrolet parked in front of her house. She says all students returning from abroad are kept under observation. Is it true?"

Sayid studied her. He didn't respond. She surmised that either he didn't know or did not want to talk about it. "It's all right. It really doesn't matter. You don't have to tell me anything."

Just then the black Chevrolet pulled up, the grubby looking man got in and the car drove a few feet up the street, squeezed itself between two parked cars and stopped. Andrea noted the license number. It was different. Change of shift she presumed. She closed the curtain and turned, shaken.

He approached her, reached for her hand and caressed it. He looked into her eyes. "These men play deadly games. I was hoping you'd be spared the knowledge. Unfortunately, short of suicide there's very little anyone can do to avoid them." His tone was emotionless.

The realization that everything she'd heard was true, sent shock waves through her. "It gives me the creeps."

"My advice to you is to be careful. Very careful. Don't discuss any subject but the weather and the traffic no matter who you're talking to. And please do not go visiting strangers especially if the person you meet happens to be a general's wife."

Incredible, stupendous were the words which popped into her head. How could he know who she'd met? "I don't recall mentioning meeting a general's wife." Her voice quivered. "Did you have spies following me?"

"No. As a matter of fact I was asleep. I didn't know you'd gone for a walk."

"You're not making sense. Someone told you?"

He led her gently to the single chair in the room and he sat on the bed. His eyes never left her face. "Andrea, please listen to me. This is not a place for you or for Kelly. Go back home before it's too late. If you need money or anything else, all you need to do is ask."

She searched his face vainly for an explanation for the drastic action he'd proposed. There was none. Only a stony expression. She shook visibly and was angry for doing so. "Why? Why do you want me to go away? How could I?"

"You must."

"Sayid, you've not given me a single answer. I've been here a week. You want me to pack up and leave. You won't tell me why. I . . . I don't understand."

The television was on full blast. Their hushed tones were consumed by the noise. Sayid rose and closed the door. He approached Andrea, put an arm around her shoulders giving her a gentle hug. "Leave," he said. "Leave before it's too late."

"Too late for what?"

He sighed resignedly, his expression that of a man begging for understanding and trust. "Why do you ask so many questions?"

"Sayid, I'm sure you have our best interest at heart. I can see you're bothered by the fact that I'm not cluing in as fast as you'd like me to. But be serious. How can you expect me to do what you want me to without giving me a logical explanation."

He paced the room, worked his fingers through his hair and rubbed his chin. An occasional glance in her direction made her feel restless, uncomfortable.

He walked back to the bed and sat down. "There's a lot you don't know and I prefer you never do. I could spend the rest of my life explaining the problems of a much abused nation. But what for?"

"You forget. Your nation is also my nation. My husband happens to be an Iranian. My daughter is half Iranian. Don't you think it would be better if I knew what was going on?"

"Yes of course. Your husband. How could I forget. And your daughter. What a pity."

His manner, his words upset her more than she was willing to admit. "I don't need anyone's pity." She was calm. "I'm quite capable of taking care of my problems."

He laughed, a nervous sounding, short laugh. "I didn't mean pity in the sense that you interpreted it. Ignorance and prejudice have roots sealed in cement here. Kelly will suffer and you will too."

Andrea remained silent. She had to admit that from what she'd witnessed, his remarks were understatements.

He approached her and put his arm on her shoulder. "I remember how involved you were at the University with social causes of the sixties. I remember you telling me about the brotherhood of man and how you as a person would do your best to bring about change."

"I still do." Andrea was surprised that he remembered after so many years.

"Forget it," he quipped. "It's great in theory. In practice it stinks. Brotherhood among brothers is quite impossible much less among strangers."

His cynicism shocked her. But before she replied he said, "That's a luxury afforded by people who have passed the stage of worrying about survival. We've got a long way to go to get there."

"I'd like to be a part of that process."

"No." His voice rose. "No. You mustn't."

She eyed him suspiciously, unable to comprehend his

vehemence.

He took her hand. "Why?" His voice pled, "Why won't you listen to me? I would have preferred to spare burdening you with unpleasant details. Unfortunately, you leave me no choice. Do you know that I was woken up and told of your every move from the time you left the house this afternoon until you returned? Do you realize that this is not a situation which is going to change? Those men out there . . ."

The door flew open. Mani stood in the doorway with a savage expression on his face. "What the hell are you doing in my room, with my wife!" He approached his brother threateningly. Then turned to Andrea. "Go take care of your daughter," he shouted. "My mother has no obligation to you or to her."

Sayid shoved him aside. "Think about what I told you." He started to leave.

Mani poked his brother's shoulder angrily. "You have no right to tell her anything. Get out of my room!"

Sayid didn't budge. He stared at Mani.

"Are you deaf? I told you to get out of my room."

Sayid spread his feet and put his hands on his waist. Without raising his voice he said, "This is my house and this is my room. I agreed to let you use the room temporarily. Make note of the word temporarily."

"Like hell it's your house," Mani snapped. "In case you've forgotten I'm the first born son. Most everything my father owned is mine."

"Except your father owned nothing when he died unless you consider a huge medical bill as inheritance."

Mani threw a punch. Sayid caught his arm in mid air and shoved it away. "I'd watch my temper if I were you." He walked out.

Farhad, stood at a safe distance and watched the scenario with a contented grin on his face. Seeing him seemed to have incensed Sayid. Sayid spun around and told Mani, "Get this parasite out of my house immediately."

"I'll see you dead before I take orders from you," Mani retorted.

Andrea approached Mani. "Darling." Her voice was soft. "I asked him to come in. We were just talking. There's no need to be upset."

"I don't need you to tell me how to behave. You stay out of it. Do you understand?"

She chose not to dignify his words with an answer. She descended the stairs, her head held high, in total control of herself. She cradled Kelly, returned to their room, and tucked her in bed.

Meanwhile Sayid descended the stairs.

"Hey, you," Mani shouted after his brother. "I'm not through with you yet. I want to settle this business of who owns what right now."

Mani rushed downstairs and turned the volume of the television down.

Farhad settled himself on top of the stairs from where he could see the living room.

Andrea walked out of the room, thought of trying to say something to pacify her husband, hesitated then caught Farhad's eyes following her.

"Come sit next to me," he said. "I love a good fight. Don't you?"

Andrea's mind raced. She wanted to find out what caused the sudden confrontation between the brothers. They'd have to speak in Farsi since Naene did not speak English. She decided to accept Farhad's offer. If her intuition was correct, he would be glad to oblige.

Mani spoke angrily, the words pouring out in rapid succession.

"Your mother-in-law is very angry with both her sons," Farhad explained dutifully.

After Mani finished his monologue, Mrs. Abbassi turned her attention to Sayid. She spoke at length, occasionally turning both palms up, as though requesting divine guidance accentuated by tears which she dutifully wiped away with her hands.

"She says an irrelevant issue such as money should not be a point of contention between brothers," Farhad told Andrea.

Mrs. Abbassi continued. Once in a while Mani said something but it was mostly the mother who spoke. She spoke firmly and authoritatively. Neither son seemed to object. Her words were mostly directed at Sayid who puffed a cigarette and stared into space.

"Sayid has made her very angry. She says he broke his promise to his father," Farhad whispered in Andrea's ear.

"What promise?"

"Before Mr. Abbassi died four months ago, apparently he made Sayid promise him to take care of his mother and never do anything to hurt Mani."

"I see."

"She says she is master of this house regardless of who paid for it and that Sayid has no business imposing his will on his brother."

"What did their father die of? Was it a stroke?"

"Shush. She's speaking again."

Farhad listened. The smile on his face broadened. "You'll love this one," he told Andrea. "She says the two brothers are being pitched against each other not because of money but because of you."

"What?"

"Don't get excited. She's an old woman."

At that moment Mrs. Abbassi turned her head and her open palms in the direction of the stairs. She made eye contact with Andrea. Rocking her body back and forth, she pounded her chest with her fists and repeated the word "negis" . . . "negis" like someone in a trance.

"What does that word mean?" Andrea asked.

"It means unclean. Someone who contaminates everyone around."

Sayid still didn't speak. Instead, he rose and walked out

the front door.

Andrea watched as Mani's mother beckoned for help. Mani rushed to help her rise from the armchair. She wobbled to the bathroom, mumbling to herself, grasping furniture whenever she could.

Mani sauntered up the stairs, a triumphant look on his face. "Let's go Farhad," he said. "The worm dug a hole. Too bad the earth he dug fell on his head and choked him to death."

"I love it when you're poetic." Farhad leapt to Mani's side. "You should be congratulated for teaching a lesson to that arrogant fool."

"Mani," Andrea interrupted, "I'd like to speak to you for a moment, alone, please."

"Not now. Can't you see I'm busy."

"It's important."

"I told you. Not now."

"It's important," Andrea repeated firmly.

He turned to Farhad. "I'll only be a minute."

He followed her into their quarters, closed the door and faced her with apparent annoyance. "What's so important that it can't wait."

She walked to the window, parted the curtain just barely and asked him to step closer. The black Chevrolet was there. "Look over there," she said. "The black Chevrolet with the tinted windows. I was told only the secret service is permitted to use cars with tinted windows. That's why I asked Sayid to come in."

Mani looked. Suddenly, the color drained from his face. He pulled back and whispered in a terrified voice, "Oh, my God," staggered and fell on the bed.

Chapter 4

Mani lay motionless on the bed, staring at the ceiling, one hand dangling from the side of the bed. His face was waxen.

Andrea stood next to the window observing, wondering. The events of the past few hours should have convinced her her husband was involved. There was no other explanation for the intensity of his reaction. However, she'd never permit emotions to cloud her logic, nor would she dismiss the possibility blindly. Too much was at stake.

It had been ten minutes since they'd looked out the window. It felt like more than an hour. Andrea did not know how much longer her husband would remain in the state he was in. She heard a hard knock on the door.

Instantly, Mani jolted from the bed and stood with a terrified look on his face.

"I'll see who it is."

"Don't touch that door," he spoke through clenched teeth.

There was another knock, harder, louder.

Andrea looked at her husband questioningly. He acted too scared to explain.

Farhad opened the door and walked in. "What's keeping you so long?" He sounded annoyed.

"We . . . we have a problem," Mani replied.

"Solve your problems later. We've got to go. We're already half an hour late for the meeting?"

Mani shook. He tried not to look at Farhad. "We . . . we can't go. They're outside."

Farhad studied him. "Who? Who's outside? What are you talking about?"

Mani dropped to the bed helplessly. "Go look out the window, to the left."

Farhad walked to the window. "Where?" he asked. "It's dark. I can't see anything."

"Look about seven or eight yards to your left. A black Chevrolet. Can't miss it. It's the only big car around."

Farhad waited until a car came up the street. When he spotted the Chevrolet he turned to Mani. "Do you know how long it's been there?"

"I have no idea. Andrea pointed it out to me."

Farhad threw a sharp glance at Andrea then drew the curtain. With a somber expression he said to Mani, "We're in bad trouble."

"I know."

Farhad sat on the chair his fist under his nose, lost in thought. Suddenly, he stood. "How did you know who they were?"

Andrea gave a brief account of her encounter with Layla. Both men listened, engrossed. When she was through, Farhad said, "Yes. I know of the case. But I didn't know his widow lived in the neighborhood. She'd know. Her husband was an innocent victim, a bystander."

Andrea perspired profusely. Then felt a chill. It was over in a few seconds.

"What are we going to do?" Mani's frightened voice pleaded.

Farhad shook his head. "Stop whining and let me think."

A few moments later, he spun and addressed Mani. "How many chaddors does your mother have?"

Mani bolted upright. "I don't know. Many I presume. I've seen her use different chaddors when she goes out. Why?"

"Don't ask questions. Listen carefully. I'll keep her occupied while you sneak into her room and grab two chaddors."

"I hope you're not thinking of doing what I think you're thinking."

"Have you got a better solution?"

"No, but . . ."

"But what?"

"Suppose they stop us. Then what do we do?"

"I have my gun."

Mani rose and paced the small room. "I can't believe it. I can't believe they're onto us so soon. They don't need an excuse. They . . ."

Farhad cut in. "Stop your moaning. It won't help solve the problem. We've got to go underground. A month. Maybe two. We've got to shake them off. So think."

Andrea, totally absorbed listening, observed Farhad's mind at work. Human behavior never ceased to fascinate her. Farhad seemed to have all the qualities of a leader. He took control of the problem immediately, wrestled with it for a few seconds and was ready with a solution. He was quick, sharp, decisive and fearless. She liked men of action. Yet something in his manner reminded her more of a tyrant than a leader. There was no apparent room for other opinions or compromise in his decisions.

She also noted that she was being ignored.

Farhad's next remark recalled her attention. "Your mother must not know. We'll tell her we're going to the movies or something. Yes. That's it. We're going to the movies. She must not wait for us. We'll probably be late."

"She's certainly going to wonder what we're up to if we leave with chaddors on our heads."

"Nah. We'll wait till she's fully involved watching television. We'll sneak out quietly."

"Why not tell her?" Mani asked. "She'll cooperate. She'll do anything for me."

Farhad shook his head. "It's not your mother I'm worried about." His voice conveyed annoyance. "It's better for her not to know. They'll be here to question her. You can be sure of that. If she doesn't know, she can't tell them. Can she?"

"You're right. I didn't think of it that way."

"I'll do the thinking," Farhad quipped. "I'm far more familiar with what goes on in this country than you are. You do what you're told."

Andrea's confusion mounted. If they were not involved, what prompted Farhad to take such drastic measures? If they were, why was he so concerned with Security questioning the mother but not her? And why was Mani taking such a passive role?

She knew she was being deliberately ignored. Nonetheless, she felt she needed clarification. She faced her husband. "Mani, what's this all about?"

Farhad cocked his head to one side. Giving her a condescending grin, he said simply, "You saw nothing, heard nothing. Can you handle it?"

Mani said nothing.

Andrea's confusion was giving way to anger but she managed to be in full control. Once again she turned to her husband. "Mani, what's going on."

"I don't know. You heard Farhad. Why can't you let me be?"

Farhad motioned for Mani to follow him and they left the room.

Incensed, Andrea closed the door. She turned off the light and cautiously approached the window. The black Chevrolet had not moved. She wanted to see for herself if, as Farhad had proposed they would manage to sneak out of the house without being detected.

She waited for over fifteen minutes. Nothing happened.

She thought perhaps they'd changed their minds. She was about to move away from the window, when the front door cracked slowly. Two figures completely covered with chadors walked casually up the hill.

Soon after, the door of the Chevrolet opened. A young man stepped out. He looked in the direction of the two dark figures walking up the street. Apparently puzzled, he returned to the car. A few seconds passed. The door on the passenger side opened. A heavier set man in a dark suit stepped out. He too looked up the street. The street was quite dark. Andrea couldn't make out the men's features or see their expressions. By then, Mani and Farhad had walked past the point where she could see them but she knew they could not have reached the main street. There hadn't been enough time.

The security agent's gaze didn't waver. Andrea felt her pulse quicken. Could he have surmised that something was amiss?

The man standing outside turned around and tapped the window of the car. When it was lowered, he stuck his head in. A few seconds later, he pulled his head out, stood to one side and the car drove away.

Andrea's fears were confirmed. The agents were suspicious. Even to an uninitiated person like herself, Mani and Farhad didn't look like two women casually walking up the street. They were too big to pass for women and certainly walked differently.

There was no time to waste. She dashed down the stairs, opened the front door and rushed outside turning the porch lights on on her way out. If only her heart would stop pounding so loud.

The lights and the opening of the door did what Andrea had hoped for. The Chevrolet stopped in the middle of the street, right next to her. The man she'd seen first jumped out, followed by the man who'd been standing outside.

Andrea kept her eyes glued to the pavement pretending to be looking for something.

"What are you looking for?" It was a male voice with forced charm.

She spun around as though taken by surprise. "I seem to have lost my ring."

"When did you find out it was missing?" asked the man.

"About half an hour ago. I wanted to have dinner. I went to wash my hands. I always take it off when I wash my hands. I reached for it. It was gone."

"Did you check the house thoroughly?" the second man asked.

Andrea hoped she looked distraught. "I've looked everywhere. It's not in the house. I must have lost it this afternoon when I went for a walk."

The agents exchanged a quick knowing glance.

I doubt I can keep this charade going on much longer she thought. I wonder if Farhad and Mani have reached the main street. She searched frantically, keeping her head bent, fearful something in her manner might betray her.

"Did you have visitors this afternoon?" one of the men asked.

With difficulty Andrea managed to look up. "We always have visitors." She hoped her voice sounded normal. "About this afternoon, I don't know. I was gone. Do you think one of the visitors might have found it?"

The man ignored her question. "Two women left your house a few minutes ago. Do you know who they were?"

Andrea was not sure she could trust her voice but she knew if she took her time to answer she would arouse their suspicion. "No. I don't know anyone who comes to the house. They are family friends and relatives. But I couldn't tell you who is who. Why do you ask?"

The heavier set man looked older and talked with more authority. He turned to the younger man and said something in Farsi. The younger man walked back to the car, turned on the ignition and drove up the street.

"I doubt you'll find it."

"I should have had it fixed long time ago. It was loose on my finger. My grandmother gave it to me. It was my favorite ring."

"Are there visitors at the house now?"

"I don't think so. I was up in our room taking care of our daughter. When I felt hungry, I went to the kitchen to find out what there was for dinner. My mother-in-law was watching television. I don't know if the maid is still there or not."

"Let's go check."

She stopped and waited for an explanation. There was none. It was apparent he was testing her. She decided to go on playing the game. She said, "I don't think my mother -in-law would appreciate a stranger walking into her house . . ."

He flashed his badge. She took a quick look.

"You're welcome to come in if you like. I don't mind. But I don't know about my mother-in-law. I don't speak Farsi. Whatever it is you want to know, you'll have to ask her."

The agent's attention was momentarily diverted as the Chevrolet returned. It stopped next to them. The window lowered and the two men talked. A quick look inside the car relieved Andrea's anxiety. The only occupant was the driver. Trouble still loomed though. If the agents insisted on going inside and questioning her husband's mother, she'd have no choice but to tell them her son and his friend had been there earlier. Slowly, still searching, she moved up the street a few feet away from the men conflicting thoughts crowding her mind.

"Is your husband home?" asked the older man.

Andrea stopped her search for a moment and looked at her tormentor.

"No." Her voice was controlled. "He's not home. If he was, he'd be helping me look for my ring."

"Do you know when he'll be back?"

"Probably soon. Last night he mentioned something about wanting to go to the movies. That is if we don't have visitors."

The older man stood on the sidewalk, feet apart, scrutinizing every move she made. He reached into his coat pocket, pulled out a pack of Winstons, lit one without taking his eyes off her.

"I wish I had a flashlight," Andrea murmured.

The older man motioned. The younger man retrieved a flashlight from the glove compartment. It was powerful.

"Thanks," Andrea said gratefully. "I'll take a quick look around. Then I'll give up."

"When did you say you returned home from your walk?"

She smiled. "I didn't. About six o'clock." She made her answers brief. She wasn't sure she could trust her voice.

The agent checked his watch. "It's over two and a half hours since you returned. Your chances of finding it are nil." His voice was toneless. "That is unless a true Muslim found it."

Andrea had heard about true believers who returned anything they found regardless of its value. However, since Savak was notorious with its distrust of the public, it occurred to her that it might be interesting to find out if the agent believed what he said. "What do you mean by a true Muslim? Are there different types of Muslims?"

He ignored the question.

Andrea wanted to return to the house without arousing their suspicion. She contemplated different courses of action while groping around, flashlight in hand.

"You're wasting your time. Why don't you go on back inside," the agent remarked.

Relieved, Andrea handed him the flashlight. "Thank you for the flashlight and thanks for your help. You're right. It is a waste of time. I'll just have to forget about it."

She took a few steps in the direction of the house. She was about twenty feet away from the door when she heard the older man laugh, a laugh full of nervous tension. Then he approached her and walked with her to the door.

"Do you have a key?" he asked.

"It's not locked."

"It's been nice talking to you." He sounded like a long lost friend. "I'm sorry you didn't find your ring."

The malicious grin on his face was enough to precipitate a stroke in a person with less self control. Struggling to keep calm she answered, "It's all right. These things happen."

He smiled broadly revealing a gold front tooth. She shuddered. Then he stuck his face in hers. "Yes. These things do. Fortunately, sometimes they happen when we want them to."

Keep your cool. Keep your cool. Andrea repeated to herself. He can't prove anything. Be calm. He doesn't need proof. Another voice interjected. Remember what Layla told you. They treat the innocent and the guilty alike. Fear. That's the essential message they want instilled in the public.

He extended his hand. She felt obliged to extend hers. He gripped it. Gripped it hard, hurting her, smiling to let her know he meant to hurt her. Then abruptly, he let go. With a cynical smile and an equally cynical voice, his eyes bored into her flesh. "Don't worry. You accomplished what you set out to do." He turned and strolled toward the Chevrolet.

For an instant her head spun. The pavement under her feet seemed to melt away, and her legs refused to carry the rest of her body. She knew they were watching her. Any show of weakness on her part would confirm further what they already were quite sure of. Trembling uncontrollably, she opened the door and quietly sneaked up to her room. She groped her way in the darkness to her bed, threw herself on it, fighting to bring together the different parts of her body which seemed to have developed an instant will of their own. After a while, the trembling stopped, her body went limp, her brain cells refused to function and she drifted into a semi-sleep.

Footsteps. She shot out of bed like a bullet, straining to hear. No. She wasn't dreaming. Someone was climbing the steps. She rushed to the window. A lone street light burned, illuminating a small circle below. With difficulty, she saw the outline of the Chevrolet. Nothing moved. It was quiet and peaceful.

She rushed out the door.

Sayid had reached the top of the stairs.

"Ah, you're awake," he said. "I shouldn't have turned the light on."

Andrea took a deep breath, relieved. "The light doesn't bother me. I heard footsteps. I thought I'd check. What time is it?"

Sayid checked his watch. "It's three forty five."

"I better go back to bed. It's too early to get up."

He stared at her. She felt uneasy.

"Is something wrong?"

He hesitated, checked his watch, smiled. "Do you always go to bed with street clothes on?"

She felt cornered, unprepared to give a logical answer. "No. Not really. I must have dozed off while reading. Funny. I hadn't noticed it. Thanks for pointing it out. Good night."

"It's more like morning." He walked slowly to his room. Then, in his now familiar monotonous tone, added, "By the way. I meant to tell you. Do you remember you went to your room to change after you returned from your walk?"

"Yes of course. Why do you ask?"

"Perhaps you misplaced your ring in one of the pockets of the sweat suit you were wearing."

Chapter 5

The mosquitoes won. Every night. No sooner did she put her head on the pillow than the insatiable pests attacked in swarms, screeching, stinging until in desperation she'd rise. She'd wield a newspaper or whatever, like a whirling dervish, in the direction she detected her tormentors were headed.

This night was worse than most. As July progressed, so did the degree of heat. Desperate for fresh air, she'd made the mistake of leaving the window open. There were no screens. Now she paid the price of her folly.

It was still dark. Nonetheless, she gave up the struggle to sleep, got out of bed and quietly made her way to the living room with paper and pen in hand. She wrote a letter to her mother giving detailed account of events since her arrival. Mani had not returned that night. A week had passed. She hadn't heard from him. But she did not mention it in her letter.

She wrote, read the pages, tore them to bits and flushed them down the toilet. Purged, she felt relieved, adventurous. Checking the street frequently, had become a part of her daily routine. To date, she'd been pleasantly surprised. The Chevrolet was gone and there was no one standing on the sidewalk looking around. Their disappearance was cause for cautious optimism, yet fear. If her assumptions were correct, the agents had left because their interest in her movements were related to her husband. And their target had slipped away. How they would react to Mani's and Farhad's escape and her helping them was a thought she'd prefer to live without. For now, they were gone. That was all that mattered.

She had a lot of studying to do, strange words to memorize. She began to read. Soon she was sound asleep.

"I'm sorry. I didn't mean to startle you," Sayid stood next to the sofa looking down at her. His eyes were bloodshot, his gait unsteady.

Andrea pulled herself up. "I must have dozed off," she said. "I couldn't sleep in our room. It's been invaded by mosquitoes."

"What about Kelly?"

Sayid had trouble speaking and keeping his posture.

"For some reason they don't bother Kelly at all. Did the light in the living room wake you up?"

"Wake me? Did you say wake me? I never go to bed before sunrise. I just got home." He lowered himself into the armchair facing the sofa.

Andrea felt awkward. Sayid's slurred speech and slow motions made him seem like a totally different person from the Sayid she thought she knew. "I'm going to make coffee. Would you like some?"

"Coffee! To hell with coffee! You look at me, you think I'm drunk and immediately you offer me coffee. Sure I'm drunk. Why not? I'm not pure like you. But then you know that, don't you?" He dragged himself out of the chair, walked slowly to the sofa and sat next to her.

He bent his head down and stared at his clasped hands. Slowly, as though having reached a painful decision, he said, "There's going to be trouble. Bad trouble. I want you out of here. I've bought tickets for you and Kelly. You must leave."

Andrea listened. She was skeptical. He was obviously drunk. Sure she'd heard rumors of disturbances, sporadic assassinations and brutal reprisals. But there really was no mass exodus of foreigners, nor any sign of escalation of hostilities other than the usual hit and run, mostly reported by Radio Israel and/or the BBC. She didn't want to argue with him. It would be futile.

"Does that mean you won't accept my advice?" His voice had an edge.

"Sayid, I have to wait till Mani comes home. I really appreciate your thinking of us. But I've told you repeatedly I cannot leave without my husband."

He got up, climbed the stairs to his room without glancing back. He opened the door, then stopped abruptly. He bent over the railing. "By the way, if I were you, I'd stay away from that woman you've been seeing daily." He went into his room and shut the door.

Andrea sat speechless, staring at the closed door, unable to think clearly. If he was right, who could she turn to for help? Jim Talbot had warned her, Irene had warned her and Sayid warned her repeatedly. Was she being naive in expecting her problems to be solved by her husband's return? A husband who had become a total stranger ever since they left the States. Was her husband himself in so much trouble that he could not even help himself much less his family? How did Sayid know there would be trouble? Sayid always left her uneasy, feeling guilty. She'd wait till he was sober and have a serious discussion with him.

She felt confused, drained. She needed a distraction. She reached for a book Layla had loaned her about the history of Iran, which she had left on the coffee table the night before. She had so much to learn. It was mind boggling. For two thousand five hundred years Iranians were subjugated, oppressed, ruled by foreigners or a native appointed by a foreign power. Yet the Iranian spirit, culture and language remained very much alive and progressive through it all. Who were these people who inhabited her adopted country? She resolved to learn all she could about them. Perhaps it would help her understand the present situation better.

Much later, when she checked her watch, she wasn't prepared for what she saw. It was ten minutes to ten. She'd been reading for hours oblivious of all else. The live-in baby sitter that Irene had helped her hire to take care of Kelly, was in bed with a cold. She hurried to her room, got Kelly fed and ready, took her and went to Layla's house for her lesson.

Layla seemed surprised to see her. "I didn't think you'd come."

"Why not?"

Layla shrugged her shoulders, then made way for the wheelchair. "Most people are scared to associate with me. They fear Savak."

"Well," Andrea said with a broad smile, pointing a finger at her chest, "Here's one brave soul who's not afraid. She's terrified."

"Were you followed?"

"I told you. They're gone."

"No, they're not. They're parked right around the corner. That's why I was surprised when you showed up."

"What could they possibly learn by keeping us under observation?" Andrea had not discussed the previous week's events with Layla nor was she willing to discuss the morning's incident with Sayid which had left her at war with herself. Sayid had cautioned her to limit her discussions to the weather and traffic. Savak had informers everywhere. Regardless. She'd let nothing interfere with her learning the language. It had become an obsession.

Layla's children stood at a distance. "Layla, this is my daughter, Kelly. The woman who's been taking care of her isn't feeling well. I hope you don't mind."

"Of course not."

"I would appreciate it if you could explain to your children about Kelly. Kelly has trouble hearing and seeing. She walks with difficulty, only a few steps at a time. But, she's a wonderful child. Always smiling, always happy."

Layla spoke briefly to her children. Sima dropped the doll she was holding, walked over and caressed Kelly's hand. Soon, her brothers joined her. Andrea could not help notice the contrast between her daughter and that of Layla. But years of pain had taught her to push such matters to a dark corner of her mind.

Every day for two hours Layla taught Andrea Farsi. Andrea spent the rest of the evening studying. Soon, she was able to decipher simple sentences. To put her newly acquired knowledge into practice, the two women left the children with Kelly's nursemaid and explored the city. The small, privately owned shops with a vast variety of goods, mostly oriental, stacked up to the ceiling were a source of amusement and curiosity for Andrea. Layla explained that almost all the stores were owned and operated by families. Whenever they entered a store, the owner quickly approached them and offered to help, often struggling to make himself understood with a few treasured English words. In turn, Andrea practiced her newly-acquired vocabulary, hesitating, stumbling over difficult words but getting the message across. This was the best time of the day for her.

The Iranians she met in the streets, in the stores, in taxis, were friendly to a fault. They went out of their way to assist anyone who asked for help, came to her rescue when she had trouble making a sentence with words from a language which endowed numerous meanings to each word depending on the context in which it was used. An old man, who sold fresh fruits and vegetables in a small store on the main street, was her absolute favorite. She taught him the names of the fruits he sold in English. He taught her Farsi. It was a game they both enjoyed, especially the time when he made a heroic effort to get her to pronounce the word "hindvaneh," meaning watermelon, correctly. He must have repeated it patiently, a dozen times, before she said it to his satisfaction, the Iranian way. He had a few teeth left in his mouth which added a lisp to his speech. But that didn't deter him from urging Andrea to pronounce every word she learned correctly.

Today Andrea had to be content with her lesson from Layla. The old man would have to wait. There was no one to leave the children with. But the last place Andrea wanted to be was home. "Let's go get something to eat. My treat."

"You're too kind. I'm afraid I have to refuse."

"Layla, you're not being fair. Please don't say no. You do so much for me."

Layla paused. "I doubt we'll find an orange cab that has room for all of us. The drivers pick up passengers along the way. Most people use cabs. It's the only inexpensive service left in this city. By the time they reach Yussefabad, they're usually full. But we can try."

"Great. Let's do it."

"Orange cabs travel only on major roads," Layla explained. "We'll have to walk there."

They gathered the children and walked to the main road.

They waited and waited. As Layla had predicted, the orange cabs were full of passengers. Kelly weighed over fifty pounds. Andrea's arms were numb from the pressure of her weight. Bringing her wheelchair would have been useless. Andrea hadn't seen a single facility geared to provide assistance to the disabled. There seemed to be a concerted effort to ignore them.

Layla confirmed this. "In our country," she stated flatly, "when we don't like something, we pretend it doesn't exist. It's simple. Then we don't have deal with it."

"What happens to the handicapped?"

"One of these days, when our visionary King has purchased all the weapons he wants, if there is any money left over, perhaps a little of it will trickle down to the less fortunate. Physical handicap is not the only deterrent to living a productive life here. There are other, more serious drawbacks.

There are also occasional blessings. The biggest blessing anyone can have is to be related to the Royal Family, even seven times removed. Then you can make it. Handicapped or not. For now, those who can't help themselves are taken care of by their families and are often hidden from the public."

Suddenly, Andrea saw the black Chevrolet crawling up the street. It parked directly under a "No Parking" sign, at the corner of the intersection where Andrea, Layla and the children waited, barely ten feet away.

"We're being watched again," Andrea said.

Layla kept her eyes focused on the road. "I wish I knew what they wanted. I can't figure out if it's you or me they're after."

"I'm sure it's me. As you said, they're probably doing their job of shadowing students who return. But, I have no idea why they're following me instead of my husband."

Layla shook uncontrollably.

Andrea was alarmed. "Maybe I should stop seeing you for a while."

"No!" Layla said emphatically.

"But you're so upset. Please think about it. Of course it would be my loss. You are helping me so much and you are my only friend."

"No, I want you to continue to come."

"All right." Andrea's voice was quiet.

Layla looked relieved. "I won't allow those bastards to intimidate me. I will go on with my life the way I see fit, regardless of the consequences. I cherish our friendship."

Andrea was deeply moved.

"Let's walk," Layla suggested. "I'll carry Kelly for a while. There's a shoe store two blocks down. He lets me use his phone. We'll phone for a call cab. They're expensive. But under the circumstances we seem to have no choice . . . unless you want to return home."

"No! I don't want to go back! I'm hungry for a pizza. Do they have pizza here?"

Layla calmed. A smile came to her face. "Oh, yes. I've seen three or four places that serve them. There's one on Old Shemran Road owned by an Iranian married to an American. They say he's the best. It's called Ray's Pizza."

"Wonderful. Let's hurry. I'm starved."

Layla extended her arms for Kelly.

Andrea handed her over. They walked down Yussefabad Avenue, which was packed with pedestrians and cars. Andrea turned around casually pretending to coax Layla's children to stay close to her and their mother, but really looking for the Chevrolet. "Don't look," she told Layla, "but they're having trouble following us in this traffic."

"Good."

Ten minutes after the phone call, a cab twisted its way in front of the shoe store. The women and children piled in. The cab sped to Old Shemran Road with its passengers giggling and laughing as though they didn't have a care in the world.

But not Layla. She looked tense, withdrawn.

The driver checked his rearview mirror repeatedly. After about five minutes, he asked curtly, "Are you women in some kind of trouble?"

"Why do you ask?" Layla asked innocently. "We're going out to eat. That's all."

Layla translated the driver's remark. Andrea's concern mounted. To think this was the way people were forced to live. They never felt safe, not like Americans could in their country.

The driver half turned his head, eyeing them suspiciously. Then turned back and kept his eyes riveted to the rearview mirror when he didn't have to watch the road.

"He can see them following us in his mirror," Layla whispered. "But he's afraid to say anything. He's not sure he can trust us."

"Is it always like this? How can people live in fear of everything they say and do. It doesn't seem possible in this day and age."

"It's possible and always with us. Fear is the most effective weapon. It has served the Shah well. So far. But one of these days it's going to explode in his face."

Andrea cringed. "Please be careful," she said gently patting her friend's hand.

"Perhaps that's what's wrong with us. Maybe we should learn to stand up for our rights despite the odds. Throughout our history we have said 'Yes Sir,' to despot after despot. They say dance. We dance. They say sing and we sing. Times have changed. We must stop relying on others to do for us what we must do for ourselves."

Andrea caught a glimpse of the driver's eyes in the mirror. She shuddered. She had assumed and she was sure Layla had assumed, that the driver did not speak English. The look Andrea saw in his eyes, told a different story. She let her eyes convey the message to her friend.

"I really don't care anymore," Layla replied shrugging her shoulders. "They can torture me and they can kill me. There are hundreds, thousands, perhaps millions more like me, smoldering like volcanoes. He can't kill us all. No. Not even he. We've got to start sometime."

Andrea didn't feel hungry anymore nor did she want the pizza. If she could turn back, she would. She felt Layla was deliberately courting trouble. Layla, herself, had cautioned her about informers and the need for absolute discretion. But she refused to heed her own advice. She was pale, angry, bitter.

The ten mile trip took them forty five minutes to cover. Andrea paid the driver, thanked him and moved to the sidewalk to help the children get out of the car. Seeing her struggle with Kelly, the driver left the car double parked, the engine running and came to help her. He carried Kelly to the door of the restaurant. His gallantry invited a furious blasting of horns by drivers stuck behind him. He apologized for not being able to help Andrea further and handed Kelly over. Touched, Andrea dug into her pocket and gave him a tip.

The restaurant was large, and looked much too expensive even if it was a pizza parlor. People of all ages occupied every inch of space, some sitting, some standing. They gulped down their drinks and devoured the food as soon as it was served. When a table was vacated, the first person to reach it, got to use it. They shoved and pushed at the sight of a vacant spot like bulldozers at work.

After waiting for half an hour, Layla detected a family getting ready to leave. "Quick. Over there," she said. She hurried to the table. Andrea and the children followed.

Layla stuck a fifty rial note in the hand of a waiter who dashed back and forth with a tray held high above everyone's head. The waiter bent his head. "The children are starved," Layla said. "Please hurry with our order."

Fifteen minutes later their pizzas were placed on the table. "It's the only way to get things done in this country," Layla explained.

"Perhaps we should attribute minor problems to what we refer to as growing pains." Andrea said with forced cheerfulness. She took a bite of her pizza. "Tastes just like the pizza at home. It was worth the trip."

Layla seemed restless, tense. Andrea watched her scan the crowd discreetly, repeatedly, then return her attention to the food in front of her. She didn't eat. A few minutes later she whispered, "The taxi driver is at the entrance. He's got his neck stretched like a giraffe looking over people's heads. He's probably looking for us."

"You don't think . . ."

"You never know."

"What should we do?"

"Keep eating. Don't look."

"I can't eat," Andrea whispered. "Too much attention spoils my appetite."

"You too, huh?"

Andrea placed the piece of pizza she was holding back in her plate.

"Damn," Layla said through clenched teeth. "He spotted us. He's coming over."

"Purple is a wonderful color on you," Andrea said loudly.

"I think so, too."

"Excuse me," the taxi driver interrupted them. "Possible speak to American lady, please?"

Andrea asked nervously, "What can I do for you?"

"Madame, check money, please."

"You asked for two hundred rials. I gave you two fifty."

"No, Madame. You give two one hundred rials and one five hundred rials. Not fifty. Please, here money." He handed her a five hundred rial note.

"Are you sure?" She looked at Layla but her face was expressionless.

"Yes. I not have money when I come work. I give money to wife. You my first customer."

Andrea and Layla exchanged glances.

Andrea felt confused and embarrassed as she glanced at the money in her palm. Was this what the Savak agent meant when he referred to a true Muslim? The driver appeared to be in his late twenties, poorly yet neatly dressed like an ordinary working man.

"Do you have children?" Andrea asked.

"Four Madame. Two boy. Two girl. God good to me."

"You'll make me very happy if you take this money and buy your kids something nice. Whatever you like. Please take it." She pushed the money into his limp hand.

The driver's eyes filled with tears. "Thank you. Thank you Madame. I will tell my mother to pray for you. May neither you nor your children ever come to harm."

"Here." Andrea gave him a small notebook and a pen from her purse. "Please, write your name. I will ask for you next time I need a cab."

Slowly, very carefully, he wrote his name in Latin letters on a piece of paper. "My name Gholam Reza," he said, as he handed her the paper.

He turned to leave, hesitated, stopped abruptly and looked at Layla like an inspector carefully examining a person for credentials. Then, he said something to her in Farsi.

The color drained from Layla's face. She became ashen.

She rose slowly. Her voice shook. "It's private enough here. My American friend doesn't understand Farsi. What did you want to tell me?"

Gholam Reza cast an uneasy glance in Andrea's direction.

Andrea busied herself cutting a slice of pizza into bite size pieces for Kelly.

The driver moved very close to Layla, almost touching her. He put his lips close to her ear. In a voice barely above a whisper, he said, "I am a Mujahed. I think we could work together. Call me." Thereupon, he bowed slightly, and left, fighting his way through the crowd.

Andrea understood every word.

Chapter 6

In early August, Layla's mother and father came from Qom to visit their daughter and grandchildren. It was late afternoon. Andrea wanted to leave but Layla wouldn't hear of it. She wanted her parents to get to know her American friend. Layla's father was a retired doctor, in his late sixties. Her mother was much younger, perhaps in her middle forties. Until Andrea left, she didn't hear the mother utter a word except for the initial greeting as she walked in.

Layla's father seemed to like Andrea. He urged Andrea to stay. Soon they were engrossed in an intense discussion about the history of the country. Totally captivated, she'd forgotten the time, dinner and even Kelly. Kelly had become a regular visitor now. Layla and her children insisted that she bring Kelly along whenever she came to their house. A quick glance in her daughter's direction convinced her it was past her bedtime. "What time is it?" she asked. "I've forgotten my watch."

"A few minutes after nine. Why don't you stay and have dinner with us?"

"Thank you, but I can't. It's past Kelly's bedtime." She

smiled. "I love talking to your father, he's a walking encyclopedia."

Andrea hurried home. She watched for suspicious-looking cars and people. A scrawny dog searched through a pile of garbage. Otherwise, the street was deserted.

She let herself and Kelly in. Her mother-in-law, Sayid and a gray-haired man were in the living room. After greeting them politely, she went to her room, gave Kelly a quick bath, fed her and put her to bed.

When she went to the kitchen to get dinner for herself, Andrea heard Naene whisper something to Sayid.

Sayid came to the kitchen. "There's a man here to see you."

"Me?" Andrea asked, taken by surprise. "Who is he?"

"He says he has a note for you from Mani."

Andrea was excited. She hadn't heard from him since he'd left three weeks earlier. "It's Kelly's birthday tomorrow," she said happily. "I knew he wouldn't forget."

The visitor gave her the note. There was a brief message scribbled on a piece of paper. "Urgent. Give ten thousand dollars to the bearer of note." It carried Mani's signature.

She didn't let Sayid see how let down she felt. She was getting used to camouflaging her true emotions. She handed the note to Sayid. "Could you please take a look. It's not at all like Mani to send me a note like this."

Sayid read the note.

Lately, Andrea had noticed a remote look in Sayid's eyes and a mask-like expression. She was disturbed by it.

He gave the note back without comment.

She heard Mani's mother mumble something but she couldn't understand it.

The mother repeated her request with more urgency shifting her gaze from her son to her daughter-in-law.

"My mother says to tell you that he's been waiting for you since five this afternoon," Sayid explained.

Andrea thought of giving reasons for her delay then

changed her mind determined to guard her privacy at all cost.

Mrs. Abbassi Sr., whom everyone called Naene, raised the pitch of her voice and regardless of who was talking to whom continued with her monologue. Sayid waited for his mother to finish. She continued with increased vehemence. Pointing her index finger at Andrea, she shook it repeatedly as though demanding a wrong to be righted.

Naene talked too fast for Andrea to understand. Also, Andrea was determined not to let anyone know she could understand the language.

"Have I done something to upset your mother?" Andrea asked calmly.

"You really want to know?"

"Yes."

"Mother says only women with no morals roam the streets at night without their husbands."

Andrea let the remark pass. She watched the visitor pace the room. "Who is this man? He looks upset."

"He's Farhad's father. He says he doesn't like what he's doing and thinks he was followed. He wants to leave as soon as you give him the money."

"Does he really expect me to hand over a large sum like that to someone I don't know just because he claims he carries a note from my husband?"

"If you don't, you will live to regret it," Sayid said coolly.

Andrea stiffened. "Are you telling me that I should give him the money?"

"I told you when you first came to this country that you should return home."

"Yes, you did. And you've told me many times since. What has that got to do with this man and his note?"

Sayid dropped his hands in exasperation. "What can I do to make you understand? How can I explain?"

"Explain what?"

Sayid threw his head back and laughed, a bitter laugh.

Andrea waited.

Naene resumed her monologue accenting her words with threatening gestures.

"Do you have that much cash with you?" Sayid asked.

"With me, no. I deposited it in the British Bank of the Middle East the day after Mani left. I didn't feel comfortable with that much cash in my purse."

"Why cash?"

"Mani insisted on cash. He wanted me to bring fifty thousand."

"He would."

"He said we'd lose money if we transferred it through a bank."

"He would."

"Oh, Sayid. Please say what you mean. It's impossible to read your mind when all you say is 'he would.'"

His expression changed suddenly. The muscles around his lips tightened. "Don't play the fool with me. You're up to your eyeballs in trouble but you wont admit it even to yourself. You think these men will stop demanding money simply because you refuse to give it to them?"

"It's my money. My father left it to me."

Sayid shook his head in disbelief. "You're stupider than I thought."

Andrea was stunned. Not knowing what else to do, she ran up the stairs to her room.

The pitch of Naene's voice had found a new higher level. She shouted obscenities, which Andrea understood. She heard them often, whenever Naene referred to her. 'Negis' meant unclean, 'khariji' meant foreigner, and 'pul' money. This night, a new word, 'Jende' was added to her vocabulary. Andrea made a mental note to ask Layla what the word meant.

Since Andrea did not hand over the money, her mother-in-law's anger was fueled with renewed and unrestrained vigor. She threatened, cursed and pleaded between sobs.

Andrea became alarmed. Perhaps Mani was in trouble

and wrote the note under duress. She had about a thousand dollars in cash with her. She grabbed her purse and hurried downstairs.

Naene stopped crying for a brief moment and gave Andrea an icy look. Then she spoke to her son while the tears continued to flow. Although Andrea understood little of what she was moaning about, it was not hard to gather it had to do with money. She used the word 'pul' repeatedly.

"Enough." It was Sayid.

Naene stopped. She was out of breath. Sayid brought his face real close to hers and said, "No, I will not give him a single rial."

He walked out.

Andrea was frightened. Sayid's presence gave her confidence and courage. She could talk to him even though he seemed to carry the weight of the world on his shoulders. Now he was gone. She didn't know whether to give the thousand dollars to Farhad's father or not. She was still debating the issue, when Farhad's father opened the front door and stomped out.

Emotionally drained, Andrea needed to be alone. She returned to her room, checked Kelly, read for a while, then tried to sleep. She slipped under the cover, tucking herself in carefully from head to toe, despite the heat. It was the only way she could avoid being bitten by the mosquitoes buzzing around the room.

Her sleep was fitful and restless. She felt she needed to go to the bathroom. She tried to get up, she couldn't. She thought she was dreaming. She tried to turn to her side. It was impossible to move. Two giant hands kept her nailed to her bed.

Someone pulled the cover off her head. Light from a flashlight pierced her half shut eyes. Then the hand on her shoulder loosened, allowing her to pull herself up. Two men in their early twenties, with black, fuzzy hair, small beards, black eyes and thick mustaches were staring at her. They looked like identical twins, except that the man who had pinned her down had a big, black mole between his eyebrows.

Andrea was petrified.

"Where's the money?" asked the man with the mole.

"What money?"

"Hit her," ordered the second man.

The man slapped her hard.

Andrea's face burned. She felt a trickle of blood make its way slowly down her chin. "It's in my purse. On the chest of drawers."

"Don't play games with us. There's about a thousand dollars in your purse. Where's the rest of the money?"

It dawned on her that these were no ordinary thieves. These men knew exactly what they wanted and were determined to get it. The only person who could have told them was Mani. Had he done so because he had to or wanted to?

"That's all I have."

The men exchanged confused glances.

Pointing the flashlight at her face again, the man with the mole said sarcastically, "Don't tell me a rich woman like you has less than a thousand dollars to her name."

"I didn't say that."

"Then, what did you say!" the man thundered. He stopped abruptly.

"You'll wake everyone up," warned his partner.

The man who had shouted checked his watch. "Who's everyone? There's only the old woman. It's five minutes to two. That vermin won't be home for another hour or more."

"Mani said sometimes when his brother loses heavily, he comes home early. I'll check the street."

He moved to the window, parted the curtain and looked outside. He nodded.

The other man approached Andrea. "We don't like to be kept waiting," he whispered softly with a frightening grin. "Now if you'll tell us where you've hid the money, we won't bother you anymore."

"It's in the bank," Andrea whispered back just as softly.

"You're lying, you bitch," growled the man slapping her face. "We know it's here somewhere. It could cost you your life if you don't comply."

Andrea's thoughts raced. She wiped the blood from her chin. Her jaw hurt. There had to be a way of outwitting these men. An idea occurred to her. "Look," she said, trying to sound sincere, "I know you're my husband's friends. I heard you mention his name. I know he's a committed nationalist and I'm all for it. I hate what my government did in Vietnam and I see we're not doing much better here. I'd be happy to give you the money. Unfortunately, I took it to the bank after Mani left. You tell me how and I'll get it to you."

Both men stared at her as though she had suddenly appeared from another planet. A moment later, the man with the mole said doubtfully, "You could be setting a trap."

"If you don't believe me, ask my husband. He'll tell you how involved I was with human rights issues. I participated in demonstrations, marches and sit-ins because I believe in freedom. Do you know my husband personally?"

Taken by surprise, the men studied her but didn't answer.

"Anyway," Andrea heard herself say, "he never told me not to put the money in the bank."

The men exchanged uneasy glances.

"How much?" asked one of the men.

"I don't know what you mean," she replied.

"I have a feeling you're playing for time."

"You're free to believe what you like."

"Listen to me. If you're hoping that your lover will come back and save you, forget it. We have men posted outside to grab him if he arrives before we're done."

Andrea wanted to ask who her lover was, but didn't. They were not through with her yet. The man with the mole seemed to be in charge. He said, "Although I'm told my English is pretty good, you seem to have trouble understanding me. I repeat. How much did you put in the bank?"

"Ten thousand dollars."

"That's not enough."

"That's all I have."

The men moved to a corner and talked in whispers. Soon, the man with the mole approached Andrea.

"When can you get the money?"

"When the banks open."

The man with the mole spoke to his partner. "According to Mani, she doesn't know Farsi. We can talk freely. What do you think? Can we trust her?"

"We've ransacked the room. The money's not here. There's no question about that. Can we trust her not to betray us? I don't know."

They were silent, seemingly searching for a solution. Finally the junior partner spoke. "Perhaps we should make a tentative arrangement to meet her tonight. Meanwhile we'll have time to consult Zia. I know we need the money for the operation and there aren't that many days left until the twenty eighth. But Mani said nothing about the possibility that she might put the money in the bank."

"You're right," agreed his friend. "Under the circumstances we have no choice. But we have to make sure she doesn't trick us. Think and be quick with it. How should we scare her so she doesn't dare double cross us?"

"She doesn't look the type. She sounds sincere."

"You're forgetting your training. You know what a person looks like has nothing to do with what she might do."

"You have a better idea?"

The leader faced Andrea, flashlight at the ready, its beams blinding her momentarily. "We'll be back tonight. Have the money ready. Don't get any bright ideas if you want to see your husband alive again."

Andrea nodded amazed at her own composure.

Both men dashed from the room and down the stairs. She heard the front door close. Shivering despite the summer heat, she walked to the window. She didn't know why, except that she felt restless and it gave her something to do. Momentarily, two shadows crept from the house to the sidewalk, gliding cautiously away from the solitary street lamp diffusing a hazy weak glow.

Two doors down, the two men were grabbed and in a matter of seconds disappeared into the doorway. There was hardly any struggle. It was like being swallowed by quick sand. They were slipping up the street one second and gone the next.

Her iron control melted. She shivered in the darkness. When the shaking stopped, she dragged herself to her bed, sat on the edge, with her face in her hands, and let her tears flow freely.

She didn't know how long she'd been in that state. She felt a pair of powerful arms lift her gently, brush a few strands of hair from her face, then tuck her in bed. She heard a man's voice whisper in her ear, "Sleep. No harm will ever come to you again as long as I'm alive."

Chapter 7

Andrea was feeding Kelly late Thursday afternoon on August 19th, when Mani strolled in accompanied by Farhad. He looked thinner than when she'd last seen him in July, preoccupied. He watched her for a while, then spoke, "How have you been?"

Farhad stood a few feet away, a cynical smile on his face.

Andrea raised her eyes and glanced at the man she'd married. "Fine. How have you been?" The words were controlled. She wouldn't let him see how vulnerable she was.

"Okay, I guess. I'd like to have a word with you, now."

"What's so important it can't wait. You disappear for weeks without bothering to get in touch with me, then you waltz in here expecting me to do your bidding. What's come over you?"

Mani looked at Farhad.

Farhad nodded ever so slightly.

Mani said, "It's important that I talk to you."

"If it's that imperative, speak. I can take care of Kelly and listen to you also."

"I'm sorry I couldn't get in touch with you sooner. You've got to believe me. My life was in danger."

What a surprise. He was finally admitting he was in trouble.

"Why should your life be in danger?"

"I swear I don't know."

Farhad nodded his head again. Andrea sensed they weren't prepared to divulge everything. It was a planned, rehearsed act.

"If that's the case, then perhaps we should return home."

"Home? This is my home. I'm not about to let a bunch of thugs drive me from my own country."

Andrea watched Farhad reach into his shirt pocket for a cigarette. He lit it. "Actually we came to discuss a business proposition with you."

"What kind of business?" She couldn't hide the dry ice in her voice.

"We want to import construction material. There's a fantastic market for it. We can double our money in no time."

"How many people are involved?" Andrea was intrigued. There seemed to be no limit to their imagination. Because two of their cronies who had visited her in the night, had failed their mission, they were trying a new approach. Should she question them about it? It was no use. They'd deny it. She chose to play their game.

"Mani and I."

"That sounds like a good idea. There's a lot of construction going on. With Mani's engineering background, you should do well."

Farhad shifted his weight from one foot to the other. "We need fifty thousand dollars."

"That's a lot of money. How will you raise it?"

"That's the problem." Farhad's voice carried despair. "No bank will loan us that much money without collateral."

"Maybe you should start small. If all goes well, you can always expand."

"That won't work. Unless we start big, we won't be able to compete. This kind of business can't be done on a small scale."

Kelly took her last bite. Andrea wiped her mouth with a washcloth, lifted the child from her lap and sat her in her wheelchair. Farhad kept talking.

"Mani tells me your father left you a large inheritance. We thought maybe you could lend us the money."

Mani stepped back, leaned against the wall with his hands behind his back and looked expectantly at his wife.

"I'm sorry. I can't."

Mani reached at her, grabbed her by the arm. "This is important." His fingers nearly pierced her flesh. "I have to have the money. Make arrangements for the transfer tomorrow morning."

"Is that why you came back?"

He squeezed her arm harder. "I told you. It's important."

"Please, let go. You're hurting me."

He pushed her away. "You know damn well I wouldn't have asked you if I had a choice."

"I'll have to think about it."

"There's no time for that. We've got to have the money immediately."

"It can't be done immediately. I will have to get in touch with my lawyer in the States, he will have to liquidate some stocks, the cash will have to be put in my account before it can be transferred."

"You're lying, you bitch," Mani yelled. "You were always tight with your precious money. What good is money if we can't have it when we need it?"

Farhad looked calm and composed. "We have a unique opportunity to buy a shipload of construction material real cheap," he said. "The merchant who imported it, is having cash flow problems. We could make a killing if we could lay our hands on cash."

"How did you hear about this deal?"

"Through a friend." Farhad gave her a crooked smile.

"It sounds too good to be true."

"Why do say that?"

"I don't know. Did he have reason to think that you have ready cash? Most people invest their money. They wouldn't have cash, not such a large sum and not on such short notice."

Farhad turned to Mani. "You have a clever wife. Her answers are not answers but questions." He faced Andrea. "How others handle their money is of little interest to us. We need money. Your delaying tactics are very clever, not to your advantage, but clever."

She'd always felt she needed to be on guard when Farhad was around. The chill of his words reinforced and escalated that feeling. It was difficult to concentrate on what he said.

Then it was Mani's voice, demanding. "Tomorrow is Friday," he said. "It's the weekend here but a weekday in the States. Call your lawyer and ask him to make the transfer."

Kelly began to cry.

Andrea took her daughter in her arms, sat in a chair and rocked the child gently to sleep. She wondered what kind of trouble her husband was in. What made a decent man turn into a beast and how dare he come back after disappearing for three weeks and demand money. Her money. Money which she would need for Kelly's medical expenses, the nursemaid to take care of the child and for herself. He had no income. And this could be the first of many demands. Jim Talbot's warning whirled through her mind, haunting her. "Once you leave this lounge, you're on your own. We can't help you."

So be it. She'd help herself. She wouldn't let them intimidate her. "I've already explained, the money is invested," she said with controlled calm. "It takes time."

"I want an answer tomorrow. Do I make myself clear?"

Farhad's hands were clenched, his knuckles white. He motioned for Mani to follow. They descended the stairs and disappeared into a room on the ground floor which Mani called his 'office.'

Andrea lifted Kelly gently, kissed her forehead and tucked her in bed. She was relieved they'd finally left. She had to think, to plan a strategy to minimize her vulnerability. Somehow, she had to find out why they needed so much money, why the urgency. To think she might have believed them if they hadn't sent accomplices two nights before to rob her.

She could do nothing but wait. Wait for what? They were probably busy plotting another elaborate scheme to get her to comply.

The walls were closing in on her. She had to get out.

She checked Kelly. The child was sound asleep. She went downstairs and called Irene.

A few minutes later, the two men emerged from the office. Mani asked the maid to serve dinner.

Andrea wondered if she'd be invited to join them. The maid set two places. Apparently not. A platter of rice pilaf and a bowl of lamb stew was brought in.

Andrea approached Mani. "I called Irene. We'd like to go to the movies."

"You want to go, go."

She was sure he'd object to her leaving. Why didn't he? What was he up to now?

"Will you be staying home tonight?"

"I don't know. Why do you ask?"

"Kelly's asleep. If you leave, can you have Fatima check her?"

Mani answered with a grunt.

When Irene arrived, Andrea was ready. She checked Kelly, said goodbye, grabbed her purse and left.

The movie, which was in English, helped distract her thoughts temporarily. But she knew it was just a distraction. Fortunately, Irene knew nothing about Mani's absence so Andrea didn't feel a need to discuss anything with Irene.

When the show was over, Irene drove her home. They said their goodbyes and Irene drove away.

Naene often slept in her armchair while watching television, so Andrea opened the door quietly. Naene's chair was occupied by the family cat. The TV was on but no one was in the living room.

Then Andrea heard an agitated voice from the kitchen. It was Farhad. "We've got to find a way," he said. "If we don't show up with the money, our credibility is finished. Finished! Do you understand? We can't wait a week or two. The plan is for the twenty-eighth. No, don't interrupt. Let me think."

There was ten seconds of silence, then the animated voice. "Mehrdad will have the check ready. We'll be at the bank when the doors open Saturday morning. But ten thousand dollars is nothing. We have to find a way for her to speed the process of transferring more money."

"How good is Mehrdad's work? Don't you think someone at the bank will become suspicious when I present them with a check for thousands of dollars with my wife's signature on it and she's not with me to verify it?"

"Don't worry. No one has detected Mehrdad's forgery yet. His work can't be surpassed."

"Farhad, that's not what I meant. Supposing they want to know why my wife is not there herself to withdraw the money. What am I supposed to tell them?"

"You know sometimes . . . sometimes you really get on my nerves. You'll find cause for worry no matter how failproof a plan is. If they ask you such a dumb question, which they won't, think of something intelligent to say and shut them up."

"Wouldn't it be easier . . .?"

"No."

"I don't like it. The manager of that bank is British. We can't buy him. If he suspects the least discrepancy, he'll notify the authorities."

"You're a pessimist. Taking risks is part of the job. How else can we advance the cause?"

"It's my neck. You won't be able to help, and she won't. I

know her. Her feelings have never been moderate. She has loved fiercely, unquestioningly, until now, because I have managed to be the ideal husband and father. Let her think she's being used, and we're finished. I know her."

"Stop saying 'I know her.' If you did, you would know she won't come with you to the bank and willingly hand over thousands of dollars without knowing why. Not even to you, even if she's crazy about you. Why should she?"

"She'll do anything for me. I'll tell her why. It doesn't have to be the truth."

Someone spit. Andrea realized she'd been holding her breath and clenching her teeth. She made a conscious effort to breathe. Farhad's voice was barely audible. "The first rule you must remember, is never to underestimate your opponent. You're overestimating yourself, and underestimating her. Even someone as simple as her, is bound to ask questions before parting with her money."

She wondered what gave him the idea that she was simple.

"I don't like it." Mani responded.

"Neither do I. Do you have a better suggestion?"

There was a pause, then Mani said, "Let's ask for a meeting. Maybe we can persuade them to postpone the operation for a couple of weeks. By then, I'm sure the transfer will have been made."

"You talk like a child." Farhad's voice exuded anger. "This type of operation takes months of planning. You want us to walk in there and admit we failed to do our duty and ask them to change their plans?"

"No, I don't. All we need is a couple of weeks. She wasn't lying. It takes time to liquidate assets."

"You should have seen to it that it was done before you left the States. You were instructed to do so."

"It's easy for you to say. You're not married to an American. They can be very stubborn."

"I'm sure it can be done."

"I tried. You tried yourself tonight. It's not easy to convince her. You think all Americans are simple. Believe me, they're not. Not when the issue in question is money."

"You leave her to me. Every one has a weak spot. It won't be long before I find hers."

She thought she heard someone sigh. Then there was absolute quiet.

Andrea's senses were on full alert. Farhad terrified her. It was his eyes, the way he looked at her, the contempt.

Suddenly, there was movement in the kitchen. For an instant she felt paralyzed by fear. Then she dashed to the front door, opened it and inserted the key in the keyhole. She fumbled with the lock, raised her head and saw both men watching her.

"Are you having trouble with the key?" Mani eyed her suspiciously.

"No, it works fine." Andrea's voice was so steady it amazed her.

She raised her head to be greeted with Farhad's twisted smile. "Perhaps the lady is not used to opening her own doors. Perhaps that's why it's taking her so long."

Did he know or was he merely hoping to corner her to find out. She pulled the key from the lock, stood straight and faced her husband.

Ever since they'd arrived, he managed to be either busy or away when it was time to go to bed. He had yet to sleep in their bed. Except for grabbing her arm to emphasize a demand, he had not touched her. She decided to try, regardless.

"Are you all done, dear? Will you be joining me soon?"

Her questions seemed to catch him off guard. "No. I'll probably be up all night."

Farhad stuck his thumbs in his belt and riveted his eyes on her. They reminded her of spotlights used by hunters to paralyze their prey. His face looked drawn, the corner of his lips curved downward. He appeared ready to attack.

She was petrified. It was best to make a hasty exit.

"Good night." She climbed the stairs.

There was no response.

She sat on her bed and shivered in the August heat. The revelations of the night spun through her head. Why the large sum of money? Why the urgency? She thought of their intention to cash a forged check and broke into a sweat. And, the twenty eighth. Farhad said the plan is for the twenty eighth. What plan? He didn't sound impressed with ten thousand dollars. Nonetheless, he was willing to risk withdrawing it with a forged check. How could she stop them? Could she block her account? They couldn't possibly go through with it. Or could they? The banks were closed on Fridays so she couldn't do anything tomorrow. If she could have a few minutes alone with Mani, she felt confident she could get him to give her a few answers. Yet a nagging voice warned her. In all probability, what she'd overheard was a small part of a larger scheme. It had to be. Farhad was much too shrewd to resort to forgery, unless their objective was of such paramount importance that no sacrifice was too big for it.

Sleep eluded her. She picked up a book and read until soft rays of sunshine pierced through the window panes. She opened the door cautiously and checked around to see if the men were still up. They weren't. She crept barefoot, down the stairs, to the kitchen, to make coffee.

Naene, Mani's mother, was at her usual spot in the living room. She was kneeling on a prayer rug, her face turned toward Mecca, reciting her morning prayers.

Andrea waited till her coffee was ready, poured herself a cup, took it, and tiptoed out of the kitchen.

She almost dropped the cup.

Naene lay on her side with a ghastly pallor, her right arm twisted under her chest. Her eyelids were half closed revealing only the whites of her eyes. Her finger nails and lips were blue. She fought for breath.

Chapter 8

The more Mani thought about the meeting that night, the more apprehensive he got. What could he tell the members of The Revolutionary Council? That his wife would not give him money? And let the members think he's a wimp? He couldn't stall them much longer. They'd order him to leave, and then . . . No one had survived dismissal. He couldn't take that chance.

Hours of internal debate convinced him he had only one choice; to reach Zia Kashani, the leader of the group and use his mother's illness as an excuse not to attend the meeting.

After a moment's hesitation, he reached for the telephone and dialed the number of the Hilton Hotel.

A woman's voice informed him the operator was on the line.

"Could you have Zia Kashani paged please?"

Mani waited impatiently pacing the living room.

After a minute the connection was cut off.

"Damn the phone system in this country," he said out loud.

He pondered over what to do next. He had to reach Zia. He had taken a chance by calling but hoped, given the circumstances, he would not be blamed too much. Every member had clear instructions: never to call or be seen in public with a member of the group unless it was an emergency. For that reason Farhad lived in their house as a friend of the family. Both men did their best not to be seen together in public.

Well, this was an emergency. He put his coat on and left.

There were few people in the hotel lobby. He glanced around. There was no sign of Zia. He crossed the lobby to the cocktail lounge. It was crowded and noisy. People of many nationalities were gathered in groups. Mani leaned on the bar and ordered a drink. In one corner, four Japanese men nursed their cognacs. They looked like businessmen. He took his drink and moved closer to three Americans engrossed in conversation. He perched on a bar stool with his back to the Americans, reached for a cigarette, lit it and inhaled it deeply.

He finished his drink and ordered another.

The bartender was a colleague. He placed a second glass of tea with ice cubes in front of Mani then turned his attention to a tall, broad-shouldered American who was struggling to fit his huge body on the bar stool next to Mani. He ordered Scotch on the rocks.

"Do you speak English?" the American asked.

"Yes."

"My name is Sam Weinstock."

"Mani Abbassi. Glad to meet you."

Mani looked around casually. He saw Zia Kashani watching him from the corner of his eye while serving drinks to customers seated nearby. What Mani knew about Zia was what Farhad had told him. Zia was an engineering student in Germany when he was recalled by the Revolutionary Council to lead the group. The Council needed a replacement urgently. His predecessor had been apprehended by Savak. That was two years ago. Soon after Zia's arrival, it became clear to him that if he wanted to keep abreast with what was going on in the country, the best place to be was the Hilton. So he had taken a job as a waiter in the cocktail lounge. The information he gathered at work, was invaluable to the revolutionary cause.

Mr. Weinstock gulped his drink and ordered another. He maneuvered himself closer to Mani talking eagerly. He told Mani he was from Orange County, California. He'd worked in Saudi Arabia for two years. He hated it. "If you didn't know influential natives, life could be hell there."

"How come?"

"No booze. No women. In desperation we flew to Beirut on weekends, spent it drinking and grabbing any skirt we could lay our hands on. The pay was very good but it ain't worth it."

"You like it better here?" Mani was listening and talking like a robot. His mind was on his next move. How to make contact with Zia without drawing attention.

"Much," replied Sam Weinstock. "Colleagues of mine who have been here longer than I, claim you can live here like a king. A few more years and this place will be as good as Europe, maybe better."

Mani watched the American drink steadily. "Have you been here long?"

"Come and go. Six months. I work for Sedco. Recruiting officer."

You're no more a recruiting officer than I am, Mani thought. He didn't trust Americans working overseas. Most had ties to the CIA: positions and titles were cover ups. Fortunately, he didn't have to worry about Sam Weinstock or whatever his real name was. The man was drunk.

He had to be careful though. One never knew.

He waited till the American turned his head to reach for his drink. Then he nodded for the bartender to bring his bill.

The bartender placed a small, silver tray with the bill in front of Mani and moved away.

Mani turned his back partially to Sam Weinstock, reached

for his wallet took the banknotes he'd prepared with a message for Zia, and placed them on the silver tray.

The bartender took the tray and placed it underneath the counter.

Soon after, Zia moved behind the bar, told the bartender to have a gin and tonic ready for a customer, glanced around quickly, put the contents of the tray in his pocket and walked away.

Mani waited for the bartender to bring the change. That would be the signal for his next move. The bartender continued taking orders and serving drinks without changing pace or expression. Mani stared at the clock behind the bar. With every passing minute, the fear in him reached new heights. Could something be wrong? Would Zia understand? He could not hazard a guess.

Four minutes later, in the course of serving a drink to a customer, the bartender brought the silver tray with the change.

Mani counted to sixty silently, then rose. "Keep the change," he told the bartender. Turning to Sam Weinstock, "It was nice meeting you. Bye."

His voice quivered as he spoke. He tried to pull himself together. It was too late to turn back. He squared his shoulders, strode nonchalantly across the lounge, to the men's room where he knew Zia would be waiting for him.

Zia stood facing the bathroom mirror combing his wiry hair furiously. With each stroke his hair ballooned around his square head. He cursed, stuck the comb in his pocket, moved away from the mirror, threw a piece of crumpled paper in the trash can and was gone.

Mani took his time washing his hands. Two Korean men were engaged in heated conversation. He had to wait for them to leave.

Still talking, the Koreans drifted out.

Mani double checked. There was no one in the bathroom.

He sighed deeply. Then with the speed of a pickpocket, he

reached for the crumpled piece of paper in the trash can, shoved it in his pocket and left the bathroom.

As he crossed the lounge to the front door of the hotel, he glanced around quickly. Sam Weinstock was not there. It surprised him. The American had ordered a double Scotch shortly before Mani left. He must have really drank it fast. Maybe he passed out. Who cared?

Mani's thoughts were on the note in his pocket. While driving home, he was tempted repeatedly to take a quick look at it. But he knew better. There was always the possibility of being followed. He had to wait for the privacy of his room.

Another sigh of relief. He was home. Finally. He rushed to his office, closed the door and read the note. It consisted of two words. "Be there." Agony replaced apprehension. He could see it clearly. A colossal mistake, one which could cost him his position in the Revolutionary Council and in all probability, his life. All because his wife, who had inherited millions, would not give him a measly fifty thousand dollars. Oh, God. If he could at least get the ten thousand, they'd know he was trying.

He burned the note in an ashtray and flushed the ashes down the toilet.

It was eight in the evening. The meeting was scheduled for ten that night. He slumped in an armchair in the living room, his fingers entwined, staring into space, waiting for Farhad to arrive.

The front door opened and Andrea walked in.

"Where have you been? Don't tell me you went for a walk again."

"I was at the hospital."

"How's my mother?"

"She's in the intensive care unit. The cardiologist said he'll know more tomorrow when the test results come in."

"Did you call your attorney?"

"I didn't have time. I was at the hospital all day."

"I warn you," Mani yelled. "Don't play games with me. I

need money and I need it now. Call him tonight. It will be morning there. You should be able to reach him."

"That's all you seem to care about lately. We have other problems. Why can't we talk?"

"Nag. Nag. Nag. That's all you ever do. Why can't you leave me alone?"

His callous manner grated on her nerves. She had planned to tell him that his mother asked about him several times during the day wondering why her beloved son had not come to see her, but she decided not to. He looked angry, preoccupied. She climbed the stairs to her room.

Mani did not move. He remained sprawled in the armchair while his wife talked to Kelly, bathed her and fed her.

The doorbell rang as Andrea descended the stairs. Mani answered it.

Farhad marched in, his chin up, his shoulders pushed back, his anger evident despite his apparent attempts to control it. "Who's here?"

"Andrea, Fatima and Kelly."

"Send them away. We need to talk."

"Fatima is getting ready to leave. Andrea came home from the hospital a short while ago. She'll probably have dinner and go to bed. Anyway, it won't matter. We'll speak Farsi."

"What about Sayid?" Farhad asked.

"His car is not outside. I'm sure he's at the hospital, not because he's crazy about his mother but because he wants to impress her. To prove he's a better son. I haven't been to see her yet."

"Why not? You had all day."

"I was busy."

Fatima pulled her chaddor over her head, said goodbye and left.

Andrea was in the kitchen preparing dinner. From the looks and behavior of her husband, she sensed something was wrong. She could easily see and hear from the kitchen which was separated from the living room by an open space. The kitchen did not have a door.

Farhad lowered himself slowly into an armchair. "Tonight's meeting is cancelled."

Mani sounded overjoyed. "That's the best news I've had all day."

"I wouldn't be so thrilled if I were you. The meeting was cancelled because of last minute complications. Zia feels he is being shadowed. Somehow Savak learned about our meeting tonight. Since only members knew about the meeting, it's not difficult to deduce that he suspects one of us."

Mani shook his head. "I don't believe it. No member of our group would do such a thing."

"You're right. All the members have been with the group for years. Except you. He doesn't know you personally and he doesn't trust you. Members suspected of treason are not asked questions. They disappear without a trace. You've got to be very careful."

Andrea's teeth sank deeper into the drumstick she was biting. No wonder Savak had Mani under surveillance. He was involved. But since when?

"Get hold of yourself," Farhad yelled. "What the hell is the matter with you?"

"I . . . I . . . went to the Hilton today."

"What? What for?"

"To talk to Zia."

Farhad shot up like a missile. "Why? How could you do such a stupid thing? You were told from the first meeting never to be seen with a member unless it was an absolute emergency? Especially not with Zia."

Lamely, Mani tried to pacify his friend. "I couldn't wait for you. You said you'd be gone all day. It would be too late."

"Too late for what?"

"I thought I'd use my mother's illness as an excuse to postpone the meeting. It would give me time to get the money."

"You don't need time. You need guts. You need to be able to stand up to your wife and demand that she give it to you. What choice does she have now that she's here? You have total control. She can't leave the country without your approval. She can't escape with a disabled child. She can't do anything."

God, how she wished he'd go away. The man was vicious, repulsive.

"I know all that," Mani explained. "I also know that she wasn't lying. Her money is invested, mostly in real estate. A little over ten thousand dollars is all the cash she has in the bank."

"I don't give a damn if she's lying or not. You've not only put yourself at risk, you've got me in trouble too. Who do you think was instrumental in getting you accepted by the group? Me. Who do you think told them about your work, your loyalty, your sacrifices? Me. It took years to convince them. And what do you do? You screw it up in one afternoon."

Mani slumped further into the sofa. His knees shook. He wrapped his arms around his knees, locked his fingers and lay his head on his knees.

Farhad paced the room and smoked. Finally he faced Mani. "Let's sort this out. You went to see Zia. How did you make contact?"

"I went to the cocktail lounge."

"Who was the bartender?"

"Velayati. I gave him a note to pass to Zia."

"Did you get to talk to Zia?"

"No. He left me a note in the trash can, in the bathroom."

"What did it say?"

"Be there."

Farhad continued pacing the room. "That means the meeting was on until then. Something else must have happened. Think."

Mani's voice sounded like it came from a distance. In short, almost incoherent sentences, he explained the events of the afternoon.

"This American you speak of, was he there when you left?"

Mani thought his head would explode. How stupid of him. He should have known. "No," he murmured. "No. He wasn't there. I checked. You think . . ."

"You think, I think. What the hell does it matter what we think. It's done now. There's nothing we can do but cool it for a while and hope the price we pay won't be with our lives. Zia is not a man who forgives and forgets. He's ruthless."

Mani's heart pounded against his ribs as though demanding release. He cracked his knuckles, bent his head and, with a voice barely above a whisper, called on the prophet Muhammed and every other prophet he could think of, to come to his rescue.

"Stop your demented rambling," Farhad snapped. "You make me sick with all that religious garbage. The only way we can save our necks is by coming up with an idea which will put us back in favor. Think."

Mani tried to pull himself together. "How much time do you think we have?"

"That depends. The target was due to return to Tehran on Tuesday but we have learned that he won't be back until Wednesday or Thursday. It gives us a little more time to plan and obtain funds. The fact that they need money desperately and the possibility that you might be able to provide it, might be our only chance to undo the damage of your thoughtless act of this afternoon. Do me a favor. Don't ever go to the Hilton unless you check with me first."

"Wouldn't think of it."

"Good. Now let's get down to business. Disregard your previous instructions. You'll receive new ones at our next meeting."

If I'm still around, Mani mourned inwardly. "Do we wait for instructions here or in Isfahan?"

"Isfahan is on hold for the time being. Our information is

that Savak has full knowledge of our activities there. We'll find out who the rat is. But until we hear from headquarters, we do nothing."

"At least one good thing came out of this mess. We won't have to return to Isfahan for a while."

"My feelings precisely."

"Does Zia know you're staying at our house?"

"Of course he does. All the members do. They also know that you are under surveillance by Savak. I should move out."

Brilliant idea, Andrea thought. Maybe then she'd get a chance to talk to her husband alone.

"You're right. We should find a place for you. We'll go talk to an agent tomorrow. With all the Americans in town, it might take a while."

"It won't. My uncle owns a real estate business. Finding a place doesn't worry me. How to pay for it, does. I have given all my money to the cause. All of us have. And if we don't do something about your contribution pretty soon, we'll be in a lot of trouble."

"I really don't know what to do," Mani said. "She's like a block of ice. She won't budge."

"You've got to be careful not to arouse suspicion. We'll start a business, rent an office, hire a secretary, do everything a legitimate business does, then present her with a fait accompli. She'll have no choice but to believe us and speed the transfer of money. It will also give us an excuse to be together and hopefully get Savak off your back."

"What kind of business do you have in mind?"

"I'll have to discuss it with Zia but what's wrong with what we told your wife?"

"It's a good idea but it needs capital. Where do we get the money?"

"Is my darling brother preparing yet for another venture?"

Both men watched shocked as Sayid descended the stairs. Sayid had his usual sarcastic grin on his face, the alcoholic pallor in his eyes and a constant mild tremor in his hands.

Farhad stared at Mani with a horrified expression. It was evident from Sayid's manner that he had heard them.

"When did you come home?" Mani asked. "How long have you been listening to us?"

Sayid did not answer.

"Where's your car? It's not outside."

"I lost it gambling last night," Sayid laughed as though it was the funniest thing he'd ever heard. "Don't worry. I'll probably win it back tonight."

"How long have you been listening to us?" Mani repeated, his irritation with his brother clearly getting the better of him.

"My dear brother, I have known about your activities for years. I have my reasons for not squealing. But you can be sure it's not because of my love for you."

"Shut up, you drunken fool. Your mouth has always been bigger than your brains."

"My dear, dear brother, get hold of yourself. I am on my way out. I shall leave you to carry on with your conniving and plotting. You're a fool among many. If I thought for a moment that you were capable of going beyond words, I would have had you behind bars long ago. Goodbye."

Sayid gave an exaggerated bow and left, closing the front door gently.

Andrea relaxed. If Sayid thought they were incapable of going beyond words, then there was no need to worry. Contributing money to the cause probably gave them a feeling of self importance. Nothing more. Relieved, she poured a cup of tea and sipped it.

"He's got to be eliminated," Farhad's fury accented every word he spoke. "We can't have drunken fools going around babbling."

"Don't worry about him. I doubt he heard anything. He likes to show off. He feels his mission in life is to make mine miserable."

"There's not much love lost between you two, is there?

All the same, he should be eliminated."

"Trust me. I have often had the same thought. But it's dangerous. His best friends and gambling partners are from Savak, including the chief. If anything were to happen to him, there would be an investigation intense enough to ruin us. Maybe, if and when he goes out of the country, then an accident, perhaps. A lot less complicated."

"You're right. Just make sure he keeps his mouth shut. I won't mention it to Zia. He's not too crazy about you. This will only make it worse."

For a few seconds neither man spoke. Then Farhad asked, "Who else is at home?"

"Andrea and Kelly."

"Your wife has been in the kitchen for quite some time now. Are you sure she doesn't understand Farsi?"

"I know she doesn't. I'll check."

Andrea remained calm. She drank the last sip of her tea as Mani entered the kitchen. She rose, washed her tea cup, dried it and put it in the closet while he stood watching her.

"What's taking you so long?" he asked.

"You told me to get in touch with my attorney, remember." Andrea checked her watch. "It's about time for his office to open."

"Give me his number. I'll call you to talk to him when I reach him."

Andrea scribbled the number on a piece of paper and handed it to him. There was no way Mani could reach him. Her attorney spent August in Europe, every year. She knew his secretary would not give that information to someone she did not know.

Andrea climbed the stairs to her room. She left the door open a crack.

Mani returned to the living room, stopped abruptly and said, "Damn it. I hate this charade. I hate being husband and father. You told me it would be for a brief period. The post of Minister of Planning would be waiting for me when I returned. Six years later, I'm still an errand boy."

"I know what you're going through," Farhad replied. "It has not been easy for any of us. You were instructed to marry along with dozens of others who were studying abroad. It was the only solution we could find to get Savak off your backs. You know it worked. All the members who married foreign girls, especially Americans, were immediately dropped off their surveillance list."

While Farhad talked, Mani dialed the attorney's number, repeatedly. He couldn't get through. All the international lines were busy. He banged the receiver in the cradle and turned to Farhad. "I know all that, but I'm fed up. I've played the role of husband and father to the maximum as ordered, but it's become more and more difficult. It's dragged on too long with no end in sight."

"We're aware of all that. There have been many unforeseen circumstances. Several defections. Many of our leaders have been forced underground. Our financial resources are dwindling. The clergy who were our staunchest supporters ideologically and financially have been bought off by the government. The government has all the money. We have only ourselves to rely upon. This is no time to let our guard down or give in to emotion. We've got a job to do. We have to pay whatever the price."

Mani listened, rubbed his hands together, then cracked his knuckles.

"If it had been anyone but you I would not have wasted time with explanations," Farhad went on. "Nothing short of total commitment is tolerated. The slightest criticism or hesitation can spell doom for a member no matter how high his post."

Mani sensed his friend's displeasure. "Forgive me. I have been under too much pressure. My wife can't be coaxed to cooperate. My mother is sick in the hospital. My sister wants me to help her find an apartment. There is nothing affordable on the market. The people are not to blame. It's our stupid King. He doesn't give a damn about the country or the people. His only concern is how best to safeguard the fortune he has robbed from the country and maintain his own glory. Did you read about the interview he gave Barbara Walters?"

"I saw it on television," Farhad said. "He claimed Iran will be the fifth greatest military power in the world! That megalomaniac should have been demolished long before he was old enough to talk."

Mani was on a roll. "In essence he said that he's the only one who knows what's good for his country and his people. Never forget. His country. His people. He said he had a vision. A vision which suits his ambitions perfectly. Bullshit!"

"You're much more like yourself now. I love to listen to you vent your opinions with so much anger. Yes, the revolutionary spirit is very much alive. The more ambitious the King's projects get, the easier it becomes to arouse the ire of the public and recruit new converts."

"Long live the revolution!"

"Let's drink to the revolution," Farhad said.

Mani went to the kitchen, fixed two drinks and returned to the living room.

Several drinks later, Farhad told Mani, "My whole life revolves around one goal, a goal for which I've been planning and working for ten years. Many of my colleagues consider the assassination of the King their ultimate goal. I am committed to the total elimination of our pseudo Royal Family, the King, the Queen, and all four children. The name Pahlavi sends shock waves through me. I want every last one eliminated so there will never ever again be a chance for a Pahlavi to 'pollute' Iran. This calls for far more complicated planning and accomplices with knowledge of the Royal schedule. Hence the delay."

"Don't you think that's a little farfetched?"

"Maybe. But it can be done. We've had bad luck so far. After months of planning, when the Revolutionary Council finally manages to get someone into the inner circle, invariably, a few days later, he or she disappears without a trace."

"I'm not surprised."

"All attempts at finding the informer or informers to date, have ended in failure, leaving the members frustrated and near hysteria. Most are ready to give up."

"Please, Farhad, forget the whole thing. At least for a while. It's too dangerous."

Mani checked his watch. It was twelve minutes after two. He was exhausted mentally and physically and ready to go to bed. But not Farhad. Again he tried to reach the attorney. The international lines were still busy.

"Keep trying," Farhad said walking toward the kitchen. "I'll fix the drinks."

He returned holding an empty bottle of Scotch. "Do you have more Scotch?"

"I don't think so. There should be Vodka in the bar."

"Sure, why not? Let's have Vodka."

Andrea shut her door and slept soon after that. She awoke startled. She'd heard a noise. She opened the door quietly and stepped out. The light in the living room was on, Mani and Farhad snored next to each other on the sofa. There was an empty bottle of Scotch and an empty bottle of Vodka on the carpet and umpteen cigarette butts in and around the ashtray. She returned to bed and was about to slip under the bed cover, when she heard footsteps. She moved to the top of the stairs and looked down.

It was Sayid. He stood erect. A tall, handsome man, with big brown eyes and long, curled lashes which reminded Andrea of half moons. He seemed poised, very much in control. She'd rarely seen him like that. Perhaps he'd quit drinking. He stopped at the foot of the stairs, looked around, then without hesitation strode toward Farhad and Mani with an impish grin on his face, and spat at them both.

"Delicious!" he murmured.

Andrea disappeared quietly into her room.

Chapter 9

Forty eight hours after her admission to the hospital, the doctors found nothing wrong with Naene clinically or pathologically and her electrocardiogram was normal. She was obese but other than that she was in good health. They had no idea what had caused her to turn blue and have difficulty breathing. She was moved from the intensive care unit to a private room.

Andrea spent all day and most of the evening with Naene listening to her complain. Naene hated hospitals. There was nothing wrong with her. Iranians did not go to a hospital unless they were dying. Being an American, Andrea mistook a mere fainting spell for a heart attack, subjecting her to unnecessary expense and discomfort. Naene wanted to go home where she belonged. She would not put up with a crummy hospital room with its disgusting food any longer. Naene complained to anyone who would listen, but mostly to the head nurse. The head nurse spoke English. Naene wanted her remarks translated for Andrea's benefit.

When Sayid came that evening to visit his mother, Andrea

returned home to be with Kelly and relax. She was grateful the nursemaid was always there to take care of Kelly whenever she was busy.

Andrea read for a while, then, exhausted from several nights of interrupted sleep, she turned the light off and slept till morning.

Mani and Farhad must have come home sometime during the night. They left the house soon after she got up. Mani did not bother to tell her where he was going or when he'd be back. To her knowledge, he had not been to see his mother. She sat at the kitchen table sipping coffee. The maid told her repeatedly, "The kitchen is for servants, Madame. You should take your refreshments and meals in the dining room." She didn't care. She brushed off the looks of displeasure and focused on how best to approach her dilemma. How to stop her husband from cashing her money? There had to be a way. Mr. Griffith, the bank manager would know.

It was Saturday. The banks opened at nine in the morning. Ten minutes after nine, she called the British Bank and asked to speak to the manager.

She was told Mr. Griffith was on vacation. His assistant would be glad to help.

Andrea had met the assistant when she deposited her money in the bank. He was a young Iranian, eager to please but uninformed in the most elementary procedures of banking. Andrea suspected he was either appointed by Savak or was given the post because someone owed him or his family a favor.

"No, thank you," she answered. "When will Mr. Griffith be back?"

"I can't say for sure. He's in London now. He might return within a few days or go on a trip for a couple of weeks. Check back next week."

The information compounded her problem. Mani would not have to worry about the Englishman. If he decided to go ahead with his plans, Mr. Griffith's assistant didn't seem to her like a man who knew enough to question them. But if he was from Savak and acting his role, then Mani and Farhad would be in real trouble. Trouble for which she would be blamed for not giving them the money.

She thought of going to the bank and asking the assistant manager to block her account, but that would aggravate matters further. She doubted she could count on her husband to react in a civilized manner if his attempts at getting what he wanted were thwarted and there was no guarantee that it would work. Farhad could easily grease the palm of a bank employee to win his cooperation. That was how almost all business transactions were carried out in the country. Why should it be different in her case? She had heard enough to convince her that their need for money was so grave and so pressing that they would stop at nothing. Farhad said the plan was for the twenty eighth. They needed the money desperately by then, desperately enough to walk to a bank with a forged check. What was this plan? Why did it require such large sums of money? By his own admission Farhad considered ten thousand dollars a mere token. He wanted fifty thousand. And Mani was completely under Farhad's spell. If only . . . Andrea still clung to a ray of hope, a faint ray but a ray just the same. She was convinced if she could persuade her husband to dissociate himself from Farhad, he would regain his sanity.

Much to her dismay, she had to admit, her sheltered life in a wealthy home, loving parents, and exclusive private schools, had not prepared her to deal with the complexities of life in the Middle East.

A disturbing thought occurred to her. If her husband went to the bank with the forged check and was refused payment, he'd come home and force her to go to the bank to withdraw the money. If she refused, he'd get violent. There was no sense in deluding herself.

She had to leave the house.

She got dressed quickly, took Kelly and went to Layla's house.

The door was opened by Layla's daughter.

Layla was curled in a corner. The dark circles under her eyes were accented by her pale face. Her long hair was in tangles.

Andrea approached her. "Layla, what's wrong?"

"Don't stay here. Go home."

The door to the bedroom was open. The room looked like it had been ransacked.

"What happened?"

"The less you know, the better off you are. Go."

"Is there anything I can do to help?"

"No one can help. It's too late."

"Too late for what?"

"They got him." Layla answered bursting into tears.

Andrea waited, gently rubbing her friend's shoulder. "Do you want to talk about it?"

"I . . . I . . . don't want you to get involved."

"Layla, listen to me. I'm an American. They might treat you roughly without giving it a second thought, but I bet they'll think twice before attempting the same with an American." Somehow her words sounded shallow, unconvincing.

After a moment's hesitation, Layla said, "Do you remember the driver who took us to Ray's Pizza?"

"Yes."

"Thursday night there was an assassination in Yazd. The mayor was killed in his home by intruders. It's supposed to be like a fortress, guarded around the clock. Yet, they managed to break in and spray him with a hail of bullets. When his wife rushed to the living room to see what was going on, she saw two masked men jump over the wall. They found the guard gagged, tied to a tree."

"There was no mention of it in the newspaper, at least not in the English daily, Kayhan."

"Of course not. The papers print what they're told to print."

"But what has it got to do with the driver?"

"He is, or perhaps I should say was, a Mujahed, a freedom fighter."

"Did he tell you that?"

"He did. He wanted me to join their group."

"Why would they suspect him for something which happened in Yazd?"

"Apparently he'd driven a customer there on Thursday afternoon."

"How did you find out?"

"Security agents paid us a visit yesterday and again this morning."

"Do they have reason to suspect you?"

Layla sighed. "They don't need a reason." Her voice quivered.

"Something must have made them single you out," Andrea persisted.

"Something did. They said they saw him talking to me at Ray's pizza. They're questioning everyone he had contact with recently."

"But he came to see me, not you."

"That was an excuse, Andrea. You never gave him the extra five hundred rials."

Andrea had suspected as much but she did not expect Layla to admit it so freely.

"Have you already joined the group?" Andrea asked worried.

"No, not yet. I was supposed to. Today."

"Does anyone know about it?"

"The driver does. And they'll make him talk if they haven't already."

Andrea was amazed at Layla's calm responses. "You mean you're not worried?" she asked perplexed.

"I've passed that stage. I'm too numb to care."

"Something else is bothering you. Right?"

Layla was silent for a while, apparently turning the matter over in her mind. Finally she said, "I told you, I don't want you to get involved."

"Tell me what the problem is and I will decide."

"I'm not worried about myself. They'll get me sooner or later. There's no doubt in my mind about that. I worry about the children. I need someone to contact my parents."

"How?"

"They live in Qom. Occasionally, I manage to reach them by phone."

"How else can they be reached."

"That's the problem. Someone has to drive there and tell them. It's an hour's drive. The children can't do it on their own."

"Maybe you should ask your parents to come stay with you for a while or you go there. Have you thought about it?"

"No, I don't want my parents to suspect anything. My father has not yet recovered from what happened to my husband."

"Give me their address."

Layla eyed her friend, disbelief apparent on her face. Then, she sprang up and embraced her. "I assure you," she said, crying tears of joy, "a better friend would be hard to find."

"On one condition," Andrea added. "You have to promise me you'll be careful."

"I promise. Now, let's get on with your lesson. That's enough of my problems for today."

Andrea left with Kelly late that afternoon, pleased with the progress she was making learning the language and leaving Layla in a better mood. Mani and Farhad were in the living room. Mani rushed at her the minute she set foot in the house. "Where have you been?"

Farhad's now familiar cynical smile, with him leaning against the kitchen door, legs spread apart, signaled trouble loomed ahead.

"Did you want something?" Andrea pushed Kelly's wheel

chair to the kitchen. Fatima was there. She told Andrea she'd take care of Kelly. Andrea returned to the living room.

"Farhad is right. You answer a question with a question. I have to admit it's very clever. Now try and answer. Where were you?"

She was determined not to let him intimidate her regardless of how little effort it required on his part to act like a tyrant lately. More so with Farhad around. She said, "I was visiting Layla."

"Next time you want to go somewhere, you let me know before you take off. I have more important things to do than wait for you to show up when you please."

"Why were you waiting for me?"

Mani threw a quick glance in Farhad's direction. Farhad nodded slightly. Andrea waited for the ax to fall.

"They called from the hospital," Mani said his voice taking a more conciliatory tone. "My mother is ready to be discharged. I need money."

I should have guessed, Andrea thought. It also meant that their trip to the bank had either been shelved or unsuccessful. Hence, the new approach.

"It's past five in the afternoon. Too late to bring her home tonight. We have to pay for an extra day just because you feel this is a hotel for you. You come and go as you please. The least you could do is leave a note."

"I would have, if I'd known you'd be home."

"I don't need excuses. I need money."

Andrea stalled. She needed time to think.

He pounced at her, grabbed her by the collar, and shoved her onto the sofa. "When I tell you I need money, it means I need money, not a lot of stupid excuses. Money. Do you understand?"

Farhad's grin broadened.

Andrea pulled her shirt down. She was determined to look unruffled despite shaking inwardly. She'd never been subjected to physical abuse before and she didn't know what to do.

He dashed at her, his face white with rage and placed a scornful stress on each syllable. "Be ready, tomorrow morning at nine. We're going to the bank. You'll withdraw the money and close your account. Do I make myself clear?"

He waited, a look of defiance and pleasure spread across his face.

She got up and tried to leave. He pushed her back. "You answer me when I talk to you." The pitch of his voice rising with every word. "I'm sick of you always acting superior to everyone else."

"She can't help it," Farhad interjected. "It's a national characteristic."

Mani smiled. His expression was that of a man who had just proved his manliness.

Andrea struggled to suppress her anger. "If you need money to pay your mother's hospital bill, and if you have no other means of getting it, I'll loan it to you. But I will not withdraw all my money and I will not close my account."

Mani turned to Farhad. "Did you hear that? Did you hear what she said? She will not withdraw the money. She refuses. Well, I have news for you. You will do as you're told or else . . ."

"Or else what?" Sayid stood in his bathrobe on top of the stairs, looking down at his brother, a murderous expression on his face.

Farhad and Mani, motionless, stared at him.

"I'll break her neck," Mani replied and glanced at Farhad for approval.

"You touch her and I'll break every bone in your body," Sayid said calmly.

Farhad spun to face Mani, "You told me he wasn't home."

"How should I know? His car is not outside. It was there yesterday."

"The bastard is clever," Farhad replied coldly. "He hides it so no one will know he's home."

Mani shook his fist at his brother. "You have no right to

interfere between me and my wife."

"Who's going to stop me? You?"

"Why don't you shut up and mind your own business?" Farhad moved threateningly toward the stairs.

Sayid descended a couple of steps and addressed his brother, "One more word out of that scum will force me to reduce him to pulp."

"You're brave today, aren't you?" Mani shouted back. "Wait till Mother gets back. I'd like to hear you talk like that when she's around."

Andrea couldn't believe what she was hearing. She'd heard her friends talk like that to their brothers and sisters when they were very young. Now she was listening to a man of thirty use the same tactic.

Sayid was unperturbed. "Unfortunately for you, she is. She's in her room. I brought her home this afternoon."

Mani's face turned red, then white. Finally, in a voice, barely above a whisper, he said, "I didn't know."

"Save your theatrics for your friends," Sayid snapped. "I heard you talk to her an hour ago."

Mani collapsed in his mother's armchair. "You," he said bitterly. "Always you. From the day you were born, you've ruined everything for me."

"No, my dear brother. You do it to yourself. Your life is governed by the lies you fabricate. Eventually, you'll have to pay the price. You cannot fool everyone all the time."

"Don't tell me how to run my life. You have a hard enough time running your own."

"I'd like nothing better. Only next time you want to squeeze money out of a helpless victim to satisfy your bosses, make sure you do it right. Didn't it occur to you that from now till tomorrow morning your wife was bound to find out that Mother was back?"

"She wouldn't have, if you hadn't tattled."

Farhad and Mani exchanged a factious look.

What was going on? Andrea was thoroughly confused.

There were too many conflicting signals to sort out.

Sayid continued to descend the stairs, then stopped, his foot stiff in mid air. There was a numbing silence. He eyed Mani.

Andrea's fears mounted. This was not a performance. Something was dreadfully wrong.

Like a man possessed, Sayid tore down the stairs and into his mother's room.

Farhad wasted no time. "Quick," he told Mani. "Let's get out of here." They ran out the house like two men hearing the ticking of a time bomb.

Seconds later, Sayid sped from his mother's room. He shook a half empty bottle of phenobarbital. "Call the hospital immediately," he ordered Andrea. "She's so heavily sedated, she's having trouble breathing."

He rushed back to his mother's room as Andrea ran to make the call.

Chapter 10

Her new life in an exotic country had turned into an exotic nightmare, her loving, caring husband, a brute who overdosed his own mother to keep her quiet. All for the sake of money. The only interest he seemed to have in her lately. She could handle that or at least she thought she could but what he'd done to his mother was unforgivable. She had to find a way out for herself and Kelly before matters got worse. But how? Horror stories of American women married to Iranians struggling to free themselves, floated through her mind. Freeing themselves and their children was almost impossible. She weighed her options. Her embassy was out of the question. She'd been duly warned and had chosen not to heed their advice.

Lately, she rarely saw Sayid, and when she did, he avoided her, presumably because she had refused his previous offers of help. Layla had her own problems. Perhaps Irene. But Irene's husband was Mani's cousin, she was an American herself, and in all probability would not want to get involved. The only solution would be to travel by land to the closest neighboring country, most likely Turkey. What would Mani do when he found out? Just thinking about it made her heart skip a beat and compelled her to admit that she was terrified of him. She'd been clinging to the past when he was an exemplary husband, making it all the more difficult to predict his behavior. It was like stepping onto another planet and living with an alien. She forced herself not to dwell on it for the time being. She'd make discreet investigations and make her mind up accordingly. For the moment, she had a more urgent matter to consider. It was August 28th.

The mere thought of the date sent shivers down her spine. She hadn't heard from her husband since he took off with Farhad after the incident with his mother. Where was he and what was he up to? Should she be concerned? Sayid said he was not worried because all his brother ever did was talk. Perhaps she was letting her imagination run wild. Perhaps that's all it was. Talk. Naene was still in the hospital recuperating slowly from her overdose of phenobarbital, and the maid was at the hospital with her. Sayid told his mother her symptoms had recurred. Nothing more.

There was no food left in the house. The maid did all the shopping for groceries daily, but she was in the hospital with Naene. Andrea was told not to shop because grocers charged foreigners double, sometimes triple the amount they charged locals. She had to. They had to eat.

She took Kelly and went up the street. After she was done shopping, they went to a small bookstore. The owner was a friendly, middle aged man who always helped her locate what she was looking for. If he didn' have it, he would get it for her the next day.

This morning, the owner replied curtly to her good morning. He buried his gaze in a folder on the counter when he saw her walk in.

Andrea wondered why she was being ignored. It couldn't be something she'd said or done. She'd done nothing out of the ordinary and all she'd said was good morning. She paid for the *Time* magazine, thanked him and left.

Although Saturday was the first day of the week in Iran, this Saturday the streets were strangely empty. It gave her an eerie feeling. She hurried home with Kelly.

Once inside, she turned the radio on to hear the news. There was no mention of anything unusual. Iranian television broadcasted news late at night, but she turned it on anyway. There were the usual programs, nothing out of the ordinary. She thought perhaps her apprehension about the date predisposed her to expect adversity in situations where none existed.

The phone rang.

"Are you home?" Irene asked. She sounded terribly excited.

Andrea laughed. "Of course, I'm home. I'm talking to you."

"Stay there. I'll be right over." She hung up.

She arrived in less than five minutes.

"Have you heard?"

"Heard what?" Andrea searched Irene's face.

Irene glanced around. "Are you alone?"

"I think so, unless Sayid came home during the night. I didn't hear him."

"We have to find out. You shouldn't stay alone in the house."

"Why are you so mysterious, Irene. What's going on?"

"A lot."

Andrea waited for Irene to calm down. Irene paced the room and then threw her hands up in exasperation. "I don't know what these troublemakers want. They had nothing. Now they have everything. And what do they do? They go around killing innocent people. In broad daylight, mind you."

"Who's they? Who did they kill?" Andrea held her breath. It felt like every red corpuscle in her body suddenly disintegrated.

"The managing director of Rockwell International in Iran,

Mr. Cottrell, and two of his associates, Mr. Krongard and Mr. Smith."

"Oh, no." Andrea eased herself slowly into an armchair.

"Wait until the foreign community hears about it. There will be absolute chaos. Exactly what the terrorists want. The rumor mills will shift into high gear and we'll have trouble. I mean real trouble."

"How did you find out?"

"Well, I wouldn't have, not so soon anyway, if it had not been for our driver. We'd given him the weekend off. It was past nine before he showed up. The first time he's been late in six years. He was hysterical. We gave him tea and after a while he calmed down. The murders happened right in front of his eyes."

The twenty eighth . . . The twenty eighth. She could hear Farhad's voice echoing in her head. No way. They couldn't have! To Irene. "How did it happen?"

"Early this morning, Ahmed, our driver, was behind a Volkswagon, in heavy traffic, in the Falakeh Vosoughi district. When he got to the square, the Volkswagon cut in front of a Dodge forcing it to come to a halt. Then he saw cars appear from two other directions trapping the Americans. Immediately, four men jumped from the Volkswagon and opened fire on the Dodge with automatic weapons, killing all three instantly."

"Oh, my God."

"You haven't been here long enough to understand. It's not just the death of three Americans which makes it such a terrible crime, but the audacity, the boldness with which it was done. Usually it's a hit and run affair. But this sounds like it was meticulously planned and executed."

Andrea wasn't sure she could trust her voice but she had to know. "Were the killers caught?"

"Apparently not. By the time Security arrived, the assailants had disappeared into the crowd."

"I'm surprised Ahmed was not held as a witness."

"There is a bizarre twist to the story. Apparently when the terrorists jumped out of their car, before opening fire, one of them ran to the Dodge and told the driver, an old Armenian man to duck, then proceeded to spray the Dodge from every angle. The first thing Security did when they got there, was to pounce on the driver. Ahmed saw his chance, backed the car to a side street and escaped."

Andrea was flabbergasted. "You mean they actually took time out to tell the driver to duck?"

"It doesn't make sense, does it? That tells you they were not amateurs. According to Ahmed, they looked like professional killers. But why would they risk leaving an eye witness behind?"

Professional killers. Professional killers. Andrea repeated the words silently. Was Mani involved? How could he be? He had no training to be a professional killer. He'd been with her the past six years. Farhad or members of his group, maybe. But Mani had to be a member. Why else would he resort to incredible means to get funds for them?

She had to stop making assumptions, jumping to conclusions. Savak, with its legendary diligence would bring the criminals to justice soon enough and the whole world would know.

Andrea sat facing a blank television screen. Irene paced the room, pulling at a tissue in her hand, reducing it to shreds.

Take your daughter and run. Run before it's too late. How? Where? Should she confide in Irene? And tell her what? That her husband overdosed his mother to keep her quiet so he could force his wife to give him money to kill Americans? Stop! You can't accuse a man unless you're sure of your facts.

Irene rattled on, "You know what this means, don't you? The government will clamp down hard to prevent such incidents from occurring again subsequently depriving innocent citizens of the few civil liberties they have left. Otherwise, the killings will continue. Because of CIA's involvement in bringing the Shah to power, Iranians blame the American government for their predicament. No American will be safe here."

"Do you think there will be a mass exodus of Americans?"

"It all depends. Following previous assassinations, our embassy offered help to all those who wanted to leave the country. Very few chose to leave. But this is different. There's a new element in the picture. The way this operation was carried out shatters Savak's shield of invincibility. It won't be safe for us to stay here unless the criminals are caught and brought to justice quickly and similar incidents don't occur in the future."

No matter how she tossed the implications in her mind, it spelled trouble. If Mani was involved, there was no telling what would happen to him, to Kelly and to her. If, as Irene suspected, Americans decided to leave, she and Kelly could not join them because they were considered Iranians through their marriage to Iranian nationals. And so was Irene. "Suppose Americans leave, what happens to those of us married to Iranians? Do you think in an emergency our embassy will help?"

"No, Andrea. They won't because they can't. In the eyes of the law we're Iranians. But I have all the necessary documents ready. They've been signed by my husband and verified by the police. I can leave at a moment's notice. You should ask Mani to do the same for you and Kelly. You must be prepared at all times with valid documents and a destination. If the country you want to go to requires a visa, you should obtain it and make sure it's current. I have a multiple entry visa for Israel where I have family. The other alternative is to go to a country which does not require visas from Iranians. Like Turkey for example. This place is like a volcano, ready to erupt anytime. We can't afford to take chances."

Andrea felt the blood drain from her face. Judging from

her husband's recent behavior, such a demand would arouse his contempt and anger, not cooperation. Without his consent she would have no choice but to resort to illegal means for her own and her child's safety and there was no guarantee that it would work. It terrified her to think about it.

The shock waves would not end with her and Kelly. They were far broader in scope. There were the families of the slain men. How would they cope? How could she face the world if there was the remotest possibility that her husband was involved in killing her countrymen? Revolting. She had to stop torturing herself.

"Andrea are you all right? You look pale."

She tried to pull herself together. "I'm all right. Do you know if they had family . . . I mean the men who were killed."

"All I know is what Ahmed told me. I'm sorry I brought you bad news, but you were bound to hear about it. This is not an incident which can be swept under the rug."

"I appreciate your thinking of me. I sensed something was wrong when I went to the bookstore this morning. The news must have traveled fast."

"Taxi drivers. They're positively the most efficient way of spreading any kind of information or misinformation."

"It certainly did not feel like an ordinary Saturday morning out there."

"I felt it too, on my way over. Listen Andrea, I have to go. I left a half crazed driver and his terrified mother, our housekeeper, to rush over here. Can you find out if Sayid is home?"

"No, his door is closed. No one is allowed to wake him up unless it is an emergency. I didn't see his car outside, but that doesn't mean anything."

"Where's Mani?"

Andrea was afraid Irene would ask about him eventually. There was no sense in confiding in her. If Mani found out he could use her indiscretion as a weapon against her. "He left with Farhad a few days ago. They're thinking about starting a business. That's what they said, anyway."

Irene cocked her head and studied her friend. "Andrea, are you having problems with Mani? Do you want to talk about it?"

"Let's say we're having trouble communicating."

"I thought as much but didn't want to pry. Don't worry. Those who have spent time overseas and return, find it difficult to decide which to chose, East or West. When he starts his business, he'll settle down. He'll have to. If he can't make the adjustment, he'll have to leave. I wouldn't bet on it though. He told us he loves it here and plans to stay."

That's more than he told me, Andrea thought.

Irene reached for her purse and rose. "You can't stay here. I came to warn you to be prepared. Security agents will pay you a visit. You can count on it. All students returning from abroad are suspect. Savak agents can be awfully intimidating. That's why you should not be alone in the house."

"I doubt Security will start investigations this soon. If they do, I'll ask Sayid to talk to them. He's usually home asleep during the day."

"Are you sure? You can come to our house if you like."

"Thanks Irene. I'll be fine. Really."

No sooner had she spoken when the doorbell rang incessantly.

The women stood up, unable to move.

The ringing did not stop.

"Who could it be?" Irene asked.

"I'll get it." Andrea walked to the door, trembling.

The caller was now banging on the door.

She opened it. An old woman stood shivering, big tears coursing down her cheeks.

Irene saw the woman. "It's all right, Andrea. That's our housekeeper. Please let her in."

"Madame, Madame, come quick," the old woman sobbed. "They took Ahmed."

Chapter 11

On Sunday, the assassination was front page news in the English and Farsi newspapers. According to Kayhan International, the English daily, clues and documents were found which would help identify the assassins.

Andrea didn't believe the news reports. She believed her sources. By all accounts, the killers were professionals. To claim that they had left incriminating evidence behind, was the authorities way of assuring the public that they had the situation under control.

The country was in turmoil. It was a specially dangerous time for foreigners and more so for Americans. She had hoped Mani would contact her. Yet she had not heard from him since he dashed out of the house with Farhad, when Sayid discovered what they had done to his mother. Was he in hiding? If so, was it because he feared his brother would make him pay for overdosing his mother or was it because he was involved with the assassination, or both? A wave of helplessness and despair swept over her. It had to have been Farhad. The Mani she knew had practically become unglued at the sight of a stray cat hit by a car a month before their departure for Iran. He had spent days nursing the animal back to health. How could he possibly become a killer in two months? But Mani knew or he wouldn't have run. Maybe she missed something. Maybe Farhad forced him to leave. Was forcing all this on him. Maybe Mani was being used, as much as she, and Mani's mother, and their lives wouldn't be worth two cents. Farhad impressed her as a man who would stop at nothing to get what he wanted. Not even killing her child. His viciousness had her in knots.

She wanted to believe all the excuses she was making for Mani but a little piece of something, buried deep inside, nagged at her. She shoved that little piece deeper. She didn't dare take it out and examine it. Proof was what she needed. Not suspicions.

Two days later, there was a total news blackout.

Late in the evenings, when the August heat abated slightly, Andrea took Kelly and walked in the neighborhood. She needed to clear the cobwebs from her head and find out how the Iranians were reacting, if at all, to the incident. She could not go to visit her mother-in-law. The nurses told her Naene did not want to see her. Naene was convinced the rift between her sons was a direct result of the curse the presence of the foreign woman brought upon them.

Iranians were coping with the incident the best way they knew how. By not getting involved with foreigners, especially Americans. The neighbors who were always warm and friendly when Andrea stopped to say hello, disappeared into their homes when they saw her approach. The storekeepers remained aloof and uncommunicative. Layla had not left her apartment since the assassination. She told Andrea she wanted to stay close to her children. Savak would take her in for questioning sooner or later. Her daughter was instructed to contact Andrea immediately.

Irene stopped by daily. Her messages were unsettling. "Don't discuss anything important over the phone. They're tapped." She'd hired a lawyer to help her find out where Savak had taken her driver. To date all her efforts were in vain. "He has simply disappeared," she told Andrea. "And when I persisted, Savak let me know, in no uncertain terms, that if I didn't stop pestering them, I'd be in trouble, too."

Even the Pars-American Club, where foreigners usually exchanged gossip on the vast grounds, because they couldn't be overheard, was deserted. Andrea had the Olympic size swimming pool and employees all to herself. But the employees were all business.

Her last hope was Sayid. She hadn't seen him since he took his mother to the hospital. He slept during the day and according to Mani, gambled all night. Friday, after repeated attempts, Andrea managed to get through to the hospital to inquire about her mother-in-law.

She was told Sayid left with his mother ten minutes before her call.

Twenty minutes later, Sayid walked in with his mother leaning on his shoulder. She looked tired but her color was good. Sayid took Naene to her room and told the maid to remain with her at all times.

Andrea waited for him in the living room. When he appeared, she greeted him. "Is there anything I can do to help?"

"Haven't you done enough already?" he replied curtly.

Andrea didn' understand the remark. But, before she could question him, he was out the door.

What's his problem? Has he been brainwashed as well into thinking that I'm a curse on their family or was he referring to something else? I can never snag him long enough to talk, really talk to him.

Then it dawned on her. It might have something to do with the assassination, the money. Fatima and Kelly were watching cartoons. She told Fatima she'd be gone about an hour, grabbed her purse and dashed out the door.

Mr. Griffith stood behind a counter talking to a clerk. He

was back. What a relief!

I have to be careful how I bring this off. If my suspicions are unfounded, I might have a lot to answer to.

"Hello Mr. Griffith. It's nice to see you."

"Well, I can't say that I'm happy to be back. I rather enjoy a lazy life."

"You look good. You must have had quite a bit of sun."

"Indeed I did. Greece is splendid this time of the year. Have you been there?"

His question gave her the opportunity she had hoped for.

"No, not yet. That's why I stopped by. I'm thinking of taking a short trip."

"Good idea. Where did you have in mind?"

"I haven't decided."

"Let's go to my office." He escorted her in and offered her a chair. "Now, my dear, you were saying?"

"I was wondering if you issued travelers' checks."

"We do, indeed. How much do you need?"

"It depends on where I go. Greece sounds like a good idea."

"How long do you plan to stay?"

"Maybe two weeks."

"If you decide to go, you should let us know in advance."

"A day or so?"

"At least. If you want more than two thousand dollars, we need forty eight hours notice. We have to inform the government. It's a new law. We can only proceed with the request if it's approved."

It didn't seem logical. A country with petrodollars pouring in needing advance notice to issue travelers' checks. "Is there a shortage of dollars?"

"No, it has nothing to do with foreign exchange. It's to make sure money taken out of the country is not used for subversive purposes, like the purchase of weapons. I'm sure you heard about the assassination of the three Americans. That's what they hope to prevent. We have to inform them of all foreign exchange transactions over two thousand dollars."

If the government had to be notified, Farhad and Mani would have to think hard before withdrawing ten thousand dollars. It eased her mind a bit but not for long. They would not have to if they had an accomplice.

But how could she find out without arousing Mr. Griffith's suspicion?

"Is your account in savings or checking? If it's in savings, you should transfer the amount you wish to withdraw into checking. It will save time if you decide to go."

"Thanks for reminding me." Now she had a perfect excuse to check her account. "I would like to transfer some money into my checking account. I need to pay my Farsi teacher."

Andrea thanked him and headed for the door.

Mr. Griffith followed her. "I'll go with you. We have few clerks who speak English."

"Please, don't bother. I'm sure you have a lot to do. Maybe your assistant can help me."

"It's no bother at all. Since the August 28th incident, business is down to a trickle."

"That was a terrible crime."

They approached the front desk. Mr. Griffith asked the clerk for Andrea's file. The clerk found it and handed it to him.

Mr. Griffith opened it, leafed through it, stopped, looked at something, checked the first sheet of paper again then closed the file. "Let's go to my office."

She wanted to know the truth but the prospect terrified her. How much could she divulge without jeopardizing her child and herself? Mani was not the only person involved. There was Farhad and a man who had forged her signature. Perhaps others. What would they do to her if they learned about her exposing their scheme? She shuddered. It was much too gruesome a thought.

She followed Mr. Griffith to his office.

He waited for Andrea to sit. Then he walked behind his desk, settled slowly in his chair, placed her file in front of him and studied the contents. He hunched over the papers, his glasses precariously balanced at the tip of his nose.

When he spoke, his tone was even, controlled. He stretched his arm across the desk. There was a check in his hand. He handed it to her. "Could you please look this over?"

It was a check for ten thousand dollars, for cash, payable to the bearer of the note. It was signed, Andrea Sorensen.

Her heart skipped a beat, pounded, then skipped another beat. The blood rushed to her cheeks. Her mouth went dry. If it was her signature on the check, it meant that she had cashed the money. If so, what was she doing inquiring about traveler's checks with no money in the bank. The mere fact that she was there was proof to the contrary. Not only would she have to give a believable explanation to the banker but she would have to face an irate husband and everyone else having anything to do with it. In addition, she had only a few dollars left in the bank.

The banker returned his attention to the file. Then he looked up, removed his glasses, and, with an expression which betrayed nothing, said, "Any ideas?"

He didn't look like a man who could be fooled. It would be wonderful if she could tell him what a creep her husband had turned out to be and even better if she could bare her soul about his best friend Farhad. But since she was a stranger, a woman with hardly any rights, and for the moment in a predicament from which she had no idea how to get out, she remained silent.

"I must say," Mr. Griffith said interrupting her thoughts. "It's a job well done. The untrained eye could have easily missed it."

"How . . . how could you tell?" It sounded like she was listening to someone else speak.

He didn't seem surprised by her question. "I'm an expert in deciphering forgeries," he said. "That's what I did for four years during the war. I prepared forged documents for German Jews trying to escape the Nazi holocaust."

"I see."

"Who knew about your account?"

Andrea hesitated. To tell him what she knew would be folly. He had a legal responsibility to inform the authorities. She said, "My husband."

"Think hard. Did anyone else know? I'm assuming that if your husband needed the money, he'd ask you to withdraw it. Am I right?"

Her husband. She didn't know who he was anymore and tired of making excuses for him. "That depends."

He studied her. "Depends on what?"

"On if it was for a business venture."

He rose and walked to the window. After a while he returned to his desk. Then, he asked his secretary to bring in his previous assistant's file. When the file arrived, Mr. Griffith glanced at the file, and closed it.

"Were you here on the twenty sixth of August when Mr. Taha left?" he asked his secretary.

"Yes, sir."

"Tell me everything you remember. Don't leave out a thing, even if you think it's not important."

"The twenty sixth of August was . . ." she checked the calendar. "Thursday. Yes, Thursday. We close at noon. A few minutes before twelve, two young men walked in. I would say they were in their late twenties or early thirties. They asked to talk to Mr. Taha. He was in his office. I showed them in. In about ten minutes, the three left together. I haven't seen Mr. Taha since."

"Would you recognize the men if you saw them?"

"Is Mr. Taha in trouble, Sir?"

Who was this Mr. Taha? An accomplice? A man Farhad bribed? And how could he disappear? Andrea was so confused, she didn't know what to think.

"No, my dear. Simply a matter of curiosity. That's all."

"I believe I'd recognize both men. It was not their first visit to this bank."

Mr. Griffith's eyebrows shot up. "Go on."

"Well, Sir. They were here once before. Last Sunday." She stopped. "Yes, definitely Sunday. They talked to Joseph. Something Joseph told them made them very angry. They stormed out of the bank."

"What makes you so sure it was Sunday?"

"I wouldn't have remembered normally. But you know how Joseph takes time off to go to church on Sundays."

"I do indeed."

"He came back from church wearing a new suit. We were talking about it when the two men walked in. They asked me who was in charge of dollar accounts and I directed them to Joseph. That's all I know."

"Thank you. You've been very helpful. Could you send Joseph in, please?"

Mr. Griffith returned his attention to the file until Joseph entered the room.

"My secretary tells me, last Sunday, you had two men inquire about a dollar account," Mr. Griffith asked. "What did they want to know?"

"Last Sunday? Two men? Oh, yes. I remember. They wanted to know if they could cash a check in dollars. I told them they could. They said it was for ten thousand. Could I give them the cash or did I have to get clearance from the manager of the bank?"

"I told them I needed clearance from the manager and the government since the amount they requested was over two thousand dollars. One of them said it was his money. He could do with it as he pleased and it was none of government's business. I told them it was a new law, they had to fill the necessary forms and if approved, we'd have the money ready in forty-eight hours. They said they'd reward me if I bent the rules and gave them the money right away. Something about the younger man having a sick mother in the hospital. I told them I couldn't. They got angry and left."

Mr. Griffith puffed on his pipe in rapid succession letting out circles of smoke which bathed the room with a sweet, pungent smell. Andrea loved the smell of pipe tobacco. It reminded her of her father. Mr. Griffith did not look like her father, yet, something in the way he talked, in the way he carried himself, reminded her of her father. She missed her father terribly.

"Have you left anything out, Joseph?"

Joseph took a pensive look, as though turning the events of the day over in his mind. "It was their understanding that you'd gone on vacation, Sir. They wanted to know who took over during your absence."

"Well, did you tell them?"

"I did. I told them Mr. Taha was in charge."

"Thank you, Joseph. That will be all."

Mr. Griffith resumed his pipe smoking. Andrea didn't know what to do. She waited for Mr. Griffith to reveal what he planned to do next.

Finally, he turned to her. With the same unaffected voice he said, "We've had this sort of thing happen before; husbands, brothers, male relatives helping themselves to accounts of women, especially foreign women, without worrying too much about legal repercussions. There's very little in the law to protect women and men can always bribe their way out. Do you want an investigation?"

Andrea stood, fighting hard to control the rage building inside her. "No. I can't see how it would help."

"I understand. But I still have to inform the authorities."

She invariably held her breath when she was upset. She made a conscious effort to relax. The matter was beyond her control.

She faced him, fighting to control her tears. "Thank you for your help."

On the way home, distraught and unable to think straight, she felt her only option was to ask Sayid for help. Without money, she could do nothing. Sayid's brusque remark had prompted her trip to the bank. It came back to haunt her. "Haven't you done enough already?"

Like a shutter opening suddenly, her mind cleared and she knew that he knew. It was the money. Sayid knew about the forgery. Or, he thought that Mani had succeeded in persuading her to give him the money. Money for which his brother was willing to see his mother die. Money which was probably used to gun down innocent people, her people.

Chapter 12

The news blackout about the assassination was lifted at the end of November with the appearance of a brief article in the local newspapers. Security forces surrounded a building downtown where the four men who had killed the Americans were hiding. The suspects were ordered to surrender peacefully but refused. Subsequently, agents opened fire and killed all four in a fierce shootout.

Savak published the names of the four men. Mani's was not among them. Nor was Farhad's. They claimed the killers were members of the outlawed Islamic-Marxist Party and that the bodies had been positively identified by the driver of the Dodge and other witnesses present at the scene of the crime. The investigation was closed.

It was news Andrea had been waiting for ever since she'd heard Farhad mention August 28th, her money was drawn from the bank, and Mani disappeared along with his friend. It was a nightmare she'd as soon forget. Through the long nights and most of the day, she had no one to talk to. Her mother-in-law wanted nothing to do with her. She hardly ever saw

Sayid, and when she did, he was too drunk to carry on a conversation. Irene and her husband had left for Shiraz in late September. Her husband was invited to teach neurology for the fall quarter. Layla was the only person she could talk to. But fear that Savak might have bugged her apartment, kept them from discussing anything of substance.

It was during this period that Andrea made her decision. She wouldn't leave, she wouldn't run away like a common criminal risking her and her child's life. She'd wait for her husband to come, confront him, and demand a satisfactory arrangement.

Two days later, Mani and Farhad strolled in. Mani said a curt hello to Andrea, asked the maid to prepare dinner, then plopped himself on the sofa. Farhad moved to an armchair across from him.

Andrea walked over and stood facing Mani. "I'd like to talk to you, alone, please."

He burst out laughing. "Look at you. You're shaking. What's the matter with you?"

"I'd like to talk to you, alone."

"Talk."

He remained sprawled on the sofa.

"All right, I'll talk. I'm not prepared to live under these circumstances. If this is going to be your lifestyle, I would like you to provide us with the necessary documents so Kelly and I can leave."

She saw Farhad nod.

Mani pulled his legs together and straightened his back. "We've had problems. Lots of problems. Impossible for you to understand."

"Try me."

"We had to go into hiding. You have no idea what long tentacles the secret service in this country has."

"Why didn't you call?"

"She's really crazy." It was Farhad. "The phones are tapped. They'd immediately trace our whereabouts."

Should she believe them? Andrea was so confused, she didn't know what to believe. "Where's my money?"

Blank expressions on both men's faces.

"What did you do with it?"

"I don't know what you're talking about."

"Uh huh."

Farhad rose, straightened his tie and buttoned his jacket. "Mani, we're late. We have to go."

A confused look momentarily crossed Mani's face. "Oh, yes." He checked his watch. "Yes, of course." He rose and buttoned his jacket.

Andrea laughed. "Nice try."

"What's that supposed to mean?" Farhad spun around like a boxer readying for a fight.

"An instant rendezvous. Perhaps you forgot that Mani ordered dinner when you walked in."

"I'd forgotten that we had a meeting," Mani said looking to his friend for approval.

"I bet you had."

"We won't be gone long. We'll talk when we get back."

"Sure."

And they left.

Christmas came and went and so did New Year. Mani did not call or come.

Soon after New Year, a soft snow began to fall on the capital, catching the inhabitants by surprise. The roads became impassable, and oil, the sole source of heat, could not be obtained at any price in a country practically floating on oil.

It snowed for days, bringing the city to a standstill. Then, one morning, Andrea woke up to a beautiful, bright, sunny day. She was hopeful that the cold spell was over and life could return to normal.

By evening, the bright January sunshine bathing the snow-covered city was gone. The night was cold and crisp. Andrea sat at the kitchen window watching the deserted streets until it hypnotized her and reminded her to throw a glance at the kitchen clock.

It was past midnight.

She went to bed, read for a while and nodded off. The cold air coming in through the cracks of the windows, made it impossible to get warm. She took one of her blankets and wrapped Kelly in it. As she did so, she heard noises coming from downstairs. She listened carefully, fearful that Naene was not feeling well and might need help.

She threw on her robe and rushed to her mother-in-law's room. The noise stopped momentarily. She opened the door and checked. The night light was on. Naene and the maid were asleep.

Then she heard the noise again. It was a cupboard door closing in the kitchen. She went to check.

Sayid turned around slowly, threw a casual glance in her direction. "Do you know where they keep the tea?"

"I'll make it," Andrea said. "I could use some too."

She put the water on the burner to boil and felt his eyes watching her. He seemed restless, nervous. "Sit," he said impatiently. "Sit down."

She did.

"Did I wake you?"

"I heard noises. I was worried about Naene."

He brought his face close to hers. "I'm sorry."

"Don't worry. I was having trouble sleeping. I can't seem to get warm."

"You're sure that's the reason?"

"Why do you ask?"

"Because you roam around the house when it's not cold and there's no noise."

Andrea smiled. "I promise to stay in my room from now on. I didn't know you could hear me."

"That's not the point. You won't admit it. But you can't sleep because there's too much on your mind."

"I can take care of myself."

"Yes, I've heard you say that often enough. But you can't in this country."

She poured him a cup of tea. "You're home early tonight," she said. "It's not two o'clock yet."

"Don't change the subject."

She heard Kelly crying. "Excuse me. I have to run to my room for a moment." She went to the room, bundled Kelly in a blanket and brought her to the kitchen.

"Her lips are blue. Our bedroom is very cold. I'd like to buy an electric heater. Where I can get one?"

"I'll get it for you. How do you expect to go shopping without a car? You know there's not a single cab to be had."

"I figured I'd walk to the main street and look for one." Then something that had been puzzling her for months, surfaced. "Early in September I received a note and a checkbook from Mr. Griffith. He states in the note that there's money in my account. That I am free to withdraw any amount I need. Would you know anything about it?"

Kelly moaned and shivered. Andrea pulled her close to her chest and tucked the blankets firmly around the child's frail body.

He raised his eyes and gave her a pained look. "You drive me crazy. You know that? Regardless of how miserable it is for you here, you insist on putting up with it. If your life means nothing to you, you should be concerned about what it's doing to your daughter. Look at her. Half frozen to death. You won't find a decent institution to put her in in case her condition becomes impossible for you to manage. Don't you ever give up?"

"You didn't answer my question."

"That's immaterial. The important thing is for you to get out of here. I can forge Mani's signature to get you the documents you need for travel."

"And then what? I can't risk flying. We have to turn in the passports to airport security forty eight hours in advance. Can you guarantee that they won't detect the forgery?"

"The name might present a problem." He seemed to be talking more to himself than her.

"You mean Mani's name, don't you? Why?"

"He's wanted for interrogation."

"Has he done something or is it routine?"

"You should ask him, not me."

"I would, if I could."

"You should go by land to Turkey."

"In this snow, with all the roads closed. You must be joking."

"You must leave."

Something in his manner, the urgency with which he was trying to impress her, made her wary.

"Are you expecting more trouble?"

"Why do you ask?"

"Because, in the past, whenever you've urged me to leave, invariably, soon after, there are rumors of disturbances."

He didn't answer. She felt something weighed heavily on his mind. "Is Mani involved?"

He gazed at her but said nothing.

"It's me you're worried about, isn't it?"

"You should be too."

"I know I have problems. Running away is not the solution. Eventually, I'm hoping he'll come back to his senses. If we can't make our marriage work, perhaps we can work out a satisfactory arrangement."

He sighed. "You simply can't admit, not even to yourself that you made a mistake, a big mistake. And, you have no one to blame but yourself."

"You may be right, but I will not leave without exhausting every possibility. I remember him as a wonderful father and a good husband and not so long ago."

Sayid stood and shook his head. Then he leaned on the table and looked her straight in the eye. "I cannot believe that a woman of your intelligence could be so blind."

Andrea pulled Kelly closer to her chest. The child was shivering again despite the double layer of blankets. She wanted to take Kelly back to her bed but this was an opportunity she couldn't afford to miss. Sayid was home early and he was sober.

"I hate to tell you this, but what you have to look forward to is more of the same. It will get worse not better. For Mani there is no turning back. That kind of commitment is final."

"How long have you known about it, Sayid?"

He said nothing. Just gave her a blank stare, rose, went to his room and returned with a bottle of Scotch.

"You take yours with water, right?"

Drunk or sober, his answers were always controlled. Regardless of how she phrased her questions, he answered mostly in generalities. "Thank you. I really don't care for any."

"Come now. I hate drinking alone."

Andrea stroked Kelly's curly hair. The child had fallen asleep. "It's late. I think we should all get some sleep."

He looked at her in a curious manner. "It's my drinking that bothers you, right?"

"Sort of." When he wasn't drunk, his good looks projected an awesome presence. What drove him to drink? Why would a man who seemed to have everything to live for pursue a course of self destruction? She had no answer.

He poured himself a drink. "You're sure you don't want one?"

"No, thanks."

He finished his drink in one swallow then reached out to set the empty glass on the table. He missed. The glass shattered on the tile floor.

Sayid picked a few large pieces off the ground, threw them in the trash can, then went to the cupboard and got another glass.

"Let me take Kelly to bed," Andrea said. "I'll be right back."

She returned shortly, found a broom and swept bits of glass into a pile.

"Stop it, please," he said.

"I'm almost done."

"Leave it. The maid will clean it in the morning."

The doorbell rang.

She stopped and looked toward Sayid. His face told her that he had no more idea who the caller might be than she.

"Put that thing away," he said as he rose and headed toward the front door. "You look silly standing there holding a broom in your hand at three in the morning."

He opened the door.

"Is Mrs. Andrea home?" It was a child's voice. Andrea rushed toward the door.

"Come inside, quickly. You'll freeze out there." Sayid reached for the child's hand to pull her inside.

"No, no, let me go," the little girl screamed and tried to pull away.

It was Sima, Layla's daughter. Andrea's heart sank. Layla had to be in trouble. "It's all right, Sima," Andrea said. "He won't hurt you."

The child sobbed but did not object when Sayid approached her.

Sayid gathered her in his arms and went to the kitchen.

Andrea closed the front door and joined them.

He sat her in his lap. "What's the matter, Sima? Are you hurt?"

Sima wiped her tears with her hands. "Mama. Two men took Mama away."

Sayid looked from the child to Andrea. "Who's she?" he asked.

"Her mother is the widow I often visit. You told me to stay away from her."

"Oh, yes, the widow," Sayid said, a painful expression sweeping across his face. "I remember the incident quite well."

"She said her husband died under interrogation by Savak."

"What else do you know about her?"

"She was worried that she too might be picked up someday."

"Yes, of course."

"What do you mean?" Andrea was astonished by his matter of fact response.

"She talks too much. She was bound to get in trouble."

Andrea went to the closet and reached for her coat. "I have to go. She has two younger brothers at home."

"You're not going anywhere."

"Sayid, I must. I promised."

"No."

"Why?"

"Because there's an agent out there who followed the child to see where she'd go and whom she'd contact. The minute you step outside, they'll grab you."

"Are you serious?"

"Unfortunately, yes."

"But, what about the boys?"

Sayid put his chin on his fist seemingly lost in thought. "Were your brothers asleep when you left?" he asked Sima.

"No, they were awake. There was too much noise."

"Do you have an aunt, an uncle, any relatives in Tehran?"

"No." Sima resumed her sobbing.

Andrea fought hard to control her own tears. "I promised Sima's mother I'd contact her parents in Qom if something were to happen to her."

He lifted the child from his lap and handed her to Andrea. "Keep her warm. I'll be back with her brothers. Don't open the door to anyone even if the caller says his name is Sayid. I have my key. I'll let myself in."

"Don't. Please don't go. I don't want you to get in trouble."

"You take care of the girl and I'll take care of myself."

Regardless of how hard she tried, she couldn't figure him out. Andrea wrapped Sima in a blanket and held her close. Soon, the child relaxed and dozed. She took her to the living room, lay her on the sofa, gave her a big hug, piled blankets on her and collapsed in an armchair next to the sofa.

An hour later, Sayid had still not returned from what should have been a ten minute trip. Had he gotten himself in trouble on her account? Did he really know anyone influential who could help? She'd heard Mani remark about Sayid playing cards with the chief of Savak and that the men were friends. If the need arose would the chief of Savak help Sayid? She thought of going to Layla's house. But the sharp, strict sound of his voice returned, "Don't leave the house or open the door." So she prepared a pot of coffee and waited.

It was morning when he returned with the two boys asleep on his shoulders. He looked exhausted.

Gently, she disengaged the children's grip from around his neck, took them to her room and put them in her bed. She checked Kelly and then Sima. They were asleep. She went to the kitchen to thank him.

He was sprawled in a chair, his legs stretched out, his hands dropped on the sides. She handed him a cup of coffee. He took it, drank a sip and placed it on the table.

"You were gone a long time. I was worried about you."

"It took longer than I anticipated." He kept his gaze focused on the coffee cup.

"What happened?"

"When I got to the house, the door was open, the boys were gone."

She shivered.

"It took a while to locate them."

Andrea felt a sudden stabbing pain in her stomach. "What did they want the children for?"

He looked at her with sad eyes, eyes that pleaded for her to stop questioning him.

She wanted to grab him, shake him, get some answers.

What would it accomplish? He wouldn't talk unless he wanted to no matter what she did.

"Do you like her?" he asked after a prolonged silence.

"You mean Layla?"

"I believe that's her name."

"Very much. She's my best friend."

"Has she been nice to you?"

"Always. Why do you ask?"

"Just curious."

"I respect her. She has principles and abides by them."

"What kind of principles?"

"She's honest, sincere and cares about others. I admire her for being so brave."

"She goes about it the wrong way."

"What makes you say that?"

"You can't voice your opinions in this country. Period."

"Actually, she's very careful. She gave me that very same advice, repeatedly."

"Then what was she doing with a known Mujahed in a pizza parlor? Being an Iranian, she should have known that if apprehended, eventually he'd talk. And, that's exactly what he did."

"He came to talk to me. He returned a five hundred rial note which I had given him by mistake."

He looked at her in a funny way. She could not tell whether he was pleased or angry. Then, he burst out laughing. "I shouldn't laugh," he said apologetically. "but that's such an old trick. You didn't fall for it, did you?"

I have a lot to learn, Andrea thought. "I saw no reason to doubt him."

"Is there any coffee left?"

She reached for the pot and filled his cup. He sipped it quietly, avoiding her gaze.

"Where could I find a cab to take me to Qom?" she asked.

"You don't need to go anywhere."

She waited for him to explain. He said nothing. He stared

into space.

"I promised to contact Layla's parents. Someone has to take care of her children."

"Someone will."

"Who?"

He got up, put his coat on, drank the last sip of coffee then turned to go. "Stay here. Don't leave the house under any circumstance. I'll be back."

"Wait. Listen to me. I have to go to Qom."

"No. You must not go out."

She was on the verge of tears. "I have her parent's phone number. Could I use the phone?"

"Don't."

"Why?"

"They'll trace the call and you'll have to answer a lot of questions."

She drifted to a chair in a daze. She didn't know what to do.

He came and stood next to her. "Does she mean that much to you?"

"Yes! Besides that, I gave her my word. She trusted me." The tears broke free.

He took her hand in his. "Please, pull yourself together. I hate to see you upset."

She dried her tears and smiled. "I'm sorry. It's been a long night. I guess the trip to Qom will have to wait."

"Did anyone ever tell you how beautiful you are when you smile?"

For a moment, she thought she saw the real man, the man she'd met at the University. Brilliant, intense, stunningly good looking. How he had changed! She laughed. "Yes, my father."

He released her hand. "I have to go."

"Supposing they come for the children, is there anything I can do to stop them?"

"I have asked for two agents to be posted outside our house. They'll see to it that no one disturbs you."

It took her a few seconds to digest the information. "Let's see if I understand this correctly. You have two agents outside; Savak agents who are to prevent other agents from disturbing me. Is that what you're saying?"

He laughed nervously. "Not bad, not bad at all. You're catching on. Please, leave these matters to me. You should rest while the children are asleep."

Incredible. "When will you be back?"

"I don't know. Why do you ask?"

"Because I'd like to know when you think it will be possible for me to reach Layla's parents."

"You don't need to."

"I . . . I don't understand?"

He stopped, looked at her, then said, "I'm going to try and free your friend."

"How?"

"Let's say I'm fortunate enough to be in a position to help."

She shook her head in disbelief. "You have me baffled. I can't figure out if you're one of them, or what?"

"I am myself, Andrea. I belong to no group and I answer to no one."

Chapter 13

It was close to noon when Sayid returned accompanied by Layla. Andrea rushed to the door to meet them. The women embraced and cried. Sayid took off his coat, threw it on a chair and went to the kitchen. Andrea noticed Layla look around with a worried expression on her face.

"Sima's in the living room and the boys are upstairs," Andrea said. "They're asleep."

"How can I ever thank you?"

"Don't thank me. Thank Sayid. I wasn't much help. Sayid wouldn't let me leave the house."

Layla turned to Sayid. "Thanks again and thank you Andrea for taking care of the children."

Sayid looked up briefly but said nothing.

The maid placed a tray with three cups of tea on the table.

"Sit," Sayid said as he reached for a cup of tea.

Andrea offered Layla a chair. "I better not. I'd like to take the children home."

"Drink your tea," Sayid ordered without looking up. "I'll drive you home when the children wake up."

Layla hesitated, then sat at the edge of a chair.

They drank their tea in silence. Andrea finished first. "I'll check the children," she said. "It's awfully quiet upstairs."

She returned with Kelly in her arms, followed by the boys. "They were entertaining Kelly," Andrea said. Turning to Layla, "Sima is awake. I think she's afraid to get up because she's in a strange place."

"I'll get her." Layla hurried to the living room.

Sayid rose, put on his coat, reached for the three year old, carried him on one arm and the five year old on the other. "Let's go."

Layla took Sima's hand, placed a kiss on Andrea's cheek, and followed Sayid out the door.

Ten minutes later, Sayid returned. He climbed the stairs, went to his room and closed the door.

Andrea didn't see him again for a month. Neither did she see her husband. She noticed a pattern which disturbed her. More often than not, whenever Mani left without saying where he was going or when he'd be back, Sayid disappeared too. Perhaps it was coincidence. Meanwhile, she spent her time taking care of Kelly, studying Farsi and planning. There had to be a way for her and Kelly to leave and she was determined to find it. The bad weather had set her back but that was over now. The snows had melted from the warmth of spring sunshine.

One sunny March morning, her long lost husband once again strolled in accompanied by Farhad. He greeted her as though he'd been away a couple of hours. Then he and Farhad sat at the dining table discussing something in whispers. Andrea waited for an opportune moment to confront him. After several cups of tea Farhad rose and went to the bathroom. Andrea put her book on the coffee table and approached Mani. "I have to talk to you."

"Some other time. I'm busy now."

"When? After you disappear for another three months?"

"We're working on a business deal. Once it gets going,

everything will be fine."

"What kind of business?"

"Questions. Questions. Quit bugging me. Can't you see I'm busy?"

Farhad returned from the bathroom. "If an American doesn't boss her husband every chance she gets, she feels deprived."

Andrea felt like smacking him. "Fortunately you're not married to one."

"Leave us alone." Mani returned his attention to a pile of papers on the table.

Andrea turned and left. She was shaking and tears welled in her eyes. But she held her head high and her chin up. She went to the kitchen, fixed Kelly's lunch and went to their room to feed the child.

Kelly beamed and gurgled when she saw her mother. Andrea lifted her from her wheel chair and placed her in her lap. "I love you sweetheart," she murmured. Regardless of how disturbed a state she was in, Kelly always brought joy to her heart. Andrea gave her a kiss and a big hug and felt much better. When Kelly was done eating, she took her to the living room to watch cartoons.

Irene came a few minutes after she was through feeding Kelly. They had made plans to have lunch together. One of the advantages of living in Iran was the full time help Andrea had for Kelly. Fatima had no family, she lived in, and took excellent care of the child.

"Hi, everybody," Irene said and headed to the dining room where Mani had his head buried in papers. "You're the man I wanted to talk to."

"Oh, what about?"

"I want to give a surprise birthday party for my husband. I was hoping you could help me."

"When is his birthday?"

"The fourteenth of March, right before the Iranian New Year. Do you think you'll have time? I'll understand if you say no."

"How can I help?"

"He'll be forty. I want it to be special. We'll do it at the Niavaran Club and invite all our friends."

"Sounds great. How many people do you plan to invite?"

"Forty to fifty couples. Here, have a look. I have the names with me."

She handed him a piece of paper.

Mani looked it over. "You want to invite the Prime Minister and a four star general?"

"Sure, why not? They're our friends. You're invited too."

"I don't think so." Mani cast a quick glance in Farhad's direction.

"Why not, Mani?" Farhad asked. "Just imagine. You'll be in the company of men who have the fate of this country twisted around their little fingers."

Irene glared at Farhad. "I take it my guest list does not please you."

"I'm a humble man, Madame," Farhad replied. "It's not for me to approve or disapprove who you associate with."

"No, it's not."

Farhad cocked his head to one side and sneered. "Mani doesn't need the company of big shots to boost his ego, nor does he need favors. He can make it on his own."

Mani fidgeted. His eyes darted from one to the other.

"You've chosen a great spokesman for yourself, Mani. I gather you'll be in business together. Hope he does as well for your business."

"Don't worry about us." Farhad answered. "We'll do just fine."

"I bet you will!"

Mani rose. "Irene . . . I . . . I." He didn't finish.

"It's all right, Mani. You don't have to explain."

"What . . . what did you want me to do?" Mani sounded like he was in pain.

Irene threw a quick glance in Farhad's direction. He

puffed on a cigarette, a contented look on his face. She turned to Mani. "Its really no big deal. The management at the club is not very good at taking suggestions from women. I thought you could come with me when I talk to them."

Mani cracked his knuckles. Then, without looking at Irene, he said, "We will probably be in Isfahan. We have to raise money for our business. Farhad has contacts there."

"That's a shame. My husband will be terribly disappointed that his favorite cousin is missing his birthday party. But don't worry. He'll understand."

Andrea listened to the heated exchange. She felt Irene's anger mounting. Hoping to find a way out before the confrontation escalated, she said, "I'm starved, Irene. Let's go."

Irene turned and walked out the door without saying another word.

Andrea walked over to Kelly, kissed her goodbye, then said goodbye to the men and followed Irene to her car.

Irene got behind the wheel. The crimson of her face paled as she drove. After a few moments of silence, she asked, "Tell me, does that . . . that creep live with you?"

"I'm told he can't find an apartment."

"I can't figure out who he hates more, Iranian government officials or Americans."

"What makes you say that?" Andrea had heard Farhad make numerous derogatory remarks about Americans and Iranians with government jobs but she couldn't fathom how Irene knew.

"We've locked horns before. I met him for the first time the night you arrived. He spent most of the evening telling anyone who would listen what idiots Americans are."

"Why would he bad mouth Americans?"

"Andrea, there are a lot of people here who blame the problems of this country on the policies of the American government. It's no secret that the CIA brought the Shah back to power in 1953 after forcing Mussadegh's government to fall."

"What have we got to do with it?"

"This man hates Americans. I made it my business to find out about him when he expressed himself so vehemently about us. He's suspected of being a revolutionary. He's kept himself out of trouble because he's very shrewd and cunning. You must warn Mani. Since you arrived, I haven't seen Mani without him. As though they're Siamese twins or something. That man is evil. Mani should get rid of him."

"How? They've been friends since childhood. When Mani goes to Isfahan, he stays in their house."

"I knew Mani quite well before he left for the States. He was a fine young man. Now he acts as though he has to wait for Farhad's approval for everything he says and does."

"Careful!" Andrea shouted.

Irene swerved, barely missing a boy who had dashed into the street after a ball.

Irene pulled the car over to a side street and turned the engine off. She was shaking. "Thaaaat was close."

They waited for a few moments until she calmed down. "I only drive when I have to," Irene said. "The worst thing that can happen to anyone in this country is to get involved in an injury accident. You're guilty until proven innocent. Meanwhile, you can rot in jail. That's why most foreigners have drivers. Unfortunately, we still don't know when Savak will release Ahmed."

"You're still shook up. Let me drive."

Irene nodded and traded places.

"Where to?"

"Pahlavi Boulevard. There's a restaurant there called Yass. Helga is waiting for us."

"Helga?"

"Yes, sorry I didn't get a chance to tell you. She's a good friend of mine. I wanted you to meet her."

"Is she German?"

"Yes. She's the wife of General Cyrus. The top General in the country. Do you know her?"

"I met a German woman by that name, married to a general, last summer. She let me use her phone."

Helga was at the restaurant when they arrived. The restaurant specialized in serving Chelo Kebab, a favorite Iranian dish served with rice pilaf.

"Nice to see you again," Helga said, as Andrea and Irene slipped into their chairs.

"Have you been waiting long?" Irene asked.

Helga smiled. "I had to leave the house an hour ago. I got thrown out. Two French experts, with special gadgets, are combing the premises for bugs, and I don't mean bugs that bite!"

"Are you having problems?"

"Enough to drive us crazy. My husband and I talk about something and a few days later it comes back to us in one form or another."

"That's incredible."

"Oh, well, it comes with the territory. They'll take care of it." Helga turned to Andrea. "Did Irene tell you what she's planning to do on her husband's birthday? She said she'd ask your husband to help her. Cyrus, that's my husband, would be glad to help, but, lately, his schedule has been unpredictable, subject to change on a moment's notice. Will your husband be able to help?"

Irene came to Andrea's rescue. "Mani is busy working on a business deal. I'll have to do it myself."

"I'm free Irene," Helga said. "I'll help."

"I thought you wanted to go to the Caspian."

"I want to, but I hate to go alone. Cyrus can't come. There are disturbances in the provinces and disgruntlement in the army. The Shah wants him on call twenty four hours a day until the situation calms down."

The Chelo Kabob they had ordered, arrived. Irene sprinkled sumac on hers. "I hear rumors to that effect frequently yet nothing is ever mentioned in the papers."

Helga chuckled. "Do you see those two men at the bar with their backs turned to us? They are the latest addition to our entourage. They go where I go. It's that bad."

Andrea and Irene looked. There were only two men at the bar. Each had a cup of tea in front of him.

Disturbances, assassinations, body guards. Words which sent shock waves through Andrea's body, prodding, twisting, torturing. The same question. Was Mani involved?

"Are the Islamic-Marxists blamed again?" Irene asked.

"No, they're blaming President Carter for his shortsighted views regarding Third World problems."

The waiter brought their order. "This smells delicious," Andrea said, "and there's enough here to feed a family."

"Enjoy it," Irene said, "and no doggy bags, please. That's considered uncouth here."

The waiter lingered close to their table. Irene bent her head toward Helga and whispered, "Isn't this the same waiter who served us at the Darband Hotel two weeks ago?"

Helga looked up, then nodded.

Irene reached for her fork. "Sometimes I feel like I live in a fish bowl."

"I bought a beautiful face cream when I was in Germany," Helga said out loud. "But it was very expensive."

The waiter drifted slowly to another table.

"They're not too crazy about listening to foreigners." Helga chuckled.

"I wonder what would happen if the government relaxed its tight grip slightly," Andrea said. "Helga, does your husband ever mention preventive measures to avoid bloodshed?"

"He's doing everything he can. It's not easy to bring about change without serious after effects."

"There's got to be a better way."

"That's what I think," Irene said. "Ghandi did it. It's called passive resistance or something."

"Iranians are not passive people. They're highly emotional. My husband's father helped the King regain his throne, so now they're blaming my husband for whatever the government does."

Andrea had not expected Helga's outspoken response. She felt uneasy. Maybe she should not have started the conversation. Sayid's warning about limiting her discussions to the weather and traffic gnawed at her.

Irene must have sensed her concern. "Don't worry. We're not making accusations. Anyway, there's too much noise for anyone to hear us."

"I've heard people get in trouble for having said much less," Andrea said.

"People seem to be bolder lately. Since my return from Germany a couple of weeks ago, I've noticed a definite change. Everyone's talking politics. It's scary."

"Maybe it's time for people to have a say in their government," Andrea said.

Helga shook her head. "The average Iranian doesn't even know how to read and write."

"But he knows there's wealth in this country and he's not getting any."

The waiter returned. "Is everything satisfactory?"

The women smiled at him. "Yes. Yes. The food is delicious."

"He knows we're not discussing face cream," Irene whispered as the waiter walked away.

"That's all right," Helga said. "Why shouldn't people be free to express their opinions?"

It was an education. Andrea had not expected the wife of the top general to be so outspoken. Helga was right. Savak had lost its invincibility as evidenced by the bold assassination of the Americans in the summer. The public had become aggressive, demanding, almost fearless.

Helga tossed her head. "Let those in charge solve the country's problems. This is the best time of the year to go to the Caspian. It would be a fabulous way to celebrate Now Ruz, the Iranian new year. Let's go after the party."

"I'm sorry, I can't. My husband wants to attend a neurosurgical conference at Massachusetts General Hospital on the seventeenth of March. He wants me to go with him."

"Oh, well, I guess I have to go with my body guards."

Irene turned to Andrea. "Have you been to the Caspian?"

"No, not yet."

"Would you like to go?" Helga asked.

"I don't know. I hadn't thought about it." Andrea felt a warmth toward Helga. She impressed her as an unusually sincere and intelligent woman.

"Then it's settled. We'll leave the day after the party."

"No, wait. I have to discuss it with my husband."

"What's there to discuss," Irene said impatiently. "You heard him say he'll probably be in Isfahan. If he can go where he wants to, why can't you?"

Andrea thought about it and realized she couldn't give a plausible answer. Mostly, he didn't give a damn where she went as long as she left him alone. "There's Kelly. I don't like to leave her alone with the maid."

"Bring her. She'll love it."

"She's in a wheel chair."

"That's all right. The fresh air will do her good."

"I'll think about it. I'll let you know."

"What's there to think," Irene said. "There will be no one left in Tehran during Now Ruz except the sick and the infirm. Everyone goes away from the capital. This place becomes like a ghost town. Go and have fun."

Irene was right. To hell with Mani. "Let me know when. I'll be ready."

"I'm delighted," Helga said. "I promise we'll have a great time. It's a pity Irene can't come. If I can drag my husband away from Tehran, well have a big New years eve party."

Andrea's attention was diverted momentarily by the waiter whispering to one of the body guards. The body guard rose, walked behind the bar and spoke on the phone. He returned quickly and conversed with his partner.

Helga was busy eating desert. She didn't notice the men approaching her.

"Is Madame ready to leave?" the body guard asked.

Helga looked puzzled. "Not quite yet. Is something the matter?"

"The General wants us to leave."

"The General?"

"Yes, Madame. He called the restaurant. He wants you home right away."

Helga shook her head. "Excuse me ladies, I guess I better go."

Chapter 14

Andrea and Irene were at the club taking care of last minute details before the guests arrived for the doctor's birthday party.

"Will Helga and the General be able to come?" Andrea asked.

"Oh, yes. They're coming. They're staying in a hotel until the investigators complete their work. There wasn't a single window left intact in their house. They were really out to get the General. He was lucky his meeting with the King lasted longer than planned."

"It gives me goose flesh." Andrea said rubbing her arms. "I hate violence."

"People here are used to it. You'll find very few bothered by the upheaval as much as you and I."

Andrea glanced around the huge reception room. "I think everything is under control."

"And it's almost six thirty. The guests are expected at eight. But if I know anything about Iranians, they probably won't appear until nine thirty. That will allow us time to shower, dress and be back in time to receive the guests."

"How about your husband? Does he suspect anything?"

"I hope not. I've asked a doctor friend he works with to invite him to the club for a drink. They come here occasionally to relax."

One last look around and the two women gathered their purses and walked from the reception room.

Andrea, in the lead, stopped suddenly. She was sure she saw a shadow sneak behind stairs connecting the reception room to a storage room one floor below. While Andrea waited for Irene to lock the door, she focused her attention to the spot the shadow had disappeared.

When Irene joined her, Andrea said, "I think I saw someone go behind the stairs."

"It could be a worker. Security gives a thorough check anywhere the Prime Minister goes. I don't think we need to worry about it."

She took Irene's word for it but was still concerned.

Irene dropped Andrea at her home and told her to be ready at seven forty five. And, since Mani had not left Tehran as he'd said he would, Andrea assumed he'd attend the party.

When Andrea entered the house, the television blared at full volume. Naene sat in her armchair holding a bowl of roasted watermelon seeds in her lap. It was a common sight. She thrust a seed between her two front teeth, cracked it open and swallowed the minute contents. Some nights watermelon seeds were replaced by roasted pumpkin seeds or sunflower seeds.

Mani was nowhere to be seen. However, she wasn't concerned. After all, he wasn't in the habit of keeping her informed of his whereabouts. She greeted Naene, inquired about her health, then went to their room to check on Kelly and get ready.

At seven forty five, Irene honked the horn. Andrea kissed Kelly, grabbed her purse, left a note for Mani, then said goodbye to her mother-in-law. Her mother-in-law grunted something in reply which Andrea couldn't understand.

The club was located on top of one of the few hills in the city. A narrow winding road coursed to the top. Irene's driver, Ahmed, back from prison, drove them to the entrance. The whole area swarmed with police and plain clothes detectives. They were asked for identification, the car searched, the occupants checked. Only then they were waved through.

The view from the garden and the reception hall was spectacular.

The guests, dressed in the latest fashions from Paris, hair beautifully coiffed, nails manicured, dripping with diamonds, trickled in at about nine thirty in chauffeur driven cars. They fascinated Andrea. She couldn't help but wonder how much planning, time and money was spent on an evening's invitation.

At about ten thirty, Andrea's stomach growled. A lot of drinks and a few snacks were served but there was no sign of dinner.

Irene casually walked toward Andrea. "I don't understand why my husband has not shown up yet. I hope he didn't have an emergency. I checked with the hospital . . ."

A waiter approached Irene. "Dr. Zangane said to tell you he's arrived."

"That's them," Irene said excitedly. "Andrea tell the guests to be ready."

A few minutes later Irene walked in with her husband. "Surprise!" the crowd yelled in unison. The orchestra played "Happy birthday" and the guests sang. The doctor hugged his wife and gave her a kiss. "Thank you all," he said. "What a surprise!" He gave his wife another hug, took her in his arms and danced. The guests followed.

At ten to eleven, there was still no sign of Helga, her husband or the Prime Minister. Andrea was starved, concerned and annoyed. Starved, because she hadn't had time to eat all day, concerned because she was still worried about the shadow sneaking behind the stairs in the afternoon, and annoyed because she was the only woman without her husband, despite his being in town.

Irene's husband approached her, smiling. He was of medium height, dark complexion, graying at the temples.

"Irene tells me you did most of the work," he said. "Thank you very much for helping her. You two did a good job."

"My pleasure. There were too many people around you. I didn't get a chance to wish you many happy returns of the day."

"Thank you. If I weren't famished, I'd probably enjoy it more."

"You too, huh?" Andrea laughed. "Is it always like this? I mean, are dinners served late at parties?"

"Normally, yes. Most of this leisurely class sleeps until late afternoon. They eat late, then attend to beautifying themselves. So they're really not as hungry as we are. But tonight, we have to wait for the Prime Minister to arrive. It's considered disrespectful to serve dinner before he arrives."

"Let's hope he's hungry too."

"Where's Mani? Irene told me there was a possibility that he might go to Isfahan."

"He's in town. I'm hoping he'll be here soon."

There was a commotion outside and a whisper circulated through the crowd.

The doctor smiled. "We're saved. The Prime Minister, the General and his wife have arrived."

Helga was dressed in a simple, black shift. She wore no jewelry except for her wedding rings and a pearl necklace. Her hair was combed in soft curls falling over her shoulders. She looked stunning, her dark hair accenting her almond shaped green eyes. She greeted the doctor, wished him many happy returns, then turned to Andrea.

"You look lovely," Helga said. "And absorbed."

"I don't think I've ever seen so much glitter in one room before. When the light from the crystal chandeliers bounces off those huge rocks the guests are wearing, the whole room seems to light up."

"Isn't that something? I remember my first party here. I kept staring at the women, totally oblivious to everything else, until my husband shook me and told me to stop. I think each tries to outdo the other."

A waiter approached them with a tray of drinks. Helga reached for a Martini. "What are you having, Andrea?"

"I better not. I've had two on an empty stomach."

"I found dinner at midnight the most difficult thing to adjust to. I should have warned you."

"The doctor said dinner wouldn't be served before the Prime Minister arrived."

"That's true. But you'll find no matter where you're invited, dinner is served about eleven. You should eat before you go."

"I'm sorry about your house," Andrea said. "Any suspects?"

"Oh, yes. Lots of suspects but no arrests yet. They did an incredibly thorough job. Had Cyrus been home there was no way he could have escaped. Remember I told you about experts coming to check our house for bugs. Cyrus had an appointment with them at noon that day. Luckily, his meeting with the King lasted forty five minutes longer than planned and the appointment had to be cancelled. You should see our house. It looks like a war zone."

"I'm sorry about your house, but it must be a relief that no one was hurt."

Helga motioned to a waiter carrying a tray of canapes. "Here, munch on these."

"Thanks."

"I don't like living in a hotel. How about leaving for the Caspian tomorrow?

Andrea had not mentioned the invitation to Mani. Since he had not gone to Isfahan, Andrea toyed with the idea of staying in Tehran, hoping to have some time alone with him. The Iranian New Year was less than a week away. Perhaps

Farhad would leave Tehran like Irene said most people did. Maybe then she could find out what was bothering him, get through to him. But she knew, deep down, the chances of it happening were practically nil. He'd either be gone by the time she got back, or Farhad would be with him like he always was. Why miss the opportunity to get away, to see other parts of the country.

Helga must have misconstrued her hesitation. "Let me talk to him. Iranians rarely say no to someone they don't know well. Where is he?"

"He hasn't come yet. Something must have happened."

Helga studied Andrea with an intensity which left her uneasy. "I'll make arrangements for tomorrow. I'll stop by your house in the morning and talk to him. I'm sure he won't object. It's a three hour drive. We'll have to leave early afternoon to get there before dark."

"I'll talk to him. I'm sure it will be all right."

A stream of waiters carrying large platters carefully made their way to the tables.

"Here they come now," Andrea said.

"This is the best time of a party in this country," Helga said. "Watch and you'll see what happens."

The two women watched the crowd attack the tables laden with food. In no time, the platters were empty and the table clothes covered with spilled food.

"Now, it's our turn," Helga said. "We eat what's left. Take it from me. Never go near a table when there are hungry Iranians around."

They laughed, approached the table, and took whatever they could find. It was an unusually warm night. The guests drifted to the garden. Helga and Andrea were alone in the room. Several waiters served wine in the garden.

The General entered. His physique and features reminded Andrea of a Greek god. He had a contented, self assured smile on his face. "There you are," he said. "Who's your charming friend?"

"Cyrus, this is Andrea. Andrea, my husband Cyrus."

The General bowed, reached for Andrea's hand, kissed it gently, then let it go. "I'm delighted to meet you, Madame. You are beautiful. No wonder my wife has not spoken of you. If I were a woman I would not introduce such a friend to my husband either."

"That's very generous of you. Your wife is one of the most attractive women I've ever met. She has no cause for worry."

"Indeed not. She's as beautiful now as the day I married her."

"You're making me blush." Helga smiled, a shy smile.

"Let's go join the guests outside," the General suggested. "On a clear and warm night like this, it's a pity to waste time indoors."

They walked toward the garden. Two waiters rushed to the General's side and inquired if he wanted a table. He said he did.

A table covered with a white linen tablecloth was immediately brought to the garden. A pretty vase full of imported flowers was placed on it. The waiters took the plates of food Helga and Andrea held and placed them on the table. They waited to seat the women and left only after the General told them he didn't need them any more.

"At last we can eat." Helga picked up her knife and fork.

The General smiled. "Helga never did get used to the crazy hours we Iranians keep. For her dinner is at six. Only lately has she learned to tolerate our unorthodox habits."

"I can't call it dinner," Helga said smiling sheepishly, "nor can I call it breakfast. I have to coin a new name for it."

Andrea took a bite of food, raised her head and saw a waiter hurrying to their table.

The waiter approached them cautiously. "Are you Mrs. Abbassi?" he asked Andrea.

"Yes."

"There's a phone call for you."

"Excuse me. It must be my husband."

Andrea followed the waiter to the entrance where the telephone was located and listened. She turned pale and started to shake. With steps reluctant to do her bidding, she managed to return to the garden.

Helga's eyes were on her. She hurried toward Andrea. "What happened? You look like you've been hit on the head."

"Could I talk to you and your husband in private?" Andrea asked.

The General rose. Helga held Andrea's arm and they walked away from the crowd. Andrea took a deep breath, fought to control herself, then said, "It was a woman. She said to vacate the premises immediately. She . . . she . . . said there was a time bomb due to go off in ten minutes. It's under the stairs leading to the room below the reception hall."

Chapter 15

It was as though a magic carpet had transported a model German home to the shores of the Caspian. Located on acres of land, filled with fruit trees, the house was built overlooking the port where the boats docked. The furniture and appliances were imported from Germany. While Andrea looked around fascinated, Helga watched her.

"Do you like it?" she asked.

"It's beautiful. How did you manage to have a mansion of this magnitude, in a country where finding a small apartment is a major achievement."

"I didn't. It was my husband's wedding present to me."

"Do you come here often?"

"I do. It's peaceful. My husband comes occasionally. He stays a couple of days, gets bored and returns to Tehran."

"It should be featured in an architectural magazine. It must be unique in this country."

"It probably is but we're hardly ever here to enjoy it. I'm sure the servants will agree with you though. People here love everything German."

"Can we go for a walk? The fresh air and the smell drifting from the sea are making my blood race. I feel good, as though the past few days never happened."

"Thanks to you we're all alive. Everyone got out of there just in time. I hear it was quite a blast. They don't know who the caller was though."

"What I don't understand is why she picked me out of the crowd to give the message to. The more I think about it, the more it scares me. I don't know of an Iranian woman . . ." Andrea stopped abruptly. Was it possible? She dismissed the thought immediately. It didn't sound like Layla. How could Layla know? Or could she?

"Forget it. Sooner or later, Savak will find out or the revolutionaries will get her for betraying them."

Revolutionaries. Was Mani involved? Was that why he had not come to the party? Where was he at the time? He was not home when she returned from the party and he was not there in the morning. Andrea wrote him a note and left. She was glad she did. It looked like an ideal place to relax.

Her thoughts were miles away when she noticed the housekeeper, shaped in a rectangle, carrying more than two hundred fifty pounds on her less than five foot frame, enter the room. She talked briefly with Helga.

"The housekeeper will take care of Kelly while we're gone," Helga said. "Is there anything special you want her to do?"

"I'll take Kelly with me. I'm sure the housekeeper has other things to do."

"We have three servants with little to do. She loves children. She'll spoil her, but we'll worry about that later."

It was a warm sunny day. They walked the beach then went to Pahlavi, a small town located two miles down the road. Pahlavi had changed little throughout centuries. Small shops, specializing in different crafts, lined narrow cobblestone streets. Hunched old men toiled mostly over pieces of wood, creating exquisite work with the most rudimentary tools. "Pahlavi," Helga explained, "is a town where no one is in a hurry. It's known for its peace and quiet."

They returned home in the early afternoon. Helga went to the kitchen to talk to the housekeeper. Andrea checked Kelly. She had been fed and put to sleep. Andrea stretched on a beach chair facing the sea. The roar and the splash of the waves aroused in her a calm she had forgotten was possible.

The next morning, the servants were instructed to prepare for a New Year's Eve party which fell on the twentieth of March according to the lunar calendar. All Helga had to do was instruct the help. The housekeeper took care of the rest. The only problem Helga had was in reaching her husband and convincing him to take time off from his busy schedule. She told Andrea, she thought he might be able to make it. For Iranians, New Year was a time of celebration. Hopefully, the revolutionaries would do the same.

Andrea went to bed early and woke up early. She fed Kelly, took her and rushed to the sea. The shore was littered with thousands of small shells and debris scattered in careless patterns on the fine, white sand. She watched as a Russian ship made its way slowly toward the port. Thrilled and excited, a child once again, she ran up the coast waving and yelling to attract the attention of the sailors watching from the deck of the Russian ship. The sailors waved back. It was a glorious day. Andrea was determined to make the best of every moment.

Meanwhile, Helga prepared the guest list and made frantic efforts to reach her husband. She couldn't. Either no one knew where he was or they weren't telling. However, she managed to reach her husband's brother who promised to bring the General over himself.

The night of the party, everyone who was invited came. No one would dare turn down an invitation from the General's wife. The Iranian custom of appearing an hour or two past the stated time of invitation was not tolerated by Helga. She told Andrea, after years of struggling, she had finally gotten the point across that she would serve dinner no later than eight thirty. Those who chose not to be on time would have to eat dinner before they came. "Iranians consider Westerners sticklers about time," she explained. "It's hard for them to understand why we're so preoccupied with it."

All the guests arrived before eight. Helga wanted it to be a surprise for her husband. The guests were instructed to have their drivers park the cars at a distance so the General would not suspect that something was up.

Andrea lingered in her room for as long as she could. She was apprehensive and reluctant to meet a crowd of strangers most of whom she assumed did not speak English. She could understand Farsi much better than she could speak. She joined the guests the very last moment when she saw from her window, the soldier posted at the gate, run up the driveway to inform Helga her husband and his brother were approaching the house.

The lights were dimmed and everyone was quiet.

When the two brothers walked in, the crowd let out a loud "Happy New Year," taking the General totally by surprise.

Someone turned the lights on.

The huge, crystal chandelier hanging from the ceiling cast an immediate bright glow, its rays bouncing in crazy patterns, reflecting the shine from the huge diamonds adorning the necks, arms and fingers of all the women present. It was the same scenario as at Irene's party.

Andrea had spent the past two afternoons exploring the town. She'd seen old men stooped over a piece of wood or a brass plate toiling in small cubicles from morning till late at night to make a living. She'd seen shacks where several generations lived without running water or power. Abject poverty was everywhere. It was impossible to miss the contrast between what she saw at the moment and what she had seen in town. She could not fathom how so many could afford such extravagance at such a young age.

I don't belong here, she told herself. I must return to my

room without attracting attention.

"Hi," she heard someone say.

She turned and came face to face with a fair skinned, black haired, tall, young man in his middle twenties. He looked different. Not entirely Iranian. Perhaps Eurasian.

"Hello," Andrea replied surprised.

"My name is Dariush. I'm the General's nephew. I don't believe I've had the pleasure of meeting you."

"Andrea. I'm a friend of Helga's."

"Don't people like her make you mad? She is annoying. When someone is that perfect and that much of a lady it makes all the rest look that much worse."

"Are you trying to be funny?"

"Not at all. She's my favorite person. Still, I'd like to see her act human someday, make a mistake, cry, get mad or something. My uncle is a bastard. A lucky bastard."

"You look like him. In a way."

"Yes, I've been told that, often."

"It's nice that he could come. Helga wasn't sure he'd make it."

"It's only a half hour flight. His airplane is ready twenty four hours a day to fly him wherever he wants to go. Helga was concerned because lately the Shah has insisted on my uncle being available around the clock. The Shah left this morning for St. Moritz to ski. That's why he could come."

Five musicians playing the latest hits from the U.S. paused while the singer announced the band would welcome requests.

"Is there a particular song you'd like them to play?" Dariush asked.

After a moment's hesitation, Andrea said, "No, not really. I'm having trouble convincing myself I'm in a small coastal town in Iran and not a big city in the U.S."

"It's the fashion. We are master imitators. We don't bother to discriminate. Nowadays, if it's Western, it's in."

"You sound cynical."

"I don't think so. I'm a realist. Let's dance."

Without waiting for a reply, he took her hand and moved to the center of the room.

They danced for a few minutes but Andrea's thoughts were elsewhere and he sensed it. "You're not enjoying yourself. You're tense. What's bothering you?"

"Nothing, nothing at all."

The music stopped.

Dinner was announced.

The guests attacked the food like a demolition crew. In a few minutes it was all over.

Andrea had seen it happen before. She was not as shocked as she was the first time she saw it happen at Irene's party. The waiters dashed back and forth frantically to replenish the food.

"Let's get out of here," Dariush said. "We'll get a couple of drinks and go to the garden."

Andrea felt relieved. Anything. Anything to get away from all those big, black eyes staring at her.

There was a mild chill in the air. Andrea shivered. Immediately Dariush took off his jacket and put it around her shoulders.

The attention he lavished on her made her feel good. It felt good to have a young man devote his entire evening to her. She had herself almost convinced that the reason her husband had lost interest in her was her fault. She was doing something wrong. She didn't know what.

Tonight had proved her wrong. The most attractive young man in the crowd had taken no notice of dozens of fabulously dressed and coiffed ladies. He had singled her out, she, with her simple dress, a light touch of make-up and no jewelry.

They drank their drinks in silence. She was aware of a delicate attraction between them but not quite sure what to expect.

"Will you be here in June?" Dariush asked.

"I don't know. Probably. Why?"

"I'm on my spring break. I leave for school next week. We get out in June. I was wondering if you'll be here when I get back."

"Where do you go to school?"

"Switzerland. I'm studying to be a pilot. I have one more year to go."

"Will you join a commercial airline when you graduate?"

"Taking decisions for myself is not a luxury I have. The Shah decides what I do after I graduate."

"Do you like flying?"

"I didn't at first. The choice was made for me. But I like it now. It gives me a false sense of freedom."

"False?"

"Of course. When I'm up there alone, I feel elated, one with nature. When I land, reality hits me like a concrete wall. The problems I left behind are there waiting for me."

"Don't you think life would be pretty dull if it was all smooth sailing?"

"You mean if we had no problems? I have no problems. It's what goes on around me that bothers me. There's too much injustice, too much pain."

It surprised her to hear a man of his social standing talk the way he did. Most wealthy Iranians seemed delighted with their good fortune and couldn't care less about others. But Dariush seemed genuinely tormented by the circumstances of his people.

"Do you like poetry?" he asked, his eyes probing hers.

"I do. I'm told Iranians love poetry and philosophy. I wish I knew how to read Farsi. I read the English version of Ferdowsi. It was good."

"I write poetry when I'm not flying."

"Then, I must definitely learn to read Farsi," Andrea said jokingly.

"I'll teach you this summer when I return. Would you like another drink?"

"I would, but I shouldn't. I'm beginning to feel the effects of the one I had."

"Life is too short to worry about little details. Let's have another."

They went to the bar. The orchestra was playing Iranian music. Andrea watched as the crowd danced. Graceful movements of the hands and body coupled with gentle tapping of the feet, invited loud applause from the onlookers.

"You look puzzled. Is it the first time you've seen an Iranian dance?"

"It's not so much the dance. It's the type of dance. It's very suggestive, sexy. I thought Islam preferred women to be less, shall we say provocative, conspicuous. What's the word I'm looking for?"

"You're very diplomatic. We are a confused nation. We don't know whether we want to belong to the East or to the West. Whether we should cling to our ancient culture or go through the rituals of Islam. If you walk down the street you will see a striking example of what's happening to the country. The grandmother will be wearing a chaddor. She'll be covered from head to toe. The mother, striving to keep pace with the times, will have her head covered with a scarf. The daughter will be in shorts or a miniskirt with a T shirt."

"Someday I hope to understand."

"Don't bother. Go change. We'll go swimming."

In spite of herself, Andrea said, "Let's."

The swimming pool was located quite a distance from the house. They met at the entrance. It was heated and ready for use year round. Helga used it whenever she came to Pahlavi and occasionally Dariush when he was home from school.

"I'll race you," he said and dove in the water.

They raced. He won. She was enjoying herself too much. She lay on her back and let her body float.

He swam in slow motion around her. "I adore your slim figure, your slender legs, your marble like skin, your goddess like face."

She loved it.

Cautiously, he touched her hand. She did not move. He moved closer, put his arms around her, kissing her lightly, arousing in her long forgotten feelings.

Her inhibitions dulled by the drinks, she made no attempt to stop him. Actually, to her surprise, she was enjoying herself. She felt no guilt, no sense of wrongdoing. If her husband had no use for her, there were others who did. At least it assured her that she was still attractive and desirable to men, to rich young men.

They swam to the ladder and climbed out. He wrapped a large towel around her and another around himself. He held her close, kissing her on her wet neck, hugging her, clinging to her.

He stopped. Cars were being driven up the driveway. "The drivers have to wait until their employers decide to leave. Iranians treat their workers like slaves."

She looked at him with an uncomprehending expression on her face. He impressed her as a complex, concerned, perhaps even bitter young man. Was he testing her?

It was past three in the morning. They could hear several couples recite an exaggerated farewell according to custom. Finally, they bowed slightly, said "Ghorbane Shema" (may I be sacrificed for you) several times and drove off.

"Goodbyes can go on forever in this country. I'll take you around the house to your room. Let's go."

They tiptoed quietly around the garden to the back of the house.

"I'll come for you tomorrow at noon. We'll go sailing. Good night." He held her close for a moment, then quietly slipped out the back door.

Chapter 16

Powerful waves at the shore rocked the sailboat as though it were a toy. Dariush managed quickly to steer it further out to where the waters were deep and the boat settled on a slow steady course.

"You're pretty good at it. Have you had your sailboat long?" Andrea asked.

"Last May my father gave it to me for my birthday. It's my favorite toy. I love to sail. I went sailing every day last summer. It gives me a chance to think."

"What do you think about Dariush?"

"Oh, mostly about the crazy world we live in."

The deep waters of the Caspian Sea were calm. There was a light breeze weaving through the morning sun. Ships from many countries like Russia, Poland, Taiwan, Turkey, their flags flapping in the wind, were docked at the harbor. Several fishing boats sailed toward the port laden with the day's catch. "Sturgeon," Dariush explained. "There's a factory nearby, owned and controlled by the Royal Family. They take immediate possession of whatever the fishermen have in their boats."

"Sturgeon?"

"Yes. For its caviar. Do you like caviar?"

"I've never had any."

"We must remedy that tonight."

Andrea watched captivated. Soon, several small boats approached the fishing boats. The fishermen from the fishing boats handed some of the catch to the men in the small boats. The small boats quickly changed direction and disappeared behind a Polish ship which seemed to be standing still.

"What was that about?" Andrea asked surprised.

"That's how the fishermen make their living. They divert part of the catch to their accomplices. Eventually the caviar finds its way to the black market. They can't fish legally. Caviar is the monopoly of the Royal Family."

"How about those guards. They couldn't have missed seeing what was going on."

"The fishermen split the profits with the guards. This way everyone is happy and the public enjoys caviar from the black market at a fraction of the cost the government charges."

"You surprise me. I thought you would be a Royalist."

"I'm a realist," Dariush quipped. "But enough of this kind of talk. Let's talk about you."

"Perish the thought. You'd die of boredom."

"Let me be the judge of that."

"What could possibly be interesting about an average girl from an average town U.S.A."

"The mere fact that you are here speaks to the contrary."

"Oh."

Dariush's attention was momentarily diverted. A small motorboat approached them at full speed. The driver of the boat slowed his engine as he expertly maneuvered and positioned it parallel to the sailboat.

He spoke quickly to Dariush then gunned the engine and raced back.

Dariush watched the speedboat head for shore. He turned

to Andrea. "The Queen is coming. She'll probably be here tonight to preside over the opening of a new hospital in Pahlavi tomorrow morning."

"What's that got to do with you?"

"When she comes to Pahlavi she stays with us. She's my cousin."

"Sort of short notice isn't it?"

"The movements of the Royal Family are never announced in advance. Even when we are forewarned about an impending visit, we don't know the exact moment they'll arrive."

"Don't you think we should return? You'll probably have a lot to do if you're going to host the Queen."

Dariush nodded, changed direction and headed for the shore.

"You don't seem too excited," Andrea teased. "If I were to receive a queen in my house I'd probably go to pieces. Don't you like her?"

"I like her better than I like her husband. But our house becomes a fortress from the moment we get word of an impending Royal visit until it's all over. I much prefer sailing."

They sailed in silence. Dariush looked as though he had something on his mind.

He said nothing until they docked. As he was helping her step out, he asked casually, "Would you like to meet the Queen?"

"Heavens no! I haven't come prepared to meet the Queen. I couldn't." Andrea was so nervous she could barely talk.

"Calm down. She is the least affected person I know. Everyone remotely related to her puts on airs and makes sure the whole world knows of the relationship but she is a very simple, and as you Americans say, down-to-earth person. You'll never know she's a queen."

"Forget it, Dariush. I couldn't possibly."

"Andrea, listen to me. This is a once in a lifetime opportunity. You'd be crazy not to come."

Andrea thought for a long moment.

"I don't have anything to wear," she said, uncertainty evident in her voice.

"Helga has closets full of clothes. Borrow one."

"Please Dariush, don't insist."

Dariush's personal servant waited to take over the care of the boat. Andrea and Dariush made their way to Helga's house.

"But I do insist," Dariush said. "Come with Helga. I'll call and let you know the time." He hurried down the road to his house a couple of blocks away.

Andrea found Helga in the living room, reading.

A servant immediately appeared with a tray. He served the women tea and snacks and withdrew quietly.

"I guess having our coffee in the kitchen is out of the question," Andrea said.

"The kitchen is the servants domain. We cannot have tea, coffee or anything for that matter in the kitchen," Helga explained. "They would be horrified. That's why I refuse to keep servants in Tehran. I don't like being a guest in my own house."

Andrea barely listened. What was she doing sailing on a fifty foot sailboat with a man whose cousin was the Queen? She didn't belong here. Borrow a dress? Meet the Queen? He's crazy!

Helga asked, "Did you have fun sailing?"

"Yes. It's beautiful and calm out there." Andrea hesitated. "Dariush wants me to meet the Queen. I get nervous thinking about it."

"Don't Andrea. She's a wonderful person. She puts everyone at ease immediately. She was tutored in royal etiquette before she was married but I'd say it comes to her naturally. If that's what's bothering you, relax. After you meet her, you'll realize how unnecessary your worrying was."

"I don't have anything to wear."

"We'll take care of that right now. Let's go to my bedroom. One more thing. You can't go without proper make-up and hairdo. My beautician will be here at seven. I'll ask her to take care of you first."

A small voice inside her cautioned her not to succumb. She and royalty were worlds apart. How did it all come about anyway?

"I can't go through with it, Helga. I'm terrified."

"You should feel honored. It's not every day that people get invited to meet the Queen. I'll fix you a dry martini. That will do it."

By eight o'clock that night Andrea was dressed in a simple, elegant, green chiffon evening gown, coiffed and made-up. The transformation left her breathless. She felt as though she was looking at someone else, someone vaguely familiar.

Still no word from the palace as to when or if the Queen would arrive that night.

At ten minutes to nine there was a blast of police sirens and a large motorcade came cruising down the street toward Dariush's house.

Andrea hurried to the street hoping to catch a glimpse.

The place swarmed with soldiers and grim looking men wearing dark suits.

Four men jumped out of a black limousine which was the first to arrive. The next car came to a screeching halt disgorging six men dressed in military uniform, submachine guns ready. A third car followed and rolled gently to a stop. A man in military uniform rushed to the back door and opened it, bowing simultaneously. The Queen, dressed in a simple blue suit, carrying a small purse, stepped out, walked cautiously, and quietly entered the house. She was followed by two men.

The door of the house closed.

Six soldiers stood outside, their hands on their submachine guns, their eyes screening the area.

Half an hour later, Dariush called to say the Queen had rested and was ready to receive guests.

Helga put the receiver down slowly. She looked like something was bothering her. "Andrea, do you have any ID with you?"

"My American driver's license. Why?"

"Let's hope they will accept it. Dariush lives a few blocks away but we have to go by car. We can't walk down the street dressed the way we are. It's not done."

They approached the house in their chauffeur driven Jaguar. Two heavily armed soldiers stopped the car before the passengers could step out. Two men in civilian suits waited idly on the sidewalk.

"ID please." One of the soldiers requested.

Helga handed over her identification papers. The soldier recognized her immediately and handed her papers back to her.

He turned to Andrea. Helga explained in fluent Farsi that she was an American, a friend. She gave the soldier Andrea's driver's license.

The soldier examined it carefully, checked the picture on the driver's license with the face in the car, checked again, walked to the two men in civilian clothes standing on the sidewalk and gave them the driver's license.

The two men conferred.

"I wish Cyrus had not returned to Tehran," Helga said reaching for Andrea's hand and giving it a gentle squeeze. "I wish he was here."

Minutes passed. Still the men conferred and the women waited.

Two more minutes passed. Still no action.

Then, the soldier who had handed the driver's license to the two men crossed the street to where the two men were standing. They talked. The soldier approached the car.

"You may go in," he told Helga. He pointed to the sidewalk. "The gentlemen over there would like a few words with your friend."

"I'll come with her," Helga offered.

"Sorry, Madame, I have my orders."

The two men from the sidewalk approached the Jaguar, opened the door on the side where Andrea was sitting and the taller man said, "Come with us, please."

Andrea looked questioningly at Helga. The pained look in Helga's eyes was enough for her to gather that there was nothing Helga could do to help. Andrea suspected Savak was an institution few dared question or tackle. The authoritative way the tall man ordered her to go with them, left no doubt in her mind that the men were from Savak.

She followed them to a car parked on a side street, in a dark corner. The tall man sat in the back of the car with Andrea. His partner got behind the wheel and after a short drive, the car came to a halt. The tall man told Andrea to get out. He spoke perfect English with a British accent.

They approached a two story building with a single light bulb at the entrance. The tall man went ahead, climbing the steps to the second floor, followed by Andrea, followed by the shorter man.

Ear piercing screams from different corners of the building stiffened her knees. She could not move. The shorter man pushed her from behind.

They entered a small room.

She was told to sit on a wooden stool.

A naked bulb hung precariously from the ceiling. The room had no windows.

The tall man sat behind a dirty wooden desk, with a dirty glass teacup and lots of papers spread across the dirty desk top.

The short man left closing the door behind him.

"Your name," the man said, leaving no doubt in Andrea's mind who was in control.

"Andrea Abbassi."

"Why are you in Iran?"

"I'm married to an Iranian."

"Name."

"Mani Abbassi."

The man wrote down every word, taking his time.

"What does your husband do?"

"He's trying to start a business. We want to live here." Andrea hoped to inject a point in her favor.

"Why?"

"Why not?"

"I ask the questions. Why are you here?"

"I already told you."

"Tell me again."

Andrea did.

"What kind of business?"

"Importing construction material, I think."

"Who are his friends? Give me their names."

"I know only one. His name is Farhad. I don't know his family name."

"Describe him."

"He's of medium height, good looking."

"Describe him."

"He has curly, black hair, dark brown eyes, athletic looking type."

"Does he live in Isfahan?"

"I believe so."

"Does your husband go to Isfahan often?"

"I think so. I don't know."

"You don't know where your husband goes when he leaves town?"

"Not always."

"By denying facts, you don't do yourself or your husband a favor. Now, let's try again. Do you or don't you know where he is when he's not in Tehran?"

After some hesitation, Andrea said, "I don't know." She did not know what else to say.

His eyes bulged. His chin quivered. He broke the pencil he wrote with into pieces and flung it across the room.

"We have ways of making you know. I don't like 'I don't

know' for an answer to any question I ask. Yes or no. Do I make myself clear?"

"Yes." He talks and acts like a Nazi, Andrea thought.

"Do you know if your husband was involved in anti Shah activities while he was studying in America?"

Somehow, Andrea had suspected the interrogation would eventually lead to this question which she feared most. She tried to stall for time, to think.

"How do you know my husband was studying in the States?" She was sorry she said it the moment the words spilled out of her mouth.

"You are very arrogant. I ask the questions, not you. Now tell me and think before you answer. Did your husband participate in any demonstrations or meetings or terrorist activities of any kind while he was in the America? You don't want anything to happen to your daughter, do you?"

Andrea felt her heart skip a beat. She shivered. The way the man looked at her left no doubt in her mind he was capable of all kinds of atrocities. Trying desperately to control her shaking voice, she answered, "Not that I know of."

"I like it. Smart woman. This time you did not say I don't know. You changed the words around. Who trained you? Your husband?"

She wished her toes would stop curling. She could not figure out whether she was hot or cold but one thing she was sure of, the less she said the less she'd have to worry about. She kept quiet.

"Speak!" The interrogator yelled, jarring her thoughts. "Who sent you to meet the Queen?"

She was questioned until dawn. The same questions over and over again.

Finally, right before sunrise, she was taken to a waiting car, driven over, and dropped in front of Helga's house.

They had been much kinder to her than they would have been to one of their own. They had even offered her a cup of tea, laced with a drug to make her talk, but a cup of tea nonetheless.

Helga had spent the night pacing the living room, waiting for Andrea's return and desperately trying to reach her husband. When a car pulled up in front of the house, she rushed to the front door. Two soldiers assigned to guard the house, were sound asleep. She woke them and had them carry Andrea in. The tea had done the job well. Andrea was completely drugged.

She slept the whole day.

Late in the afternoon, she finally opened her eyes only to shut them at once. The sunlight seeping in through the windows made it impossible for her eyes to remain open.

In that split second, she thought she saw two pairs of eyes anxiously looking into hers.

She shuddered involuntarily. Not wanting to betray the horror she felt within, she pretended to go back to sleep.

It was a futile attempt. The screams she'd heard while climbing the stairs to the interrogation room were still ringing in her ears.

Chapter 17

The next morning, Andrea heard voices in her room. She opened her eyes briefly. Helga and Dariush watched her. She heard Helga say to Dariush, "It's been over twenty four hours. The shot the doctor gave her last night doesn't seem to have done her much good. She still looks drugged. Do you think I should call another doctor?"

"Let's wait one more hour. If she's not awake, we'll fly her to Tehran. You know there are no well trained doctors in the provinces. Why bother?"

Andrea tried to prop herself up, but couldn't. Her head fell back on the pillow. Helga and Dariush rushed to her side. Helga reached for her pillow, fluffed it, and placed it against the headboard. Dariush put his arms around her to help her sit up.

"How do you feel?" Helga asked anxiously.

"Please, don't worry about me. I'll be fine." Andrea could not keep her eyes open.

"Dariush, please tell Goli to bring tea," Helga said.

"Where's Kelly? Is she all right?"

"She's fine. She's having a sunbath."

"Thank you so much."

A samovar brewed tea all day. The house boy brought their tea within minutes.

They drank in silence.

Andrea had a splitting headache. She felt as though her eyeballs were ready to pop out. "Both of you look tired. I'm sorry about the trouble I caused you. I have a headache. I think I'll dress up and go to the beach. I could use some fresh air."

"Would you like me to stay and help you get dressed?" Helga asked.

"Thank you. I'm sure I can manage."

Helga and Dariush left the room.

Andrea felt dizzy. She sat on the edge of the bed for a few moments before she could stand without falling. She put on a pair of shorts and a T shirt then went to check Kelly. The child smiled and gurgled when she saw her mother. Andrea brushed a few strands of hair from her face then planted a kiss on each cheek. Tears welled in her eyes. She was fortunate. Her daughter could not understand her suffering. She stayed with her until Kelly fell asleep.

Andrea walked the short distance to the shore. A gentle breeze from the sea revived her. She took deep breaths to clear her muddled head.

She looked back and saw Helga sitting in the living room, facing the sea. She looked dreadful. There was a vacant look in her eyes as her gaze roamed aimlessly across the beach where Andrea stood kicking shells washed ashore, back to the sea.

A few long strides and Dariush stood next to her.

Andrea continued kicking shells.

There was a prolonged silence.

Dariush searched her face. Andrea's impassive expression betrayed neither anger nor acceptance. He tried to speak but no words would come out.

She sensed his pain, his concern.

"The waves are much higher today," she said to ease his discomfort.

"Only at the shore. It's a superb day for sailing. It will do us both good. How about it?"

"Maybe later."

"I have an idea. Let's go back to the house, have breakfast, then drive to Rasht. It's a half hour drive. There's a small airport in Rasht. Our plane is parked there. I'll take you for a spin and let you have a look at the surrounding towns."

"I thought you said you didn't have your license yet."

"I don't, not until next June. But I fly any time I want to. Who's going to stop me?"

"I have a lot to learn."

"It's different here. And I'm sure very difficult for you to accept a lot of what goes on in this country, but the manipulators of our destiny get a lot of outside help."

"What do you mean?"

"What I mean is that without the help of the U.S. government, those in power in this country wouldn't last very long."

Andrea listened intently, carefully evaluating what she heard. Could it be that he was testing her? Could he be one of them? A person enjoying the privileges of royal favors hardly qualified to criticize those who made his lifestyle possible.

"It doesn't look like you have too much reason to be dissatisfied."

"Personally, maybe not. But there are thirty five million people in my country and over ninety percent of them live in misery."

"No one else seems to care. Why should you?"

Dariush stared into space.

Andrea felt a pang of guilt. She'd been hurt but that was no reason to hurt him. "I'm sorry."

She heard Dariush say, "To survive, I keep my opinions to myself. I have less to worry about that way. But I care a lot about you. I don't want to leave you with the wrong impression."

He moved about nervously, shoving piles of sand with his feet. Then, he stopped abruptly, facing her, his eyes staring directly into hers.

"I have never told anyone my true feelings. I don't trust anyone, not even Helga. I know if I talk to her, she will keep it to herself. But she is the wife of the top ranking general in the service of the Shah. It will make her uncomfortable. I want to talk to you. I have known you briefly but there is no doubt in my mind that I can trust you."

"I'd prefer that you don't. Who knows when your infamous secret service will decide to change my blood chemistry again."

"You should consider yourself lucky. Few escape their tentacles without permanent damage. You're lucky you were with the wife of a general, a general they respect and you're lucky you're an American."

A huge wave roared toward the shore where they stood. It was impossible to escape in time. They got soaked.

Dariush rushed back to the house and returned with beach towels. They dried themselves. Andrea suggested they get back to the house.

"If you're not too cold I'd much prefer to be outdoors. In Iran no one discusses anything of importance indoors. Walls have ears, servants same day information service."

Andrea couldn't help laughing. "You sound like an American."

She spread a towel and they sat next to each other.

"I learn American expressions from a classmate. He's from Boston."

"Is that who you learned your American English from?"

"Mostly. I studied in England for four years before going to Switzerland. I prefer American English though. It's much more alive, changing. I like it."

"Do you think the Shah will ask you to join the Air Force?" The spring sunshine and a gentle breeze made her feel good.

"Most probably. He has bought quite a few F14s and F15s. He wants me to go to the U.S. for further training after I graduate."

"Is that what you want to do?"

"No, not really."

"Can you say no to him?"

Dariush's eyes remained glued to her face. His answer was a sad smile.

A cold breeze from the sea sent a shiver through Andrea. "I need to get out of these wet clothes. I better go back to the house." Andrea's teeth chattered.

"Dark clouds are moving in. Most probably we won't see the sun again today. Here the weather changes suddenly. Since there are no weather forecasts, we can only guess. I hate to spend the day indoors. How about walking to the next village. There's a restaurant there which has the best sturgeon kabob and caviar in the country, right out of the Caspian."

"You're too generous. You don't have to take me anywhere. I'm fine, honest," Andrea protested weakly.

"I don't have to. I'd love to. I promised to let you taste caviar, remember? Come on. I'll go change. You do the same. Wear walking shoes and comfortable clothes. No shorts please. The villagers are not used to seeing women in shorts. It would horrify them. I'll pick you up in fifteen minutes."

They reached Helga's house. Andrea went to her room, put on a pair of jeans, a sweat shirt and sneakers, then she went looking for Helga. Helga's friendship meant a great deal to her. She felt Helga was blaming herself for urging her to meet the Queen. It was time she let Helga know she was feeling better.

Helga was in the kitchen talking to the house boy. Kelly was propped up in her wheelchair, being fed by Goli, the housekeeper.

Andrea gave Kelly a big hug and a kiss, and thanked Goli.

"She's a lovely girl," Goli said. "I enjoy taking care of her."

Helga was visibly relieved seeing her friend come to the kitchen with a semblance of a smile on her face.

"Are you feeling better?" she asked stifling a quiver in her voice.

"I feel much better. Dariush says I'm lucky to have escaped permanent damage after a session with Savak."

Helga motioned for Andrea to follow her to the living room.

"Sorry," she began, "I don't like to discuss anything in the presence of servants, especially the housekeeper. She understands English and German quite well. What she doesn't understand, she assumes."

"I'm sorry. I didn't know," Andrea said apologetically.

"Don't worry. I only mentioned it so you'll be careful. The government assigns the help the military have in their homes and offices. Mostly, they're here to spy on us. That's why we have to be very careful."

Andrea listened with quiet disbelief. It was her understanding that the privileged few had a blissful life, lacking nothing, wanting more. But recent revelations were chiseling sizable chunks from her preconceived notions.

"How can you stand it?"

"You get used to it after a while. I wish I could suggest a solution. There is none."

Dariush's footsteps could be heard in the hall. He joined the women in the living room, told Helga where he was planning to take Andrea, and asked if she would like to join them.

Helga declined, explaining she was tired and wanted to take a nap.

It was a twenty minute walk to the village. Clusters of one room mud huts were scattered around a narrow dirt road with a public water fountain located in the center. Excess water from the fountain drained into manmade ditches along the sides of the road. "The ditches are called jubes," Dariush explained. "Jube water is considered clean because it's not stagnant. The villagers use it to wash their clothes, their children, their dishes, cooking and drinking. That's why we have one of the highest infant mortality rates in the world."

A girl, who looked seven or eight years old, was washing pots and pans in the ditch. As they neared the village, the child raised her head, gawked at them, dropped the pan she was washing, and ran toward a brick house. It was the only brick building in the village besides the mosque.

Dariush seemed amused. "She recognized me even though it has been a while since I last visited the village."

"This place is so picturesque," Andrea said. "I wish I had my camera."

"I must warn you though. The restaurant is not Maxim's. It's a room with one table and eight chairs. The owner, the cook, the waiter are all one, a sixty seven year old man. You come here to eat, not to enjoy the decor. And by the way, he's spotlessly clean. A rare specimen in this part of the world."

An old man in baggy pants, and a shirt with wide sleeves, came dashing out the brick house. He had a wide, black cloth belt around his waist and wore an embroidered vest. He looked overjoyed at the sight of his unexpected guests. He greeted them, spitting words in profuse succession, obviously overwhelmed by the honor.

Dariush translated, "He knows I'm home on vacation. He says he waited for me but gave up hope. He didn't think I would come."

"That wasn't Farsi, was it?" It sounded different to her.

"Kurdish. He's a Kurd."

"Where did you learn Kurdish?"

"My nanny is a Kurd," Dariush answered. "The different races probably don't mean much to you. The only thing Kurds have in common with Persians is their religion. They are fiercely loyal and honest people and they never forget a kind deed."

The restaurant was as Dariush had described. It's saving grace was a window covering the entire front section of the room overlooking the sea. The view was breathtaking. Huge ships docked in the harbor, fishermen worked on their dilapidated boats, a few sailboats rocked lazily in the distance and a little boy perched on a rock. He held a bamboo pole with a string attached to it. He seemed seriously absorbed in what he was doing. There were no other customers in the restaurant.

Dariush did not have to order. Within minutes, the old man brought a small bowl of caviar set in a bigger bowl filled with crushed ice. He served it with toast, butter, chopped boiled eggs, minced onion and quartered lemons.

The owner's wife and two daughters helped prepare the food. It was not a meal. It was a feast. When a dish was ready, the old man hurried to the table, beaming, delighted to see his guests enjoy the food the place was known for. They had sturgeon kabob, right out of the sea, grilled on charcoal. The second dish was duck with walnut and pomegranate sauce served on rice pilaf. Next came baked eggplant with tomatoes and crushed garlic, lamb kabob and sour cherry rice pilaf. Andrea was famished. She ate like an inmate just released from a long prison sentence.

When they stopped eating, the old man cleared the table, brought clean plates and assorted pastries.

"I'm stuffed. Please tell him to stop," Andrea pleaded. "There's enough food here to feed the whole village."

"I can't do that. He'll be insulted. It's his way of showing his gratitude."

"Gratitude?"

Dariush made no reply.

The old man served them tea from an ancient samovar.

Andrea and Dariush sat back in their chairs, relaxed, taking small sips of the boiling hot brew.

When they were through, Andrea could hardly move. She was hoping Dariush would pay the owner and they could leave. She watched as Dariush took a stack of bills from his pocket and slipped it under his plate. Seeing the puzzled expression on Andrea's face, he explained, "If I try to pay him, he'll get upset. So far as he's concerned, our coming to his restaurant is a big honor. Mentioning money would be in poor taste."

"That looks like a lot of money."

"Why not?"

She didn't know what to say.

"Are you ready to leave?" Dariush asked. "I've got to move or I'm going to bust. I have to starve for a week to make up for my gluttony today!"

"Let's go."

They rose, thanked the man, his wife and daughters. They were saying goodbye when a little girl's screams put an abrupt end to their conversation. Dariush and Andrea rushed out the door, followed by the owner, his wife and daughters. The little girl pointed toward the rock and sobbed hysterically. She was the same girl who had ran to the house to notify her father when she saw Dariush and Andrea coming.

"Her brother is drowning," Dariush yelled and ran like a madman toward the rock where the little boy had been fishing. He made a wild dash through the waves, circled the rock, stopped, scanned the area, then slipped back in the water.

Andrea followed Dariush to the sea. She stood in knee-high water looking for a sign, any sign. Could the waves have taken him further out? Suddenly, she thought she saw a bunch of black hair pop up and disappear as though it was an apparition. She swam fiercely to the spot. In a moment, she grasped a limp body. She pulled the boy's head out of the water and swam to shore with enough vigor in her strokes to qualify her for a swim championship.

He was alive! Barely able to breathe, lungs full of water, but alive. Andrea shouted for someone to call an ambulance while she worked frantically to keep him breathing.

The villagers gathered around, watching solemnly as the foreigner tried to revive the boy.

"Somebody call an ambulance!" she yelled again.

Nobody moved.

Dariush edged his way through the crowd just as Andrea

was ready to explode.

"Call an ambulance, quick! I can't get these people to move. They're just standing around staring. Hurry up!"

"Forget it. There are no ambulances." Dariush reached for the boy, threw him on his shoulder and ran to the main road. "Follow me," he yelled.

"Flag down the first car you see. They'll stop." They were both practically breathless.

The child's fingertips and lips were fast turning blue, his breathing shallow and labored.

An old truck heavily laden with farm produce came climbing up the hill, creaking, ready to collapse under its load.

Andrea waved frantically.

The truck driver saw her and stopped. They got in. Dariush stuck a bunch of banknotes into the driver's pocket and told him to drive as fast as he could, to the new hospital, the hospital which the Queen had inaugurated the day before.

he hospital was very impressive looking. A life-size portrait of the King and the Queen monopolized the section above the door to the entrance. A man sitting behind a huge desk was busy sipping a steaming cup of tea.

"Where's the emergency room?" Dariush asked, concern evident in his voice.

"Back there," the man pointed. He continued drinking his tea, unperturbed.

They found the emergency room and rushed in. Except for an examination table, the place was empty. Through an open door to an adjacent room, Andrea could see a picture-perfect emergency room, the latest equipment neatly stacked in glass cabinets.

Dariush seemed to be having a hard time keeping his temper and his voice in check. "I'll look for a doctor. I don't see any medical people around."

Andrea could hear Dariush talking to the man at the desk. A heated discussion ensued after which Dariush dashed back to the room to inform Andrea that the hospital had no doctor. He had to find a doctor somewhere, somehow. He looked livid. "Yesterday, this hospital was hailed as the best medical facility outside the capital. It was front page news, praising the Shah for making it possible for the villagers to have a modern medical center at their disposal. But nobody, I mean nobody bothered to mention that it had no medical staff to run it. The receptionist is it."

"Please hurry," Andrea pleaded.

"I don't know where to look."

"Grab a cab. The driver will know."

"See if you can find oxygen anywhere."

"I will. He's hardly breathing. He'll be dead by the time you get back." Andrea snapped, her self control giving way to panic.

Dariush dashed out the door and into the street before Andrea was through talking.

Soon after, the child stopped breathing.

Frantically, Andrea tried CPR, her eyes searching for a nonexistent oxygen outlet or an oxygen tank. She shuddered involuntarily, her helplessness compounding her agony.

In desperation she rushed to the next room and tried to open the cabinets displaying an assortment of shiny medical instruments. Maybe there was a tracheal tube somewhere or something she could use to help him breathe until the doctor arrived.

She tried every cabinet. They were locked. She tried to break it open. She couldn't. She rushed back to the boy.

She could hear a crowd gathering in the hospital lobby, women wailing, more footsteps. She continued her frantic efforts to get the boy to breathe. There was no response. His lifeless eyes had ceased to plead.

Andrea reached for the boy's wrist. She couldn't feel his pulse. She pressed her ear to his chest. She could hear no heart sounds, no breath sounds. She reached for his hand, placed it on her chest and sobbed softly.

Later, she did not know when, Dariush walked in with a man wearing a three piece suit. In the lobby the men talked in whispers, the women wailed pounding their chests. Someone grabbed the man at the desk by the collar and shook him mercilessly. Was it Dariush? She wasn't sure. Nothing registered. It was all happening to someone else. She could look but she could not see.

The boy was dead.

Chapter 18

The hospital lobby was furnished with modern furniture from Denmark. Paintings of scenes depicting the ancient glory of the Persian Empire, hung on the walls. A huge crystal chandelier precariously balanced from the ceiling, poked every corner of the room with its rays.

There was the inevitable life-size picture of the King and the Queen strategically located above the entrance. The King wore his military uniform, his chest covered with assorted medals. The Queen stood next to him with a diamond tiara on her head. She wore a blue, satin, full length gown, embroidered with pearls. They looked down over on the crowd, a crowd of villagers that had suddenly materialized from what seemed to be nowhere and everywhere.

The doctor dug into his black bag savagely and emerged with a stethoscope. From the look on his face, Andrea sensed, the ritual was for the benefit of the onlookers. The boy was past the stage of stethoscopes, past doctors, past the condescending look his King and Queen were bestowing upon him, from yet another portrait appropriately located above the examination table in the emergency room. He was at peace.

The doctor placed the stethoscope unceremoniously on the boy's chest once, withdrew it, looked at Dariush, then at Andrea, and without any apparent emotion said, "He's dead."

A resigned look in Andrea's eyes met with Dariush's. Dariush's big, black eyes were not resigned. They were full of fury. She could feel its corrosive waves permeating the air as he stood motionless, raging, vengeful, like a man in a trance.

The doctor reached for his bag, stuck his stethoscope in it, closed it and explained that he had to sneak out the back door. His past experiences with death in the village had left him with unpleasant memories. "In this country," he said, "the messenger always gets blamed for bearing bad news."

Dariush watched the doctor make his exit. He did not stop him. He mumbled incomprehensibly about wanting to do something irrational; something like taking the gadget with the shiny buttons from the next room and throwing it out the window. "Why not?" he shouted suddenly, dashed to the next room, grabbed the sterilizer, and sent it flying out the window.

The crash was followed by total silence.

Slowly, with great effort, the receptionist dragged himself off the stool he had occupied without interruption, and wobbled somberly toward the emergency room.

Andrea watched as the sole keeper of the hospital eyed the damage. Dariush stood feet slightly apart, looking out the shattered window, ignoring the presence of the man standing in the doorway.

"Let's get out of here," he said, his voice sharp, forewarning against any dissent.

As they walked out, the crowd shuffled to make room for the father of the boy to advance. Dariush murmured a few words to the old man, pulled him aside, shoved a bundle of money into the man's pocket, grabbed Andrea by the arm and walked out the front door.

They waited by the sidewalk for a taxi. Meanwhile, the women drifted to one side of the lobby, wailing, pounding their chests, rocking from side to side. The orchestration grew louder and the pounding harder with each passing moment. A few feet away, in the opposite corner, the men sobbed quietly, frequently wiping their tears with the sleeves of their worn out jackets. Not to be left out, the receptionist shook his head sorrowfully.

The whole scenario seemed put-on, practiced. It didn't look like it had much to do with the boy's death. The mourners sobbed, raised their heads rhythmically, their eyes searching for approval from curious villagers who drifted into the lobby from the street. Watching the hysteria mount, Andrea caught herself seething. The boy's useless death awakened in her a feeling of resentment, of rage. Destitution amid plenty, hypocrisy of do-gooders whose only concern was self-aggrandizement. The assumption by one man that he and he alone knew what was good for "his country" and "his people." The resigned, impassive look on the faces of everyone excluding the privileged few, stirred ugly emotions in her psyche, emotions only a short time ago, she wasn't aware she had. Injustice is what these people expect and injustice is what they get, she concluded. She felt like grabbing and shaking them to knock some sense into their heads so they'd fight for their rights.

"Why are they carrying on like this?" she asked the question before she could stop herself.

"They are expected to. Whenever there is a death, they scream and holler and extol the virtues of the dead person. It's the custom," Dariush stated flatly. There was no hint of objection in his voice.

An aging orange cab, driven by an old man who should have retired decades ago, stopped at the curb where Andrea and Dariush waited.

Dariush opened the back door and let Andrea and himself in. After three attempts, the back door finally closed.

"Don't sit close to the door," Dariush advised. "There is no telling when it will swing open. It's a pile of junk."

Driving at less than twenty miles an hour, the car huffed and rambled its way to Pahlavi. Andrea was sure the car would disintegrate any moment or the old man would have a stroke. She could hear him wheezing with every breath he took. Dariush did not look worried, just distant, lost in thought.

Two miles short of their destination, the car made a feeble sputter and quit.

Dariush paid the driver the full fare plus a handful of bills and told him to be sure and get his car fixed before he put it on the road again.

Overwhelmed by his passenger's generosity, the driver grabbed Dariush's hand and kissed it repeatedly.

Dariush drew his hand back slowly, looking slightly annoyed and terribly embarrassed.

"Do you mind if we walk the rest of the way?" he asked. "I feel an urgent need for fresh air."

Andrea nodded.

They walked over ten minutes. Neither spoke. Finally Dariush asked, "You look annoyed. Why?"

"Not annoyed, puzzled."

"You mean you're having trouble putting a label on me. Americans love to do that, don't they? Well, I'm afraid you're wasting your time. I don't fit any mold. If you know what I mean."

"No, I don't know what you mean. Should I?"

They continued walking through the littered path. Huge rocks had found their way to the narrow, gravel path, the only space available for walking. Andrea tripped and lost her footing. Dariush caught her just in time. Otherwise, she would have fallen in a pile of manure neatly deposited on the side of the road.

"Are you hurt? Can you walk?"

"Thank you. I'm fine." There was an edge to her voice.

"Please forgive me," he said. "I did not mean to upset you. Like most people I'm far more complex and changing than this fast paced world will allow. Don't be angry with me. What puzzles you today will be irrelevant tomorrow. What is relevant and irreversible is death, of which we have had enough for the time being."

Andrea regretted her curt reply. "You're right. Today's events have given me the jitters. It scares me to think how delicate the balance between man and nature is."

"Nature only wins when man is ignorant. I can accept nature's ravages. It's man's greed I abhor. My countrymen, especially those in power, seem to be blessed with megadoses of it."

"Do you still wonder why I'm puzzled?" Andrea kept her eyes on the path. The ratio of garbage to gravel was in direct proportion to the distance from the village. The closer they got to the village the harder it became to find a spot to step on. Cars zoomed in both directions, on the only two lane paved road, at any speed they could muster, showering pedestrians with whatever size rock their tires could propel.

"It must be difficult for you to understand my unorthodox behavior. I don't suffer injustice graciously."

"That's a very tall order you have prescribed for yourself, especially in this country."

"It must change."

She felt it was best not to dwell on the subject. She asked half in jest, "What do you think our chances are of reaching the village unharmed?"

"With the dawning of the automotive age the Iranian male has an unprecedented tool with which to impress the world with his manhood. The harder he presses on the gas pedal, the manlier he feels. The villagers ride their donkeys through back paths. They won't risk the shorter wider main road. But I'm afraid we have no choice."

When they reached the village square, Dariush asked Andrea to wait for him. He wanted to talk to the village chief about the boy's death. "Dying in Iran is easy," he explained. "The formalities and the bureaucratic red tape which follow, are senseless and endless."

Dariush entered a roadside tea house. A few moments later he emerged with an old man balancing himself on a stick improvised from the branch of a tree. Andrea watched as the men talked. Once again Dariush dug into his pocket, took out a wad of bills and gave it to the man. He crossed the square and joined Andrea. "The village chief will take care of the formalities and see to it that the boy is buried within forty eight hours. We don't have morgues. Early burial prevents the corpse from rotting and spreading disease."

"Makes sense. What doesn't make sense is you giving money to practically everyone you talk to."

Dariush shrugged. "Why not? It's my way of pacifying my conscience. These people are poor, illiterate and often helpless. Whole families work from dawn to dusk. Yet all they can afford is bread and tea. Sometimes, they get lucky. They have a little left over to buy cheese."

"Why? There's so much oil revenue. Where does the money go?"

Dariush's deep set, black eyes seemed to sink deeper. Andrea was not sure if she had angered him or reminded him of an unpleasant fact.

He chose not to answer.

A few minutes later, they arrived at Helga's house.

She was waiting for them. "Cyrus is here," she said. "He arrived unexpectedly. He's upstairs showering. I've told the cook to prepare dinner. Can you stay for dinner Dariush?"

"I have to go home first. I need to talk to my nanny. Ahmed Agha's son drowned."

"Ahmed Agha who has the little restaurant?" Helga asked.

"The same."

"Isn't he the one who had nine daughters from three wives before he had a son?"

"That's right."

"Oh my God!" was all Helga could say.

Dariush left and Andrea went looking for Kelly. Kelly was on the back porch being entertained by a servant. Andrea thanked the servant then lifted Kelly into her arms. She could not control herself any longer. The tears rolled down her cheeks.

Soon, Helga was by her side. "Do you want to talk about it?"

Andrea reached for a tissue, dried her eyes, raised her head and studied the face of the woman she admired. Dariush was right. Helga was an exceptional person, capable of holding her own despite many adversities. "Oh, Helga," Andrea said sobbing. "It was terrible. I can't forget his eyes. I see them wherever I look. There has to be a way to help these people."

Helga put her arms around Andrea. "You mustn't torture yourself. You did all you could. It's a harsh life for these people. I do all I can and yet, at times, it pains me so much, I can't stand it. I leave. I go to Europe, somewhere, anywhere, to get away from it all."

"There's no excuse for it. It's such a rich country." God! If only her tears would stop running down her cheeks. It was embarrassing.

"Time. Maybe time will help. For the moment, I worry about Dariush. He's much too sensitive."

Andrea pulled Kelly closer to her chest deriving an unexplainable comfort from the child's warmth. "I thought he was going mad in the emergency room when he threw the sterilizing unit out the window. I can't blame him though. It was mind boggling to watch a child die in front of our eyes, in a brand new hospital, surrounded by millions of dollars worth of equipment and not a medical person in sight."

"This may sound callous to you Andrea but, Reza is neither the first nor the last to die a useless death. Life has very little meaning in this part of the world. For males, a little, maybe. Females are tools for producing males. Neither their birth nor their death is registered with a government agency."

"Isn't it ironic though that they made such a fuss over the inauguration of the hospital? Doesn't anyone stop to ask what good expensive buildings and equipment are without medical people?"

A bitter, understanding smile lingered on Helga's face. "It accomplished its purpose," she said. "It was front page news. The people were led to believe their monarch is working for their welfare. Few will question the outcome."

"It's scary. I was assured there was good medical care available."

"Only in Tehran," Helga replied. "And only if you have money."

It was easy to blame the monarchy. Andrea felt the problem was far more complex and deep rooted. The apathy, the resigned outlook, the corruption, the greed, the lack of reverence for human life, were the symptoms, not the disease. The disease itself was of epidemic proportions having afflicted almost the entire society.

"Greetings," Cyrus said, smiling broadly. He was dressed in a pair of black gabardine slacks, a knit Pierre Cardin sweater and a white, neatly cut sport jacket, his cologne preceded him.

When the women did not respond in kind he became angry. "Why the solemn faces," he demanded.

"Reza, Ahmed Agha's son is dead," Helga explained. "He drowned this afternoon. Andrea and Dariush were with him in the hospital when he died."

"C'est la vie," Cyrus answered shrugging his shoulders. "Some have to die so others live. Ahmed Agha will soon marry again in hopes of having another son. Forget it. Let's have a drink."

With great effort, Andrea tried to hide her feelings behind a blank face. Helga said nothing.

Cyrus offered the women wine and poured himself gin and tonic. He stretched on a deck chair and sipped his drink. Andrea watched Helga wondering what kind of reaction, if any, she'd have to her husband's callous remark. If she was upset, nothing in her manner betrayed it. Andrea did not know whether to admire or envy her. Did Helga have an insight, a grip which eluded other Westerners from accepting or tolerating the adversities they faced in an alien culture? Damn! How does she do it? And for so long. Nine months and I'm ready to explode!

Cyrus's relaxing was over in a few minutes. He was a restless man in perpetual motion. "What's keeping Dariush so long," he demanded. "I'm going over to their house. Have dinner ready. I've something to tell you."

Helga excused herself and went to the kitchen to talk to the cook. Andrea left for her room to put Kelly to bed and change for dinner.

Half an hour later, Cyrus and Dariush came up the street. Cyrus was laughing and gesturing, seemingly without a worry in the world.

"My husband has only one preoccupation in life," Helga said matter-of-factly. "It's called having a good time. All else is irrelevant."

An elegant dinner, prepared according to the General's specifications, served by a professional butler, enhanced the General's good mood. "I flew to Monte Carlo yesterday afternoon, gambled all night and flew back this morning," he said with an impish grin on his face. "Wine, women, and songs make life worth living." He slapped his thigh, laughed out loud, then stopped abruptly. His audience seemed to lack in enthusiasm. "If you don't snap out of it, you're going to give me indigestion. You're acting like teenagers. Are you going to spend the rest of your lives mourning the death of a child?"

"Please Cyrus, let's finish our dinner in peace," Helga said. "Did you win or loose in Monte Carlo?"

Even though the General got angry quickly, he could reverse himself in no time and be in a jovial mood again. "I won!" he exclaimed.

"No wonder you're in a good mood," Helga said smiling.

"That's part of the reason. I told you I had something to tell you. We're leaving tomorrow morning for Beirut, Lebanon. It's sin city. I love it."

Chapter 19

It was time to leave. Andrea did not want to remain in Pahlavi while Helga was in Lebanon.

She excused herself after dinner and went to her room. She piled Kelly's clothes on the bed, next to her suitcase and started packing. In the morning, she would somehow get herself and Kelly to a taxi stand. She'd heard about passenger cars which commuted between Pahlavi and Tehran. It would not be the same as the trip over in an air-conditioned Jaguar, but it would have to do.

There was a knock on her door. "May I come in?" It was Helga.

"Sure."

Helga looked puzzled. "I don't think we should take Kelly with us. She'll be fine here with Goli. We'll only be gone three days. Beirut is fun for its nightlife and the sea. You should have some time to yourself."

Andrea stopped packing. "Kelly and I will leave for Tehran in the morning."

"Don't you want to come with us?"

"Come with you? I didn't know I was invited. I'm sure Cyrus meant you and him."

Helga looked surprised. "He wouldn't have mentioned it in your presence if he didn't want you to come."

Andrea laughed nervously. "You know I can't go. I have no ID, no passport, nothing. They took my American passport at the airport and my husband has yet to get me an Iranian one. And how can I leave without my husband's permission. Isn't that the law of the land?"

"Try calling him," Helga suggested.

"It's no use, Helga."

Helga thought for a moment then said, "He doesn't have to know. Beirut is a great place to have fun. On previous trips we hardly slept a couple of hours a night. I'd love for you to come."

"I can't. Tell me all about when you come back."

Helga was crestfallen. "I forget where I am sometimes. Let me talk to Cyrus. I'll be right back." She hurried out of the room.

She returned accompanied by Cyrus. Cyrus had a broad grin on his face. He seemed carefree, exuding charm, leaving no doubt in anyone's mind life's problems were for others. He could not be bothered with such trivia. If faced with one, he found the quickest way out.

"What's this I hear about you not coming with us?" he asked. "If I thought there would be a problem I would not have invited you."

Something in the General's manner unsettled her. He displayed no insecurity, no uncertainty. Andrea found it hard not to be affected by his presence. He expected and got everyone's attention. Andrea was no exception.

"Thank you for the invitation but there's no way I can go. Kelly and I will leave in the morning."

Cyrus's smile broadened as though he found Andrea's response amusing. He leaned against the open door, smiling. "I have to deliver a message from the King to the President of

Lebanon. We have an airplane at our disposal. We fly in, a representative of the President meets us and takes us to the hotel. You're my guest. No one is going to question you."

Andrea looked at Cyrus astonished. Slowly, the General's words sank in. We fly in. We are driven to the hotel. No questions asked. The man's crazy!

No, she could not risk it again. The last time she was urged to do something against her better judgement, she had landed at Savak headquarters. A trip to Beirut was very tempting but the consequences could be disastrous.

As though reading her mind he walked over and gave her a friendly hug. "I know you're upset about what happened to you when you went to meet the Queen. I learned about it too late. They'll never bother you again. You have my word."

Andrea burst into tears and immediately was annoyed at herself. She could feel the effect it was having on Helga. She couldn't bear to see Helga saddened. Sounding more cheerful than she felt, she said, "Let's forget it. I'd rather look forward to the future than dwell on the past."

"But we'd like you to come with us," Helga said with a pleading voice. "First Savak, then Reza's death. It's not what I had in mind when I invited you. The change will do us both good. Let's call Mani."

Andrea tried until midnight. She could not get through. Although American Bell had installed automatic dialing service a few months prior between Tehran and the northern provinces, the lines were few and the callers many. For most Iranians automatic dialing was a new phenomenon which gave them great pleasure. Once they got through, they spent hours chatting. Cost was irrelevant. Those who could afford black market prices for telephones, could afford the long distance phone bills.

Andrea's reward was a sore index finger.

She gave up and went to bed.

At five in the morning, Helga knocked on her door. "Make sure you pack a swim suit," she said. "The Phoenicia has a fantastic swimming pool. Don't worry about evening wear. I packed enough for both of us."

"I don't know what to do Helga. I couldn't reach Mani. I tried for hours."

"Don't worry about it. It's a short trip. We'll be back on Monday. He'll probably be delighted that you had an opportunity to enjoy yourself."

"I don't feel right about it."

"I could send my driver to Tehran with a note to let him know, if you'd like."

Andrea decided against it. It would mean a five hour drive, probably in vain. She'd hoped Mani was in Tehran when she telephoned the night before, but she really didn't know where he was. And the only time he was interested in her whereabouts was when he needed money. "Thank you. That won't be necessary. I'll tell him when we get back."

"Great. Let's go."

Dariush joined them at six thirty. Andrea was surprised. Then she remembered Dariush was having dinner with them when the General spoke about the trip. She assumed that meant he was invited too.

They drove to the airport and at seven flew to Lebanon. Two and a half hours later, they landed at Beirut International Airport, on a secluded runway.

Cyrus had not exaggerated when he said a representative of the Lebanese government would meet them upon arrival. The representative was waiting with his French wife and a huge bouquet of flowers for Helga.

They were whisked to town in a diplomatic limousine with dark windows, the driver following two policemen on motorcycles, their sirens turned on full blast. They arrived at the Phoenicia Hotel in record time, less than thirty minutes.

The Phoenicia was known to most travelers as the ultimate in luxury. Its huge, lavishly decorated lobby aroused the curiosity of the most sophisticated visitor. Each corner was uniquely designed. Phoenician motifs of ancient ships bedecked the walls under bright spot lights. A group of Arabs from the neighboring Sheikhdoms sat Buddha style around low, round, hand carved, silver tables, sucking on their water pipes. Two men dressed in black, baggy pants tied at the waist with a string, a collarless white shirt and a craftily designed vest, circled among the guests in the lobby, around the clock, serving spoonfuls of very strong, very bitter coffee. Above, an immense, glass swimming pool displayed slim beauties in microscopic bikinis, gracing its waters like mermaids.

A peculiar sense of awe swept through Andrea. She stood mesmerized, wondering if it was real or her imagination was playing uncanny tricks on her. I must remember this scene, she told herself. This is how to live. Not the one room prison I've been condemned to.

She was jolted from her reverie by Cyrus. He was talking to them but it did not register. She was totally absorbed in her surroundings. She felt a gentle nudge at her elbow. It was Dariush.

"We have to go to our rooms," he said. "They have the lift door open. They're waiting for you."

Andrea rushed to join them. "I'm terribly sorry," she said.

Helga chuckled. "I did the same on my first visit here."

The elevator came to a halt on the top floor, a floor reserved for special guests. Three uniformed bellboys ushered them to their rooms.

Andrea stopped at the entrance and looked around. The small hall led to a large living room. She could see two rooms, one on each side of the living room. One was a bedroom, the other a study. All the rooms were furnished with Louis XIV furniture. The bathroom had wall to wall mirrors, a sunken tub, carpet an inch thick, and fresh flowers in a crystal vase. There were perfumed candles in crystal candle holders arranged around the tub and the smell of burning incense. The floors of the living room and the other two rooms were covered with Persian rugs. There was a huge basket of flowers on the dresser, another basket filled with fruit on the coffee table.

It must be a mistake. The bellboy was probably misinformed. Dariush said room not suite. She'd wait before she unpacked.

There was a knock on her door. Helga and Dariush entered. Dariush was carrying a package.

"Cyrus just finished talking to the President," Helga said. There was a touch of concern in her voice. "His wife is a friend of mine. They invited us to spend the day with them and said something about dinner tonight."

"Hey, don't worry about us," Dariush said. "I know this city very well. I promise to take good care of Andrea. Go ahead and attend to your stuffy obligations. We'll rent a boat, go way out, and bask in the sun."

Helga looked relieved. "Great. Here are the keys to the car you can use. The concierge knows which car to give you. I don't know when we'll be back. Bye." She headed toward the Presidential suite.

"Let's go," Dariush said impatiently. "We must not keep the blue Mediterranean waiting."

Dariush's enthusiasm was infectious. Nonetheless she had to question him about the suite. He found her misgivings amusing. "Of course you're in the right place. Where did you think you'd be, in a room in the cellar? Come on, put these on." He gave her the package he was holding.

"What is it?"

"Open it."

She looked at him, not quite sure what to expect, then opened it. There was a boating outfit complete with a pair of shorts, a designer top, a special terry cloth robe, sunglasses, an Italian straw hat and sandals.

He saw her hesitate. "Try them on. I got them from the boutique in the lobby. They'll exchange anything you don't like."

"I . . . I can't accept it. You shouldn't have."

He gave her a long hard look. It was apparent she'd hurt his feelings. "In the Middle East, refusing a gift is considered an insult. Please, take it."

Everything fit. He was dressed in a matching outfit he had bought for himself. They crossed the lobby of the hotel, their looks strikingly similar to Vogue models. Sheikhs strained their necks and eyes to get a better glimpse of the handsome couple. Andrea could feel their penetrating gazes and was surprised to find herself enjoying them.

They crossed the street to the St. George Hotel. Dariush rented a speed boat, got behind the wheel and started the engine. A few minutes later they were miles away from the shore. Dariush cut the engine and let the boat rock on the gentle waves.

It was a warm spring day. Andrea stretched facing the sun, basking in its warmth, totally relaxed.

For almost half an hour neither spoke. Occasionally, Andrea threw a glance at him. He sat behind the wheel, silent, motionless, staring into the deep waters as though searching for an answer which could only be found in the depth of the sea.

It was noon. The sun's rays were piercing Andrea's skin far more fiercely than she'd imagined possible in early spring. She reached for her robe and wrapped it around herself.

A while later, she thought of asking him to turn back. Her skin was bright red despite all the suntan lotion she had used. He had not moved. He sat like Moses, his chin cupped in his hand, still staring.

She was bothered by the sudden change in his mood. She tapped him gently on the shoulder. "Do you sleep with your eyes open Dariush?"

"I was not sleeping. I was thinking."

Something was bothering him. Dariush had a face which registered freely the slightest change in his mood.

"Did I do something to upset you?"

"Your whole existence upsets me."

Shocked, Andrea searched her mind for something she may have said or done. At a loss for words she mumbled,

"What do you mean?"

Their eyes met, his piercing hers in a steady gaze. She did the same. She had to know.

Slowly, tenderly, he held her hands in his. "I love you, Andrea. I know I shouldn't. I've struggled. I've fought with myself every moment since I met you. It's no use. I love you and I want you. I will do everything I can to get you."

Watching the pain in his eyes, Andrea was filled with an aching sadness. "It's the blue Mediterranean, the sunny skies and this boat which have put you in a romantic mood. We hardly know each other?"

"I need someone to care about. Someone who will care about me for who I am and not for what I have. I have lots of friends. The wealthy always do. I know we've known each other only a week, but there is no doubt in my mind that my wealth means nothing to you."

"You're right on that point, but that should not be a major factor in your decision."

He moved closer. "I'm failing miserably. I don't know how to make you understand what's going on inside me. The way you walk, the way you talk, your attitude toward life, your reaction to the death of a total stranger, your inability to accept the inhumanity of man to man, your sensitivity, your deep caring for others, have aroused in me emotions I would have denied I had a week ago. I feel human when I'm with you. Is that very difficult for you to understand?"

He was fighting back tears. Ordinarily, Iranians avoided revealing their true feelings and were genuinely surprised when Westerners expressed themselves freely, without reservations. Andrea was deeply moved.

"I understand you well Dariush, but I am married, and I do have my daughter to think of. Don't you see how it complicates matters for me?"

He looked at her strangely, hesitated, then said, "Your daughter will be my daughter. If you're worried about your husband, you can relax. That's not a problem. He can be easily silenced. What disturbs me is not knowing whether you care about me or not. I have two rough months ahead of me in school. I can't think straight. Promise me you'll think about it. That's all I ask."

She hardly heard what he said after he told her not to worry about her husband; that he can be easily silenced. What did he mean by "silenced." What sort of crazy society had she become part of? Was it characteristic of the ruling oligarchy to dispose of whoever did not suit their fancy?

"What does it take to silence a person Dariush?" she asked fighting to keep the irritation in her voice under control.

"A telephone call. Why?"

"Just wondering."

"There are two ways of silencing a person in my country. Money and bullets. I have to admit bullets are used more often than money. Beheshte-Zahra, our famous cemetery is full of people who'll never talk again."

"And you approve?"

"Andrea please, you've got me all wrong. When I referred to your husband, I meant money. I hear he's desperately looking for funds to bankroll his anti government activities."

Stunned, she almost fell out of the boat. "How do you know? Have you met him?"

"I made it my business to find out."

"And?"

"I don't want to discuss it. If you don't know who the man you married is, you're in bad trouble."

"What did you do? Call Savak to give you a rundown on my husband."

"Please, Andrea."

"I'm serious. A friend said she feels like she lives in a fish bowl in Iran. I'm beginning to understand why."

He put his index finger under her chin and raised her head up. "Listen to me. You must be a fool to think that anyone can be involved in terrorism in Iran and keep it a secret. Half the national budget goes on silencing dissidents."

She was lost for words. The atrocious was not the exception, it was routine. How could there be such numb acceptance? Such acquiescence. And yet she felt as helpless as those she was accusing. There seemed to be no way out. Like her, Dariush seemed to be groping for answers. It wasn't fair to blame him for the way things were in his country.

He had turned his face away from her, watching the calm sea gently rock the boat.

"Friends?" she asked.

He did not answer.

"Please, Dariush. I hate to see you upset. Let's forget Iran while we're here. Agreed?"

He turned around slowly. "If you promise to think about what I told you."

"I promise."

"Can you keep it a secret?"

She had to laugh. "There are no secrets where we come from. Remember?"

"Except one," he said happily. "No one knows I love you."

He jumped up, grabbed her and they tumbled into the water in a spontaneous embrace.

Chapter 20

Mani read the note from Andrea, crumpled it and threw it in the trash can. He felt relieved. She wouldn't be around to nag him for a while. Questions. Always questions. Where's my money? When can we go for my passport? How come you don't sleep in our bed? You're always disappearing. Why don't you tell me where you're going? Why don't you call? He'd had enough. Hopefully, someday soon, it would be over. He had enough to worry about. Since the bomb incident at the Niavaran Club, he was under more intensified surveillance by Savak, Farhad stayed with a friend temporarily until security agents shifted their attention to other suspects, and Zia had sneaked back into the country and given him an ultimatum; either he contributed soon, or he was out.

He poured Scotch in a glass, added a couple of ice cubes and settled in his mother's armchair to watch television. No one was home.

After a while he dozed.

He was awakened by the ringing of the door bell and was instantly gripped by fear. He wasn't expecting anyone. Could it be Savak? If so, he better open the door quickly. Security agents hated waiting, they were there because they knew he was home and they'd get in anyway.

He opened the door.

A foreign looking man, holding a briefcase, asked, "Mr. Mani Abbassi?"

Mani's heart stopped pounding. "Yes."

"My name is Phil Conrad. I'm from the American Embassy. Could I talk to you for a moment?"

Mani despised Americans more than he despised the Shah and the Shah's entourage. His conviction was firm. Americans were responsible for the plight of his countrymen. Without their meddling there would be no Shah and therefore no suffering Iranians. But he had to keep his hatred under control. Those were his orders.

"Come in please," he chirped with a plastic smile instantly planted on his drooping lips. He directed Phil Conrad to the sofa in the living room and he sat in an armchair facing his guest.

"Can I get you something to drink?"

"No, thank you. This won't take long. You're married to an American, Andrea Sorensen, correct?"

"Correct."

"Is she home? Could I talk to her?"

"I'm afraid that's not possible. She's not in town."

"When will she back?"

"I don't know, Mr. Conrad. I was away on a business trip. She left a note but there was no mention of when she'd return."

"Please call me Phil. All my friends do."

Mani smiled a twisted smile. "Phil, yes of course. A difficult American custom to get used to; calling a person by his first name minutes after being introduced. I never did get used to it. In Iran, it's considered rude. We address only family and close friends by their first name."

He noticed Phil Conrad's expression change. He had to be

more careful.

"Perhaps you could help me. Was your wife sick recently?"

"Sick? No, she's fine. Like I said, she's vacationing in Pahlavi with friends."

"That's strange. I have with me the copy of a letter which your wife's mother, Margaret Sorensen claims to have received from you. It states that her daughter is sick in the hospital and that you need money for her hospitalization."

Phil Conrad opened his briefcase, took out the letter and handed it to Mani. The letter was typewritten. "Is that your signature?"

The color drained from Mani's face. He glanced at the letter, threw it on the coffee table and pointed his finger at Phil Conrad. "It's a lie I tell you. A vicious, disgusting lie. That woman hates my guts. So did her husband. They didn't want Andrea to marry me. Her father threatened to take her out of his will if she did."

"But he didn't. Your wife got half of a sizable fortune."

"Yeah, what's the use. It's all hers. I didn't marry her for her money. Her parents insisted that I sign an agreement. I think it's called prenuptial agreement."

"So it's your contention that you did not send this letter."

"Of course not. Margaret's a bitch. She was livid when she found out we were leaving for Iran. She'll do anything to break up our marriage."

"I'd like to hear what your wife has to say. The friends she's staying with, do they have a telephone?"

"Why do you want to call her? She'll be back soon."

"Because her mother has received a second letter demanding her to comply and threatening her with harm to her daughter if she doesn't. I seriously doubt that Margaret Sorensen would write such letters to herself."

Mani fought to control his rage. He pushed his shoulders back then said, "I'm sorry. If you want to talk to my wife, you'll have to wait for her return. You'll be wasting your time though. I'm sure she doesn't know any more than I do."

"My job is to look after the welfare of Americans living in Iran. If there's a threat, I have to look into it. Here's my card. Please have her call me when she gets back."

Mr. Conrad rose and headed for the door. He thanked his host, said goodbye and left.

Mani rushed to the phone, called Farhad and insisted that he come over.

Fifteen minutes later Farhad let himself in.

"You were hysterical like a woman. What happened?"

Mani told him.

"Damn!" Farhad spat. "She didn't go for it. And now we have that bastard on our backs. He's not here to look after the welfare of Americans. Our contact at the American Embassy assured me that he is. But now, I'm not so sure he knows what he's talking about. I think this man is a spy. They all are."

Mani cracked his knuckles. "What do we do now? He's determined to talk to her. She'll know it's my signature."

"Damn!" Farhad spat again. "Let me think. You didn't give him the General's phone number, did you?"

"I don't have it to give it to him. But he won't have trouble locating her. Pahlavi is a small place and there are such few foreigners that if Conrad decides to locate her, he won't have trouble."

"You idiot! Did you tell him where she was?"

Mani felt a chill run through his spine. "I . . . I . . ."

"Shut up. Let me think. If he knows where she is, we've got big trouble."

"Why? What . . . what difference does it make? He'd talk to her when she got back."

Farhad stopped pacing the room and glared at Mani. "Because it would give us time. Time to consult Zia. But since you don't think before you talk, we have to come up with a plan immediately."

Mani cracked his knuckles and stared into space. Lately, he could do nothing right regardless of how meticulously he planned it. Invariably, a factor, impossible for him to foresee, cropped up and forced him to alter his course of action or drop the matter completely. It demoralized him when he failed. Especially with the job at the Niavaran Club, which, had it succeeded, would have given him an excellent standing with the Council. Instead, they were betrayed, Savak rounded six of the Council members, dozens of so called suspects were apprehended and the pay of informers doubled. All activity by the Revolutionary Council had to be put on hold. And now this.

"Call the operator. Use your charm. See if you can get the General's number in Pahlavi."

"Suppose I get the number, what do you want me to do?"

"Talk to your wife. Convince her it's to her advantage not to recognize your signature."

"She won't do it."

"Try. If bad comes to worse we'll threaten her with harm to her daughter. She'll do it."

Mani tried to get the number. The operator said he did not have it.

"That's that," Mani said.

"You've got to reach her. If Conrad can't reach her by phone, I bet he'll drive there first thing in the morning. If he gets to her before we do and she verifies your signature, they'll open an investigation and we'll have a mess on our hands. We don't want a bunch of Americans snooping into our business."

"It's past nine. Short of driving there in the middle of the night, I don't see how."

"Think. Do you know anyone who might have the number?"

Mani's face brightened. "Irene. I'm sure she has it."

He called Irene's house. The housekeeper informed him Irene and her husband were in Boston.

Mani slouched on the sofa, next to the telephone, drained.

Farhad lit a cigarette and paced the room. Suddenly, he

stopped. "The guard. There's always a guard guarding the General's house. He'll know. Go ask him."

Mani rose slowly. "I'll go, but I doubt he knows, and even if he does, I doubt he'll give it to me."

"Tell him your wife is staying with them. You have an urgent message for her from the States. Tell him it's an emergency."

Mani returned after ten minutes triumphantly waving a piece of paper. "I got it. I got it. It took a lot of convincing but I got it."

"Good. Call her. Start by telling her you miss her, you miss your daughter, you've started a business and you think you'll do real well soon. Promise her whatever she wants. Don't quit until she agrees."

Mani dialed the number. Talked in Farsi briefly, then slowly put the receiver down. "She's gone. The housekeeper said she left with the General, his wife and a nephew of the General. They left Friday morning, with suitcases."

"That means they have left the country. But how could she? You told me she has no ID. You said you didn't get it for her."

"I didn't. All she has is her driver's license."

Farhad fidgeted like a man who had a terrible itch he couldn't reach. "Damn," he yelled and spat. "Damn. Your wife travels high class. How could you permit such a thing to happen? No need for ID, no need for permission from her husband, a free trip. What more could she ask?"

"I wasn't here to stop her."

"The whole thing stinks. With friends like that, she won't give a damn if she has an ID or not. Nor will she bother to ask you for permission. She'll go where she wants, when she wants. We've got to put a stop to it. This calls for drastic action. Something she'll never forget."

"That's easy," Mani said, an arrogant expression sweeping his face. "But what do we do now."

"Did the housekeeper know where they went?"

"No. They didn't tell her."

"That won't be much of a problem. We have contacts. We'll find out. Did she know when they'll be back?"

"No."

"That could be a problem. The travel plans of top government officials are always secret and often subject to change. But we've got to find out."

"With all the turmoil in the country I doubt the General can afford to stay away too long."

"Damn!" Farhad lit a cigarette and inhaled it deeply. "There's got to be a way. Pour me a drink, will you?"

Mani poured drinks for both of them. "Think of it this way. If we can't reach her, neither can Conrad. For now, all we can do is wait."

Farhad took a big swallow from his drink, placed the glass on the coffee table then turned to Mani. "Sometimes you boggle my mind. It should have occurred to you that our information about Conrad could be wrong. I bet he's with the CIA and I bet he knows exactly where the General went. And he'll soon find out your wife went him. All he has to do is call Pahlavi."

Mani felt irked by his best friend's constant belittling of him. "You assured me Conrad was a simple employee. You said I worry too much. But, assuming what you say is true, he still has to wait for her to come back to show her the letter."

"Maybe, maybe not. It all depends on how he views the matter. Since he knows your wife is not sick, he'll wonder why you wrote those letters. Don't you think he'll find a way to contact her before you do?"

Mani finished his drink in one gulp but it didn't help calm his nerves. "What the hell do you propose we do. It was your idea to send those letters, remember?"

Farhad collapsed in an armchair. "There's nothing we can do but wait. Wait and plan. I don't like rude surprises. We must see to it that it never happens again."

Chapter 21

Dariush and Andrea spent Saturday exploring downtown Beirut with the help of the driver the General had provided for them. It was a crowded, dynamic city, tall, modern buildings next to shacks, banks everywhere.

Dariush was like a little boy in an amusement park. "Beirut is my favorite city," he said. "I love dancing, sailing and mountain climbing. I can do everything I want in Lebanon. All it requires is money. It's great when I travel with my uncle. The Iranian government picks the tab. No questions asked."

They drove along the beach, then downtown. The driver asked, "Is there any place in particular you'd like to go?"

"The Souk," Dariush said.

"What's the Souk?" Andrea asked.

"The gold market. I want to buy my mother a gift."

The Souk was a narrow, covered, cobblestone street, about a hundred yards long, lined with small shops on both sides, packed with shoppers. The six feet by eight feet shops looked almost identical except for the owners names written in Latin and Arabic letters above the entrance. Handmade gold jewelry displayed in every window glittered under bright lights. Dariush saw a bracelet he liked in one of the windows. They went in and he bought it.

Late in the afternoon they returned to the hotel.

"Let's rest a while," Andrea suggested.

"Later on tonight I'd like to take you to the 'Cave du Roix.' It's a nightclub famous for its food, decor and orchestra. We'll have dinner and dance. How about it?"

"Sounds good to me."

Dariush told the driver to come for them at nine thirty.

The nightclub was lavishly decorated, the food was good, the prices exorbitant. But it did not seem to bother Dariush. Dawn was breaking when they left. After a cocktail, wine with dinner and after dinner drinks, Andrea felt dizzy and sleepy. She could barely keep her eyes open.

Dariush had dismissed the driver. They took a cab to the hotel.

Andrea waited near the elevator while Dariush got the keys. She heard the clerk at the desk mention her name. Dariush said something. Then the clerk gave Dariush a small envelope and he headed toward the elevator.

"Was that for me?" Andrea asked looking at the envelope in Dariush's hand.

"Someone called while we were out." He gave her the envelope.

They took the elevator to her suite. He opened the door and they went in. She kicked her shoes off, plopped herself on a chair, opened the envelope and read the message.

"There must be a mistake." She felt like a dozen cobblers were hammering nails into her head. "I don't know a Mr. Philip Conrad. He wants me to call him in Tehran or contact him as soon as I get back. I wonder what for?"

"It's four thirty in the morning. I suggest you wait a while before you call."

"Right. Now I want to sleep. It can't be about Kelly.

Helga instructed Goli to contact her husband's assistant if she needed to get in touch with us. Anything else can wait. Good night." She fell asleep a few seconds after her head hit the pillow.

She was the first to wake up. It took her a few seconds to realize where she was. She was still dressed in the gown she had worn the night before. Her watch claimed it was ten to three. Night or day? She parted the curtains slightly and looked out. The bright sunshine blinded her momentarily. The sun, the traffic noise, the crowds in the street below, infused her with exhilaration. Another beautiful day.

She walked to the bathroom. As she did so she noticed Dariush asleep on the couch in the next room. He awoke immediately. They looked at each other and burst out laughing. He too had slept in his clothes.

She sat next to him on the couch. He took her in his arms. She did not resist. He ran his fingers through her hair all the while staring intently into her eyes. A strand of hair fell on her face. He lifted it gently and tucked it behind her ear. She closed her eyes. He planted a tender kiss on each eye. When she opened them, she saw a man overwhelmed with passion, excitement, and a craving for love.

How long had it been since Mani had said a kind word or touched her? Years, not months. She had been lying to herself. She could easily count the number of times he had made love to her in the seven years they'd been married. When was the last time? She strained to remember. Strangely, it did not matter anymore. She saw her life as she should have seen it years ago. Mani wanted U.S. citizenship and her inheritance. He got the citizenship but not the money. She was a means to an end to be discarded when her usefulness was over.

A gentle, probing kiss made her shudder. The thoughtful expression on her face was replaced with a sparkle in her big, green eyes. She needed and wanted to be loved.

Tenderly, between kisses and caresses he took off her dress, her pantyhose and her bra. He kissed her eyes with a savage passion. "Those eyes have pierced my soul and weakened my resolve despite myself," he whispered. "They follow me everywhere I go. More so when I try to sleep." He kissed her nipples, devouring her breasts with a consuming hunger. She felt ecstatic. He undressed quickly and retook her in his arms. They held each other tight wanting to be one for a timeless moment. Sensations not felt for years swept inside her, carrying her to heights she had not experienced before.

Her urgency became unbearable. He kissed her neck, her shoulders, her breasts, her nipples, wild with the euphoria of actually experiencing rather than dreaming about it, kissing until she could stand the blissful sensations no longer. Then he was inside her, pushing, pressing, wildly. He held her waist pulling her closer, penetrating deeper.

Soon her breathing became uneven, her senses soared and her heart pounded. She could feel his heart beat against hers. He was moving faster until an avalanche engulfed them.

She was a woman, a woman born again.

He held her close, stroked her hair, examined her face. "Your eyes change color when the sun hits them," he said caressing her. "They tantalize and torment me. I'm supposed to be an international playboy, immune to such temptations. How dare you destroy years of hard earned reputation."

He sat up lazily, pulled her robe from the chair next to the bed, put it on and wiggled around on tiptoe, imitating the transvestite they had watched the night before at the nightclub. She laughed until tears ran down her cheeks. She reached for him and kissed him.

As she moved, she realized there was blood smeared on the bed sheet where Dariush had been. She asked him to turn around. His back was covered with scratches and a few spots were bleeding.

"You won't be able to go swimming for a while," she said teasingly. "One look at your back will let everyone know what you've been up to."

"You vicious cat, you," he countered, covering her neck

with kisses.

"I'm a cuddly kitten," Andrea curled herself into a ball.

"You're a kitten who needs her claws trimmed." He tickled her mercilessly. "My love life is ruined. No Lebanese beauty will ever entice me again."

She was exhausted from laughing. She rolled to the far corner of the bed. "Time out. I need to catch my breath."

"Only if you promise not to look at me that way. As of this moment I give notice. I'm not responsible for my actions if you keep looking at me with those . . . those . . . tempting, haunting eyes."

"It's a deal."

She lay back to rest.

He moved to the window. The street lights had come on. He checked his watch.

"It's past six o'clock. I wonder where Helga and Cyrus are. We have not heard from them all day."

"Yesterday she said something about spending the day with the minister who met us at the airport. His wife and Helga are old friends."

"I was hoping we could go to the Casino du Liban. It's a must. The show is imported from France. It surpasses many shows in Europe. Then there's the gambling casino. We can't leave Lebanon without trying our luck."

"I'd rather not go out tonight."

Dariush pressed his hand on his chest. "My stomach is protesting. Its rumblings can be heard all over town. How about dinner."

"Super idea."

"Room service okay?"

"Perfect."

He called and ordered dinner for two to be served in half an hour. "I want to shower and get dressed."

"Me too. Would it be all right if I call Tehran?"

"Sure. Ask the operator to get the number."

The call went through. A woman answered. She asked for

Mr. Philip Conrad. "Eshtebah," was the answer and the line went dead.

"Eshtebah means wrong number, doesn't it?"

"It does," Dariush said. "Let me try."

He did and got the same answer. "Long distance calls are almost always full of interference. The clerk might have heard the numbers wrong."

"It had to be important or he wouldn't have called."

"Not that important. He says as soon as possible, not urgent."

"True. But how do I reach him when I get back if the number is wrong?"

"Your embassy might know."

"They might. I'll try when I get back."

He put on the suit he was wearing the night before, kissed her lips gently and left.

She showered, wore a pale blue dress, fixed her hair, applied a light touch of make up and returned to the living room.

He returned shortly, dressed in a custom tailored suit. He looked more handsome than she'd seen him before, an air of confidence enveloping him.

Andrea knew he would have no trouble getting most any woman he fancied. A disturbing thought crossed her mind. Was sex all he wanted from her?

He came and sat next to her on the couch. "I'll be leaving for Geneva a couple of hours after we return to Iran. I'll be gone a little over two months."

She was lost in thought. Reality would be waiting for her return. This was a temporary diversion, a dream, a lie. "I know."

There was a knock on the door. Dariush opened the door. The waiter came in pushing a cart piled high with food.

They ate in silence for a while, then suddenly Dariush said, "I want to marry you when I return." There was no hesitation in his words, no doubts, no restraint.

She trembled but managed to appear calm. "I'm already married."

"Divorce him. We'll leave for Geneva immediately after your divorce. Iran is not the right place for you or Kelly."

She had no answer to give him.

When they were done eating they moved over to the sofa in the next room.

He put an arm around her and with the other raised her chin. "Look at me. Do I look like a man who wants to play games with you? I love you. Can't you understand that? Can't you see what it's doing to me?"

"You'll get over it. Switzerland is another world."

She sensed outrage welling up in him. His face looked drawn.

Pronouncing each word slowly, deliberately, while holding her face in his hands, he said, "I love you my crazy kitten and I want you to know I never take no for an answer."

"Please stop," she pleaded tears streaming down her cheeks. "I can't. I'm attracted to you. I can't deny that. But I'm not sure I love you."

"I'll wait." If he was perturbed, he gave no indication of it.

"Don't."

The way she said it, the finality of it, made him pull his hands away from her face. "Forgive me. I'm a foolish person. I should not have assumed that because I love you you felt the same way about me."

He got up to leave.

"Wait. Please don't go."

"Why not?"

"I promise to think about it."

Overjoyed, he rushed over and carried her in his arms circling her around the room, covering her cheeks, eyes, forehead and neck with kisses.

Finally, he set her down in a chair and kneeled next to her. "Please smile. I never want to see you sad again. You're always beautiful but more so when you're happy."

She smiled a tortured smile. Her thoughts raced. How could she break the news to Mani? No doubt he'd react violently and she'd be at his mercy. She had few options. Nonetheless, she decided to put those thoughts aside and concentrate on showing her gratitude to the man who was doing all he could to make her happy.

"Could we keep it to ourselves until you return in June? I feel it's premature to tell Helga or anyone else."

Dariush hesitated. "Would you mind if I tell my mother?"

"Your mother?" Andrea asked surprised. He'd mentioned her once. When he wanted to buy the bracelet.

"My mother is Swiss. She lives in Switzerland. I've lived summers in Switzerland and winters in Iran since I was three years old. Now I live winters in Switzerland and summers in Iran because my school is in Geneva."

"What about your father?"

"When I was three years old, my mother decided to call it quits. She couldn't stand life in Iran or my father. She hasn't been back since. My father loves to roam the world, loves women and gambling. He's not choosy in what order he gets them. Occasionally, our paths cross." He said it without bitterness or regrets but rather with total detachment.

Dariush's statement about his father made Andrea think how different her father had been. Always there when she needed him. Always loving. Always caring. Tears welled in her eyes. Dariush was quick to sense the change in her mood. "What is it? Did I say something to upset you?"

"It's nothing. I guess I'm homesick."

"Perhaps this will help," he said reaching in his pocket. He held her hand and slipped the bracelet he had bought from the gold market on her wrist. "You'll have something to remember me by."

She shook her head baffled. "You said it was for your mother."

"I lied."

"It's crazy. I can't accept it." She pulled the bracelet off.

He put his elbows on his knees and covered his face with his hands.

She didn't know what to do. He looked distraught.

"I'm sorry if I hurt your feelings. I didn't mean to."

"Then put it back on. Either that or I'll throw it out the window."

She slipped it back on her arm. Who was this strange man? And what price her folly? An urge to be a little girl again, to rush into her father's waiting arms, overwhelmed her. He would know. But her father was no more. The tears flowed. She made no attempt to stop them.

"Please don't cry." he took her in his arms. "It'll be over in two months. I promise."

"Yes . . . two months."

Chapter 22

It was their last night in Lebanon. The General had made reservations for dinner and the show at the Casino du Liban. They were driven in a chauffeured limousine to a hilltop which housed three large buildings overlooking Beirut. "The Casino is the main tourist attraction," the General explained.

They had dinner, the lights were dimmed and the show began. Every table surrounding the stage was occupied by sheikhs except for the table reserved for the General and his party. "Iranian V.I.P.s contribute just as generously as the sheikhs to the coffers of the Casino," the General said, "so we're given the same privileged treatment."

The sheikhs seemed frozen in their chairs, eyes glued to the stage, mustaches twitching uncontrollably, the tempo directly related to the nudity on the stage.

"It's hard to decide what to watch," Andrea joked. "I can't decide whether our neighbors are more captivating or the dancers."

The General roared with laughter. "Wine, women and songs I always say. I've seen this show often enough. It's more fun to watch the crowd."

He turned towards Andrea. "Can you see that man holding small, velvet sacs?"

Andrea's eyes searched the front row.

"You mean the Arab at the next table with the pockmarked face?"

"Yes. I've seen him here before. Whenever a dancer tickles his fancy he throws a sac of gold at her. It's his way of letting her know he wants her for the night. An advance payment if you will."

"There are at least a dozen sacs in front of him. What does he do? Line them up and chose the one he wants." She was enjoying herself immensely, her worries temporarily forgotten.

The show went on for two hours. For the finale, the queen appeared wearing a huge feathered hat, a G string and little else, parading her wares provocatively, circling the stage. Now she was standing a few feet away from the Arab with the pockmarked face.

"Helga look!" It was Cyrus nudging Helga.

They watched as the subject of their attention grabbed a couple of velvet sacs, jumped on the table and from the table on to the stage. He grabbed the queen from her waist, shouting, "Habibi! Habibi!" (my darling) All the while shoving the little bags at her stomach.

A pro at her job, the queen looked down at the man embracing her, a head shorter than herself, his perfume of rose water mixed with his perspiration unfolding in waves, increasing in intensity with his every move.

The Arab clung to his newly found treasure. The orchestra increased its tempo to deafening heights and the performers exaggerated their movements to distract the overzealous admirer to no avail. He was busy kissing her bellybutton.

The queen seemed annoyed. She cupped her hands on his ears, lifted him up like a rag doll, stepped over to the table and plunked him down.

As though following a prearranged signal, the men in the audience jumped to their feet clapping and shouting, "Bis! Bis! Encore!" They seemed to have enjoyed the impromptu performance far more than the elaborate show on the stage.

The Arab remained slumped in his chair. His gold had failed him. He knew no their way.

"This is getting boring," Cyrus said. "Let's go to the gambling casino." He rose and walked out, followed by Helga, Andrea and Dariush.

"A guest is King here until he runs out of money," the General said.

Cyrus and Helga decided to try their luck at chemin de fer. Dariush wanted to play roulette. Andrea did not want to play. She had no money.

"I'll make a deal with you," Dariush said. "You tell me what color to play, red or black. If we lose, we lose. If we win we split fifty fifty."

"You're weird."

"Quick. Red or black." The ball was rolling.

"Red."

Dariush placed his chips on red.

The ball rolled and stopped right where Dariush had stacked his chips. He won.

"Beginner's luck," Andrea said.

"No dear. The games are rigged. They make it so initially those who place big bets win to encourage them to keep playing. The rest of the night will take care of their earnings and more. Let's move to another table."

As they moved from the table, the Arab who had made a spectacle of himself, tapped Dariush's arm and spoke.

Dariush shrugged his shoulders at the man's words and continued walking.

The Arab asked a passing waiter to translate.

"He says the lady with you brings good luck. He would like you to be his guest so she can tell him what to play."

"He can't be serious," she whispered to Dariush.

"Tell him the lady is busy," Dariush replied.

The waiter translated.

Andrea and Dariush walked away in search of Helga and Cyrus.

"Sir, sir." It was the waiter accompanied by the Arab.

"He's certainly a persistent fellow," Andrea said, her voice betraying her irritation.

"The Prince says he's ready to pay her. All she has to do is tell him what to play."

"He's a prince, huh?"

"Yes, sir. These people are superstitious. He's convinced she holds the key to his winning. The money means nothing to him. He always gives it away. It's the joy of winning."

Andrea stared at the so called 'Prince' waiting impatiently for her consent. "I always thought princes were supposed to be tall and handsome," she said to Dariush.

"Watch what you say," Dariush teased. "He's not only a prince, he probably has more money than most banks."

Andrea was in a silly mood. "Let's humor him."

"You really want to?"

"Sure."

"Tell the Prince we'll join him in a moment," Dariush told the waiter.

The Prince looked ecstatic. He marched to the roulette table and spoke to an aide.

The aide returned with a stack of chips. A Frenchman was in charge of the roulette table. He announced the start of the game. All bets had to be placed right away.

The Prince beckoned Andrea, his expression filled with anticipation.

"Thirteen."

The ball rolled. The Prince lost. If he was bothered by the loss, he showed no sign of it.

For two hours he bet and lost.

Andrea got bored. She turned to the aide. "Please tell the Prince we'd like to leave. He'll probably do better without me."

The aide relayed the message.

The Prince's reaction was one of disbelief. The aide translated. "His highness says he does not care how much he loses. He needs to win once. He's convinced he'll win if you stay."

Andrea gave Dariush a questioning look.

"It's up to you," Dariush said. "I'm going to get chips for myself. If you'd like to play I'll get chips for you too."

"No, thank you. I'm afraid my hunch was good only once. His indifference to his losses is mind boggling."

"That's because he hasn't worked for it. There's plenty more where that came from."

Another game was starting. The Prince waited for Andrea.

"Ask the Prince how old he is," Andrea said to the aide.

"Twenty four." The aide translated.

"Let him play twenty four."

The Prince bet fifty thousand dollars worth of chips on number twenty four.

There was an ominous silence.

The ball whirled and whirled and came slowly to a halt. The tension around the table mounted to unbearable heights.

The Prince lost again.

Dariush had missed the heart stopper. When he returned, the group around the table had funeral home expressions plastered on their faces. All but the Prince.

"What happened?" he asked Andrea.

"He just lost fifty thousand dollars."

Dariush had had enough of the Prince. "You're only good for me," he said half-jokingly. "Your verdict, please."

"My luck has run out. You choose."

Presently, Cyrus and Helga joined them. They said they had both won initially but kept playing and lost it all.

Dariush placed his chips and waited for the croupier to announce "Rien ne va plus." No more bets.

He lost.

Cyrus checked his watch. "It's almost three in the morning. We fly to Tehran at seven. We better get going."

The Prince realized they were about to leave. He pleaded with Andrea to give him one last tip before she left.

She hesitated, then said, "Twenty five. That's my birthday. I wish you luck."

The Prince tossed a huge pile of chips on number twenty five. The ball rolled, all eyes followed it. It stopped on number twenty five.

The onlookers could have easily been mistaken for patients with catatonia. Slowly, the Prince turned around, extended his hand, shook Andrea's hand and said something.

"He thanks you," the aide translated. "He says he knew his intuition was right. He knew he'd win."

"I'm happy for him," Andrea replied. "He sure has perseverance."

Cyrus and Dariush went ahead to get the coats the women had checked in. Helga and Andrea waited for them to return when they saw the aide rushing towards them carrying a briefcase.

"Thank God I caught up with you. The Prince would have killed me. He wanted your address but in the excitement I forgot to ask you for it."

"What does he need my address for?" Andrea asked surprised.

"He wanted you to have this." The aide pressed the briefcase against Andrea's chest and without waiting for a reply, hurried down the hall.

The two women looked at each other. Helga asked, "What's in it?"

"I've no idea."

Dariush and Cyrus approached with the coats. Dariush eyed the briefcase. "Where did that come from?"

"The Prince's aide brought it," Andrea said. "I don't know what's in it. Should we open it?"

"No," Cyrus said curtly. "I know what's in it. Let's go back to the gambling hall. You should return it."

They searched everywhere. There was no trace of the Prince or his entourage.

"What do we do now?" Andrea asked.

"Let's ask a waiter. They might know if he's still around or where he's staying."

"The Prince and his companion left a few minutes ago," the waiter told them.

"Do you know where he stays when he's in town?" asked Dariush.

"The Bristol Hotel, usually."

"We'll have to wait till he gets there," Cyrus said. "We'll call when we get back."

They were driven to the Phoenicia Hotel, sleepy and tired but they could not go to bed. They had to check the contents of the briefcase and locate the Prince. Cyrus had vetoed the idea of opening the briefcase in the car. He did not want to tempt the driver, if, as he suspected, there was reward money in it.

There was.

Thousands of Lebanese pounds.

Meanwhile, Dariush called every hotel in town. The Prince was nowhere to be found.

Shocked, Andrea found herself stuttering, "I . . . I . . . didn't know it contained money. How am I going to explain it to my husband?"

"Let's count it," Helga said. "We'll change it to dollars at the airport. If you're worried about your husband, I'll keep it for you."

The General was busy counting. "There's close to four thousand dollars here."

"You keep it for me," Andrea told Helga.

"I will."

"Women!" Cyrus said angrily. "Why don't you use your brains. Assuming Helga kept it for you, how can you prove that you ever gave it to her?"

The women looked at each other, their looks betraying

their naivete.

"I trust her," Andrea said.

"It's not a question of trust. She could be killed crossing the street. If you're worried about your husband finding out, Helga should keep this money for you in the bank. In the meantime, she should give you a check for the approximate amount. The exact amount you could work out later. You're too vulnerable. You should learn to protect yourself."

"Cyrus is right," Dariush added. "It's not a question of trust. It's better not to take chances."

"Let's get it over with and go to bed," Cyrus said. "Give me the dollar check book, Helga."

Helga took the checkbook out of her purse and handed it to him.

Cyrus wrote a check for four thousand dollars in Andrea's name and placed it on the coffee table. "Let's go," he told his wife impatiently. "And bring the briefcase with you."

Helga followed him quickly, briefcase in hand.

Dariush said good night and left.

It was past four o'clock in the morning.

Andrea stared at the check dazed, "Why me?" she asked of the empty room and collapsed on her bed.

Chapter 23

The plane touched down on a runway at Mehrabad airport reserved for military use. Four sleepy passengers stumbled out. A senior Iranian government official waited for Cyrus.

Cyrus conversed with the official briefly, then turned to his wife. "I have to go to the palace immediately. The King wants my report."

"Have you made arrangements for our transportation home?" Helga asked. "I told Ibrahim to bring Kelly to Tehran to our house but I didn't want him to come to the airport. The less he knows the better."

Cyrus conferred with the official.

"There's a car parked about a hundred yards from here. The driver will take you home after he drops Dariush at the V.I.P. lounge. Dariush's flight is on time. His servant is in the lounge with his luggage."

Cyrus got into the limousine and the car sped off.

The parked car headed in their direction. It stopped near them. The driver got out and opened the doors. Helga sat in the back seat.

Dariush and Andrea faced each other for an uneasy moment their eyes riveted on each other.

"I'll miss you," he whispered.

"I'll miss you too. Bye Dariush," Andrea said quietly.

"I love you. Don't forget what we discussed."

"I won't."

They got in the car. Andrea sat in the back with Helga. Dariush sat in the front with the driver.

The car stopped at the V.I.P. lounge. Dariush said a quick goodbye and hurried to the lounge without looking back.

During the drive home, Helga was quiet.

"Is something the matter?" Andrea asked.

"I don't know. I have an uneasy feeling. I hope the servants did not talk. We didn't tell them where we were going but I had to tell Goli we would be gone for three days. I wish we'd been able to reach your husband."

"We tried. I'll explain when I see him." Andrea wondered how he would react when he learned his wife had left the country without his knowledge or permission.

They approached the General's house. There was a crowd outside the front door. They heard the housekeeper yelling hysterically, like she was quarreling with someone. But they could not see who. Their view was blocked by the crowd.

Helga asked the driver to stop. She rolled the window down and stuck her head out. Then she turned to Andrea. "I think Goli is fighting with your husband."

Helga and Andrea got out of the car and made their way to the house. Goli stood her back against the door, both arms outstretched, blocking the doorway.

"No one enters this house without my mistress's permission," she shouted, her face red with rage. "No one. Least of all a bastard like you."

"What is it you want?" Helga's words, spoken in English, cast an immediate spell on the crowd. Everyone was quiet. Several men who had been urging Mani to hit the woman who dared raised her voice against a man, melted instantly into the crowd.

Mani whirled around, an expression of surprise and panic sweeping his face. "I . . . I . . . want my daughter. She won't let me have her. I asked her nicely."

Goli was white with anger. "What's he saying Madame?" she asked disgust apparent in her voice. "He's a liar. He attacked me the minute I stepped out of the car with Kelly. He shoved me to the ground and tried to grab the child from me. I don't know who he is. I wouldn't let her go. He got mad and kicked us, repeatedly. Kelly is hurt bad. She's bleeding from her nose. I told him I expected you home soon. For him to wait. His answer was more kicks. Even beasts should not be allowed to give birth to such a monster."

Goli gathered her long skirt around her legs with both hands and spat a glob of spit where Mani stood.

Andrea felt stark terror in her heart. "Oh my God, Helga, is she saying Kelly is hurt? There's blood all over. Where's Kelly? Where did they take her?"

Helga asked Goli where Kelly was.

"Ibrahim took her inside. He's trying to reach a doctor."

Andrea did not wait for Goli to finish. She tore her way to the house like a woman demented. Ibrahim was in the kitchen talking on the phone. Kelly was on the kitchen floor, her face and chest covered with blood.

Helga entered the kitchen. Goli bolted the front door and followed her mistress in.

"Have you reached a doctor yet?" Helga asked the driver.

"Not yet."

Helga took the phone from Ibrahim. She turned to Andrea. "I'll call Cyrus' brother. He's not a pediatrician but he'll help till we get hold of one."

Andrea murmured something incomprehensible. She grabbed some ice from the freezer, wrapped it in a towel and placed it on Kelly's nose. Kelly screamed.

"Could we take her to an emergency room?" Andrea pleaded.

"We can if you want but it won't do her any good. There may or may not be a doctor available. The nurses are not trained. You'll be taking a chance. She's bleeding profusely. We need help now."

"The doctor said he'll be here shortly."

Helga helped Andrea lift the child and take her to the kitchen sink. They washed her face and neck with cold water. The bleeding was heavy from the nose. They packed it with cotton then turned their attention to her left ear which was also bleeding but less acutely than the nose.

Andrea sat on a kitchen stool with Kelly in her arms. Kelly's eyes roamed from her mother to Helga, a warm expression of love and gratitude flooding her delicate features.

The doctor arrived twenty minutes later, checked Kelly and gave her a shot to stop the bleeding. "She'll be fine," he said. "It's not as bad as it looks."

"What about the bleeding from her ear. Should I have a pediatrician take a look?"

"There's no need. The bleeding will stop but the bruises will take time to heal. Sorry, I have to go. I left a clinic full of patients."

Andrea thanked the doctor and asked him to please send her the bill.

"Forget it," the doctor said and walked out.

Gradually the bleeding stopped. Kelly fell asleep in her mother's arms. Andrea's anxiety mounted with each passing moment. Where could she go? Who could she turn to for help? Did the doctor know what he was talking about when he said Kelly would be fine?

The phone rang. Helga answered it, put the receiver down, then turned to Andrea looking distraught. "That was Cyrus. There have been more bomb threats. The King wants us to move to a safe house near the palace immediately. They're sending a military escort to follow my car. What are you going to do?"

Andrea raised her head, looked at Helga, saw the pained expression on her face, chose to say nothing.

"You can't go home. I don't trust that husband of yours. I know it's impossible to get accommodation in any hotel, but we could try. Would you like me to?"

"I'd appreciate it. Thank you."

Within the hour, the military escort arrived, while Helga, frustrated and upset couldn't find a single vacancy in all the hotels she had been able to reach.

Andrea lifted Kelly and stood. "Well, I better brace myself. It's time to find out what my husband has in store for us."

"Bye Andrea," Helga said, stifling a sob. "Our address and phone number are secret but I'll be in touch. I promise."

"Thank you for everything." She walked over to Goli. "Thank you for taking such good care of Kelly. I hope you're not hurt. Please see a doctor. I'll pay for it."

Goli burst into tears.

She thanked the driver and walked out.

She rang the doorbell and waited. No one opened it. Her arms tired under Kelly's weight.

She rang it again.

Nothing happened.

She shifted the child's head to her shoulder freeing her right hand, searched for the key in her purse, found it and let herself and Kelly in.

The house was quiet. Mani stood erect in the living room, chin up, fists clenched.

Andrea ascended the stairs to their room. She changed Kelly's bloody clothes and gently eased her into her bed.

Mani paced the living room. She could hear his labored breathing. She had witnessed his temper once before. When her parents advised her not to marry him. It was like a volcano smoldering, gathering momentum with each passing moment, then erupting suddenly with uncontrollable rage.

Andrea's heart skipped a beat. The check. She had to find

a safe place to hide it, away from his prying eyes. In her concern over Kelly she'd forgotten about it. She grabbed it from her purse and was about to tuck it in her bra when Mani barged into the room.

"Where were you?" he demanded harshly, his voice full of contempt.

Her back was turned to the door. Had he seen the check. She wasn't sure.

She flashed him a cold stare.

He walked over and grabbed her hair. "I asked you where you were. Answer me."

"Let go. You're hurting me," she said, hoping her voice did not betray her panic.

Tightening his grip more, he pulled her hair savagely forcing her to face him.

"You'd better start talking and fast."

"Let go of my hair."

Her stubborn refusal made his blood boil. He shoved her to the ground and kicked her hard. Again and again.

She felt a warm trickle of blood flowing down her cheek. She tried to get up but the blows kept coming. He was like a mad bull stomping his victim.

"You're a whore," he screamed. "How much did the General pay to sleep with you? How much? When I'm through with you no one will look at you. Not even the garbage man."

The blows kept coming.

Andrea lost consciousness.

She didn't know how much time had passed when she heard voices. Someone was yelling but it didn't sound like Mani. She got up slowly, feeling dizzy and nauseous. The door to their room was partially open. She crept out, stood in a corner hidden from view and looked down. Farhad stood in the living room, his appearance intimidating, his rage directed at Mani.

She heard him say, "Your temper is your downfall. If you don't learn to control it and soon, you're out. I can't cover up for you any more. You've ruined everything. She won't give you a penny. You've tried her mother. You've gotten nowhere. The woman hates you. So what do you do? You beat the daughter unconscious. Forget it my friend. It's over. Finished."

"I'll make it up to her." Mani's voice shook.

"Are you kidding me or yourself? If that wife of yours had any sense she would have left you long ago. It was lucky for us she thought she is a liberated woman. She thought she is defying convention by marrying a foreigner. But you've pushed your luck too far. One of these days she'll find out who you really are. Then you can kiss years of planning and hard work goodbye."

Andrea was so stunned and appalled her mind went blank.

Her roaring lion of a husband remained crouched in a corner looking more like a petrified animal than the beast he was only a few hours earlier when his victim was weaker.

"She loves me too much," he said trying to sound convincing. "Believe me she'll forget. She's like a dog that has been kicked. If you give her a bone, she'll be delighted and won't remember the kick."

"Enough!" Farhad yelled. "You're so smart you think you know everything. With foreigners there is no telling how they'll react. Americans are worse. They'll surprise you every time."

There was no response from Mani.

Andrea's head throbbed. Her right eye was swollen shut. Was she imagining they were saying what they were saying or was her marriage, in reality, a preplotted arrangement to accommodate terrorists and their deadly games. For all their cunning and shrewdness they had not come to check on her. Surely they must know that by now she was either dead or conscious and able to hear what they're saying, especially since they spoke English. But her mother? What had they done to her?

Her brain cells were on strike. They demanded time out. She felt an insufferable need to sleep, to shut the world out. If only Farhad would stop screaming, go away, do something, anything. Sleep. It was an alluring feeling.

She wanted to return to bed when she heard Farhad say, "Give me the check. It's not much but it will do for the time being."

Sleep took an instant second place to her curiosity. Could it be the check Cyrus had given her? She stuck her head cautiously out the door. She saw Mani give Farhad a check. She dug in her bra. The check was gone.

Her first impulse was to rush downstairs and demand that the check be returned to her. But if she did, they'd know she had overheard them. The consequences could be disastrous. She thought of contacting Cyrus or Helga to stop the check from being cashed. But how could she do it without an address or phone number.

"It doesn't make sense," Farhad said. "Why would the General give her a check for four thousand dollars? Why not two or three or whatever? Why four?"

"I don't know. She won't talk. I found the check near her head when she passed out. She must have hidden it in her bra."

"There has to be an explanation," Farhad persisted gruffly.

"I'm sure there is."

"It's not for you to find out. Your methods are barbaric and counter productive. Leave her to me. I think they've paid her to spy on us. No doubt the General is well informed about your past. He'll make it his business to learn what you're up to at present."

"It still doesn't make sense," Mani replied. "He must have used her. Everyone knows what a womanizer he is."

Farhad studied his friend with disdain. "Your stupidity is phenomenal. He doesn't have to pay women to sleep with them. They throw themselves at him. That money is a down payment, a retainer fee. Savak is not strapped for funds. They have all the money they need and they pay their informers handsomely. Who better than a woman who lives with you and who hasn't had much to be happy about lately?"

"That may be so. If she hates me enough she'd probably do it. But not for money. She doesn't need it. She has enough of her own."

"But she's not stupid enough to transfer her money here so you get it. She's biding her time. Given the opportunity, she'll escape without giving you a second thought. I think the only reason she hasn't done so so far is because of the child."

"What . . . What makes you say something like that? She doesn't know what's going on."

"You think so huh? Well, I know otherwise. She's been making inquiries. Very discreetly, but inquiries . . ."

The conversation stopped abruptly. After a few seconds, Farhad asked, "Are you sure Sayid is not home?"

"Positive. I checked his room."

"I heard a noise. Did you hear anything?"

"No, nothing."

Andrea rushed to her room and snuck in bed.

"Let me think . . . It could be her. Go check. If she's awake, don't say a word. Come back immediately."

Mani climbed the stairs quiet as a cat. He could not afford another blunder.

Andrea was in bed, her back turned to the door, her eyes closed. Mani tiptoed downstairs.

"She's sound asleep. I left the door open so we'll know if she wakes up."

Farhad seemed lost in thought. Eventually he said, "You must return the check. We can't cash it. When she finds out it's missing, she'll inform the General. If we cash it before she has a chance to contact him, they'll trace the check to us. Put it under her bed. She'll think she dropped it when she undressed to go to bed."

Mani looked at the check with sorrowful eyes. He loved money, any amount. He wanted that check real bad. But he knew better than argue. He climbed the stairs once again and placed the check under his wife's bed.

"You're sure she's asleep?" Farhad asked.

"Sure I'm sure. She's either dead or asleep."

Farhad gave Mani a penetrating look. "Hope your brother doesn't find out what you've done to her. How come he's made it his business to be her protector?"

"He was madly in love with her when I suddenly appeared on the scene and married her. He left the States the day before we were married. He's hated me since."

"Is he still in love with her?"

"I don't know and I don't care."

"Does she know he's in love with her? If she works with him against us, we'll have more than we can handle."

"Don't worry. She's never been in love with anyone but me."

Farhad slumped on the couch and checked his watch. "I doubt she's still in love with you. It's been an exhausting day and I'm in no mood to discuss your love life. It's five minutes to eleven. They should have called by now."

"Would you like a drink?" Mani asked.

"Bring the Scotch."

For a while, neither man spoke. Andrea thought they had slept.

The phone rang.

She heard Farhad's voice answer it.

Overwhelmed with curiosity, Andrea tiptoed to the door.

Farhad had a monstrous grin on his face. He put the receiver down and announced triumphantly, "Our brothers have succeeded. Two American officers are dead. They were gunned down while waiting for their bus. Let's celebrate." He finished his drink and poured another.

Mani stood rooted to the spot, his face a study of pure ecstasy. "Success at last. Yes, let's celebrate." He raised his glass and downed the contents following Farhad's example.

Stunned and thrown off balance by what she'd witnessed, Andrea felt her knees buckling under her. She reached out blindly and gripped the door knob to steady herself.

Slowly, she pulled herself together, her eyes turned cold, her manner resolute. She would never be the same again.

Chapter 24

She fell into a deep sleep almost immediately after going to bed, the pain and exhaustion temporarily dulled by a feeling of numbness. She needed sleep. Before her marriage she'd never been exposed to the harsher aspects of life, protected by her parents, the immense wealth they had, and the insularity of the U.S. Northwest. She'd been shocked into reality by what she'd seen and heard but the brutalizing experience would have to wait. There would be time enough to deal with it.

She checked Kelly before going to bed. The bleeding had long since stopped. Kelly looked pale. Her pallor was more pronounced than usual, but Andrea had no way of knowing how much blood the child had lost or if the loss was significant. The doctor insisted the fall was not as bad as Goli had led her to believe. Regardless, in the morning, she'd have her checked by a pediatrician.

She woke up a couple of hours later with a throbbing pain in her right eye and realized she'd been dreaming. She dreamt the same dream whenever she was troubled but tonight's dream had a different ending.

She was a little girl, dressed in a pink dress, walking in a wheat field, humming a tune and keeping step with the rhythm. Music flooded the field from everywhere. She looked up and saw her father dressed in his Sunday best come toward her, arms outstretched, waiting to embrace her. She loved him so much. She ran into his arms. He lifted her off the ground and pressed her against his chest.

"Please, Daddy, don't press so hard. You're hurting my eye." She tried to open her eyes but only the left upper eyelid would part. Her right eye was swollen shut. It was the size of a plum and looked like one.

She got up and looked in the mirror. She looked like a boxer who has just lost a fight. Ice. She needed ice to help reduce the swelling.

She had not expected to find her husband in their bed and she wasn't disappointed. She didn't know where he was.

She checked her watch. It was three twenty two. It was better to get the ice before anyone woke up. Mani's mother was always up at dawn reciting her morning prayers. She had not seen her mother-in-law the night before, nor had she seen the maid. No one had approached their room while Mani was yelling and beating her. Could they have gone on a trip?

Groping her way cautiously in the dark, she descended the stairs. The kitchen was a few steps away. The light in the kitchen was left on all night for Sayid. He turned it off before going to bed. Tonight, the house was in total darkness. She did not want to turn the light on in the hallway. There was always the possibility that someone could be asleep on the living room sofa and that someone could be her husband. The last thing she wanted for him to see was what he'd done to her and gloat. Maybe not outwardly, but she was sure he'd gloat.

Probing carefully, she located the light switch in the kitchen and turned the light on. She glanced quickly in the direction of the living room. An empty vodka bottle and two empty glasses were carelessly thrown on the rug. There were two ashtrays full of cigarette butts and a bowl half full of pistachios. No one was asleep on the couch. Had Mani and Farhad left?

She was reaching for an ice tray when she heard a key turn in the lock of the front door. No surprise there. Sayid came home at odd hours.

She wanted to flee to her room but there was no time. Before she could reach the light switch to turn it off, Sayid was in the kitchen. The kitchen was next to the front door. Sayid always went to the kitchen when he came home, got himself a glass of water, and climbed the stairs to his room.

She prayed he would leave. She did not want him to see her bruised face. There was no telling what he'd do if he found out what had happened.

She waited, her back turned to him, pretending she was searching for something in the freezer.

He didn't move.

She had no choice. She took an ice tray and walked to the sink.

He watched her.

She expected him to be drunk but if he'd been drinking, it didn't show. She took a few ice cubes, wrapped them in a washcloth and tried to leave the kitchen.

He grabbed her arm as she walked out.

"Who did that to you?" Anger lined his voice.

She struggled to pull her arm from his grip. A sharp, shooting pain in her shoulder put an abrupt end to her struggle.

Gently, he sat her in a chair, his gaze never leaving her face.

"Do you want to talk about it?" he asked softly.

She put the ice pack on her eye keeping her head bent. She had not looked at him nor did she intend to.

"You don't have to tell me," he said in an expressionless voice. "It's not hard to guess."

Andrea moved the ice pack lower where she felt the

swelling press on her eyeball, sending sharp, shooting pains through her head. If she could make it to her room, she'd take a couple of aspirins to help relieve the pain. But it was not likely that Sayid would let her go without first insisting on knowing what had happened.

What had Mani told Farhad the night before? Oh, yes! She recalled their conversation word for word. "He was madly in love with her when I appeared on the scene and married her. He left the U.S. the day before we were married. He's hated me since."

"Is he still in love with her?"

"Who knows?"

Her recollections of the previous night's encounter between her husband and Farhad were quite vivid. She thought they were real amateurs because they always carried on their discussions in English. It was as though she didn't matter or exist. Consequently, she had to deduce that they chose to speak English because Mani's mother could easily overhear them from her room. That had to be it. Mani could not afford to disillusion his mother. She was convinced Mani was the perfect son and he liked to keep it that way.

Sayid sat across the table from her, his hands cupped around a glass, his gaze focused on Andrea's hand holding the ice pack to her eye.

She got up, poured herself a glass of water and walked out of the kitchen.

He didn't stop her.

She closed the door to her room, took a couple of aspirins, then eased her body into a chair. She hurt all over. It was difficult to move her head. The back of her neck was excruciatingly painful. Mani had kicked her in the head several times. There was a big lump at the base of her skull. It was sore. If he used as much force to kick Kelly, then, regardless of the way she looked, she had to get her daughter to a doctor. First thing in the morning. But how? How could she face the doctor looking the way she did? What would the doctor think?

She checked the child, caressed her forehead, planted a light kiss on her cheek and returned to the chair. It felt like the least movement sent sharp pains from the base of her neck to the top of her head. She moved the improvised ice pack from her right eye and placed it on the swelling on her head.

Suddenly, she heard a commotion downstairs. Someone was yelling and kicking at a door. It sounded like Sayid.

She opened her door and took a peek.

The door of the room which Mani referred to as his office was the target of Sayid's fury. It was closed. He kicked and banged on it cursing in Persian.

A droopy-eyed, totally naked Mani opened the door and looked at his brother through alcohol reddened eyes.

"What do you . . ."

He did not finish his sentence. Sayid knocked him to the ground with a blow meant to kill.

A scream let out by Mani as he spinned down startled Farhad bolting him out of bed. He too was naked.

Knocking his brother down did not seem to satisfy Sayid. He picked Mani off the ground like a rag doll and kept punching him until he fell down practically lifeless.

Mani remained slumped on the floor. Blood from his mouth trickled down his chin. Farhad made no attempt to intervene. Sayid's hobby was boxing. He'd trained in England and was good at it. Those who knew him knew about his hobby. They also knew how vicious he could be when provoked. Few provoked him.

Sayid seemed intent on finishing the job now that the opportunity had presented itself. It was obvious he would not stop until he had hurt his victim badly.

Once again he reached and grabbed Mani by the hair forcing him to stand up and was getting ready to deliver what seemed like the last blow when he heard Andrea scream.

"Stop it!" she yelled from the top of the stairs. It was not her love for her husband that prompted her to yell but the realization of Sayid's enormous strength and his lack of qualms about using it. Also, the consequences of his action disturbed her. No doubt the family would blame her for sawing dissent between the brothers. And if Mani were hurt bad, her mother-in-law would make sure that Andrea paid the price.

She didn't come downstairs. Farhad standing in the room naked looked so silly that despite the gravity of the situation, Andrea had a hard time suppressing a smile.

Sayid raised his eyes and looked at Andrea for a long moment, then he said wearily, "I've wanted to do this for years. I've been waiting for the right moment. Everyone would be better off without such trash littering the world. I restrained myself because you are too young to be a widow."

Mani's groans escalated. "Somebody help me," he cried.

Sayid's face, a picture of hatred and disgust, looked at his brother. "Next time you have an urge to hit someone,try me. But you're too much of a wimp to do that, aren't you?"

Farhad helped Mani to a chair.

Sayid grabbed a robe and threw it at Farhad. "Put this on your lover," he ordered, "and get out of this house. If I ever see you here again I'll break every bone in your body."

Sayid words had a drastic effect on Andrea. She froze on the spot, her grip tight on the banister, her knuckles white. What was Sayid talking about? No, it's impossible. I must have heard wrong. But they were in bed together, naked. I'm losing my mind, imagining things.

Farhad grabbed a robe and put it on.

She heard Mani say, "You heard what Mother said. This is our house. You have no right to make him leave."

"Stop me!" Sayid hollered.

"I'm the first born son. Legally this house belongs to me. I don't care who paid for it."

"And I'd like to remind you," Sayid quipped disgustedly, "it doesn't matter whose house it is. Homosexuality is against the law. I can have you both rot in jail for years to come."

"You'll have to prove it first."

"I'm sure it can be arranged," Sayid retorted coolly.

A door slammed.

Andrea had heard enough. Sayid was no fool. He'd made sure the argument was in English. No doubt he wanted Andrea to find out every gruesome detail of her husband's lifestyle.

She was stupefied, unable to think. The situation seemed surreal, absurd. She drifted giddily to the only chair in the room and fell into it. It was all so futile, so senseless. She felt trapped. A stranger in a strange country surrounded by people with manners impossible to comprehend, consumed with complex hatreds embedded deep in their psyche, to be tapped at will.

Instantly she pulled herself together. Self pity was not for her. She'd gotten herself into this mess, she'd get herself out of it. Her father had often told her, "Defeat only comes to those who let themselves be defeated." Her manner became resolute. This was a man who had turned her world upside down. She'd find a way to get even with him and make him pay for it dearly.

She felt as though the four walls of the tiny room were closing in on her. She paced the room, opened the window, shut the door, went to the window, came back and opened the door. Mani had collapsed in an armchair in the living room, his head thrown back, the naked hatred boiling inside him reflected on his face.

Quietly observing him now she recalled how courteous, charming, friendly and ready to oblige he'd always been in the past. Her perceptiveness should have easily pierced the facade behind which he'd taken refuge until the present, yet she'd had no reason to suspect he'd been putting up a relentless show to camouflage a mediocre mind, obsequious, devoted to death and destruction. His commitment was total. There was no room in his life for much else.

She had to stop deluding herself. Her mind was made up. The details she'd work out later. She closed the door and went and lay down on her bed. Her head felt like a cobbler's workshop, her eye throbbed mercilessly. She put the ice pack on it.

She could hear Sayid's slow, deliberate steps on the stairs. The familiar steps invariably stirred inexplicable sensations in her. He was a bear of a man, taller and bigger than any Iranian she'd seen. Yet, he was gentle and kind when he felt the situation called for it and incredibly versatile in his cruelty with those whom he felt preyed on victims weaker than themselves.

He reached the top of the stairs and knocked on her door.

She didn't stir.

He knocked again.

She hoped he'd tire and leave. Too much had happened in one night. She wanted to be left alone.

He knocked again.

Reluctantly, she got up and opened the door. She did not want his persistent knocks to wake Kelly up.

"I wanted to tell you that if you want to move out, I'll help you."

She tried to answer him but no words would come out.

"Good night," he said and walked to his room a look of infinite sadness in his eyes.

Sunlight seeped into the room through a tear in the curtain. Andrea parted the curtains and looked outside. Dawn was breaking, peacefully, innocently, oblivious of humanity's follies. The street below, strewn with garbage was deserted except for emaciated, half starved dogs savagely searching through the trash for food.

Suddenly, the silence was shattered.

Three cars raced down the street and stopped abruptly in front of their house. Two men in civilian clothes got out of each car. They looked at the house, then at a piece of paper one of them was holding. The other four men positioned themselves, surrounding the place.

A man dressed in a charcoal-gray suit approached the door and rang the bell.

It's got to be Savak, Andrea figured. Just like in a bad detective movie, the leader is dressed in dark gray and they travel in pairs.

She checked the living room. Mani's mother was saying her prayers, her head turned toward Mecca. She knew Naene would not interrupt her prayers for any reason. Someone else would have to open the door.

The ringing continued.

Andrea found the scenario intriguing. The men outside waiting impatiently for the door to be opened; Naene carrying on with the recitation of her prayers regardless of who rang the bell and for how long; Sayid definitely not asleep since he'd been talking to her a few minutes earlier, provided an unexpected diversion. Since she had overheard Farhad and Mani celebrate the assassination of the American officers earlier, there was no doubt in her mind who the secret service men had come for. If Farhad and Mani knew who was at the door, they'd run for their lives.

The man ringing the doorbell conferred with his colleague standing close by. He motioned to a third man to approach, then whispered something in his ear. The third man went to a window facing the street and pounded it with his fist while his colleague pressed the door bell.

A few minutes later, the door opened slowly.

Mani stood in the hall, face swollen with a robe hastily tied around his waist.

One of the men shoved him aside and pushed his way in. He was followed by the man in the gray suit who walked with authority, head held high, very much in command.

"What can I do for you gentlemen?" Mani asked. His voice cracked.

"Is your name Mani Abbassi?" asked the man who had spent the past few minutes ringing the bell. He eyed Mani suspiciously.

"Yes."

"Where's Farhad Moussavi?" It was more an order than a

question.

Mani hesitated.

The same man shoved Mani aside and approached the closed door of Mani's office. He kicked it open. Farhad had his pants on and was busy buttoning his shirt. He pretended to be startled.

"Both of you move over here." The man in the gray suit ordered. Over here was the living room.

Although Mani's mother was through with her prayers soon after her uninvited guests had barged in, she lingered unobtrusively in a corner. She didn't escape detection. When the agents had both men in their presence, they ordered her to go to her room.

"Where were you last night?" the leader yelled with a malevolent glare.

Farhad made inaudible sounds, then looked at the men, saw the murderous expression on their faces and immediately found his voice. Andrea had never heard him speak so softly before. "We were here all night," he said.

The leader seemed to find Farhad's meekness particularly irritating. "You were getting dressed," he snapped impatiently. "Where were you planning to go this early in the morning?"

Farhad seemed paralyzed by fear. He could barely talk. But remaining quiet could cost him his life. Everybody knew that. "Nowhere," he murmured.

"Why were you dressing up?"

"I . . . I . . . heard voices outside."

"Do you always dress up when you hear voices outside?" his tormenter demanded in an accusatory tone.

Farhad shuffled his weight from one foot to the other. He opened his mouth to speak but what he said was unintelligible. He was trembling.

The leader turned to Mani. "Put your clothes on. Both of you. You're coming with us."

Andrea saw Mani cast a worried glance at Farhad. There

was no reaction from Farhad. Seeing the shape he was in, forced a sad smile on Andrea's lips. Farhad, her husband's boss, his lover, his genius friend who was always full of advice and brilliant suggestions, stood white as a ghost, almost catatonic ready to pass out.

"Please," Mani said, "you don't have to take our word for it. My wife is American. She was home. I'll go wake her. She'll confirm what I've just told you."

Quietly, Andrea closed her door and slipped into bed.

A few seconds later, a distraught Mani barged into the room. "Andrea, wake up!" He shook her forcefully. "Wake up." He was having trouble breathing.

She opened her left eye grudgingly and looked at him. "Put your robe on and come down right now. It's an emergency."

He dashed downstairs.

"I bet it is!" she said out loud.

She took her time with her robe then descended the stairs slowly, making sure she looked and acted sleepy.

Instantly, the eyes of the men in the room were riveted on the slender figure approaching calmly, possessed with a cool poise and confidence. Seeing her swollen eye they exchanged quick, knowing glances.

"Gentlemen," Mani said with a rush of excitement. "This is my wife, Andrea. Ask her any question you have, in English, please. She doesn't speak Farsi." He took a step back, looking pleased with himself. This was his stroke of genius. Maybe now his colleagues would have more respect for him.

Andrea didn't move.

Mani approached his wife, held her gently by the arm and led her to where the man in the gray suit stood.

The man stubbed out his cigarette slowly while carefully studying Andrea's bruised and swollen face.

She remained unflinching under his steady gaze.

The air vibrated with tension.

The man cast a disdainful glance at Mani's anxious and strained face, then half turned and asked in perfect English, "Madam, were you home all night last night?"

Perhaps because of the rapid succession of events, or nerves, or reasons which she failed to understand, Andrea found herself suddenly in a taunting mood. She wanted to prolong the drama. She put on a disarming smile and said provokingly, "Sir, you speak English superbly." She moved closer to him smiling innocently. "I can't place the accent. It's British, isn't it?"

The man in the gray suit did not seem amused. "Madam," he retorted angrily, "answer my question. Were you home all night last night?"

"Of course I was. Where else would I be?"

"Were these two men in this house all night?"

The eyes of everyone in the room were focused on her.

She glanced at Mani. He did not seem worried. He looked expectantly at her, his expression revealing his trust, the certainty that she'd never let him down.

Calmly and deliberately Andrea flashed an icy glare at him. She faced the agent. "I have no idea. I was sound asleep."

Chapter 25

A visit by somber looking men, always traveling in pairs, knocking on doors any time of day or night, invariably portended doom. Iranians lived in dread of that moment, guilty or not. Any law in the country could be bent or broken. However, the law assuming a person guilty until proven innocent was a way of life few dared question or challenge.

Mani's mother was no fool. She had been banished to her room by Savak agents when her son was being questioned but that had helped fire her imagination and put her senses on full alert. Those men were treacherous and despicable. Her son helpless, innocent, victimized. It was imperative for her to know exactly what was going on, her duty as a mother.

She was a shrewd woman. She decided not to make a fuss when told to make her presence scarce in the hopes that if she did not attract too much attention, the agents would forget her.

They did.

Hidden behind a slightly open door, she listened and watched with absolute concentration.

So it was that immediately after the agents left with her

son and his friend, she dragged her multi fat-layered body convulsively into the living room in a state of hysteria, crying, pulling her hair, calling on Mohammed the prophet and the Almighty God to come to her son's rescue. She sat on the carpet in the living room, legs folded, a soiled handkerchief in her hand used to pound the carpet and wipe her tears. Andrea knew the theatrics was more for Sayid's benefit than Mohammed's or God's. It was a tactic Andrea had witnessed before with hundred percent success rate.

Naene never referred to Andrea by her name. Special derogatory words like negis, meaning unclean, khariji, foreigner and pedar seg, fathered by a dog, were her words of choice for her daughter-in-law. Her laments were full of those words.

The wailing continued, her hysteria feeding upon itself, gaining in intensity and vigor with each passing moment.

As always, her plan was right on target.

Sayid descended the stairs and walked over to where his mother had prostrated herself, flat on her face. He lifted her onto the sofa and sat next to her. "Stop your crying," he said. "You're giving me a headache."

"A headache!" she yelled back her voice full of disbelief. "A headache! You're worried about a headache when your brother is facing death. This house is cursed, unclean. Get her out of here. Out. I don't want her in my house another minute."

She stopped crying, went down on her knees, pleading, begging, "You're the only person who can save Mani. I beg of you. Do it for me. Don't let me go to my grave with a broken heart. Your conscience will gnaw your guts, destroy you like a malignant cancer."

Andrea felt sorry for Sayid. It was clear she'd nag until she got him to comply. And, under the circumstances, time was crucial. She pressed on. "He's your brother. You've enough contact in Savak to free him with one phone call and you're sitting here doing nothing. What black days have descended upon us! God have mercy." She renewed her sobbing with increased vigor.

Sayid rose, his face an expressionless blank. He climbed the stairs and knocked on Andrea's door. Without waiting for her to answer he said, "You'd better pack your things."

"Did she order you to throw us out?" Andrea shot back angrily.

"I don't take orders from anybody. I have to free her darling son, otherwise, she won't shut up."

"Lucky for him he has a brother like you."

"I didn't have any choice in the matter," he retorted icily.

"You have a choice now. Why don't you let him get what's coming to him. It might teach him a thing or two."

"You don't know what you're talking about. If they decide they need a scapegoat to pacify the American government or to prove to the Shah that they have not lost their touch, no one in their grip will escape permanent damage. They play rough with their victims before they dispose of them. Ordinarily, I wouldn't give it a second thought even if it involved my brother but my mother has already been through it once . . ." He stopped, looking horrified at his own indiscretion.

There was a chilling instant. Andrea's thoughts raced. Who could it be? Was it a factor in her husband's consuming hatred of the Shah?

"Was it your father?" It seemed strange to Andrea that their father's death was never discussed.

"My father died of a stroke," Sayid said stiffly. His manner forbade further discussion.

Mention of Savak's excesses reminded her of Layla. Andrea had not seen her since before Irene's party. Aside from wanting to reach a pediatrician for Kelly, she wanted to locate Phil Conrad and check on Layla and her children. But the succession of events had made it impossible.

"Pack up. You don't want to be here when your husband and his friend return." Sayid was not an alarmist. He continued with the same monotonous voice, "If he does not make you pay for your indiscretion, his friends will. I'd keep a low profile for a while if I were you."

Andrea shook uncontrollably. Her mind had turned into a jungle. "Where do you propose we go?"

"I'll make arrangements for you to stay at the International Hotel. It's relatively clean. We'll register you under a different name."

She knew he was right. The atmosphere was too charged for Kelly and her to stay in the house and her mother-in-law wanted her out. "There's not much to pack."

"I'll make arrangements for a room."

"How?" It was common knowledge. Hotel rooms were almost impossible to get. Foreign companies doing business in Tehran paid exorbitant sums to middle men to reserve rooms for their people.

"In this country everything is possible. It works on the whom-you-know system of personal connections. I happen to know a few."

He left and was back in less than five minutes. "A room will be ready for you within the hour. The number is three thirteen. Take the key from the receptionist, go to your room and stay there until I let you know it's safe to leave. Don't give your real name to anyone. If you have problems, call me at this number." He scribbled the number on a piece of paper and gave it to her.

Naene must have gotten tired of waiting for her son to finish pampering the foreigner. "Come down," she yelled impatiently. "Let's go."

"There's no need for you to come," Sayid shot back. "I'll get him out. Don't worry."

"I want to come. I'm an old woman. I've been to Mecca. They'll know I don't lie. They'll believe me when I tell them my son and his friend were home all night, in this house."

Sayid tried to convince his mother nothing she said or did would make the slightest difference but his mother was adamant. She insisted on accompanying him to wherever Mani was being held and telling them her story. According to her, no true Muslim would doubt the word of a Hadji, a person who had made the pilgrimage to Mecca, cleansed herself of past sins and lived life in strict adherence to the teachings of the Koran.

"Sit down and wait," he replied with an exasperated tone of voice. "I don't know where they are. There are dozens of interrogation centers. I have to call before we go. Say your prayers. It might do us both good."

Her expression was a perfect blend of scorn, churlishness and wounded pride. She muttered a few incomprehensible words, her lips compressed, her brows knitted. Moving back and forth the living room as fast as her heavy frame would permit, she pulled her chaddor over her head securing it in place with her teeth. The message was clear. She was ready to go.

Sayid went to Andrea's room, picked Kelly from her bed, then took her and placed her carefully in the back seat of the car.

Andrea picked up her suitcase and walked down the stairs. She ached all over and could hardly walk. She was having trouble keeping her balance and her sanity.

He rushed over, grabbed the suitcase, held her arm and walked her to the car. Andrea wanted Kelly in her lap. He lifted her from the back seat and placed her in Andrea's arms.

Paradoxically, it had been easier to think of him as a drunken, good-for-nothing, ill-tempered gambler. Sayid's human side, left her confused, uncertain of what to expect. It was like dealing with two persons.

Before he could drive off, Sayid's mother intercepted their departure, planting herself directly in the path of the car. She was livid. Froth poured from her mouth in a mass of bubbles. "Let her take a taxi and go where she wants. We have no time to waste when your brother's life is at stake. The longer we delay going to his rescue the worst off he'll be."

Andrea saw Sayid's expression change from disapproving silence to icy fury. The contractions of his eyebrows grew denser. He swallowed hard, slowly, fighting to stay calm. But the calm was deceptive. Andrea felt it coming. He could defy tradition, deeply ingrained in all Iranians to respect their elders, and vent his fury on the woman who seemed to have no idea when to stop.

He gave her a long hard look. "Do you want to see your son alive again?"

"Are you threatening me?" Naene yelled incredulously. "Who's more important, your brother or a worthless woman who betrays her husband?"

He'd had enough. His patience taxed mercilessly, he exclaimed with unusual harshness, "Shut up woman. We'll go when I'm ready. If that's not to your liking, go on your own. But for God's sake stop pestering me!"

She burst into tears casting hurried glances up and down the street. Passers by stopped and stared. A captive audience guaranteed, she raised her arms high, palms open, all the while shouting lethal threats at Westerners and begging her merciful God to relieve her of the corrosive, putrefying influence of nonbelievers.

Sayid got out of the car, walked over, held his mother by the arm and took her inside.

A few minutes later he returned, sat behind the wheel and drove off.

The fifteen mile ride took over an hour in the horrendous, unruly, Tehran traffic. Sayid checked the rearview mirror repeatedly. Andrea thought of asking him to stop briefly at Layla's house so she could check on them, but decided not to considering the mood he was in.

There was no place to park. Sayid double parked and told Andrea to wait in the car. He gave the suitcase to a bellhop and went in. Andrea looked at Kelly. The child was still asleep. She'd slept through all the commotion and the noise. Strange. Kelly was a light sleeper.

Sayid opened the car door. "Sorry about the delay. It's a good thing I checked. There was one bed in the room after I specifically told them to have two. They brought a cot for Kelly. Here's the key. The elevator is across the hall. Go directly to your room. I'll bring Kelly."

The hotel was an unpretentious building. The reception area looked clean. A mixture of Iranian carpets and imitation European furniture decked the lobby. A few dust laden paintings hung asymmetrically on gray walls.

Andrea opened the door to a sunny, small room with standard, boring hotel furniture. There was one window. It overlooked the heavily trafficked main street. It didn't have a screen. She hadn't seen screens anywhere in Tehran or Pahlavi in spite of the myriads of insects which plagued the inhabitants.

Sayid arrived promptly carrying Kelly. "Have you touched Kelly's forehead?" he asked.

"Yes. Why?"

"I'm no expert on children but she looks drowsy, her forehead and body feel hot."

He placed Kelly on the cot. The child opened her eyes briefly then went back to sleep. He turned to Andrea, his eyes betraying his sleeplessness, the thick black eyelashes holding the eyelids down covering his eyes half shut. "I have to go. Hopefully, my mother's laments did not invite the neighborhood over for a consolation party. She's not very patient when her favorite son is involved. Call me if you need me. Bye."

Andrea walked over to Kelly. She touched the child's forehead. It was hard to tell whether she had a fever or not. She didn't have a thermometer. The hotel was in a part of town she wasn't acquainted with. She didn't know if there was a drugstore within walking distance and the idea of leaving Kelly alone in strange surroundings did not appeal to her. She rang for a bellboy, gave him a large tip and asked him to buy her a thermometer.

She was ready to collapse physically and emotionally. Yet

an intense stabbing pain shooting down her spine reminded her of the maniacal beating she had been subjected to. A consuming hatred mushroomed in her for the man whose monumental poverty of mind and soul had snuffed out the last ray of hope she had of adjusting to a world where diversity and adversity, cultural, social, religious and political battled to coexist unsuccessfully.

Her internal debate convinced her to fight. It was unthinkable to condemn a whole nation because of the twisted mind of one man. She was the product of a generation which believed in the brotherhood of men, fight against war and prejudice, with love. She couldn't alienate herself from those beliefs. Yet faced with seemingly unsurmountable obstacles, she found it hard to accept it as a regular diet and return for seconds. It was an oppressive atmosphere which mindlessly suppressed higher thought.

Presently, the bellboy returned with a thermometer. It was in centigrade. Andrea took Kelly's temperature but couldn't interpret the reading. She had to get hold of a doctor.

She called the desk. The doctor was in the operating room with an emergency. He would call her soon.

She took two aspirins and tried to relax, to untangle the jumble which her thoughts had become. She dozed.

But not for long.

She was startled by a knock on the door. Impossible. Only Sayid knew where she was. Why would he return so soon? Were they followed? Was that why Sayid checked his rearview mirror repeatedly?

There was another knock.

No need to be alarmed. It could be a hotel employee checking to see if everything was in order.

Another knock.

She got up, opened the door a crack. A man stood in the doorway. He looked like a foreigner, an American perhaps.

A genuine look of pleasure brightened the man's face.

"Andrea?" he asked. "Andrea Sorensen?"

Chapter 26

"Who are you?" Andrea asked.

"Philip Conrad. U.S. Embassy. May I come in?"

Andrea looked at a man in his early thirties, tall, with light brown hair, blue, intelligent eyes. He was dressed in casual clothes projecting an air of gruff masculinity.

"Oh, yes. I tried to reach you but couldn't. I was given the wrong number."

"I'd like to talk to you."

Her vision was cloudy. She tried to wipe her left eye, but the blur remained. The throbbing in her right eye had ceased but the swelling would not permit any movement of the eyelid. It remained shut.

"Is it urgent?" She turned her face. She didn't want it scrutinized.

"No. It can wait. I'll come back later."

She hesitated, her face tensed up, then looking at him quizzically, she asked, "How did you find us?"

His friendly smile was an invitation for her to relax. "I'll tell you about it tomorrow, around eight in the evening.

Would that be a good time for you?"

"I think so." The internal injuries were easy to hide but her swollen face and eye were testimony to her agony.

"Is there anything I can do to help," he asked.

"No, thanks."

"Bye."

She closed the door and stretched on the bed, struggling to stay awake, waiting for the doctor's call.

She awoke feeling apprehensive. The room was dark. A look out the window affirmed her guess was correct. She had slept through the day.

Kelly! She had neglected the child. She switched on the light. Kelly was awake. She rushed over and embraced her. The child moaned. When she tried to lift her, Kelly let out an ear-piercing scream. Perhaps she had a fracture. She undressed the child and checked her. Goli said her father had kicked her head and her side. Could she have internal bleeding?

A nagging thought resurfaced from a murky corner of her mind. Kelly had refused to eat or drink since her fall. Now she was gagging and trying to throw up but her stomach was empty. Nothing but froth dribbled down her chin.

She called the desk. The receptionist assured her he was doing his best to locate the doctor. It was six twenty three.

By eight o'clock there was still no sign of a doctor. She called the desk again only to be told that the shift had changed and the receptionist on duty knew nothing about it.

"Could you please try?" Andrea pleaded.

"Right away, Madam."

By nine o'clock Andrea's frustration had turned into fury. Kelly's moans and the froth from her mouth had increased. She called again. The receptionist assured her he was working on it.

"Call another doctor or an ambulance. I don't care which. I need help and I need it now."

"Yes, Madam."

At ten thirty, a bold, old man, breathing with difficulty finally arrived. His examination of the child lasted less than five minutes.

"There's nothing wrong with her," he said. "She's coming down with the flu. It's going around. Do you have aspirin?"

"Yes." Andrea's fears were not assuaged. Her anxiety was building to a pitch. Kelly needed competent medical attention. Not a superficial examination.

"Don't worry. She'll be fine." He closed his medical bag and walked to the door.

"Is there a drugstore nearby?"

"No, and even if there was, they'd be closed now. Aspirin is all she needs."

"Is it possible to find thermometers in Fahrenheit?"

"No."

"Do you have a moment? Could you tell me how to read a centigrade thermometer?"

"You don't need a thermometer," he replied impatiently. "Give her an aspirin. I'll leave the bill at the desk."

"Thank you. Sorry to have bothered you this late at night."

His reply was a grunt as he made a hasty exit.

Kelly's cheeks were red. The usual pallor which had always been a part of her complexion had moved down to her body. It looked waxen. She rested, her breathing faster than usual.

She tried to coax Kelly to swallow an aspirin. It prompted an immediate reflex inducing her to vomit. Exhausted, she relapsed into a deep sleep.

It was almost midnight. Andrea paced the small room, forcing herself not to panic and assess her options. Should she call Sayid? She didn't feel comfortable imposing on him. According to Mani, Sayid gambled every night. He might resent the intrusion.

She approached Kelly's bed. Her pale, little hands were on her chest, where her mother had placed them. An angel,

Andrea thought. A sweet, lovable, harmless, innocent angel. God, how I love her!

"I hate to disturb you Kelly." She always spoke to her. It was irrelevant that Kelly could not answer. "I'd like to check your diaper dear."

It was dry except for a drop of blood.

Ashen-faced, she looked at it again and again. It couldn't be! Where did the blood come from?

She replaced it with a fresh diaper then tried to change her position.

Kelly shrieked.

It was then that she saw blood on the pillow where Kelly's left ear had been resting.

Paralyzed with fear, she remained transfixed, her eyes glued to the red blotch on the pillow. There was no mistake. It was blood and it was fresh. She called the desk. "How long will it take to get an ambulance?"

"I'll check and call you back soon."

An hour later she still hadn't heard. Time had little meaning in Iran. Soon could mean anything from an hour to weeks to months.

She called back. "Do you have any idea how long it will be?"

"Soon, I hope."

Faced with a brick wall of incompetence and indifference, she decided to take matters into her own hands. She wrapped Kelly in a blanket, grabbed her purse and descended the stairs to the lobby, making her way quickly to the sidewalk in front of the hotel.

Transportation was difficult to find during the day but more so at night. There was no public transportation system to speak of except for a few run down busses with no known routes or time schedule. She thought of calling a cab but the call cabs were notoriously unpredictable. She decided to wait for an orange cab. Luckily, soon, an orange cab came crawling down the road. She waved frantically. The driver stopped and told her to get in. Ordinarily, orange cabs picked customers along the way. Andrea offered to pay the full fare if he'd drive to a hospital without making stops.

"What hospital?" he asked.

"Do you know a good one?"

"Pars Hospital."

"How much?" Andrea asked. The fare had to be agreed upon by passenger and driver because foreigners were often overcharged.

Ignoring her question he asked, "Daughter sick?" He sounded genuinely concerned.

"Yes."

"Don't worry. We go hospital."

He seemed like a kind, old man until he uttered his last sentence. The fact that the child was sick seemed to have given him an instant license for lunacy. He drove maniacally, his hand on the horn, through red lights, over sidewalks and when he could not carve enough space on the road for his small, Iranian made Peykan, he stuck his head out, cussed and yelled.

Andrea clung to Kelly, petrified of the near misses and the sudden stop and zoom driving which seemed to characterize most Iranian drivers, but this was the worse she'd ever encountered.

He must have realized how terrified she was. "No be afraid. This only way to get to hospital. Ambulance no good. Nobody move. I make noise they know somebody sick. We go, yes?"

Finally, they reached the hospital. She could see the sign. Pars Hospital. She sighed relieved.

The driver turned the engine off, rushed back and opened the door.

"I take her," he offered, reaching for Kelly. "You go talk, yes?"

He's probably expecting a big tip, Andrea thought.

The admissions' clerk informed her there were no beds

available in pediatrics or surgery. She could take the patient to the emergency room. A doctor would see her soon.

"I hate that word soon!" Andrea said to no one in particular and without waiting for an answer went to the lobby to fetch Kelly.

She took a five hundred rial note from her purse and offered it to the driver, a day's income for most drivers. She felt she owed it to him since he offered to help without being asked.

An impatient, perplexed look clouded his face momentarily. He pushed her hand away gently yet with a force and finality which surprised her. "Where we go?"

"Emergency room."

The nurse helped the driver place Kelly on the examination table. The driver slipped out of the room quietly. Assuming that he was ready to go, Andrea asked the nurse if she could leave Kelly with her for a couple of minutes. She wanted to pay the driver. The nurse said she wasn't needed until the doctor came.

The driver refused to leave and he refused the money.

"I'd like to stay, help," he said simply.

"Don't you have work to do?" she asked, her confusion growing in direct ratio to his kindness, a rare experience lately.

"No work," he replied shrugging his shoulders. "I make sure daughter good, yes?"

Something about him made her think of her father. Perhaps his simplicity, his honesty, or the concern he had for others without expecting anything in return, a rare quality in a country which thrived on extracting what they could from whoever they could.

She stood watching him, not knowing what to say.

He spoke, his voice tight with emotion, "Please, no go. My daughter, she die. Ten year old. I love her. Iran, men want boy. I want girl. I have one. She die. Cholera. Much people die. Very bad."

Andrea watched as slowly a few tears found their way down his bony cheeks.

"I'm so sorry," she said, giving his hand a gentle squeeze.

He wiped his eyes with his hands. "Me, no go."

A doctor was being paged for the emergency room.

"I have to get back," Andrea said. "I'll talk to you later."

Pars Hospital was privately owned by a group of American trained doctors. It was well equipped and well staffed. The emergency room, although not quite up to American standards was nonetheless the best in the country.

"How long has she been sick?" the doctor asked.

"Two days."

The doctor examined Kelly carefully. He turned to Andrea. "I have to catheterize her. Her bladder is very distended. Has she had any fluids?"

"I tried. She couldn't keep it down."

"We have to admit her. She has to be kept under observation and we need to run tests."

"I was told at the desk there were no vacancies."

"Dress her, please. She'll be admitted to the intensive care unit."

He returned shortly. "You need to sign the admission form. But your signature alone is not enough. We have to have her father's signature as well."

"I'm sorry. I'm afraid that's not possible."

"The father's signature is required by law," the doctor said. "In his absence that of the next male kin is acceptable. But you have to prove the father is either deceased or out of the country."

It was impossible to forget how intensely male dominated the society was.

"Let's say we're separated and I don't know where he is. Does that mean you won't admit her?" She fought to quell the tears welling in her eyes.

He studied her for a moment, started to say something, then stopped. He sighed heavily like a man who is given multiple choices yet no choice at all.

"I'm only a doctor. I can't make or change the law. Your daughter is very sick. My duty is to treat her. Your duty is to make sure the paperwork is in order. How you do it is your business. I have given orders for her admission. If she's not admitted today, she won't make it through the next."

The depth and the intensity of his remarks felt like a screw driver poking an open wound. She nodded mutely, sick with fright.

An orderly brought a stretcher and Kelly was transferred to the intensive care unit. There were four beds in the room. A young woman was asleep in one bed. The other two were not occupied.

The nurse started an intravenous solution on Kelly. Andrea was advised to stay with her daughter. The man who had followed her to the ICU had to leave.

"I'll wait outside," the driver offered.

"Please go," Andrea said, again offering money. "It's late. I can't thank you enough. I don't even know your name but I'll never forget your kindness."

"My name is Vartan," he said proudly. "I wait."

She couldn't understand his stubbornness, nor his pride in his name but she felt it was useless to pursue the matter further.

The doctor came in. He inserted a catheter in Kelly's bladder, attached it to a tube leading to a bottle to drain the urine. "May I have a few minutes of your time, please. I have a few questions about her past medical history and about her present condition."

Andrea had dreaded the moment, but it was inevitable. She gave brief answers to his probing questions.

Exasperated, the doctor pulled the stethoscope from his neck. "I don't know who you're protecting or why. Your reluctance to cooperate is not good for you or your child."

Andrea was silent. She knew he was right. The truth would be revealed eventually. All he had to do was look at her eye. The swelling had decreased but there was a purple circle around it. She had worn dark glasses during the day but had to remove it when it became difficult to see at night in the dimly lit halls.

"I think she has intracranial hemorrhage," the doctor continued. "A simple fall could hardly cause the extensive bleeding I suspect she's having. Blood on the diaper means internal bleeding, most probably due to trauma. We have to do an electroencephalogram, blood, urine and stool tests and take it from there."

She was devastated. Her skin felt clammy, her hands began to tremble. She was quiet, mulling over his words, fearful her voice would betray her feelings. But the seriousness of the situation demanded her cooperation. "When will you know?"

"When all the tests are completed."

"What are her chances of recovery if she has internal bleeding?"

He remained silent.

"Please tell me," she implored. "I want to know."

The doctor shrugged helplessly. "It would be much easier to give you a tentative prognosis if I knew the cause. Handicapped children are prone to pneumonia. They don't respond to treatment as well. We'll consult a neurosurgeon tomorrow." Then as an afterthought he added tersely, "That's if you agree."

Forcing herself to remain calm, she asked, "Somehow I get the feeling you don't trust me. Why wouldn't I want a neurosurgeon to check her?"

"Okay. I'll be blunt with you. Your daughter couldn't have fallen and hurt herself this badly. So how do you explain the massive bleeding in her head. She's also having internal bleeding. You can see for yourself. The catheter from her bladder is draining blood. Kidney damage most probably. Either from trauma or infection. In any case, because of the seriousness of her condition, the police have to be notified.

It's the law."

She felt like she was in a cold shower in sub zero temperature, numbed, uncomprehending. "Do you have to notify them right away?"

He gave her a long, compassionate look. "I should but I could be busy and not have time. Looking at you, at your daughter, and from your cautious replies, it's not difficult to surmise who did it. My wife is American. I've lived in the States for many years. Even so we have trouble reconciling our differences. Conflicting expectations gain in intensity in this environment where East is supposed to meet West. In reality they clash, often fiercely, leaving in their path disillusionment and chaos. For the moment, the child's well-being is what matters. For that she needs her mother. Notifying the police will have to wait."

"Thank you for understanding doctor," she said relieved. "It would be me my word against his. I doubt my word would mean much."

"It won't. I'll tell the nurse to give you an ice pack. Put it on your eye. Good night."

She pulled a chair and sat facing Kelly, her cold hand lifeless in hers.

She did not know how long she'd been sitting there, limp, consumed, unaware of the possibility of life beyond the bed she was staring at.

"Madame."

She sprang to her feet.

Vartan stood in the doorway.

He had a broad grin on his face. "I brought you something to eat. My wife make soup. Fresh Barbari bread. You eat."

He removed a small pot which was wrapped in a rag and placed it on the bedside table. Then he dug into his coat pocket and presented her with a spoon. The bread was loosely wrapped in an old newspaper. It was still warm. Overcome by his excessive, unexpected kindness, she threw her arms around him and hugged him.

He beamed like a little boy receiving praise for a good deed.

"You have renewed my faith in humanity. I'll never forget this."

"No forget. You eat, I happy. Yes? I come tomorrow. Good night."

"Good night." She felt elated for the first time in years, her belief in the goodness of man reconfirmed.

Chapter 27

Andrea spent the night on a chair next to Kelly's bed, dozing on and off. Kelly slept peacefully.

The doctor came in the morning, checked her and ordered X-Rays and tests. There was no change in the child's condition.

After the doctor left, Vartan appeared in the doorway.

"Daughter good today?"

"The doctor says she's about the same," Andrea replied. Then seeing Vartan's face droop, she added, "They're running tests. Maybe when they start treatment, she'll get better."

Vartan was quiet for a while, then suddenly, his face lit up as though he had stumbled on a discovery. "This Sunday, I light candle, in church. You know, candle, church?"

Andrea was touched and confused. Most Iranians were Muslims. They did not light candles in churches. Yet here was a man who seemed convinced that lighting a candle in church would help her daughter recover. Maybe he was Christian. His name did not sound Muslim.

"Thank you. That's very thoughtful of you."

"Maybe God busy, yes?" he continued eagerly. "Maybe he sleep. Light from candle wake him up, yes?"

"I'm sure it will."

"I come see you tonight."

After he left, she was alone with her thoughts, battling the doctor's words still ringing in her ears. If his tentative diagnosis was confirmed by tests, the road to recovery would be slow and expensive. She was determined not to transfer money from the States. Despite Mr. Griffith's objections, Mr. Taha was back working at the bank, an ideal arrangement for Mani and Farhad. The money Mr. Griffith informed her was in the bank for her, had to have come from Sayid. Sayid had done too much for her already. She had not and would not take advantage of his generosity. She had retrieved the check for four thousand dollars which the sheikh had given her from under her bed where Mani had placed it. But if Kelly needed surgery or long term treatment, four thousand dollars would not last long, especially if she had to pay hotel bills.

The only solution she could think of was to remove her belongings to the hospital and cancel her reservations at the hotel. If she followed this course and Kelly got better, they'd have no place to go.

A nurse entered the room.

"There's a gentleman in the lobby. He says he wants to talk to you."

"Me?" No one knew she was in the hospital except Vartan.

"You are Mrs. Abbassi, aren't you?"

"Yes. Did he say who he was?"

"I didn't ask. He said it was important."

"Please ask him to come up."

A few minutes later, the elevator door opened and Philip Conrad stepped out.

Andrea waited outside the intensive care unit. She saw him approach. She was scared. If Philip Conrad could locate her, so could her husband.

"Remember me?" he asked smiling broadly.

"Yes."

"Is there some place we can talk?"

"The waiting room."

They sat facing each other in vinyl-covered armchairs.

"You're a difficult person to keep track of," he began amiably. "I learned from the hotel clerk about your daughter's illness. I think I've been to every hospital in town."

"How . . . how did you know about the hotel? Who told you where to find us?"

"I went to your house to talk to you. Your husband said you were in Pahlavi. I knew the General and his wife had flown to Lebanon but I didn't know you'd gone with them. I called. The housekeeper informed me you had. I've come to apologize. I'm afraid my conversation with your husband must have prompted him to call you."

So that's why Mani had called and that's how he knew she'd left the country. But how did Philip Conrad know?

"I'm sorry about your daughter," he continued. "I feel terrible."

The more he talked, the more the extent of his knowledge baffled her. "How did you find out?"

"I'm in charge of the General's safety. And I'm a friend of the family. Helga told me about your daughter and asked me to find out how she was. She couldn't come because she's leaving for Germany this afternoon. Her father had a stroke."

"I'm sorry to hear that. Please thank her for me. They're running a lot of tests on Kelly. She's in X-Ray now. We won't know until the results come in."

"Can I help? Please allow me. Probably none of this would have happened had I not gone to your house and talked to your husband."

"But you said you went there to see me. Why?"

"Your mother called the Embassy. She asked us to contact you. Your husband has written two letters asking for money. He claimed you were sick in the hospital. He needed money to pay the bill."

So that's what Mani had been up to.

"Did my mother do so?" She had overheard Farhad mention Mani's failure to make her mother comply, but they might have tried again.

"No. She wanted us to contact you first."

Andrea felt relieved and spent.

There was an easy way about Philip Conrad, a warmth which soothed her nerves. She felt she could trust him, confide in him. Ordinarily, she would have preferred indifference to concern but these were not ordinary times. The problems were far too complex, the events too unpredictable and the results intolerable. There were too many details crowding her mind, demanding immediate attention. Her husband's unquenchable thirst for money and persistent efforts to get it, had to be stopped. Under no circumstances should her mother be duped by her son-in-law. She wondered if her visitor knew or suspected why Mani needed funds.

She had to take a chance before it was too late. Mani would find out soon enough about Kelly's illness and use it as an excuse to extract money from her mother. He'd have no trouble getting a statement from the hospital in support of his claim or forging her signature.

She felt she could and had to trust the man who was scrutinizing her but she was not sure he trusted her. "It's difficult for me to leave my daughter alone. There are no mailboxes in the city that I know of. I'd like to send a message to my mother. If I wrote her a note could you mail it for me?"

"No problem. I can do better than that. We promised to call her when we got in touch with you. We can give her the message over the phone tonight." Then, almost as an afterthought, he added, "Unless of course you don't want us to know what the message is."

She knew her suspicion was well founded. He did not trust her. "When you talk to my mother," she said calmly, "please tell her not to send any money to my husband. Ever."

"Consider it done." He studied her for a moment, then added, "Legally our hands are tied. We can't help you. You're an Iranian subject. But that could change."

Intrigued, she asked, "How?"

"If you cooperate with us . . ."

"Cooperate? What do you mean?"

It seemed like forever before he spoke again. "We need your help. But before we proceed I've got to be certain, very certain about your allegiance. There are matters in your past which give us reason to be cautious."

"Oh?"

He did not hesitate. "Our information is based on your life with your husband in the States," he said noncommittally. "We think you knew your husband belonged to a cell bent on the destruction of the monarchy in Iran. We are fully aware of his activities and so is Savak. If our assumption is correct, you married him and stayed married to him knowing he was a terrorist."

"Your assumption is wrong. I had no idea and no reason to suspect him. You can think I was naive, blinded by love or whatever. I heard rumors of course, and I questioned him about it. He dismissed them as a smear campaign by Savak to intimidate students abroad."

"That's true to a point. Our main concern is the safety of our citizens who live here. That's where you come in."

"How?"

"A few more assassinations and it will be impossible to recruit employees to come here. Many of our companies are heavily committed with long term projects and millions of dollars in investments. Terrorist activities make people nervous."

"That may be so but there's a lot of resentment toward the present regime. Don't you think change is long overdue?"

"We're working on it. In our opinion, gradual change is better than revolution. We all know the Shah is an absolute dictator but he is pro West and he is ruthless with communists.

For the time being, that's all we can hope for."

"What about human rights? Should we close our eyes to what goes on here because not to do so would threaten our interests? And that's not to say that I agree with the tactics used by the opposition."

He stood up and paced the small waiting room, his face taunt, a grim expression betraying his thoughts.

"May I call you Andrea?"

"Please do."

"Call me Phil. I understand your concern. It's ours as well. However, violence is not the answer. There are more acceptable alternatives, slower perhaps but definitely less destructive."

"So you agree with the goal of the opposition but not the means they're using to achieve it."

"Precisely. Working through the existing government is the only logical solution."

"Do you really believe that?"

"Absolutely. If I didn't, I wouldn't be here."

"And you are here because you think I can help. Can you be more explicit?"

"I would have preferred to discuss it with you some other time. Unfortunately, time is a luxury we can't afford. We have reason to believe that there will be a rash of killings in the very near future. We have our informers and we have Savak fully alerted. That does not mean we can sit back and relax."

"What else can you do?"

"We need inside information from people we can trust. The number of revolutionaries has more than quadrupled in the past year alone. There are too many of them and too few of us. The King refuses to acknowledge the problem. He has surrounded himself with officials who tell him what they think he wants to hear. When we present him with facts, we are dismissed as alarmists."

"If that's the case, how do you expect to work with this government to bring about change?"

"We have to. We have no choice. If the King does not relax his grip and if the revolutionaries succeed in overthrowing him, we'll loose a close ally, and our foothold in a very strategic area. We have to work out an arrangement which will be satisfactory to all parties concerned."

"It sounds like mission impossible to me."

"Nothing's impossible, Andrea. Look at what we did in Europe and Japan after World War II."

"What do you expect from me?"

"Do you speak Farsi?"

"I do. Quite well." she replied without hesitation.

"I know what I have to say could have a drastic effect on you. But we need your help. We have to have more information about your husband's group. We think they murdered the two American officers a few days ago, but we don't have a shred of evidence."

Andrea chuckled, a nervous chuckle. "What's wrong with Savak? It shouldn't be difficult for them to take care of the matter."

"Like I said, there's too many of them and we are no longer dealing with amateurs. These are well-trained, disciplined, dedicated militants. We did not know who their leader was until your husband and his friend were interrogated. Unfortunately, he left the country right after the assassinations took place. Destination unknown."

Her eyes turned cold. Maybe her husband had not actually pulled the trigger to kill the American officers. But what difference did that make? "You've got problems. Right?"

"You bet! But with your help, we hope to solve a few. I learned from Savak that when their agents came to your house after the officers were killed, despite your husband's pleas, you did not confirm his alibi. That told me a lot about you."

A deceptive tranquility engulfed her. She was numb. Her feelings for her husband had deteriorated from love, to contempt, to total indifference. But to spy on him? She didn't live with him anymore and wanted nothing to do with him. Yet he had to be stopped before more innocent people paid with their lives to satisfy his sadistic pleasures.

Recollections flooded her memory. The phone call the night of the murders, Farhad's and Mani's exuberance. Their drinking themselves to stupor. Mani's perpetual need for money. His frequent, unexplained "business" trips. His sudden reversal from a seemingly Westernized person to one of instant Iranianization and his recently surfaced rabid hatred of Westerners, revealed an inescapable conclusion. He was a committed terrorist. Like Sayid said he was. The bits of information which she had been storing and sorting out crystallized, wiping out in its wake all elements of mystery and doubt that had taunted her for months. The era of self-delusion was over.

Phil wondered over to the window overlooking the boulevard on which the hospital was located his attention temporarily claimed by men behind wheels protesting vociferously with their horns against the murderous, chaotic traffic.

She approached him. The cacophony of sounds from the street below claimed her attention briefly. His eyes met hers, challenging, warning, hoping.

"I don't believe any sane person should sanction terrorism," she said calmly. "Give me a few days to think about it. I'll let you know."

Chapter 28

The fourth day after her admission to the hospital, Kelly lapsed into a coma. The process came on like night following day, gradually, without fanfare, without struggle. Andrea watched in quiet desperation, frustrated with her helplessness, her blood percolating with rage at the man who had destroyed the one person she dearly loved.

When the doctor came for his rounds that morning Andrea waited impatiently to talk to him. She wanted to know the truth. Irene had occasionally discussed the problems her husband faced in treating Iranians. Unlike doctors in the States, doctors in Iran minimized or avoided relating factual details to the patient or next of kin. Most patients and their relatives were expected to and did react violently. If the information was not what they wanted to hear, they became hostile, uncooperative. Or, they moved the patient, regardless of his condition, to another facility. If the patient took a turn for the worse, it got attributed to the will of Allah.

She wondered if Irene and her husband had returned from their trip to Boston. She knew Irene's husband worked at Pars

Hospital. Although she liked him, she did not want him to know what had brought about the deterioration in Kelly's condition. After all, he was her husband's cousin.

The doctor was through with his examination. "Some of the test results are in," he said. "Her prognosis is poor. It will be a miracle if she pulls through. I consulted a neurosurgeon last night. He thinks surgery might help. We'll observe her for twenty four hours. If there is no improvement in her condition, we'll have to operate."

She thought the merciless bombardment of unexpected events and their aftermath had dulled her senses. She had tried to prepare herself anticipating the worst, yet when she was informed of it she was not prepared for it. She listened, worry clouding her face, in dazed disbelief.

She felt giddy, her vision blurred. The room would not stand still. Instinctively she gripped the back of the chair next to the bed to steady herself and force the room to stop spinning. Neither the room nor her body would yield.

She felt the color drain from her face. The doctor put his arms around her and gently lowered her into a chair. Slowly, she regained her senses and forced a smile.

He reached for her hand and gave it a gentle squeeze. "I'm sorry," he said apologetically. "I rarely tell my patients the blunt truth. But I had to tell you. I felt you'd want to know."

"I appreciate it. Thanks for your help."

He was paged to go to the emergency room.

"I have to go but I'll be in the hospital for the next twenty four hours. Call me if you need me."

"Sorry I took so much of your time doctor. There's something I'd like to discuss with you when you have a free moment."

"I'll stop by after I'm done with the emergency room."

"Thank you."

He returned after an hour.

"What I'm about to say is in no way a lack of confidence

in you," Andrea said. "I have absolute trust in you. But for my own peace of mind I need your advice and reassurance."

"What about?"

"Do you think Kelly's chances of recovery would be better in the States?"

He gave her a long appraising look, the prematurely entrenched lines on his forehead tightening, a casualty of the suffering and pain he attended to. "You're free to take her anywhere you like. Unfortunately very little can be done for her here or elsewhere. It's a long trip. It might kill her. The decision is yours. I can't force you to keep her here."

"I understand."

"There's also the problem of your husband," he continued quietly. "I've made a few discreet inquiries. You can't leave without his permission. If my information is correct, he won't oblige."

It's amazing how fast news travels in this country, Andrea thought. It's more like a small town than the capital of three million people.

"If it's a question of life or death for my daughter, I'll find a way doctor, trust me."

"What for? Her care is the same here as it would be in the U.S. and she's in no shape to travel."

"Thank you for your honesty. I had to know."

"I've delayed informing the police, but eventually I have to. They'll want to know who did it. Prepare yourself for a lot questioning."

"I'm sure you've guessed by now her fall was no accident. My husband pushed her to the ground and kicked her when my friend's housekeeper refused to let her go because she did not know who he was. There were many witnesses."

"That does not mean they'll testify against him," the doctor replied. "Witnesses here have a way of developing instant amnesia, especially when the person involved has the reputation your husband does. They fear reprisal."

"I'm sure the housekeeper will. She was very fond of

Kelly."

"Get in touch with her and let me know."

"I will."

She tried several times. There was no answer.

Andrea's thoughts were murky from lack of sleep and nervous tension. There was a cot in the room. Andrea had yet to use it. The sleep she got was on the chair next to Kelly's bed. It was brief, irregular and happened only when her body and brain rebelled against the undeserved abuse they were subjected to.

Unable to think or act logically she returned to the chair, checked Kelly, put her head on her folded arms next to Kelly's chest and promptly fell asleep.

She shot up like a missile. She had no idea how long she'd slept. Kelly looked the same. It was six thirty. The doctor had left their room around nine in the morning. She couldn't have possibly slept over nine hours!

A few minutes later, Vartan peeped through the door. He came every evening with something for her to eat and when business was good, he brought her fruit.

"Kelly good, yes?" he asked expectantly.

She could not bring herself to tell him the grim truth. "She's okay."

"Eat." He placed the pot on the bedside table. "My wife cook Borscht. She from Russia. Borscht very good."

Andrea did not cease to be amazed by this wonderful, warm, loving, giving human being who had appeared from nowhere and inconspicuously worked his way to her heart. With a grateful smile she took the spoon he had fished from his coat pocket. "Please thank your wife for me."

"No thank you. Eat."

She knew he wouldn't leave until she did so. It was delicious. She told him so. He beamed.

His self-appointed mission accomplished, Vartan reached for the empty pot. "I come tomorrow night see you. Yes?"

How many more tomorrows? No one could tell. Perhaps

it was best to check out of the hotel. There was no sense in paying hotel bills and hospital bills.

"Are you busy tonight?"

"No busy."

"Could you please drive me to the hotel."

He looked perplexed. "Hotel?"

"Yes. Check out. Bring suitcase."

He nodded.

The nurse assured Andrea it was all right to leave Kelly. She'd watch her.

Vartan drove her to the hotel.

The clerk gave her the key.

She walked up the stairs to her room, opened the door and walked in. The lights in the room were on, a pair of pants and a man's shirt were piled on a chair. Assuming that she had entered the wrong room, she went back out and checked the room number. It was correct and the key fit the lock.

As she reentered the room she came face to face with a man who had just stepped out of the shower. He had a towel around his waist and was curiously looking at the open front door. He seemed as surprised to see her as she was seeing him.

"There must be a mistake," she said. "This is our room."

"One moment, please." He reached in the closet for a pair of pants and a shirt and retreated to the bathroom.

He returned dressed. "You say this is your room?"

"Yes. My daughter is sick in the hospital. I didn't realize they'd give the room to someone else without me having vacated it first."

"It's the way they operate. You can have it if you want. But first, I've got to get my money back."

"Have you already paid for the room?"

"No. I bribed a clerk to get a room. Expensive! Wow! There isn't a room to be found in this city."

Should she take it back? Her dilemma was not knowing how long Kelly's recovery would take. The chances of an early recovery were minimal. It was best to tackle one day at a time.

"You don't have to leave. I came to get our suitcase. It was in the closet. Have you seen it by any chance?"

"A suitcase," he asked surprised.

"I'll check with the desk. I'm sorry to have barged in on you like this."

Andrea walked out. He followed her. "I'd like to go with you."

They took the elevator to the lobby. He introduced himself. His name was Dino, an Italian working as manager for a construction firm in Ahwaz. He was in his early thirties, of medium height, light brown hair and eyes attractive in an uncommon way.

"You needn't have bothered," she said to break the silence. "I'm sure I can manage."

He chuckled. "I've dealt with these people for years. You won't get a straight answer from them, especially hotel receptionists. They will not go out of their way to help a woman."

They approached the desk and waited. The young man behind the desk ignored their presence until Dino tapped him on the shoulder. "We'd like to talk to the manager, please."

The receptionist raised his head and looked at Dino and then at Andrea. "He's not here."

Dino's eyes bulged. He grabbed the clerk by the collar. "Find him. You have five minutes."

The clerk resumed shuffling papers lying on the counter.

His eyes bulging even more, Dino said with a threatening voice, "The lady and I are going to have a drink. We'll be sitting on the sofa across from you. You now have four minutes." He turned, reached for Andrea's arm and walked away.

"There are two ways to get a message across to these people. Money or might. If you're lucky, one of them will work."

The manager arrived before the drinks.

Andrea watched fascinated as Dino put on a charm mask. His moods seemed to shift from one extreme to the other effortlessly, on an instant's notice. "My friend here needs her suitcase."

"Your friend?"

"Yes. You gave me her room. I didn't know it then, but she had not checked out." There was an edge to his voice.

"I'll see what I can do." The manager headed down the hall, back to his office.

It was taking a lot longer than Andrea had anticipated. Vartan was double parked. "Excuse me. I have a cab waiting. I'd like to let him go."

Vartan had found a spot to park his cab. He was waiting for her in front of the exit. She tried to pay him and urge him to leave. "No go, Madame. Vartan wait."

Andrea returned to the lobby.

An hour and half later Dino ordered his fourth drink and Andrea's second. There was no sign of the manager. The more Dino drank, the more he talked about all the crazy, mixed-up experiences he had dealing with unskilled peasants working on prefabricated houses for employees of oil companies in Ahwaz and Abadan. He laughed at his own jokes and simultaneously banged his right fist into his left palm.

She tried to be attentive, but it was a distracted concentration brought back from its wonderings through conscious effort.

"Do not look so sad," Dino said and stopped abruptly. His bald head held high, his belly protruding like a Halloween pumpkin precariously set on two short legs, the manager was headed their way.

"I'm sorry," the manager said. "No one seems to know anything about a suitcase. Maybe the day shift put it in storage someplace. I've checked with housekeeping. There's nothing there. Maybe tomorrow. I'll call you."

Andrea sank in her chair. Everything she owned she had brought with her from the States, items impossible to get on the local market.

It was late. Nothing more could be accomplished. She had

to return to the hospital. This was the best organized disorganization yet, but she knew it was not the last.

"I'll call you," she told the manager. She neither had the inclination nor the desire to let him know where to reach her. Most probably, an employee had disposed of it at a sizable profit. There was no sense in agonizing over it.

Dino watched her as she got up and reached for her purse. His exuberance and charm changed to belligerence. He grabbed the manager by the shoulders and lifted him off the ground. "You find her suitcase Mr. Toqi. You find it quick or I'll beat the shit out of you."

Carelessly, he let go of his victim thus permitting the ashen faced man's tiny shoes to return to ground.

"Yes, sir," Mr. Toqi whimpered, shaking. "I'll do my best. Tomorrow. I promise."

"Your best better be good," Dino yelled. "There's a limit to how much nonsense your guests will put up with. Right now you've passed that limit."

Dino shoved the man away from him.

Mr. Toqi pulled himself together as he cast a quick glance around as though assessing the damage of his guest's indiscretion. Every eye within hearing distance was glued on them. He straightened his tie with a jerk, pulled his jacket back on his shoulders and marched to his office.

He banged the door shut.

Dino had already turned his back to the crowd focusing his attention on Andrea. "He'll find it. I'll check first thing in the morning. We'll find it even if we have to turn this hotel upside down."

"Thank you. You've done more than enough. I have to go."

"Wait. You did not tell me where I could reach you when they find the suitcase."

"They won't. With all the threatening you did, the manager could not locate it. It's gone. Forget it."

Dino grinned broadly. "Don't be such a pessimist. What's

your phone number."

She told him where she could be reached, thanked him, and hastened out the door.

Vartan saw her return. He opened the door, made sure she was seated, then drove off. He did not question her.

At the hospital, she paid him, thanked him and took the stairs for the intensive care unit.

Kelly was in the same position. Her tiny features had taken on a deathly gray hue. An occasional twitching of a facial muscle, coupled with shallow breathing was the only detectable sign of life.

Overcome with emotion and in desperate need of someone to hold and hug, she dug her way through the tubes surrounding the child and pressed her chest gently against the inert body beneath hugging and kissing her. "I love you my baby. I love you more than life itself. Please get well. Please. I need you." She broke down sobbing.

She pulled herself away and dried her tears. She stopped, an expression of disbelief sweeping her face. Was it possible? She could have sworn Kelly opened her eyes and smiled at her. Even though her vision was fogged with tears, she knew she was not imagining it. Kelly had responded. She had actually smiled.

Chapter 29

Kelly remained in a coma. Andrea changed her position every two hours and watched her. The doctor urged Andrea to take breaks. "Go out. Get some fresh air. It will do you good. There's nothing more you can do for her."

Her clothes were stinking and she needed a shower. The hospital allowed her to use the guest shower but putting the same clothes back on was not very appealing. Ready to wear was difficult to find. The importation of most consumer goods was strictly forbidden to protect the local industry. Translated, it meant shoddy goods for consumers and enormous profits for producers.

She had asked Vartan to come for her in the afternoon. He took her to several stores. She could find nothing that fit. Desperate, she realized she had no choice but to return to the house. She had a key to the front door. Hopefully she could sneak in and out undetected. Mani was hardly ever home in the afternoons, Naene always took a nap and it was too early for Sayid to be up. She told Vartan to drive her to the Abbassi residence.

She was in her room within seconds.

She was frantically throwing whatever she could find into a suitcase, when she heard her mother-in-law's voice mournfully placating Mani. The Persian room, right outside Andrea's and Kelly's room, overlooked the living room and three rooms on the ground floor. Overcome by curiosity, Andrea stepped out.

The door to Mani's "office" was open. Mani was in bed, his face swollen, his abdomen partially covered with a sheet, his feet bandaged. The bandages looked caked with blood. Farhad smoked in the next bed. She had trouble recognizing him. He looked pale, unshaven.

She heard Mani scream while Naene tried to remove the bandages from his feet.

"Mother," he yelled, "my feet are infected. I have a fever and I can't stand this pain any longer. Call a doctor."

Farhad nodded in agreement. "Mani is right. My scrotum is infected too. This is not a job for you. Without medical care we'll never get well."

"God have mercy on us," Naene cried, hands raised, palms open. "May the Prophet hear my prayers and take revenge. Thank God Sayid intervened. You probably would not have lived to see the sun rise again if he had not come to your rescue."

Andrea had never heard Mani speak harshly to his mother but her praising Sayid must have irked him. "Mother, you may think that your son did us a big favor but he sure took his time getting there."

"He said he did not know where they'd taken you."

"I bet he knew exactly where we were," Farhad interjected. "He probably delayed his arrival to give Savak time to do their job."

"Sayid would never do a thing like that," Naene sounded angry. "He promised his father not do anything to hurt his brother. He took that bitch and her child somewhere. He did not get back until noon."

"Mother, please call a doctor."

Mrs. Abbassi shook her head dismayed and walked out the room.

Mani sighed. "If I could lay my hands on her, I'd tear her apart. Can you believe it? My stupid brother made me promise not to touch my wife in the presence of two Savak agents."

"That bastard!" It was Farhad. "He must be gloating watching us suffer."

"Don't worry. I'll get even with him and with her," Mani replied. "I was delirious with pain. I would have agreed to anything. I'll break it when I want to."

The door bell rang.

Andrea was seized with panic. She withdrew quietly to her room leaving the door partially open.

"My name is Bahram." It was a man's voice. "I'm Mani's friend. May I come in?"

Naene ushered him in.

Andrea did not recognize the voice or the name. She tiptoed back to the Persian room.

Bahram looked to be in his middle twenties. He was of medium height and had a gaunt face. He had thick, bushy eyebrows which extended from one temple to the other paralleled with an equally thick mustache which looked as though it was glued precariously to his lip. He was wearing a pair of faded jeans and a T shirt with University of St Louis inscribed across the chest.

Mani and Farhad stared at the visitor.

Naene deposited herself carefully on the carpet and studied the visitor.

There was a brief moment of uneasy silence.

The man who called himself Bahram, glanced in the direction of Mani then Naene. "Get rid of her." He spoke English with a heavy accent.

Mani lifted his head slightly. "Mother, this gentleman has business to discuss with us. Would you mind leaving us alone for a few minutes, please?"

Naene cast an indignant glance at the intruder, rose and left the room.

Bahran slammed the door shut.

Andrea crouched behind the love seat.

Naene wobbled around the living room, talking to herself. "There's no respect left for elders. This generation has no fear of God. Why can't a mother be present when her son discusses business? Business! What nonsense! So far there's nothing to show for it. I must alert my son not to get involved with impolite, brash young men like this."

She retraced her steps and approached the door straining to listen. After a few moments, she shook her head, returned to the sofa and resumed her monologue. "My son is the best son. He's loving, attentive. Never said a harsh word to me in his life. Had I been with him I wouldn't have allowed him to marry that foreigner. My poor child. He has to attend to business even when he's sick."

The maid headed toward the room carrying a tray of tea. She opened the door and went in.

"You know me as Bahram." Andrea heard the visitor say. "I'm replacing Zia." He spun around, took the tray from the maid, grabbed her by the arm and shoved her out. He had the appearance of a hyena on full alert.

"Who's in this house besides your mother," he asked.

"My brother is usually home around this time but you don't have to worry about him. He sleeps. He's too drunk to hear anything."

"If you leave the door open," Farhad said, "we can hear him when he wakes up."

Bahram threw a contemptuous look at the men. "How much did you tell them."

It was quiet for a second, then she heard Farhad's voice. "Nothing."

"I'll ask you one more time," Bahram yelled. "How much did you tell them?"

"The terrible shape we're in should be sufficient proof

that we did not talk."

"You did not talk," Bahram repeated Farhad's words. "You did not talk and those kind, obliging gentlemen at Savak released you the same day. Is that what you'd like me to believe! Perhaps they went down on their knees and begged your forgiveness. After all, not even Savak could doubt the integrity of two such illustrious gentlemen!"

Andrea crouched behind the love seat. Her mother-in-law had poor vision but the maid could easily spot her from the living room. When the maid returned to the kitchen, she took a quick peep. Bahram paced the room and smoked.

Mani said, "My brother . . ."

Bahram interrupted. "You shut up. You're nothing but a pain, an insignificant, loathsome appendix. If it wasn't for your wife's money, the organization would never put up with a useless person like you. Tell me. What have you contributed to the cause so far besides ten thousand dollars and empty promises?"

There was no answer.

"Answer me!"

"My . . . my brother has connections. In very high posts. He got us released."

"Released? Why don't you tell me something I might believe. That son of a dog brother of yours was running around with an American woman at the International Hotel the same time you were being interrogated. I saw him with my own eyes. I was assigned to follow him. He did not leave the place until noon. I lost him in traffic. Now do you want to tell me the truth."

Sayid must have suspected as much. Andrea recalled how frequently he checked the rearview mirror on the way to the hotel.

"Did . . . did you say American?"

"What's your problem? Are you hard of hearing?"

"I . . . I wanted to be sure. I was afraid my brother had smuggled my wife and daughter out of the country. What you said gives me hope. He must have moved them to a hotel before getting us released. Thank God he came. Neither one us could have endured much more."

"Your lies will get you nowhere."

"He's not lying." It was Farhad. "His brother has connections, worthwhile connections. He got us out the same day."

"If he has such fantastic connections, why did it take him eighteen hours to get you released?"

"The chief of Savak is my brother's close friend and so is his deputy. My brother said they were both out of town. It took a while for him to locate and clear us."

Naene rose and went to the kitchen. Andrea moved closer to the bannister to take a good look at the man who called himself Bahram.

Bahram's mustache was twitching. He said, "The chief was in town and so was his assistant. When Americans get murdered the man in charge of Savak does not leave town. Your brother wanted Savak to have time to teach you a lesson. How can you be so dim as to believe the words of a man who has been the enemy of everything we stand for?"

Mani looked troubled, like a man with too many problems on his hands and no ideas in his head. His swollen eyes darted from his friend to the visitor. "We suspected as much but at least he came."

Bahram stubbed out his cigarette and approached Mani. "If you hadn't been such an ass, Savak would not be on your trail."

Naene returned from the kitchen to the living room. A moment later the maid stepped out holding a cup of tea. Andrea ducked behind the love seat.

"None of this would have happened," Mani said, "if my ungrateful wife had not betrayed us. When I'm able to stand on my feet, I'll teach her a lesson she'll never forget."

"You're an even bigger ass than I thought." Bahram's voice got louder the angrier he got. "Years of indoctrination were wasted on you. If you had done what you were told to do, she wouldn't have turned against you. You can't treat her like an Iranian. Americans have long memories. They remember the good and the bad. You should know that. You lived in that country long enough."

The phone rang. There was only one telephone in the house. It was in the living room. Naene answered it. She talked briefly then walked to the room. She stopped at the door. "The doctor will be here in an hour." She returned, took the empty teacup and went to the kitchen.

"What doctor?" Bahram asked.

"Our wounds are infected," Farhad said. "We need treatment. We asked her to call a doctor."

"Cancel it!" Bahram dashed to the living room, then the kitchen. He spoke to Naene. "Call the doctor's office. Tell him not to come."

"Why?"

"My brother is a doctor. He'll come. He doesn't charge my friends."

"Thank you." Naene sounded pleased. "No charge is good. House calls are expensive. I'll cancel it."

Bahram returned to the room. "I expected you to have better sense. It will not take a doctor long to figure out how you got your wounds. And it will not take long for that information to become public disqualifying both of you from further membership in the organization. Was that very difficult for you two to figure out?"

"Our wounds are badly infected." It was Farhad. "No one from the party contacted us. What were we supposed to do?"

"Wait." Bahram said and slammed the door shut.

For a couple of minutes, Andrea could not hear a thing. Either they had stopped talking or their voices were so low that she could not hear them. Then suddenly the door swung open and Andrea heard a body fall.

"I thought so!" Bahram said. "Send her to her room. I've no time to play games."

Andrea looked down. Naene was on her face, her legs

buckled under her abdomen.

"Mother, please go to your room. I'll tell you everything in Farsi later."

Naene dragged herself away from the door, marched to her room and slammed the door shut.

"I'll ask Dr. Fakhran to come see you. He's one of us."

"Thank you." Mani sounded relieved. "When I'm able to stand on my feet I'll deal with my brother and my wife."

Bahram spun around. "What does it take to make you understand?"

"Understand what?"

"Understand that you're not to touch your wife. You're not to tell her a single harsh word. Get in touch with her, apologize, convince her you're madly in love with her. You have to win her back."

Mani looked stunned. He tried to answer but couldn't.

"She won't cooperate." Farhad said. "From what she did to us it's obvious she hates him."

"He'll have to try that much harder. Won't he?"

Andrea rose and looked down. She had to see Mani's face. He looked distraught.

"My . . . my relationship with my wife has deteriorated to a point from which it can't be redeemed. I doubt there's anything I can say or do that will change her mind."

You're right there, Andrea said to herself.

"Then you're out," his visitor replied.

For an instant Mani remained transfixed. Bahram smoked incessantly dropping the ashes on the carpet.

Mani sounded desperate. "Please, I'm ready to do whatever you want. Please, ask me to do anything you like except play husband again. Maybe I can sell the house."

"It's not yours to sell. It belongs to your brother. We've checked."

"I'll find something else."

The look on the man's face was murderous as he stepped close to the bed and yelled, "You'll play husband for as long as we want you to. We don't need your advice. Your impertinence, if not curbed, will cost you your life. No sacrifice is too big for the cause. You do as you're told or perish."

Mani slumped further in his bed.

Andrea felt a twinge of pity for him. He looked like he had been handed the death sentence. How could she have been so blind for so long?

But, his tormentor was not through with him. Not yet. "I won't be coming here again. Your house is under 'surveillance. I took a chance today. Just as we suspected, you made a dumb decision like calling a doctor. If you need to contact the organization, go to the mosque in Ekhteyariyeh. Ask for Mullah Hamid. He'll be your contact from now on."

Andrea heard the sound of a door lock.

Instinctively, she slipped behind her partially open door.

A moment later, she saw Sayid creeping down the stairs, barefoot.

Bahram had his back to the door. "You should pass all information to Mullah Hamid. Your questions and problems should be directed to him." Then turning to Mani, he said, "Make sure next time we meet you have something tangible for us. We're tired of listening to your stupid excuses. Do you unders . . ."

Andrea crept back out. With Sayid home, her fears diminished.

Bahram must have seen the sudden, horrified look on the men's faces. He whirled around, pulled a gun from his belt and pointed it at Sayid.

"Put your toy away," Sayid said unperturbed. "You might hurt yourself. Or better still give it to Mullah Hamid. After today, he'll need it. Now get out and don't ever step in this house again."

Bahram stuck the gun in his belt with a disgusted look on his face and dashed out the door.

The front door slammed with such ferocity it shook the whole house.

Andrea rushed back to her room and hid behind the partially open door.

Sayid climbed the stairs slowly, stopped at her door and knocked.

She hesitated.

He walked in.

"Why are you here?"

"To pick up the rest of my stuff."

"Take it and go. Now, while my mother is in her room. If you need help let me know."

Andrea grabbed her suitcase, raced down the stairs and hurled herself into Vartan's cab.

Chapter 30

The next day was Friday, time for devout Muslims to pray. The noon prayers drew the largest crowds. The mosque in Ekhteyariyeh was packed with worshippers in their stocking feet, facing Mecca, prostrating themselves in unison, a sea of shoulders rising and falling, proclaiming Allah's greatness.

Mani and Farhad inched their way slowly to the front of the hall. Mani struggled to keep his balance as best he could on improvised crutches. Farhad walked with his legs apart, like a toddler in diapers. With each step, the cigarette burns on his genitals sent sharp, shooting pains up his spine. The doctor promised by Bahram did not come. Their wounds festered. In desperation, they decided to contact Mullah Hamid.

"I hate religion and everyone remotely involved with it," Farhad whispered. "But I especially despise mullahs. They're the perpetrators of misery and ignorance. The suckers of the blood of the poor. Their only interest is to line their pockets. All in the name of God. They are vile, despicable men. They can't be trusted. They've sold their conscience to the King in return for guaranteed Swiss bank accounts."

"Everyone knows about their reputation," Mani said soothingly. "But I'm sure there are exceptions."

"My hatred for the Shah is nothing compared to the hatred I feel for what others call 'God.' Those who believe are weaklings in mind and soul. It's this reliance on Allah and the fatalism advocated by our religion which has hindered progress and led to apathy. Our country is the best example. All you have to do is look around."

"We have to forget our personal feelings for a while. It could be that the Revolutionary Council chose to work with a mullah because they know something we don't. We'll have to go along. No member will come to our house again. Not with my brother around."

"I can't wait to get rid of that bastard."

"Allah u Akbar." The chant reverberated through the hall.

Mani and Farhad joined the worshippers in prostrating themselves and solemnly bending down to touch the ancient carpet with their foreheads.

Mani cast a discreet glance at his friend. Farhad looked like a man who was having trouble controlling an attack of violent emotional paroxysm.

"What's the matter?" Mani whispered.

"The dressing is tearing my scrotum every time I bend."

"Just be patient. It'll be over soon."

Farhad cursed through tightened lips, "Damn this mentally handicapped religious oligarchy. They inflict such mindless demands on the public."

"But it works. It has worked for centuries."

"You bet it works. It's the best tool there is for subjugating and controlling the masses. Anything is possible in the name of God. Look around you. Have you seen a more disgusting sight?"

Mani cast a quick look around. "Be careful. Many people nowadays understand English."

"I still can't believe that an organization like ours would use clerics. Any cleric caught inciting the public is bound to face justice a la Shah. Do you think these cowards will risk their lives to help their fellow men?"

The congregation rose to its feet. Farhad let out a sigh of relief. Mani and Farhad drifted to a corner while the worshippers exited in one uninterrupted wave.

They waited for ten minutes for someone to contact them, but no one came. The prayer hall was empty.

They made their way to the anteroom where shoes were taken off before entering the prayer hall. Because of his swollen feet, Mani had come in slippers. Farhad's shoes and Mani's slippers were the only footwear left.

Farhad cringed with pain as Mani helped him with his shoes. Then Farhad held the crutches for Mani. While Mani tried to balance himself, a voice from behind startled them, sending Mani crashing to the floor. Mani turned his head. He saw a young man holding a cane. The man's face was covered with smallpox marks. He was blind.

"Follow me," the young man said.

Mani scrambled to his feet. They followed the man in silence.

They crossed an adjacent room, walked down a narrow corridor to a small bare room. The young man tapped his cane until he found a wooden door. He opened it. They descended a steep staircase which led to a closed door.

The man tapped the door with his cane. He said, "In there."

The door was opened by a cleric in his early thirties. He was almost as wide as he was tall. His small, intense black eyes were shadowed by thick, bushy eyebrows, his chin lost in layers of fat and a volume of curly hair shielded his chest.

"You've caused a lot of problems for us," he said brusquely, without preliminaries.

Neither man spoke.

"You must move out of that house immediately," the mullah continued. "We've rented a large apartment in the north of the city. You'll be among thousands of Americans. Savak will not look for you there."

He waited. There was no response from the men.

"Any questions?"

"Why a large apartment?" Farhad ventured. "I thought we were short of money."

"Large because Mani has a wife and a kid you stupid," the mullah retorted angrily.

Turning his back to Farhad and pointing his forefinger at Mani, he said disgustedly, "Your brother is a snake. He slithers in and out of your house the slimy bastard. Soon he will meet the fate he deserves. In the meantime, you'll live with your family in the apartment. We can't afford to lose any more members. Do I make myself clear?"

Mani was stunned. Was he referring to Bahram? Was he caught? Was that why the doctor had not come? And how much longer did they expect him to play husband? There had to be a way out.

"My wife left me," he said, planting an instant mournful expression on his face.

The mullah placed his teacup carefully on the wooden table separating him from his visitors and gazed at Mani like a beast in a jungle with a cornered prey.

"So your wife left you," the Mullah repeated with icy sarcasm.

"I don't know where she is."

"Save your theatrics for a more gullible audience. Your wife did not leave you. She had to escape. And your brother helped her. Make it a policy never to lie to us."

He was short of breath and had to stop. He added two more cubes of sugar to his tea, stirred it and sipped it, slurping noisily.

"Grab a chair and sit down, both of you. What I have to say will take a few minutes."

Mani and Farhad did as they were told.

The mullah poured himself more tea from a samovar on the table. He then went to a small cabinet behind the desk, took out two small glasses and poured tea for the men. His breathing was noisy and rapid.

They waited for the mullah's labored breathing to abate. The least exertion seemed to make him short of breath and purple around the lips. He lowered himself, with great difficulty, into the immense chair behind the desk, put his head back and relaxed.

The men sipped their tea.

"Your orders are not open for discussion. The apartment will be your base of operation. It's safe. Your wife must live with you. It's imperative that she does. It's the cover you need to avoid suspicion. She's an American living in an American neighborhood. Without her, Savak will be on your trail the moment you move in."

The dissertation sent him into a paroxysm of cough which lasted over a minute. Mani grabbed a glass, poured some water and gave it to him. The mullah drank it.

When he regained a measure of control over his breathing, he resumed his monologue. "You'll be assigned subjects to observe and follow. All information comes to me. I'll be in touch."

"What should we be looking for?" Mani asked.

"Now you're thinking," the mullah replied pleased. "We have made changes in our plans. We will target Americans we feel will make the most impact. We will attack when and where least expected. This is where you come in. You have to keep a detailed record of their movements, their routines, when they leave their homes, what they use for transportation, their cars, the license numbers and any details you might observe."

"I love it!" Farhad exclaimed. "I love action, violence. It makes my blood boil."

The mullah ignored him directing his comments to Mani instead. "That's not all. We have added prominent Iranians to our list." He sat back, his small, black eyes scrutinizing the men.

"It's the day we've been praying for," Mani said, his voice cracking. He wanted to say waiting for, but changed his mind. Praying would sound better to a cleric. "Farhad suggested this course of action to our leaders repeatedly. They objected. They said the adverse publicity would damage our cause."

The mullah turned to Farhad. "Agha Farhad, from the look on your face, and based on your previous record, I can tell you like the idea of extending our struggle to Iranians."

Like Mani said, I've been an advocate of this policy for years. We should rid the country of the enemies of the people."

"Do you have any particular individuals in mind?" the mullah persisted.

"The Prime Minister is a Bahai," he said cautiously. "He should be our prime target. He's a traitor. I volunteer for the job. Excluding the Royal Family, nothing would give me greater pleasure than to see his blood flow."

Farhad spit. "Excuse me. I always spit after mentioning the Royal Family. It's my way of cleansing myself."

The mullah seemed captivated by Farhad's enthusiasm. "You bring joy to my heart. Go on. Who else?"

"The Minister of Foreign Affairs, the Mayor of Tehran and at least half a dozen officers."

Mani cringed. It could be a trap. Farhad knew better.

"Who from the officers do you have in mind?"

"Generals. The Shah's stooges. It can be done. For years I've dreamt of nothing else. With careful planning, reliable inside information and the right person doing the job, there is no reason for us to fail."

The mullah threw his head back and laughed uproariously, the masses of fat encircling his short neck bouncing up and down to the rhythm of his laughter. "I like you. You've got guts and no scruples. Exactly what we're looking for."

Farhad was on a roll. "A Bahai. Why should a Muslim country have a Bahai Prime Minister? Does the bastard who crowned himself king want us to believe no Muslim in this country has the qualifications to be Prime Minister? Is that why he chose a Bahai? Or is it his way of impressing the public that he does not give a damn about their opinion. He does what he wants so long as he has the backing of the Americans. As a Muslim, and a clergyman, to be ruled by a Bahai, a religion you despise, must be more than you can bear."

"What you say is true," the mullah replied. "Unfortunately, our hands are tied. The King has stripped the clergy of all power. All of us are under strict observation. That's why you were not given my real name. For now, I'm Mullah Hamid. Tomorrow, God knows. Not that I don't trust you. But because Savak can make anybody talk." He stopped to catch his breath, then added, "There are ways though, and we shall find them."

"The Bahais are systematically bleeding our country of its wealth. We must send that infidel two meters underground."

Mullah Hamid rose slowly. "Your ideas are very good. Very good indeed. I like them. But ideas are just that, ideas. Carrying them out would be thrilling, a glory to God, a worthy service to the nation. The important thing is how. Anybody who's somebody is heavily guarded. The Prime Minister makes it a point not to be where he's supposed to be, when he's supposed to be. He keeps no schedule, has no close friends, no routine, not even a servant."

The mullah wiped the perspiration beading on his forehead with his sleeve. "Abbassi, what's your opinion?"

Mani was caught off guard. It was rare for anyone to ask his opinion. He hesitated, then said, "We've all vowed to sacrifice our lives for the cause, if necessary. I think it's time we stopped talking. Unless we pursue our goal aggressively, the little momentum we gained with the assassination of the Americans will be lost."

"You're absolutely right," the mullah said, "I have to admit a positive outcome would be a big blessing for our people and a monumental achievement for all of us, especially the clergy. We have endured years of humiliation. Revenge would be delicious. I can almost taste it, feel it. Yet we cannot act in haste. The repercussions could throw us back years. Do you agree?"

Mani had never seen Farhad so happy. He was beaming. "We don't have to act in haste," Farhad said. "Initially we should target officers who hold highly visible posts but don't have top ranking positions. We have to strike with lightning speed."

Mullah Hamid's expression changed suddenly. He rose, grabbed Farhad by the collar. "Names. Give me names. Not sermons. You say we have to take action. We all want action. Who are the officers you have in mind?"

Farhad took a step back. The smile was gone from his face. "We don't have anyone definite in mind. We'll look into the matter and get back to you."

"I thought so," the mullah replied. "Meet me here next Friday, same time. Meanwhile, think of a few concrete proposals. We need action, not talk and vacillation. I need names of intended victims, names of volunteers for the job, where and when."

The mullah reached in his desk drawer and handed Mani a bunch of keys.

"The keys to your apartment. Move today. Dr. Fakhran will be at your place sometime tonight."

"What about me?" Farhad asked.

"What about you?"

"Where do I stay?"

"Your permanent address is Isfahan. You are Mani's guest when you're in Tehran. I want that clear. If you act as though you're in his house to stay, his wife might object. Take your clothes, only. The apartment is fully furnished."

He reached for the Koran on his desk and began reading.

The men got the message. The meeting was over. They left.

They waited impatiently for an orange cab. After about ten minutes Farhad said, "Bombers, we have. Tanks, yes.

Taxis, no. Let's walk."

"I can't walk on these crutches. My armpits are sore and the soles of my feet have no flesh left on them."

"I'm hurting too. But we have no choice. Not until we get rid of those who inflicted this torture on us."

"I couldn't agree with you more. Our brothers are beginning to see the wisdom of your ideas. Hopefully we'll see action soon."

"You're wrong," Farhad quipped. "You assumed that the man was truthful because he's a clergyman. He's not. He's a shrewd, conniving, unscrupulous bastard. His religious garb makes his job easy. All he wanted to know was the names of the Iranians we want eliminated. That's why I talked in generalities. I don't trust him."

"For a while there, I was worried too. But you're becoming paranoid. Your hatred of religion makes you suspect anyone remotely associated with it. I can't believe the organization would use someone unless they had positive proof of his loyalty."

"The organization is made of human beings. They make mistakes. I bet this is one of them."

"I hope you're wrong. I never thought I'd hear myself say so, but I hope you're wrong."

"I know I'm not. Didn't you notice how angry he got when I wouldn't mention anyone by name. 'Names. Give me names. Not sermons.' It's not for us to decide which Iranian officer lives and which one dies. He knows that. Why was he so eager to learn their names from us?"

"I don't know."

There were no free cabs on the main boulevard either. Exhausted, they stopped at a small tea house by the roadside.

"If we had a government which took minimum interest in domestic affairs, we would have better city planning and a few parking lots. We wouldn't have to leave my car parked in front of the door, nor would we have to roam this chaotic city in search of an illusive cab."

"But my dear brother," Farhad replied, his voice full of sarcasm. "Our King has majestic visions for his country." He stopped to spit. "His country. Never forget that. How else can we become the fifth military power in the world? I'll tell you how. By giving back to the Americans the money we make from oil. Americans take our oil and give us arms. Everyone's happy. Who cares what happens to thirty five million Iranians?"

The waiter placed two cups of tea and a bowl of sugar on their table.

Farhad leaned close to his friend and whispered in his ear, "At our next meeting, I'll propose General Cyrus as our next target. He's very close to the King." He spit again. "His death is sure to create tremendous upheaval. The skeptics will know we mean business. After that no one can stop us. Mostly though, I want it for you. Isn't that what you want?"

Mani was speechless. The teacup, which had yet to reach his mouth, remained in mid air. "Reading my mind is as easy for you as it is for others to breathe."

"Never fear. We'll do it."

"Andrea changed radically after he took her to Lebanon. He brainwashed her. She would have never betrayed us. She has always been an ardent supporter of human rights everywhere."

Meanwhile, Mullah Hamid handed a small Koran to his faithful assistant, the blind young man. It was a job his assistant performed routinely. The Koran had a skillfully concealed cassette which had recorded the mullah's conversation with the two men. Within the hour, the cassette was in the hands of Savak.

Chapter 31

"Andrea, Dr. Hedayat will be joining us in a few minutes," said Kelly's doctor, Dr. Nazari. "He's the neurosurgeon I consulted. We will examine Kelly, evaluate her condition, and let you know what we recommend."

Dr. Hedayat was Irene's husband.

Dr. Hedayat walked in with a pleasant smile, greeted Andrea, then spent the next forty minutes examining Kelly and the lab data. The pleasant smile was gone from his face when he addressed Andrea, "I recommend immediate surgery. The bleeding in her brain has to be stopped to relieve the pressure."

Andrea listened wondering why Dr. Hedayat was acting like a total stranger. After all, he was Mani's cousin and they knew each other socially.

"You must get hold of your husband immediately," said Dr. Nazari. "We have to operate as soon as possible."

"Do you want to explain the procedure to her or would you rather I did?" Dr. Hedayat asked Dr. Nazari.

"I can't do it until later. I have to do my rounds first."

"I'll do it." Turning to Andrea Dr. Hedayat said, "Come, let's go to my office."

Dr. Hedayat closed the door, then motioned for Andrea to take a seat.

"How did it happen?"

She told him.

"That's almost impossible to believe," he said, then topped. "Well, maybe not so impossible. I don't know what's come over Mani. I don't recognize him anymore."

"Neither do I."

"Is he in town?"

"I think so."

"I would have called him and talked to him myself but I was advised by Savak not to have anything to do with him. I have not told Dr. Nazari he's my cousin."

"I understand."

"We don't have much time. Every minute we delay the surgery decreases her chances of recovery. Without surgery she probably won't make it through the night."

"I'll try to reach him right away."

"I wish Irene were here to help you take care of Kelly. But she won't be back for a while. She went to Baltimore to visit her folks."

"Thanks. I'll manage."

Andrea returned to the intensive care unit, thinking, planning how to approach her husband. What could she say or do to convince him to put aside their differences for the sake of their daughter's welfare. He had shown no interest in the child since they left the States. Their daughter's well being seemed to be the last thing on his mind. Nonetheless, she had to try.

She went to the nurse's desk and asked to use the phone. She called the Abbassi residence. Naene answered. Andrea asked to speak to Mani. A succession of curses was followed by the receiver being slammed in her ear.

If she went there herself could she convince him to sign? Could she risk it? He'd said he'd tear her apart if he laid eyes on her and Naene was bound to make a scene. But if she went with someone who had seen him kick the child and was willing to testify, he might relent. Hopefully, Goli was still in Tehran. She dialed Helga's number. Goli answered.

"Goli, I need your help," Andrea said. "I'm calling from Pars Hospital. Kelly is very sick. Would you be willing to go with me to the Abbassis? It will only take a few minutes. All you have to do is tell him you're ready to testify if need be."

There was absolute quiet for a long moment. Puzzled, Andrea asked, "Goli, are you there?"

"I'm here."

"What's wrong?"

"Madame, you're asking me to do the impossible. I'm a poor woman. I have to support five children with the money I make. I'd like to help you but I can't."

"Why? All you have to do is tell the truth."

"The truth as you call it might mean a few broken bones and bruises for me, if I'm lucky. I can't take that chance. Your husband is a brute. No, Madame. You'll have to forgive me. I saw nothing, heard nothing."

Dr. Nazari had warned her but she hadn't believed him.

"Do you think Ibrahim feels the way you do?"

"Madame, forget it. You're wasting your time. When you marry a vile, wicked man like that you should accept the consequences."

"I have," Andrea snapped. "Thank you for your help."

The only option she had left was to telephone the Abbassis until she got through to Mani.

She called every fifteen minutes. There was no answer. To her surprise, she was relieved. She needed time to think, to gather her thoughts. Mani was in no shape to go out. Maybe he was asleep. She'd try again.

She did, until six in the evening. There was no answer. Either they had unplugged the phone or Mani's condition had worsened and they had to hospitalize him. She could think of no other explanation.

She decided to wait a while. Vartan would be there soon. She'd send him to their house with a note. If that didn't work, she'd go herself.

Vartan came an hour later, smiling. "Very good day today, Friday. I make good money. My car not break once." Then seeing the worried look on Andrea's face, he asked, "Kelly no good?"

"She's about the same."

"Why you so sad?"

"Not sad. Just frustrated. I've been trying to reach my husband but no one answers the phone. Can you help?"

"I ready. What you need?"

"Please take this note, go to the Abbassis, and ask for my husband. Tell him it's an emergency. He should call me immediately. The number is in the note."

He returned an hour later, note in hand.

"No one home. I wait. No one come. No one go. Neighbor give water to garden. I ask if he see Mr. Mani Abbassi. He say Mr. Mani go in car. He not alone. A man go with him. Two big bag, how you say? Oh, yes, suitcase. They go. Maybe three, three thirty this afternoon."

"Oh my God!" Andrea said. "He must have left the country."

Dr. Nazari had come and gone. On Fridays he did his evening rounds early. Andrea reached him at home and gave him an account of where matters stood.

"Try contacting the next of kin," he suggested. "If your husband has left the country, his father or brother are legally acceptable substitutes."

It was close to nine p.m., still a chance to catch Sayid at home. Ordinarily he left the house at ten at night and returned at dawn. He answered after the second ring. She told him her problem.

There was a long pause. Andrea waited, her nerves raw, not knowing what to expect. Finally he said, "He couldn't have left the country."

"What makes you so sure?" Andrea asked astonished.

"He has not been cleared by Savak."

"Why would he leave with two suitcases if he was not leaving the country?"

"I don't know. I was asleep."

"Maybe your mother knows," Andrea suggested. "Could you ask her?"

"She's not home."

"What do you suggest I do?" She hoped her voice did not betray her panic.

"Let me see if I can locate Mani. I'll call you back."

Andrea ordered a pot of tea and went to the waiting room expecting a long wait.

She was not disappointed. It took two hours before Sayid called. "He's moved to an apartment in Sultanatabad."

"Did you talk to him?"

"I did. That's why it took so long. He said he had nothing to do with Kelly's illness. He refuses to sign. He said he did not want to be involved."

"What's that supposed to mean?"

"He insists that you've done something to Kelly to rid yourself of the burden he claims she is for you. Apparently you have powerful friends who fly you in and out of the country when they want to have fun with you. He claims you left the child in Pahlavi when you were gone and that if something happens to his daughter, he'll sue you for everything you've got."

"You're not putting me on, are you Sayid?"

"No, I'm not. Those were his exact words. He said a lot more, ranting on and on about your unfaithfulness, your selfishness and how little you care about the child."

"Was he drunk?"

"He was not drinking when I was there. To me he seemed like his normal self, obnoxious."

"I guess it's my problem now."

"Yes. That's what your husband said. It's your problem."

"Why do you think he's doing this. I mean, what could he possibly gain from it?"

"You wouldn't ask such a question if you knew how his mind works. He's looking for an opportunity to make money. Either he's holding out to force you to pay him, or, if that fails, he'll threaten to sue you. He's confident he'll succeed, one way or the other."

"I'm not giving him money. No way. Let him go ahead and sue me."

"He won't. I promised him a special cell in Evin Prison if he tried."

"Do you think if I were to go there myself I could persuade him to change his mind?"

"Don't even consider it. He's full of hatred toward you and me. He's in pretty bad shape. Especially his feet. He blames us. He's not about to oblige."

It took a lot to dampen Andrea's spirit and a lot had happened that day. She fought to control the rage building inside her and the helplessness engulfing her. Yet every door she tried to open slammed shut in her face. There was nowhere left to turn.

She heard Sayid say, "Are you still there?"

"I'm here. Thank you for your help. I'm sorry I troubled you."

There was no response from Sayid.

"I have to check Kelly. Good night Sayid."

"Would you mind if I came to see you for a few minutes?"

"Now? It's almost midnight."

"I won't stay long. There's something I'd like to discuss with you which can't be discussed over the phone."

Andrea never knew what to expect from Sayid. His behavior was always at odds with the norm. What was there to discuss which he preferred not to do over the phone and at midnight.

"Aren't you late for work?"

"Don't be so creative with your insults. I don't work. I

play."

"Whatever. If you feel it's important and can't wait for tomorrow, come."

"I'll be there in half an hour."

Kelly slept peacefully. Her breathing was shallow, irregular, her color ashen.

Outside, spring rains were pounding against the window panes. It was a welcome sight. Heavy rains were uncommon in the desert climate. The sight of raindrops revived her, reminding her of her university days when life was simpler, her only worry being getting her assignments in on time. No, that's not true she reminded herself. Most of my time was taken up by social causes. Love and brotherhood of men. What a laugh! No one told me there were monsters among the so-called brothers. And lucky me, I married one.

Half an hour later, Sayid had yet to come. Despite her best efforts, her eyelids kept closing like automatic shutters. She washed her face with cold water and returned to the waiting room.

Sayid found her slumped in a chair. As always, his expression was that of a man in torment, making it impossible to tell what mood he was in.

"Sorry I'm late. I was at the admission desk convincing a sleepy clerk to let me sign the permission slip."

"What do you mean?" Andrea's eyes popped open.

"I signed it. Call the doctor and advise him everything is in order."

"It's too late. He said after midnight it would be impossible to operate because they'd have trouble reaching the staff. He'll be here early in the morning. But how did you do it?"

"I swore my brother was out of the country. They have my ID number and a statement from me accepting full responsibility."

Andrea was stunned. "Why? Why did you do it? I've never done anything for you."

He did not answer. He stood motionless, staring at the

bare wall.

"You're asking for trouble. When Mani finds out, there's no telling what he'll do."

His gaze shifted slowly from the wall to her face. "Mani can go to hell."

"I think you should go back and tear up the papers you signed. I'll get hold of him tomorrow. I'll make him sign. I don't know how, but I'll find a way."

He continued staring at the blank wall.

"Please Sayid," Andrea pleaded, "I simply can't allow you to stick your neck out for us, especially when we're dealing with someone like Mani."

His manner remained unchanged. The implication was clear. He was not about to change his mind.

"Are you sleepy?" he asked unexpectedly.

"Not any more."

"I've got a bottle of the best brandy available in this country in my car. I think we both need a drink."

She watched him walk to the elevator, immaculately dressed, the same pained expression his constant companion. She'd never seen him smile. The only change she'd noticed was a deepening of the lines on his face whenever he drank heavily. On rare occasions, when she was in the living room with her in-laws, still new to the place and quite naive, she'd seen her mother-in-law shake her head in a distraught manner as she watched her son descend the stairs. Soon after he left the house, she pounded her chest with her fist, and lamented disdainfully. Surprised, she'd asked Mani's sister what the problem was. "She says that she sent a young, energetic son, full of life, to the U.S. He came back all shrivelled up inside," Mani's sister explained. "All he does is drown himself in alcohol and pursue mind and soul deadening activities."

At the time Andrea had dismissed the mother's remarks as exaggeration. Later, her own experiences with him left her confused and bewildered. She never knew what to expect. It was as though she was dealing with two different personalities, diametrically opposed, a recluse when drunk, unpredictable when sober.

He returned with two small glasses which he had coaxed a nurse to give him and a bottle of Remy Martin.

Andrea took a sip and stopped. Her stomach was empty. She'd forgotten to eat. The food Vartan brought was still on the bedside table. But he drank steadily. Enough for both of them. In an hour, the bottle was empty.

Her frequent trips between the intensive care unit and the waiting room did not seem to bother him. Each time she returned, he asked if there was any change in the child's condition. After her sixth trip, she collapsed in a chair, unable to keep her eyes open.

He rose. "I hope my presence was not too much of an imposition on you. Call me if you need me. You have my number." With that he turned around to leave.

Spontaneously, she extended her hand and held his. "I want you to know how grateful I am. Maybe I'll be able to do something for you someday."

"You already have."

"How you can say that? I've never done anything for you."

"Oh, yes, you have."

"How?"

"By being yourself."

"I don't follow."

"When I first saw you on the university campus, you stood out in the crowd. You looked different, in control, full of confidence, full of life. Later, when you became a part of the sixties crowd which plagued your country, you lost direction. It's the only plausible explanation I have for what you did to yourself."

"I presume you're referring to my marrying Mani."

"You're right. I am."

"And you feel that now I'm my old self again."

"I may be wrong, but I sure hope so."

"You're absolutely right," she answered without hesitation. "I hate to admit it. But you are."

"You better get some rest. It's two in the morning. You might have a rough day ahead of you tomorrow."

"Friends?" she asked smiling.

"Always." He whirled around and hurried down the stairs. But, he was not quick enough.

She caught a glimpse of the tears welling in his eyes and she knew she had witnessed love in its purest form, ready to give, no strings attached.

A deep sigh gave her momentary relief. Her body and mind were limp with exhaustion. In her present state, she was of use to no one. She needed rest before she could function again. She pulled a chair and sat next to her daughter's bed. Since both doctors had told her Kelly's condition might deteriorate without warning, she decided sleep had to be postponed. She had to keep an eye on the child.

The early morning hours brought a slight chill. Andrea got a blanket and wrapped herself in it.

She fell asleep immediately and dreamt the same dream she always dreamt whenever she slept fitfully. She was a little girl, in her favorite pink dress, strolling in their wheat fields, without a care in the world. Her father was always there, waiting with open arms to embrace her. She ran to him as fast as she could. He picked her up. She threw her arms around his neck, burying her face in his chest.

There was too much noise, too much traffic in and out of the room. Voices, whispers, squeaking shoes. Hospitals are no place to rest, she told herself and pulled the blanket over her head.

She felt a strong hand shaking her. Someone said, "Madame, Madame, wake up. It's Kelly. She's dead."

Chapter 32

People came and people stayed. When the living room at the Abbassi residence filled to capacity, part of the crowd drifted to the back yard, men in one group, women in another, children roaming everywhere. They ate and they drank and conversed in whispers. Andrea watched numbed, uncomprehending. Women she'd never seen before, walked in and dutifully kissed her on both cheeks. The men shook her hand, striving to portray the mournful look expected of them. Tradition dictated a rigid set of rules to be observed whenever a death occurred. Everyone was expected to abide by those rules and did.

For Andrea, it was a study in human behavior exemplifying the hypocrisy of men, trapped by ancient customs, unaltered by time, robotic, pacified by motions accepted unquestioningly. Few had known or met Kelly. It was a party, an opportunity to meet acquaintances they probably saw only on similar occasions.

Two servants hired for the day, circled through the crowd serving tea and assorted sweets.

Mani had a black suite on, a black necktie and a black look. A master at concealing his true feelings, he carried on with his duties as a model husband and host.

Naene sat in her favorite armchair. She accepted the condolences of her guests, frequently dramatizing her grief by bursts of sobbing. It was late in the afternoon. She was being served her third meal of the day when Mani ushered a mullah in.

Naene invited the cleric to join her. The room was packed. Two guests sitting on the sofa where Andrea sat, rose, greeted the cleric and offered him their seats. A few minutes later, the maid placed a large tray of food on the coffee table. Naene invited the mullah to help himself. The mullah obliged after declining the offer several times. To attack the food right away would be in poor taste. Visitors had to show reluctance and the host had to insist. It was a ritual without which few Iranians knew how to function. It was known as "taarof." Its purpose easily eluded the uninitiated. It had not ceased to amaze Andrea.

When the contents of the tray was reduced to a pile of chicken bones, the cleric sat back on the sofa, raised his head and studied the crowd with intense, black eyes. A signal from him brought Mani scurrying to his side. The two men talked in hushed voices.

"I've instructed my assistant to take care of the formalities," the mullah said. "The burial has to take place tomorrow. As your religious leader, it's my duty to remind you that Islam urges its followers to bury the dead as soon as possible."

"I understand, Mullah Hamid," Mani replied. "I have no objections."

"To avoid problems in the future, you should make sure your wife agrees."

"Why shouldn't she agree? The dead have to be buried. What else?"

"She might want to take the body to her country," Mullah Hamid snapped impatiently. "I've had a few unpleasant experiences with foreigners in the past. Not one would permit us to entomb their deceased in this country."

"She was my child as much as hers. In my house I make the decisions. Please proceed with the necessary arrangements."

"You converted to Christianity to marry her. Therefore the child is Christian. She can create trouble for us."

"My conversion to Christianity was just a show for her father's benefit. She doesn't believe in religion. I do. I pray five times a day. My religion is my life."

Andrea was ready to explode. Lying came so naturally to him.

"Beheshte-Zahra has to be the cemetery," Mullah Hamid continued. "It's the prestigious thing to do. A little more expensive but well worth the honor it will bring the family."

For a moment Mani looked pensive, then he asked, "Is that where my mother wants her buried?"

"Yes. If the authorities permit us to do so. Legally you are Christians. Beheshte-Zahra is reserved for true believers of Islam. A sizable contribution is in order."

Mani glanced apprehensively at his mother. She was busy eating her dessert. He turned to the mullah.

"She was a child without sin," the cleric continued, "even if her mother is a nonbeliever. Her burial in Beheshte-Zahra will assure her a spot in heaven. We can't punish the child for the mistakes of the parents."

"You're right. Excuse me for a moment, please. I'd like to inform my wife."

Mullah Hamid sat back. He wiped his mouth and beard with his hand and lit a cigarette.

There was no room on the sofa. Mani crouched next to Andrea. "The funeral arrangements will be made for tomorrow noon. Kelly will be buried in Beheshte-Zahra. Don't bother to argue."

She remained motionless, staring vacuously into space.

"Answer me, you bitch," he ordered through clenched

teeth. "Does it give you pleasure to humiliate me in the presence of all these people?"

"You said don't bother to argue."

He raised his head. Mullah Hamid's eyes were focused on him. Gently, he placed his hand on hers. She saw the "watch me everybody I love my wife" act coming on. "These are hard times for both of us. Please forgive me. I know I've treated you badly. It won't happen again. I promise."

She pulled her hand away slowly. "What is it you want?"

"I want you to forgive and forget."

"I'd rather leave. It will be better for both of us."

"We will dear," he said soothingly. "Just be patient. I've rented an apartment in Sultanatabad. It's beautifully furnished. We'll start over."

"I want to return home, to the States. Not move to an apartment."

Unperturbed, he continued, "You'll see. Everything will be different. We have to stay here until the funeral is over. Then we move to our new apartment."

"You and me and Farhad. Right?"

Stunned, he was speechless for a moment. "What . . . what makes you say something like that?"

"It's true. Isn't it?"

"That damn brother of mine. It has to be him."

"Why? I can judge for myself. You've had nothing to do with me or your daughter since we arrived. Nothing but demand money."

"My sexual preferences are my business. Maybe I like being bisexual. If you don't like it, tough."

"Don't flatter yourself," she said calmly. "You're not bisexual. You're gay. But you're a pretty good actor."

After an awkward pause and a nervous shrug, he rose and moved away, his head high, his chin jutting forward, his manner defiant. He advanced toward the entrance to greet a family who had just arrived.

As he had done with previous guests, Mani described his

feelings of loss and pain to the newcomers. He had not yet finished when Farhad tapped him on the shoulder. "There's an American waiting at the entrance. He wants to talk to you."

Mani cast a quick glance at the doorway. With a voice barely above a whisper he said to Farhad, "I find it particularly irritating that this man makes it his business to appear when he is least wanted." He headed toward the door. "Mr. Conrad. Please come in. What an unexpected pleasure."

Andrea chuckled inwardly. Iranians were expected to treat all visitors with warmth and cordiality. But for Mani acting in direct contradiction to his feelings seemed to come as naturally as breathing.

"I hope I'm not disturbing you," Phil Conrad said. "I'm here on behalf of our Embassy. We'd like to extend our condolences to you and your wife. How is she?"

"She's as well as can be expected under the circumstances. Would you like to talk to her?"

"If I may?"

"Certainly. This way please." Mani directed Mr. Conrad to the sofa in the living room. Andrea pulled herself to the edge of the sofa to make room for Phil Conrad. The rest of the sofa was filled by the mullah.

"Mr. Conrad. This is my wife, Andrea. Andrea, meet Mr. Phil Conrad. He likes to be called Phil. He's here on behalf of your embassy."

Andrea extended her right hand and shook hands with Phil Conrad. "Pleased to meet you."

"It's been an exhausting day for Andrea," Mani said. "Not knowing the language and the local customs are an additional burden on her. But she's taken it surprisingly well. It would be impossible to tell by looking at her that she's the one who lost a daughter. Most of the crying and wailing is done by my relatives who never knew Kelly."

More guests arrived. Mani left to greet them.

Phil spoke to Andrea in hushed tones, his eyes incessantly probing the crowd.

"Have you reached a decision?" He could have as well been discussing the weather.

"Yes."

"The cleric next to me is fluent in our language. Keep your voice as low as you can."

"Do you know my brother-in-law, Sayid?" She raised her head. Mani was eyeing them nervously.

Phil must have noticed it too. "Ignore him," he advised. "He's worried. He can't figure out why I'm here."

"He doesn't bother me any more. I was asking you if you knew Sayid."

"I do, quite well."

"Have you talked to him recently?"

"I do daily. He works with us."

"Did he tell you about Mani's refusal to sign the permission slip for Kelly's surgery?"

"He did."

"It's his contention that I wanted Kelly dead."

"I heard."

"Then you understand my willingness to work with you. He killed her. We have to put a stop to his killings."

"Are you sure? Have you considered the implications?"

"Absolutely. Any doubts I had vanished with Kelly's death. There's too much at stake."

"I'm delighted. But you mustn't underestimate him. He can't be a member of such a radical group and not be ruthless. You have to be very careful."

"His curiosity is getting the better of him," Andrea whispered. "He's coming toward us."

Phil shifted his eyes to his hands lacing them together.

Someone called Mani. He spun around.

Mullah Hamid's blind assistant stood in the doorway holding what looked like forms. Mani took the man to his office.

"Let me tell you quickly what we want you to do," Phil said. "Move to the apartment with him. You agree to stay with him until an arrangement can be worked out. Meanwhile, insist on his letting you go. You have no desire to stay here. You want to return to the States."

"Supposing he agrees."

"He won't. He can't. He has orders to do everything in his power to win you over. They need money."

"That's going to be his next move."

"Can you handle it?"

"He can pressure me. But legally there's nothing he can do. My parents made him sign a prenuptial agreement."

"That's fantastic. How come he agreed?"

"He had no choice. And at the time, it didn't seem to matter. He was sure of my love and he was right. I was willing to do anything for him."

"Here he comes now," Phil said in a low voice.

Mani came and stood next to his wife.

Phil rose. "Thank you for your hospitality, Mr. Abbassi. I have to leave now. If there's any way we can help, please let me know."

"Thank you for coming." He accompanied Phil to the door.

Farhad came in from the back yard. He spoke to Mani in Farsi. "Did he leave?"

She could easily overhear them.

"He left," Mani answered. "I don't trust him and I don't trust her. I know they're plotting something. Probably arranging to sneak her out of the country. That man is a smooth operator. I must get more information on him."

Without waiting for a reply from Farhad, he hesitated, then pretending to be exhausted, casually sat on the carpet next to Andrea. She could sense his discomfort.

"It was nice of Mr. Conrad to come."

"He came as a representative of my Embassy. I'm sure they do the same for all Americans."

"You think so?"

"Why are you so nervous? Why should a simple visit by

an emissary upset you so much?"

"What makes you say that. All I said was it was nice of him to come."

"You don't have to say anything. You were coming apart at the seams watching him talk to me. Not everyone goes through life like it was a war zone full of men with perfidious schemes. It must be very hard on you."

Instinctively he raised his hand to hit her but quickly regained his self control. He rose and walked over to Farhad.

"I'd like to stomp her to death. Her and that turbaned mullah who ordered me to be nice to her. What do they know about being married to an American? Everyone thinks marriage to an American is a one-way ticket to paradise. What they don't know is how vicious they can be once you step on their toes."

"Calm down," Farhad interrupted. "You're hysterical."

"I can't calm down. I'd rather rob a bank, prostitute myself or become a mullah and steal from the poor than subject myself to this abuse."

"This is neither the time nor the place for you to have a fit. Mullah Hamid is watching. Pull yourself together. Here. Drink a cup of tea then go talk to her. Nicely." Farhad reached for a cup of tea from the tray on the coffee table and gave it to Mani.

Mani looked around casually. Mullah Hamid's eyes were glued on him. He drank the tea, placed the empty cup on the coffee table then returned and crouched next to Andrea. He put his hand on her thigh. "Please forgive me. It's all my fault. Kelly's death has brought me back to my senses. I see life in a different perspective now. Give me a second chance. Can you find it in you heart to forgive me?"

The man was amazing. To achieve his objectives, he cajoled, coaxed, lied, seduced or threatened as the situation demanded, and on a moment's notice.

Something in her snapped. "Don't you ever give up? Your antiquated tactics are counter productive. How dare you use the death of your child for your vile, despicable schemes."

Mani's chin quivered. He pulled his hand away, rose and stomped out of the room.

He returned, spotted Farhad a few feet away from Andrea drinking beer.

"It's useless," he whispered. "The lamb has turned into a lion whose cub has been snatched from her. It doesn't matter what I say. She doesn't believe me."

"She'll come around. Don't worry. It's a matter of time."

"We don't have time. How will we know what that bastard's interest is in her?"

"You worry too much. While you were in your office, I talked to our contact at the American Embassy. He assured me Conrad is a simple employee. His job is to look after the welfare of Americans in Iran. Nothing more."

Mani looked dumbfounded. "I . . . I can't tell you how relieved I am. I . . . I can actually feel the knot in my stomach ebb away. She was telling the truth. She always does. I should have believed her."

Chapter 33

"The important thing for you to remember is to act normal," Phil said. "You want a divorce, you want your passport and you want to leave the country. You have no interest in your husband, his activities or his friends. Occasionally, you might have to play the deeply wronged innocent."

They were in the living room of the apartment which had been rented for Mani. It was beautifully furnished with imported furniture and Persian carpets of exquisite design and workmanship. Andrea walked on the carpets with bare feet. Soiling gorgeous pieces of art was intolerable to her.

"That shouldn't be too difficult. They're hardly ever here. Coffee?"

"Yes please. Black."

Andrea went to the kitchen.

It was the eleventh day after Kelly's death. She ached for the child and was constantly tortured by her brutal death. The killings had to be stopped. That was the sole motivating force which kept her going. Maybe then, the ever-present agonizing episode would recede into the background and liberate her.

Kelly's death made her that much more sensitive to the pain Layla suffered with the loss of her husband. The second day after moving to the apartment, Andrea went looking for her. Someone she didn't know answered the doorbell. It was the landlady. "Layla moved out on New Year's day," she told Andrea. She did not know where.

Andrea was not overly concerned. She was probably with her parents in Qom. She had Layla's parent's phone number.

She called. Repeatedly. No one answered.

Maybe they went on vacation, Andrea told herself. But there was no way Layla could locate her. Andrea had moved. If Layla contacted the Abbassis, she knew Naene would not give her the phone number to the apartment.

She returned from the kitchen with two cups of coffee.

"This apartment is for use by anti-government activists," Phil said. "We would like you to make a mental note of what's said, what's done and by whom. The most recent information we have suggests an escalation of assassinations and bombings are in the works this very moment."

"Then what?"

"Then comes the hardest part. Passing that information on to me without arousing suspicion."

"Is this place bugged?" Andrea asked.

"No. We knew they'd check. They did."

The implication was clear. It was her responsibility to gather and transmit information. She was gripped by an uneasy foreboding. She felt the color drain from her face.

"You look awfully white. Are you sure you want to go through with it?" he asked.

"I'd like nothing better."

"You're really determined, aren't you?"

"Absolutely."

"In that case let's proceed. Still, if you change your mind, let me know."

"I won't change my mind."

"I didn't think you would. Nonetheless, it's my duty to make it clear to you that you'll be dealing with assassins, revolutionaries who will stop at nothing, men who are willing to sacrifice their families without flinching."

She felt a sudden chill tingle her spine. "I understand."

"I'll admit, your help will be invaluable. We're never sure of the loyalty of the locals. Few are committed royalists. Most oblige the highest bidder. The information they provide is often exaggerated or downright false. That's how we lost the two Americans last month."

"I'll do all I can."

"Subjecting an inexperienced young woman to a bunch of fanatics for whom brutality is an appealing form of amusement, fills me with immense pain. They are not burdened by religion, morals, scruples or ethics. Their one goal is to get rid of the Shah - at any price."

She shivered. "Do you mind if I close the window? I feel kind of chilly."

"Go ahead. You can't be cold. You're nervous. It's eighty degrees outside."

She nodded absently, closed the window, and returned to the sofa.

"I'm not trying to scare you but I do want you to know what you're getting yourself into before it's too late. It's frightening- and true."

"I'll be fine. Please go on."

"Your husband and his friend Farhad are pawns, underlings. The real jobs are done by rebels trained in Lebanon by Palestinian commandoes. Three week ago we received word that six Iranians who have undergone extensive training in Lebanon have returned to Iran. I have their pictures with me."

He took an envelope from his coat pocket and handed it to her. "Please commit their looks to memory. If they come here or you see them any where else, get in touch with me immediately."

She took a quick look and gave them back.

He looked surprised. "Please study them carefully. You won't get a second chance."

"I have a photographic memory for pictures, faces and numbers. I'll keep you informed."

"Score one for us," he said. "That's fantastic. A priceless advantage. We can sure use it."

"How?"

"What do you mean, how?"

"In the event I see these men, how do I contact you?"

"Oh, that. I'll give you instructions on that later. Let me first tell you about the six men. They've gone underground. They sneaked in through the Iraqi border."

"Any leads?"

"A few. Not very reliable. We know they're members of the Revolutionary Council. We have reason to believe they're preparing a major assault of some sort. We don't know what. We need to know before it happens. We're often kept in the dark even after an event takes place, particularly if the victims are Iranian."

"Why?"

"To avoid panic in the public and not to give undue cause for rejoicing to the rebels. The government's policy is total censorship."

"Sounds like overkill," Andrea commented.

"By our own standards, yes. By Iranian standards, it hardly matters. Freedom of the press is a barbaric Western concept which a Middle Eastern dictator can ill-afford."

"What are we looking for?"

"To draw the attention of the world to their cause, it's reasonable to expect they'll target Americans. The propaganda advantage is immense. Neither the King nor his censorship will be able to prevent word from leaking out."

"It gives me the creeps," Andrea murmured.

"We have issued directives to all our people to deviate

from their routines and be on the lookout for suspicious characters. There are fifty thousand Americans here, almost all living in the north of the city. We can only provide security to a select few."

"Since we're not wanted, why don't we pack up and leave."

"Because we have too much invested here and because geopolitically being here is of great advantage to us."

"So we stay and fend for ourselves as best we can."

"That's about it. Americans living in foreign countries expect a certain degree of resentment and are rarely disappointed. It's when resentment brews and becomes lethal that our job becomes complicated. Complicated but not impossible. At present it's to our advantage to support the Shah. There's no better alternative."

"It boggles my mind. We support a one-man tyranny and manage to alienate thirty five million people in the process."

"These people are not ready yet. For democracy to function, you need a mature, discriminating, well-informed public, otherwise, there will be chaos."

"And yet there would be no terrorists if there was no demand for blind subservience."

"You are young and eager but hardly naive. Your inquisitiveness is remarkably direct. I like it. I prefer working with someone who is well informed and logical."

"Thank you. I can't commit myself to a cause unless I'm fully convinced it's deserving and worthy of preservation."

"Precisely. However, since freedom is an experience which has eluded Iranians throughout history, it has to be introduced gradually, in small doses. The proper antidote is not terrorism but education."

"You're talking decades."

"I am. The alternative is anarchy. Democracy is an unaffordable luxury, tantamount to mob rule. Evolution not revolution is the only sensible approach."

"And you feel we're doing our share to help achieve this

goal."

"Don't let anyone fool you. We're here to make sure the country stays pro West and we're here to make money. We are not missionaries by any stretch of the imagination."

"Thank you for your honesty," she said. "I hope my questions were not too exacting. I had to be sure."

"I'd be concerned if you hadn't asked."

"What about top Iranian officials. My concern is for Cyrus. Mani hates him."

"Short of a miracle, it would be very difficult to get him. His movements are unpredictable, his whereabouts known only to the King."

"I gather Helga is still in Germany."

"She is. Cyrus wants her to remain there until it's safe for her to return. That reminds me. There was a message for you from the General's nephew. I believe his name is Dariush."

Andrea felt the heat rush to her cheeks. "Oh? What did he have to say?"

"I didn't ask. You have to cut all relations with him immediately. It's too risky. At the moment, you can't afford any complications in your life. Especially, if you're serious about wanting to help us."

She did live in a fish bowl. Before long, Mani would hear about it. She had to agree. "I have no objections."

"Good. The General told him not to send any more messages. Hopefully, he'll heed the General's advice."

Andrea was eager to change the subject. "Mani left this morning but he did not say when he'd be back. When should I expect them?"

"Four days. Maybe a week."

"What is he up to now?"

"Abadan. Their instructions are to incite the workers of the oil fields to strike, to paralyze the economy. They're going for the jugular."

"I don't think there will be a strike."

Astonished, he stared at her. "What have you got?"

"Bits of conversation I heard last night. Mani and Farhad came in about midnight. They were up till three in the morning. I gathered the workers were reluctant to go on strike for fear of reprisals. The plan is for some workers to call in sick and for the rest to report to work. Those at work will be instructed to work slowly, very slowly."

"You're incredible."

"Farhad mentioned the name Parish twice. You might want to check it out."

"I will."

"I'm starved. I want to fix myself a sandwich. Would you like one?"

"No sandwiches," he said. "Let's go to the Intercontinental Hotel. The rooftop restaurant has a terrific rotisserie. We'll celebrate."

"I'd love to. I'll be with you in a few minutes."

She emerged dressed in a pink linen suit with a touch of make up, her long hair bouncing in graceful curls as she walked.

"Before we go," he said, "I should tell you how to pass on the information you gather. Have you noticed a small apartment next to the main entrance of this apartment building?"

"Yes."

"It's occupied by a middle-aged man employed as the concierge."

"I've seen him."

"He's an American of Greek origin. He's been here eight years. Speaks the language fluently. As a matter of fact he speaks several dialects. Everyone thinks he's Iranian."

"I would have never guessed. He certainly looks Iranian."

"He's one of us. The name is Mohammed. He's your contact."

"A Greek named Mohammed?" She couldn't help laughing.

"It sounds funny but it works. You should watch him pray. He's even got the mullahs fooled."

"What about Sayid?"

"What about him?"

"If, for some reason, I need to contact you urgently and Mohammed is not around, should I talk to Sayid? You mentioned he works with you." Sayid was constantly on her mind. A puzzle she couldn't solve. She was anxious to learn all she could about him.

He took his time answering her. "Sayid has always been an enigma for us. He has always come through whenever we've needed him. Savak swears by him. But I'm convinced he is his own person, an exact opposite of his brother. His loyalty is to justice. Not to an institution or a person."

"There's something mysterious about him. I can never predict his behavior."

"There's a lot you probably don't know about him and yes there might be occasion when you have to reach me through him. So you might as well know. His father was killed by Savak and yet his best friends are from Savak. He left his studies in the States abruptly. We don't know why. His wife was killed in a head-on collision with a drunk taxi driver. The driver was also killed. Sayid has supported the family of the taxi driver since."

The shocked look on Andrea's face made him stop. "What wife?"

"Sorry. I thought you knew. When he was twenty, the daughter of a wealthy industrialist in this country fell madly in love with him. She was sixteen. An only child. Sayid did not want to marry her but in the end he agreed. Rumor has it that his father-in-law placed millions of dollars in a Swiss bank in Sayid's name the day of the wedding."

"Did they have any children?"

"She died two months after they were married."

Andrea was quietly turning the information over in her mind. Maybe his wife's death was the reason for the perpetually pained expression on his face, his chronic dependency on alcohol, his gambling, his melancholy. Why had Savak killed his father?

"I asked Sayid about his father's death. He said his father died of a stroke. I had not heard about his having been married?"

"Probably because money was involved. In the Middle East people hide their wealth. It's too risky. They can't rely on the government for protection or fair taxation. His father did die of a stroke but only after Savak worked him over."

"Why? What did they want from his father?"

"I really don't know. I haven't asked and he hasn't mentioned it."

"There's a lot about him I don't understand."

"He is very tight lipped. Sayid is probably the second most powerful man in Iran."

"You're putting me on."

"No, I'm not. Our information is that he saved the King's life while the King was on a visit to London. The King was supposed to hold a press conference in the Savoy. Sayid learned from a dissident group that a time bomb, hidden in the lobby, was due to go off within minutes after the King's arrival. It seems at the risk of his own life, Sayid managed to save the King and scores of others unfortunate enough to be there."

"That's incredible. He never talks about it."

"We're told Sayid is the only man the King trusts implicitly. Apparently, what amazed the King most was, when he asked Sayid what made him do it, Sayid told him simply that he hated violence."

"I can't believe it." Andrea shook her head.

"Believe it and forget it. Only a handful of people know about it. The King has lavished him with gifts and unprecedented power. He gives the gifts to charity and has turned down government posts which others kill for. The only offer he has accepted is to keep an eye on the excesses of Savak.

Human rights is a major concern of the government lately. The King wants to mollify his critics, especially President Carter. Sayid has done a fantastic job of keeping Savak in line."

"I'm amazed the terrorists haven't killed him yet. I mean for saving the King."

"The incident was kept quiet. Only a few people know. You must keep it to yourself."

"Thanks for trusting me."

"Contact him in case of an emergency. If you can't reach Mohammed."

"The reason I asked about Sayid is because of an incident which happened yesterday afternoon. I don't know if it's relevant or not. I wanted to check with someone but didn't know who. A grubby looking young man with a tool box in his hand, rang the door bell and insisted I let him in. He said he needed to check the air conditioning unit. I told him to come back when my husband is home. He was furious when I wouldn't let him in."

"That surprises me," Phil said. "Mohammed has strict instructions not to let anyone enter the building without his permission."

"Well, someone did. He was here again, this afternoon."

"We better check it out. Let's go talk to Mohammed."

Mohammed's door was closed.

They knocked. There was no answer.

Phil turned to Andrea. "Come to think of it I did not see him when I came in. I thought he went to get supper or something."

He tried the lock. The door opened. The place was dark. He groped and located the switch. A bare bulb hanging from the ceiling lit the room. A pool of blood covered the tile floor.

Phil moved swiftly. There were only two rooms. The door in between was open. He rushed to the next room. There was a body on the floor face down. It was

Mohammed. There was blood around his lips and nose. The back window was open. Phil checked Mohammed's pulse and breathing. Mohammed was alive. Barely. There were no stab wounds or bullet wounds.

He handed her his car keys. "Down the street. Two blocks south. Park in the back. Keep the engine running."

Andrea rushed over to take the keys, stumbled, and fell. She got up impatient with her clumsiness, her eyes searching for whatever it was that made her trip.

A black tool box identical to the one she'd seen that afternoon, lay carelessly on the floor partially hidden from sight by the semidarkness of the room.

Chapter 34

Phil's information was correct. Four days later, in the afternoon, Mani walked in with Farhad and another man in his early thirties. Phil had instructed her not to call the hospital to inquire about Mohammed and pretend she knew nothing about the incident. Fortunately, minutes before her husband's return, Phil called to let her know Mohammed was showing signs of consciousness.

"Hi, Andrea," Mani said with forced cheerfulness. "How have you been?"

Andrea was reading a book. "Fine thank you."

She cast a quick glance at the third man and immediately returned her attention to her book. It took superhuman effort to do so. She'd never seen anyone like him before.

He was a tall, thin man. Very tall by Iranian standards, with a long, thick neck stretched to a curve. Almost as an afterthought, an elongated head appeared with patches of black crinkly hair which failed to cover several bald spots. Andrea had often seen bald spots before in adults and children. She was told it was a common ailment, alopecia, mostly due to unsanitary living conditions, sometimes stress. Few bothered to treat it.

The man had a black eye comfortably resting in the left socket. The right eye was grayish, protruding fiercely, as though ready to pop out. The narrow face came to a point with a thin, sharp nose giving him a triangular profile, broken only by an irregular, bony mass between his eyes. Thick lips boasting a wing-shaped moustache and bushy, bulging eyebrows made him look like a prime candidate for a horror movie.

"How are you doing, Andrea." It was Farhad smiling slyly, a look of, "I've won; you've lost" on his face. "Hope you weren't too lonely when we were gone."

His affrontery did not surprise her. He could be rude, intimidating, charming or disgusting, effortlessly. Mani tried to imitate him, but he had to work at it. She chose not to dignify his sarcasm with an answer. She returned her attention to her book.

Mani and Farhad conversed in whispers. Then Mani approached Andrea. "I'm expecting a few business associates. They'll be here any moment. We have a meeting. Could you go shopping or for a walk or something."

"I have done my shopping and my walking. You said when we move to the apartment, we'd start over. You didn't mention anything about using it as your office. Can't you rent a place for your meetings?"

"Why don't you rent it for me and deny me the pleasure of disturbing you?"

"There's a better solution. Let me leave the country and you'll be free as a bird."

"What do you take me for? A fool."

The doorbell rang.

Mani hurried to the door.

Two policemen waited to be let in.

"Which one of you is Mani Abbassi?" One of the men asked.

Andrea knew the sight of any law enforcement officer terrified Mani. She watched him as he turned white and remained glued to the spot. He could not talk.

Farhad came to his rescue. “Gentlemen, please, come in. We were about to have tea. Please join us. We have delicious sweets from Isfahan which will melt in your mouths.”

“Thank you, we have not come to visit,” said the same policeman. He must have surmised which of the men was Mani. He pointed at him. “You, come with us.”

“Why?” Mani stuttered.

“She must be your wife,” The policeman said ignoring Mani’s question.

Andrea stopped short of answering. She had to remind herself that she did not understand or speak the language.

“Does she understand Farsi?” the policeman asked.

“No.” Farhad volunteered.

Rubbing his hands on the pockets of his uniform, the policeman shifted his weight from one foot to the other eyeing his partner who seemed to be totally absorbed with Andrea, practically devouring her with his eyes.

“Both of you have to come with us to the police station,” the same policeman said.

Farhad translated.

“Why?” Andrea asked.

She was ignored.

“Why?” Farhad asked the officer in Farsi.

“They’ll find out when we get there. Our job is to deliver them to the station for questioning.” His partner’s eyes remained glued on Andrea. Her presence seemed to have induced an acute case of discomfort in him. His right hand remained busy rearranging his genitals, the smile on his face betraying how delightful the discomfort was.

Farhad translated.

Mani had slumped in a chair, a blank expression on his face, looking into space.

“Please tell the gentleman,” Andrea said, “I’m not going

anywhere, with anyone, without a lawyer."

Her words brought a delinquent smile to her admirer's face. "Madame, you not worry. I take care of you. I captain."

"I'm sure Mr. Abbassi can tell you everything you need to know."

Mani cringed.

"No," said the captain. "Madame come."

"I'm not going anywhere."

The captain grinned, exposing a gold tooth on each side of his mouth. He spoke quickly to Farhad, in Farsi.

"The captain says you have to go with them."

She glanced around. Mani sat in a corner in stony silence, studying his hands.

"Mani, please call a lawyer."

He did not move.

She reached for the phone and dialed Sayid's number.

If she was lucky, someone other than Mani's mother would answer.

Mani's mother answered and slammed the receiver in her ear.

She turned to Farhad. "Please get Sayid on the line for me."

"What makes you think he can help? These men are not from Savak."

"Please try."

"It's four in the afternoon. He sleeps. Remember? He'll be furious."

"Let me worry about that."

Mani continued studying his hands.

Farhad dialed the number. Mani's mother answered. He asked for Sayid then handed the receiver to Andrea.

"Hello."

"Sayid, this is Andrea. Sorry to disturb you. But we have a problem. There are two police officers here who insist your brother and I accompany them to a police station for questioning."

"Is Mani there?"

"He's here."

"What's he doing?"

"Studying his knuckles."

"I should have known."

"Can you recommend a lawyer or someone who can help?"

"What can a lawyer do?"

"I don't know. They said it's their job to take us in for questioning. That's about it."

He interrupted her. "Stall them. I'll be right there."

He was. Within twenty minutes.

"Gentlemen, could we talk outside?"

The policemen followed him out.

He returned shortly. He said to Andrea, "Stay here until you hear from me." He turned to Mani. "Don't get any ideas in your head. The captain is accompanying me downtown, the other policeman is remaining behind to make sure neither of you leaves."

"Thank you Sayid," Andrea said.

Sayid left.

Andrea went to the kitchen to prepare coffee.

The doorbell rang three times and stopped.

Farhad opened the door and ushered two men in.

They were young, in their early twenties at the most.

Mani looked revived. He greeted them with a smile. They moved to the dining room.

Andrea glanced at the newcomers. She knew who they were instantly. Phil had shown her their pictures four days prior.

"We almost didn't come," said one of the men. "There's a policeman at the entrance of your building."

"Did he question you?" asked Farhad.

"No."

"He's there to make sure my wife and I don't leave," Mani said.

"Why?"

"Something about taking us to the police station for questioning. I have no idea what it's about."

One of the newcomers caught sight of Andrea in the kitchen. "Why is she here?"

"She can't leave," Mani replied. "That's what the policeman at the entrance of the building is there for. To make sure neither of us leaves."

The tall, sullen faced man said authoritatively, "It doesn't matter if she stays. Mani assures me she doesn't understand our language. It will look suspicious if we insist. Let's get on with our work."

"Gentlemen," Mani said clearing his throat. "Mullah Hamid advised me to be a model husband again." He wiggled in his chair restlessly, as though unsure of the reaction the men would have to the proposition he was about to make. "Mullah Hamid insists she can be a valuable asset."

"How?" asked one of the newcomers.

"He says because she's an American, Savak will not question our living in this neighborhood and we can use her as a courier. They will not suspect her."

"From what we hear," Manucheir interjected, "she's not too crazy about you lately."

Mani shifted his position again. "It's only a matter of time. She'll change. She's upset because I didn't sign the permission form for our daughter's surgery."

"Why didn't you?" asked the man with the curved neck.

The eyes of the four men were on Mani. "Agha Mehdi," Mani said with a frightened voice, "I thought if I hold out she'll offer me money. The child meant a lot to her."

"You're stupid. You know that," Agha Mehdi said with uncontrollable rage.

There was a brief silence.

Andrea sipped her coffee and pretended to read her book.

Agha Mehdi turned his attention to Farhad. He asked, "What do you think? Can she be trusted?"

Andrea listened without raising her head from the book. Farhad was too much of a diplomat and too shrewd to commit himself. He had never made a secret of his hatred and distrust of mullahs. He said, "A few months ago I would have agreed with Mullah Hamid without reservations. She's committed to social justice. I'm sure she would have joined us eagerly. But since then, unfortunate incidents happened, none of which could be foreseen. I suggest we wait. She's convinced Mani was the cause of their daughter's death. Mani had nothing to do with it. The child was a vegetable. Sooner or later, she would have died." He stopped, scrutinized the faces of the men, then continued. "An Iranian mother would have been overjoyed to have such a burden lifted from her. Foreigners are different. I believe once she realizes how much more freedom she has, she may not admit it, but she'll like it."

Andrea wished she could smack him.

"What's your opinion, Kurosh?" Agha Mehdi asked the other visitor who had yet to say a word.

"I agree with Farhad. Let's wait."

Agha Mehdi stretched his long neck allowing his protruding gray eye to roam from face to face. "We are in the early stages of planning. We don't need her yet. Try to win her over. Especially for this mission. We could sure use her. If everything goes as expected, the hawk should return before the end of May. Our brothers are following his every move. We have planted contacts in Swiss Air. They will inform us of his travel plans when confirmed."

Hawk? Swiss Air? Was it possible? Andrea's thoughts raced.

"I disagree," Kurosh interjected curtly.

Andrea decided to nickname Agha Mehdi, Emu. From her seat in the kitchen she could see all four men, but Agha Mehdi sat directly across from her in the dining room. The unexpected reaction from Kurosh made his gray eye bulge even more and his face turn purple.

Manucheir took over. "As I see it, this job can't be preplanned as proposed by our esteemed brother, Agha Mehdi. The hawk is an impulsive, restless animal. He does what he wants on the spur of the moment. Our agents should be given freedom to take advantage of any situation which might present itself unexpectedly. It's the only way it will work."

Mehdi's voice was squeaky and thin sounding like it was being forced through a narrow metal tube, like the whine of a hungry hyena. Banging his clenched fist on the table he shouted, "They forgot to teach you discipline while you were training. I give the orders. You'll do well to keep that always in mind."

Andrea repeated the names. One was Manucheir, the other Kurosh. She wondered if these were their real names. Hopefully, Phil could sort it out.

She herself was dying to know who the hawk was.

Kurosh, it seemed was not easily thwarted or intimidated. "That may be so," he replied, "but this is one situation which demands instant decision making. We should strike the moment we feel we have a chance to succeed. I must insist."

One look at Emu and Andrea was sure the men would come to blows.

Farhad, always the mediator, intervened, oozing charm. "Gentlemen. Please. We should put our differences to work for us – not destroy us. Achieving our goal is what matters. Let's pool our ideas together. I'm sure we can find an approach acceptable to all."

Meanwhile, Emu regained his composure. "He's a hothead. He doesn't know what he's talking about. It's not like before. Anybody who is somebody is heavily guarded. In all probability it will be a suicidal mission. Loss of trained commandoes sets us back years. In situations like this, shrewdly calculated and logically executed plans are the only ones that work."

"I'm sure there are other alternatives," Mani offered eagerly.

"Like what?" Kurosh asked, his voice full of sarcasm.

"Like the new mansion he's building," Farhad interjected. "Reliable sources inform us that the mansion has forty rooms, two movie theaters, three swimming pools, an underground garage with parking facilities for hundred fifty cars, its own TV tower and the whole place is monitored by closed circuit TV. Apparently there's nothing like it in the whole of Asia. It's been under construction for five years and is still far from being finished."

"I investigated," Mani interrupted excitedly. "There are hundreds of workers on the premises and more being hired. Maybe one of us could be planted as a construction worker or a gardener or something. It shouldn't take long after that."

It must be the King's brother, Andrea surmised. No one else would dare embark on a project of that magnitude. The King would not tolerate it. Phil will know. There can't be too many mansions like that. For a moment she thought it might be Helga's husband. Once before she'd heard Farhad refer to the General as the hawk and Helga had mentioned that her husband was building a house for the past five years which was still far from completion. But why would the General build a forty room house?

Yet, Emu had stressed the fact that they needed her especially for this mission. Why? A piece of the puzzle was missing. She loved figuring out how different minds worked. It fascinated and intrigued her. Minds like these were unique with their ruthless determination, ferocious enthusiasm, and firm conviction that death for the cause was the noblest of achievements man could strive for. The thought of outwitting their treacherous schemes filled her with a mixture of cautious excitement and apprehension.

Emu was not pacified. Reducing his voice to a whisper, he said, "You gentlemen overlook a major factor when you propose plans without regard to time. It's best to strike when the iron is hot. The two Americans are dead. Savak is in confusion, their credibility badly tarnished. Now is the time to strike. We can't wait for the hawk to return when it pleases him, hope that he will employ one of us, and pray the right moment will come sometime in the future."

There was stony silence.

To Andrea's surprise, it was Mani who broke it. "We don't have to wait idly. Farhad and I succeeded beyond our expectation in winning the cooperation of the workers in the oil fields of Abadan. Next week, following our brother Mehdi's advice, we shall do the same in Ahwaz. Kurosh and Manucheir can easily restore panic by eliminating a few Americans here in Tehran. That's sure to bring the hawk back."

Andrea felt a massive currant course through her body and a merciless pounding in her head. "They are a bunch of cold blooded, ruthless criminals," she said to herself white with rage. "They've intensified my resolve. I'll do everything I can to stop them."

The doorbell rang.

The men cast worried looks at Mani.

"Quick. Down the hall. To my bedroom." Mani ran to his room, opened the door, and let the men in.

He ran back and nodded.

Farhad opened the front door.

It was Sayid.

Chapter 35

"Where were you Monday afternoon?"

"What's it to you?"

"Nothing," Sayid replied. "I hope you have a convincing alibi for the police."

"What police?" Mani sounded terrified.

"That's for you to find out. The reason I'm warning you is because I don't want to be burdened with bailing you out again."

Mani cast a quick glance in Farhad's direction. Farhad continued reading a newspaper.

"Don't look at him," Sayid said in the same monotonous voice. "He's in as much trouble as you are."

Farhad put the newspaper on the coffee table. "What's that supposed to mean?"

"It means that the concierge of this apartment building is in critical condition in the hospital. Monday afternoon someone hit him on the head while he was praying. Police are investigating everyone in this building."

Andrea saw a hint of satisfaction in the eyes of both men.

But only for a split second.

Farhad reached for a cigarette. "Since when did the misfortune of a concierge become a matter of concern for the police?"

"Why don't you ask them. I'm not their spokesman."

"Oh, really. I thought you knew everyone and everything. Is your star fading by any chance?"

"With mentally handicapped people like you around my star can only rise."

"Go to hell," Mani yelled.

"If I do, I'll reserve space for you."

"Forget whatever your convoluted mind is concocting," Farhad said returning his attention to the newspaper. "You're not convincing me."

"We're not idle like you," Mani added. "We've got things to do. What did you come for? To hurl insults at us?"

"My esteemed brother," Sayid said bowing in mock courtesy. "I would not dream of insulting such illustrious company."

"Go to hell," Mani retorted angrily.

"I prefer to go after my business," Sayid commented dryly. "Unfortunately, your wife called and asked for my help."

"My stupid wife has learned something new. Every time she is faced with a small problem, she cries for help."

"Come, come Mani," Farhad interjected. "She doesn't cry for help from just anybody. It's always him. Any excuse is good enough."

"It wouldn't be necessary for me to ask for help if my husband had taken care of the matter."

"My fair lady, pray tell us. Why do you always call him?"

He grinned lecherously at her.

"If you have something to say," Sayid said quietly, "say it to me. Don't pick on those you consider weaker than yourself."

"I'll say what I please to whomever I please. Who's gonna stop me? You?"

"I don't like to soil my hands." Sayid turned to Andrea. "Can you get ready please. We have to go."

"She's not going anywhere with you." It was Mani.

"That's fine with me. You take her. It's mostly you they want to talk to. Her case is just routine."

"What do they want to talk to me about?"

"I already told you. The police are questioning all the occupants of this building."

"I don't live here," Farhad exclaimed happily.

"That's funny," Andrea said. "I thought you did."

"Check your lease."

"I didn't know we had one."

Sayid walked to the door. "Take your wife and go to the police station in Farmanieh. I convinced the police to leave. For now. But if you don't show up, they'll be here to get you. A second trip here is sure to sour their disposition."

"You take her. I'm busy."

"I can take care of myself. Give me the address Sayid, please."

"Getting there is not the problem," Sayid said. "Any taxi driver knows where the Farmanieh police station is. No one at the station speaks English except for the captain. His knowledge is limited to a few words. You need someone to translate for you."

Mani sauntered off to the kitchen and returned with two glasses of tea. He offered one to Farhad, settled on the sofa, cupped his hands around the glass teacup and slurped his tea. An act which had never failed to irritate Andrea before.

She ignored him. His coarse behavior had frequently bothered her in the past. But the past was history, history best forgotten. Blinded by what she had assumed to be love, she had found excuses or tailored explanations for all his faults.

"I'll manage somehow," Andrea said.

"Why don't you learn the language," Farhad said, forcing

his voice to squeak.

"Oh, but she is," Mani said mockingly. "Haven't you noticed that she disappears frequently in the afternoons around two?"

Astonished, everyone looked at Mani questioningly.

"You didn't know I knew, did you? I make it my business to know." He turned to Farhad. "She goes up the street to that small shop that sells fruits and vegetables. I've heard the owner has nine boys and four daughters. She gathers the children around her, teaches them English and they teach her Farsi. All in all a neat arrangement. Wouldn't you say?"

Andrea was horrified. The man was a menace. Fortunately, he did not seem aware of the real reason for her trips. The pain from the loss of her child intensified with each passing day. Surrounding herself briefly with children dulled it temporarily. Another matter, which never left her thoughts, was the whereabouts of Layla. The grocery store was owned by the old man she and Layla often visited. Maybe, just maybe, Layla might come or leave word for her with the grocer.

"Why should my teaching a few children English bother you? What would you rather have me do? You refuse to let me get a job."

"A job is out of the question. I will not have people say my wife is working to support me."

"You never objected before."

"We never lived in Iran before."

Farhad stuck his empty tea cup in front of Mani. Mani went to the kitchen, refilled it and brought it back. He turned to Andrea. "You seem to be very fond of the plain, ordinary folk here. Had the children been older, I would have sworn you were in love with one of them."

Andrea shook her head in disbelief. She didn't know what to say.

Her silence drove him to distraction. He rose, grabbed her chin and forced her to face him. "If you love filthy, uneducated peasant children enough to spend hours teaching them English, why can't you have any love for me or my family?"

"Let go of me. You're hurting me." She tried to pull her head back. As she did so, she caught a glance of Sayid's face. He had turned around. The expression on his face frightened her.

"Yeah, let her go," Farhad tuned in. "Can't you see her protector is here?"

Mani let go of her with a shove. "My dear woman, if you want to learn the language, there are other ways."

"I don't need to. I don't plan to be in this country any longer than I have to."

"You'll stay as long as I want."

"Why? I'm only in your way."

"How much does your freedom mean to you? Offer me a price."

A look of approval from Farhad seemed to be all the prodding Mani needed.

Andrea wondered if her husband's excessive belligerence was for the benefit of the men hiding in the bedroom. Perhaps not. Mani's bedroom was way down the hall. With the door closed, it would be difficult for the men to hear much. Most likely it was to impress Farhad.

"How much? Answer me." Mani persisted.

"I don't have any money to give you."

"You'll give it," Mani answered confidently.

"We'll see."

"Shut up, woman. You're giving me a headache."

She desperately wanted to stop the argument. But he wasn't through with her yet.

"You feel pretty brave, don't you? You think you have powerful friends who will take care of you. You'll soon find out they are neither powerful nor your friends."

"That's for sure," Farhad added.

Sayid opened the door. "Do you want me to take her or not?"

"I don't care." Mani shrugged his shoulders. "It's her problem. Not mine. She was here. We weren't. We were in Abadan. We left Monday morning."

Suddenly, all color drained from Farhad's face. He flashed an icy glare in Mani's direction.

"You were?" Sayid's voice was full of sarcasm. "Then you have even more to answer for. Only it won't be to the police"

Horror registered on both men's faces. Farhad was the first to speak. "You say one word of what you heard to anyone and you're as good as dead."

"Afraid, are you?"

"It's nobody's business where we were," Farhad shot back.

"Of course not. Except that there's a sit-down strike in Abadan, oil production has come to a standstill, and people are waiting in line for hours to buy gas in a country which floats on oil. And you just happened to be there the day before. Sing that song to Security."

Mani collapsed in a chair like a body weighted down by a block of cement, the magnitude of his indiscretion had finally caught up with him.

"There is no way for Security to know unless you open your big mouth," Farhad hollered.

"You took all the necessary precautions I presume."

Mani leaped from the chair. "Of course we did. Only a few trusted friends know. And now you."

"Sit down," Sayid said. "Your limp brain bores me. Let's go, Andrea."

He turned to go.

As he did so, Andrea saw Farhad nod. Suddenly, both men jumped him from behind. Mani hit hard, with raw animal rage. Farhad delivered the coup de grace knocking the wind out of Sayid.

Andrea's mouth went dry. Horrified, she couldn't move.

The blows kept coming, swinging Sayid back and forth

between his brother and Farhad. Sayid collapsed, face down, on the coffee table. His face smashed in an ashtray full of cigarette butts and ash.

"Stop it," Andrea pleaded. "Stop it or I'll call the police."

"Shut up, bitch," Mani yelled. "He had it coming."

Blood coursed down Sayid's ash-smeared face. There was a brief lull. Mani and Farhad had stopped to catch their breath. Andrea rushed to the bathroom, grabbed a towel and wiped Sayid's face.

Farhad laughed. "Don't do that. He looks like Hadji Firouz. Have you seen Hadji Firouz, Andrea?"

"No, I haven't."

"Hadji Firouz is a man who smears his face with ash, once a year, before the Iranian New Year. It has nothing to do with Islam. It . . . it . . . Why aren't you listening?"

It's worth it if it will stop the fight, Andrea thought.

"It's fascinating. Please go on."

"It's a tradition of many centuries. Men cover their faces with black ash and go around the neighborhood banging a spoon on a metal plate. They dance in circles to lure the inhabitants to give them sweets, pastry or money. They claim they can ward off evil and foretell the prospects of the donors for the coming year. True to Iranian custom, the donors' fortunes are predicted to match their contributions. Don't you think he looks like Hadji Firouz?"

Sayid tried to pull himself together.

Farhad and Mani knocked him down.

"Stop it," Andrea shouted, shaking uncontrollably. "Stop it, please."

"We've waited a long time for this opportunity." Farhad rubbed his knuckles.

Andrea reached for the telephone. Mani leaped over the coffee table, grabbed her wrist and twisted it.

She dropped the receiver. "Let go. You're hurting me."

He twisted it harder.

The pain was so intense, Andrea felt giddy. Tears welled

in her eyes and her hand went numb.

Still, he wouldn't let go.

She had had enough. "Kick." A voice within her urged. "Kick his balls." She raised her knee and whacked him in the groin.

Mani screamed and doubled over. He crawled to the sofa, cupped his hands over his genitals and moaned with pain.

Farhad's concentration was momentarily diverted. Sayid grasped the opportunity, punched Farhad on the jaw and sent him flying across the room.

Seeing his beloved crumpled in a corner was more than Mani could bear. He seemed to have forgotten all about his own pain. He plunged forward, grabbed a chair, and smashed it on his brother's head.

Sayid staggered and fell.

Andrea rushed over. He was bleeding from his mouth and nose. His lower lip had a nasty cut. His eyes were glazed. Then he passed out.

It was like watching a bad movie. This sort of thing was supposed to happen in movies, on television, or to others. And it wouldn't have happened had she not asked Sayid for help. If she couldn't cope on her own, she was in bad shape indeed! Had she made yet another mistake by accepting to stay and work for Phil? Should she have attempted to escape? A glance at her husband told her a different story. He watched his brother's fall with glee, his eyes protruding, his chin jutted forward, his thick hair tangled like a bird's nest. Someone had to stop him.

When he felt confident that his brother was in no shape to attack him, Mani dashed back, cast a mournful glance at Farhad, then rushed to the kitchen. He returned with a glass of water. He tried but could not make Farhad drink. He cradled Farhad's head in his arms and cried, "Speak to me. Say something."

There was no response from Farhad.

Tears flowed down his cheeks. "Talk to me. It's me,

Mani."

There was no response.

"You bastards," he yelled. "You damned bastards. You killed him. You'll pay for it. Inch by little inch. Call on your Christian God to help you. Call on all your gods. You'll need all the help you can get."

Andrea reached for the phone and dialed.

Chapter 36

Sayid stirred, opened his eyes, took a quick look around, collected himself and left.

Andrea dialed several phone numbers she had committed to memory in hopes of locating an ambulance. Mani was too overwhelmed by concern for Farhad to pay attention to what was going on. Farhad was not dead. Soon after Sayid left, he pulled himself off the floor and sprawled on the sofa.

He whispered in Mani's ear.

Mani rose, went to his bedroom and returned with the men.

"What happened?" Emu asked.

"It was nothing," Mani replied. "My brother insulted Farhad. They had a fight."

Emu stared at Farhad, then at Mani, then at Andrea holding the receiver. He turned to Kurosh and Manucheir. "Let's get out of here. That brother of his is sure to return with the police."

As they walked out, Andrea heard Kurosh say, "We won't be able to reach . . ."

She couldn't hear the rest. She resumed her dialing.

Mani walked over, grabbed the phone from her hand and shoved her aside.

"I'm trying to get an ambulance," Andrea said. "He might have a fracture."

"When are you going to understand that you are not in the States?" he quipped angrily. "We have F14s, not ambulances."

"I've seen ambulances. There's got to be one we can reach."

"Yeah, how? By asking an operator who couldn't care less and who will be hostile because you disturbed her permanent tea break. Or by consulting a nonexistent directory?"

Andrea ignored him. She had seen an ambulance at Pars Hospital. She tried them next.

"It's broken down," she reported hopelessly.

"We don't need an ambulance. He'll be fine."

"He will not be fine. He should be seen by a doctor."

Mani returned to the sofa.

Farhad motioned. Mani put his ear close to Farhad's face. Farhad whispered in his ear.

Mani went to his room, brought a clean shirt and helped Farhad put it on. Farhad's eyes and the left side of his face were swollen. He looked like a boxer who had just lost a fight.

Mani told Farhad to wait and he ran down the stairs.

Andrea moved slowly to the kitchen window and watched the street below.

It was nine thirty. The streets were deserted.

Soon Mani drove his car up the street, parked it on the sidewalk, left the engine running and dashed upstairs.

He took Farhad's right arm, put it around his shoulder and with his left arm held him by the waist. He stopped and glared at Andrea. "Farhad tripped and fell on the stairs, understand?" They walked slowly to the door and down the stairs.

They got into Mani's car and drove off.

The sudden silence in the apartment was a welcome change. She reached for the coffee pot. A sharp pain in her wrist alarmed her. Because so much had happened afterward, she'd forgotten her own pain. She took an ace bandage from an emergency kit she had, and wrapped her wrist. Brutality had become a mainstay of her life. How much longer could she endure it? She could not hazard a guess.

Her mind drifted to the recent past. Helga, Dariush, the fun times they'd had together. Phil was right. She mustn't have contact with Dariush. If Mani ever found out . . .

Occasionally she called Goli to inquire about Helga. Goli said her mistress called twice. Her father was better. The second call came from Switzerland. Helga was in Switzerland visiting Dariush's mother. She didn't know when Helga planned to return to Tehran or where the General was.

Suddenly, it all fell in place. Since Helga was in Switzerland, it was highly probable that the General would join her. Then the General was the hawk. But why? Why would they want to kill Cyrus? A shrill voice within her jolted her upright. How stupid of me. I should have known. Mani hates the man because of me and because he has power. They wanted to assassinate high ranking officers who did not have or did not want secret service protection. Helga often expressed concern over her husband's refusal to have bodyguards. They had mentioned Swiss Air. A contact they had planted at the ticket office to keep them informed about the hawk's travel plans. But the General flew his own plane. Maybe she was imagining things. Maybe, but not likely.

She tried to recall in detail the conversation the five men had in the apartment. "Try to win her over," Emu advised Mani. "We need her especially for this mission." Why? Why this mission?

And then Mani's description of the mansion.

It was all wrong. The hawk had to be the Shah's brother. Helga said they were building a house, not a mansion. But why would the Shah's brother fly Swiss Air when he had his own airplane?

She admonished herself. I'm becoming paranoid. I search for meaning and interpretation in situations which exist only in my mind. I'm losing track of reality. I must get my act together.

Phil would know. But how could she reach him? She had not heard from him since he let her know about Mohammed. Phil did not call or come when Mani was home. Mohammed was in the hospital and Sayid, her emergency contact, probably needed to be after the brutal fight he was subjected to.

Her mind was a jumble of bits of overheard conversation. No matter how she arranged the pieces, a clear pattern refused to emerge.

What if it was Cyrus? Or the Shah's brother for that matter. She'd never forgive herself. She had to reach Phil. Hopefully, he'd contact her if and when Farhad and Mani left.

Her reverie was shattered by footsteps climbing the stairs, barely audible, but footsteps nonetheless. The police are back! What now? She listened. There was a gentle tap on the door. She did not move. It had to be someone else. The police did not knock gently.

The tapping was repeated after a brief wait. She sensed a rhythm to it. She approached the door, peeped through the magic eye, and saw two men waiting. The stairs were dimly lit. It was impossible to tell who they were. It couldn't be the police. They were not in uniform. They could be detectives in plain clothes or her husband's friends.

She checked her watch. It was ten thirty two.

The tapping was repeated again with the same rhythm, with renewed urgency.

Andrea took one more peep. She noticed they were carrying briefcases. Most everyone who came to the apartment to talk to Mani and Farhad, came with a briefcase. Their persistence meant they were expected.

She thought of going to bed and pretending she was asleep. But that would mean she would not have a chance to see the men. If she stayed up, she would have to explain to Mani why she had not opened the door.

She decided to wait in the living room until she heard Mani's footsteps.

It was past midnight. There was still no sign of Mani. Another look revealed the men had finally left. Andrea went to bed.

Mani and Farhad did not return that night or the next day. By evening, restless and apprehensive, Andrea waited and read. She stopped frequently in mid sentence to listen to steps she thought she heard. She figured sooner or later the police would come. The only choice she had was not to open the door. She had decided to stay home. The police could be in the building questioning tenants or at the entrance. If she stepped out, they might grab her and she would be at their mercy. If they broke the door and came in, she didn't know what to do. But somehow, she felt less vulnerable inside the house.

A few minutes before nine, the phone rang.

"You need not worry about the police," Sayid said. "They will not disturb you."

Andrea heaved a sigh of relief. "Thank you. Thank you very much."

"Don't leave the apartment."

"I understand."

"Did you receive your mail?"

That was the code Andrea waited for. "Yes. Yes. Yes, I did." Repeating yes three times meant three persons not seen before had visited the apartment.

"Bye."

"Wait a minute. I've been worried sick about you. How are you?"

"I'm fine. Take care of yourself."

The line went dead.

By midnight, her vision got blurred from reading. She went to bed.

By Iranian standards, it was a large apartment. It had a living room, dining room, and three bedrooms. Two of the bedrooms were large, located at the end of a long, narrow hallway. Mani insisted on having the larger bedroom down the hall so there would be room for Farhad. He used the second large bedroom as his office. Andrea's bedroom was the smallest of the three, located directly across from the living-dining area. It wasn't her choice but she was pleased to have it because of its location. She could hear clearly most of what went on in the living-dining area and the kitchen.

She did not expect Mani to return. Whenever he feared the arrival of police or Savak, he and Farhad promptly disappeared.

This night proved to be different.

Loud, angry voices jolted her upright in bed. Among them voices she hadn't heard before.

She was instructed by Phil to take a look at everyone who came to the apartment and listen to what was said. She decided to risk it.

She pulled her housecoat over her nightgown, opened the door and stepped out. "Gentlemen, please lower your voices. It's one in the morning."

They were gathered around the dining table. She spotted Emu, Kurosh, Manucheir and two new faces. The instant she opened her door, one of the new comers turned his face. But he was not quick enough. Andrea caught a glimpse and recognized him immediately. She closed her door and returned to bed.

The new faces did not belong to the pictures Phil had shown her but the man who had turned his face, was the man who had claimed to be a technician. The technician with the tool box.

She heard whispering, then Mani's voice. "It's Mullah

Hamid's idea, not mine."

"Mullah Hamid knows what he's doing," one of the men replied.

"He's one of our best assets. Thanks to him, we get good inside information about our adversaries."

Someone said angrily, "You don't have to look at Farhad in that manner. Majid knows what he's talking about. Mullah Hamid's honesty and devotion to the cause is indisputable. Unless you have solid proof for doubting his loyalty you shouldn't act as though you don't approve."

For a moment, no one spoke. Then Mani explained, "I have nothing but respect for our great religious leader. As a matter of fact, I insisted that he be the one to conduct the religious services for our daughter's burial. But I was shocked when he insisted that I live in the same apartment with my wife. He knows she hates me."

Emu's squeaky voice rose above the others. "You are a very shortsighted person. She's not bothering anyone. She's not nosey. She doesn't ask any questions, does she?"

"No," Mani admitted.

"Then what's the problem?"

"She won't cooperate."

"She will. You don't know how to handle her. You have to change your attitude toward her. Otherwise, you're out. Finished."

Andrea imagined the expression on Mani's face. Poor guy, she thought. No matter what he does, he does it wrong.

"I promise everything will change," Mani said. "I'll do my best."

"Don't take the rest of your life doing it," one of the men replied. "We are not noted for our patience."

"Bring the vodka and let's get on with our business."

There was a lull.

"Ali," said Manucheir, "the plans are in your briefcase."

She heard two clicks then shuffling of paper.

"At dawn, Thursday, we leave for Ahwaz, by car," Ali

began.

"Why by car?" Mani interrupted. "It's too long a drive."

"We know how long it takes," Ali retorted angrily. He cleared his throat and continued, "For your information, Savak has the picture of every one of us who participated in the slow down strike in Abadan. We have an informer. We don't know who, yet. But we'll find out. From now on we're traveling by car. In different cars, rented. Two in each car. We'll meet at the house of Mullah Hamid's sister. It's all taken care of. We'll arrive in groups of two. From midnight till two in the morning. We use the same code. Any questions?"

"I don't think Farhad will be well enough to travel by then," Mani said.

"He'll be fine," Majid said.

"He's hurt bad," Mani protested.

"Are you suggesting that he should not participate in our next project?" Ali demanded.

"I bet he does not want to come either," interjected Majid. "He probably wants to stay with Farhad. After all, someone has to be around to hold Farhad's hand."

She couldn't hear Mani's response.

Then someone spoke. The words were stressed and spoken slowly. "We have no time or patience to concern ourselves with your endless problems. First your mother was sick, then your daughter, now your friend. You're either in or out. Decide."

She heard Farhad's voice for the first time that evening. "Give us our assignment, please."

"That's settled then," one of the men said. "You and Farhad must find a car and a driver. Preferably someone you know. Someone who can keep his mouth shut. You leave Tehran at three in the morning on Thursday. Any questions?"

"If we can't find a driver we can trust, should we rent a car from a rental agency and drive ourselves?" Mani asked.

"Only if you've exhausted all other possibilities and only

through a third party."

"That could be a problem. Who?"

"You'll have to figure that yourself, Mani?" said Majid. "But under no circumstances are you to rent it yourself. Even if you give them an assumed name, Savak will have no trouble tracing it to you."

"Maybe I can convince my wife to do it for us."

"Why don't you think before you talk?" Ali said angrily. "Your wife has already been interrogated by Savak. They know her quite well. How long do you think it will take them to make the association?"

There was no response for a while.

"I didn't know," Mani mumbled finally.

"They got her in Pahlavi, trying to see the Queen."

"Then her usefulness to us is very limited," Mani moaned.

"Oh, no it isn't," interrupted Ali. "Savak has strict instructions not to bother her again by none other than the hawk."

Andrea's mouth hung open. Oh, my God! She said to herself. Cyrus is the hawk. What the hell am I going to do?

Majid said, "We should not use her for minor errands like renting a car. That's unnecessary exposure. We have more important matters for her to handle."

"What?" It sounded like Farhad.

"The question is not what but how." Again Andrea could not distinguish the voice. "We must first win her over. Convince her ours is a worthy cause worth sacrificing one's life for. But how can we do it? She's treated like dirt by her husband. Do you blame her for not wanting to have anything to do with him? By extension she won't want to have anything to do with us. What are you going to do about it, Mani?"

"She's upset because of our daughter's death. She'll get over it soon. I'll see to it that she does."

"Mani is being blamed for a lot of things over which he

had no control," Farhad said. "Let's forget the past. We'll both work on her. She's very intelligent. She grew up in the sixties. We know she was involved in social issues while attending the University of Washington. That whole generation was. Her thinking is fair and liberal. We have to show her our struggle is the struggle of a whole nation against tyranny. She's been here long enough to realize the degree of oppression, corruption and lack of basic human rights which all Iranians are forced to put up with."

"Well said, my friend," said Ali cheerfully. "But she's not Iranian. Sooner or later she will return to her country. Why should she risk her life for us?"

"Precisely because she's not Iranian," Majid said. "Americans take individual freedom very seriously. It's their politicians who are screwed up. We have to rekindle her sense of fair play. The rest is easy."

"Let's hope so." Ali did not sound convinced. "Let's go on with our work. We took care of every detail for our next move in Ahwaz. Every detail except one. Mullah Hamid's sister has agreed to let us use her house. But we have to give her advance notice. She doesn't want to be home while we're having our meeting. The plan is for her to take her family to her sister's house and spend the weekend there. Any suggestions as to who we should send to inform her? She doesn't have a phone, and, even if she did, communicating messages by phone is out of the question."

She heard Mani say, "If our meeting is on Friday, we don't have much time."

"No, we don't," replied Ali. "The messenger has to fly."

"Any suggestion?" asked Majid.

There was a brief silence followed by someone clearing his throat.

"We should send a woman," someone suggested.

She heard noises in the kitchen. Probably Mani refreshing drinks. It promised to be a long night.

"I wonder why Zia is late," Ali said. "Should we continue

or wait?"

Soon after, Andrea heard a knock, the same kind of knock she'd heard earlier. The door was opened and closed quickly. The person who came in spoke in an agitated voice. "I was followed," he reported excitedly. "It took me two hours to shake them off."

"That's impossible," Ali said. "No one knew about this meeting except the five of us present in this room. Mullah Hamid said he made sure of that."

"We have an informer," Majid said. "We've got to find out who. We assumed it was the concierge. It was a far fetched possibility. We know now it couldn't be him. He's in the hospital."

"We have to finish this meeting soon and disperse," Zia said. "I'm quite sure I lost them but one never knows."

"We've taken care of all the details," Majid said, "except who to use as messenger. I suggest we use a foreigner. I suspect Savak got wind of our operation in Abadan through the messenger we sent. It's just a suspicion. I have no proof. But we better play it safe."

For Andrea, the implication was clear. So far as she knew she was the only foreigner around.

Mehdi said, "We can't do that. Not unless the foreigner accepts to wear a chaddor. Otherwise, she'll be too obvious."

"The problem is not the chaddor, it's the foreigner," Majid replied. "The only foreigner we know is in the next room and I have my doubts she'll even consider."

"Maybe she would," Ali suggested enthusiastically. "I bet with the right approach we can have her fighting with us side by side."

Mehdi's thin voice rose above the objections of the others. "Don't get carried away, Ali. It's a gamble. And, the only person who can approach her is her husband. We have to stay out of it."

"What if she betrays us?" Mani protested.

"Don't be stupid," Mehdi snapped. "If she wanted to

betray us, she had the opportunity to do so before. This is not the first meeting we have held here. You're not worried about that. You don't want to ask her. Isn't that the real reason?"

"She won't accept," Mani said.

"You won't know that until you ask her. Do you?" Majid persisted.

"We'll both talk to her in the morning," Farhad said. "Maybe one of you can stop by tomorrow afternoon or evening. We'll let you know."

"Majid should come," Ali said. "She might recognize me if she sees me again. I don't think she recognized me tonight."

"It doesn't matter," Mani said. "I don't think she's met the concierge. Even if she has, she won't suspect anything. She doesn't know he's missing."

"I'll come after dark," offered Majid. "You better have good news for us."

"In less than half an hour, the sun will rise," Zia said. "We have to go. Let's space it at five minute intervals. You go first Ali. Mani check the street."

A few seconds later, Mani said, "It's clear."

"Keep looking," Zia ordered.

Ali said a hasty goodbye and hurried down the stairs.

A couple of minutes later, she heard Mani calling the others. His voice cracked. He sounded hysterical. "Come," he yelled. "Come. Quick."

There was a commotion. She opened her door a crack. The men ran to the kitchen window. Zia looked down first then turned to Mani. "What happened?"

Mani stuttered. "A . . . li. A . . . li. The second . . . the second he stepped out the building, four men jumped him and shoved him into a car. The car . . . appeared mysteriously from around the corner."

Chapter 37

After Mani's announcement about Ali's apprehension, the men reassembled around the dining table and conferred in whispers. Andrea fought sleep and listened. She could not hear. Her attention drifted to the sound of raindrops landing on the window panes. A warm feeling surged through her. After years of rainy weather in Seattle, she was surprised to find herself actually enjoying watching raindrops fall. The raindrops wiggled and twisted like little worms followed by more drops coursing aimlessly down paths of least resistance. It rained occasionally in Tehran, not hard, and hardly enough, but whenever it did, it invariably kindled in her visions of life, rebirth, growth, continuity and Kelly. Almost everything reminded her of the child and her brutal death. Sleep became a luxury. She searched for an excuse, any excuse not to go to bed. The child's adoring, grateful eyes, followed her to bed, piercing her soul, forcing her to see herself as she truly was. Hurt, angry, resolved to do all in her power to stop her husband from inflicting pain and death indiscriminately on others. She couldn't leave the country even if she wanted to. She had to stay and do what it took to stop him.

A few minutes past six in the morning, the phone rang. Farhad answered. She heard movement, whispering, the front door open, the sound of steps on the stairs, then silence.

Did the phone call let the men know it was safe to leave? Had they left?

She waited till seven before venturing to the kitchen for a cup of coffee. She came face to face with Mani. His eyes were red, his face drawn. No one else was around. If the men were still in the house, they had to be hiding. Mani had coffee ready, the table set, the eggs washed just like Andrea always insisted that they be. It was the first time since they'd come to Iran that he had done any work in the kitchen and the only time he'd entered it for reasons other than ice for drinks. He ate his meals in the dining room. Kitchens were for servants, not the man of the house.

"Good morning," he chirped cheerfully.

"Good morning."

"I washed the eggs in Roccal. That's what you said the doctor told you to do. Right?"

He was not a man noted for his patience. It amused her to watch him struggle to put her in the right frame of mind whenever he wanted something from her. She could not imagine a less talented person entrusted with the job. He was so transparent, he did not stop to take into account what effect the sudden reversal of his behavior would have on her. She poured herself a cup of coffee, sipped it, and watched the rain.

"I'm sorry about last night," he said. "Does your wrist hurt?"

She looked away.

"May I take a look."

"It's wrapped."

"Do you want to have it checked?"

"I don't think it's necessary. Thank you."

"I said I was sorry."

"Let's forget it."

"You're not being very cooperative," he said sharply.

"My presence seems to anger you. I better leave."

"Please don't," he pleaded. "That brother of mine always brings out the worst in me. I don't know why."

"Probably because he's always bailing you out."

"No. That's not it. Farhad felt that if he knew we were in Abadan, he would report it to Savak."

"I think Sayid knows about everything you do. Have you ever had reason to suspect that he gives the information out? He hardly talks regardless of what the subject is. If anything, you should be grateful he's around and has friends in positions that matter. Where would you be now if he had not bailed you out the last time Savak paid you and Farhad a visit?"

"He doesn't do it out of love. Believe me."

"But he does it."

"What do you want me to do? Kiss his feet?"

"No. Just leave him alone. What have you ever done for him? You're the older brother. It's supposed to be the other way around, isn't it? I'm told that's part of your culture. Think about it next time you get ready to lose your temper. You almost killed him."

"Hell. I don't know what to think. Everything is a mess. We lost another one of our men last night. We're racking our brains but can't come up with an explanation."

"There was more than one man here last night. Where are the others?"

"They left."

Farhad walked in carrying a bagful of groceries. He placed it on the kitchen counter and sat down across the table from Andrea.

"Sorry, I'm late. The new supermarket was crowded. Somehow the owner got hold of American ketchup. Within minutes every last bottle disappeared. I wanted to get one for

Andrea but couldn't. I bought fruit instead."

"I'll wash the fruit," Mani said.

Farhad gave the bag of fruit to Mani, then turned to Andrea. "Have you been to the new supermarket?"

"No, I haven't."

"You should. It's called Super Shilan. Occasionally they have imported stuff. You might find something you like."

Andrea wondered if he realized how phony his charm was.

"I remember you mentioning that you liked cereal. I saw a box of cornflakes. I bought one for you."

"Thanks. That was very thoughtful of you."

Cornflakes. The mere mention of the word reminded her of Kelly. Kelly expectantly watching her mother fix breakfast for her every morning. Her eyes brightened whenever her mother approached with a bowl of cereal, her favorite food. Tears welled in her eyes. She rose and walked to the window. She did not want anyone to know how terrible her suffering was, least of all her husband and his friend.

"That building belonged to us. My father sold it when he was transferred to Isfahan. It has doubled in price in two years."

"That was a big mistake," Mani said. "If he had waited, he would be a rich man now. At the rate foreigners are pouring into this country, prices will triple and quadruple."

Farhad pondered quietly for a second. "That was not his only mistake. Remember the so called 'man of God' he rented the second floor to?"

"You wrote to me about it."

Farhad approached the window. "I wish you could meet this man," he said to Andrea. "He was some kind of zealot. Jehovah's Witness or something. He spent hours trying to convert me to Christianity. Me or anyone who would listen."

He waited for Andrea to show some kind of reaction. She continued looking out the window. It was customary for Iranians to speak in circles. Centuries of subjugation had ingrained in them a strong sense of caution. Speaking one's mind was a luxury few dared risk.

Mani and Farhad did not speak in circles. They spoke in spirals, especially Farhad.

Andrea listened patiently and wondered when Farhad would finally reach the end of the spiral.

"Can you believe it?" he continued. "This man actually spent his life telling people that their only salvation is through Jesus Christ. If they did not believe in Jesus, they could not be saved."

"What did you tell him?" Mani asked.

"I said I did not choose to be born a Muslim. Why should I burn in hell for something I had no control over? Are you telling me that only Christians can go to heaven? What happened to your merciful God?"

He fixed his eyes on Andrea. She did not comment. She did not want to start an argument.

"Was there any truth in what he was preaching, Andrea?"

She knew he wouldn't give up.

"I take religion in stride," she said calmly. "Religion becomes a problem for those who hate it with a passion or worship it with fanaticism."

Farhad and Mani exchanged puzzled looks.

"Andrea," Farhad tried again. "He wanted me to believe that Christianity was a tolerant religion. One which forgave and forgot. Its adherents were won over by love, not by the sword like Islam."

"What are you getting at?"

"I wonder what makes some of us love, some of us hate, and some of us take it or leave it. Not only religion but most major issues."

"Philosophy is not one of my strong points. You should have asked the missionary."

"I'm asking you to see how much forgiveness you have."

She sipped her coffee. "I don't like to discuss religion or myself."

"Relax. You're much too tense," Farhad said. "You need a vacation. Iran is not Tehran and Pahlavi. There are many ancient, historical sites people come from all over the world to see. You should go."

I bet one of them is Ahwaz, Andrea thought. "Maybe some other time."

"Why some other time, Andrea," Mani said amiably. "You've been through a lot lately. It will do you good. Why don't you hop on a plane and go someplace. Shiraz, Isfahan, Tabriz, wherever you want."

"You should," Farhad urged. "There's more to life than reading books."

"You don't need to worry about me. I'm fine."

Mani leaned against the kitchen sink. He turned his back and proceeded to peel an apple over the kitchen sink. Farhad stared at her.

"You make it very hard for us to be nice to you," he ventured cautiously. "We're living under the same roof. We might as well be friends."

"I don't live here by choice."

"You're a Christian, aren't you? Isn't forgiving part of your religion?"

"Why are you so involved with religion this morning?"

"I don't know how else to get through to you."

"Why should you want to?"

He looked confused, unsure of himself. She'd rarely seen him like that.

"We need your help," he said softly.

"My help? You must be joking."

"Not at all. It's something you could do easily. But if we tried it, it might cost us our lives."

"Like what?"

"Delivering a message."

"Are you telling me that you want me to get involved in your illegal, murderous activities?"

"I told you it was hopeless," Mani interjected.

"Of course it is. You want me to help you get people killed?"

"It's not what you think," Farhad murmured.

"Really?"

"We're not planning to kill anybody."

"That's a relief."

"Honest. I swear it's the truth."

"If you were to tell me snow is white, I'd wonder what the motive behind your statement was."

There was an awkward pause.

"All we want you to do is get on a plane, go to Ahwaz to a certain address and say Friday, in Farsi, to somebody."

"Why?"

Farhad sighed. "We are freedom fighters. Our cause is noble, just. We're ready to sacrifice our lives to liberate our people. We're not asking anything for ourselves. On the contrary, we have given everything we have so our people will have a better future. What's wrong with it? Didn't your countrymen do the same? Don't you believe human dignity is worth fighting for?"

She said with forced calm, "It surprises me to hear you talk about human dignity. You who have robbed me of mine ever since I set foot in this country. From what I've seen, violence seems to be your weapon of choice. I want no part of it."

"You've got a better alternative?" Farhad quipped.

"Gandhi won independence for his people from the British with passive resistance. Why don't you give it a try?"

Farhad threw his head back and roared with laughter. "Did you hear that Mani? She says passive resistance. She thinks the Pahlavis are like the British. If you pressure them enough, they'll come to their senses. You're crazy if you think that anything short of bloodshed can dislodge that megalomaniac's grip from the throne."

"You won't know until you try."

"We have a much better plan," Mani said.

"What's your plan, Mani?"

"We want to rid this country of the Pahlavis, establish a democratic government, and give the people back their dignity."

"That's a noble cause. Let's suppose you succeed. Then what?"

"Then we take over. Every member of The Revolutionary Council will have a ministerial post. The government will be run by us instead of a puppet appointed by the CIA."

Farhad let out a short, nervous chuckle. "Just imagine. You could be the wife of a minister."

"I prefer to be Andrea Sorensen."

Farhad glared at her. "I suggest you help us. It will be to your benefit in the long run."

He didn't have to say much more. The vicious expression on his face conveyed the rest.

She had to get away, to think, to reach Phil for advice. It was not a decision she could make on her own. Phil had given her a number to use in case of emergency. She could, but not from the apartment. Since her husband's admission that he had her followed, she didn't know what to do. But she had to get away from them, especially Farhad. The man symbolized death and destruction.

"I'm going for a walk." She went to her room, put her sweats on and walked out. As she did so, she heard Mani muttering obscenities using the same words his mother used in reference to her.

When she neared the exit of the building, she saw the young woman who lived on the first floor, come out of the concierge's apartment.

She stopped. Was Mohammed back? She had to know without arousing suspicion.

"Good morning," the woman said.

"Good morning."

"I've been meaning to stop by to say hello to you but

something always comes up. I'm Shirin."

"Happy to meet you. Andrea."

"If you're not in a hurry, how about having a cup of coffee with me?"

"Thanks. That will be great."

"Come in, please." The hall was packed with boxes. "Please excuse the clutter. It's a temporary arrangement. We're building a home. It was supposed to have finished months ago. My fiance got tired of waiting. So we got married and moved here. My father said we could use this apartment for the time being."

"Your father?"

"Yes. My father owns this building. He's in the construction business. He can't keep up with the demand. We had a hard time getting him to come to Israel for the wedding."

"I've never been to a Jewish wedding."

"It was absolutely smashing."

Shirin pulled a chair for Andrea at the kitchen table and one for herself. She had big green eyes, fair skin, light brown hair and a slender body. She was attractive in an unusual way. Perhaps it was the smile, the smile of innocence, youth and love of life. Something Andrea had but lost. Somehow, she reminded her of Layla even though the women had nothing in common in appearance except their youth. Where was Layla? And why had she disappeared without a trace? She racked her brain but could not find an answer.

"Were you planning to go for a walk?"

"Yes. Would you like to go with me?"

"I hate walking in this city. I don't like to deal with pot holes, car fumes and crowds."

"That's true. But I need the exercise."

"I have a better idea. Let's go to the Imperial Country Club."

The club was the most exclusive in the country, frequented by VIPS and wealthy businessmen with connections to the monarchy. Andrea had heard about it from Irene.

"Are you a member?"

"My father is. We can do anything you like. Tennis. Golf. Swim. Ride. Whatever."

"Sounds like fun. I'd love to."

But her thoughts were with Mohammed.

"I'll ask the housekeeper to fetch the driver." Shirin rose. "He parks wherever he finds a spot. Let me know anytime you need a ride. My husband refuses to let me drive in this crazy city. So we keep a driver."

Andrea listened admiring the woman for her ability to take wealth in stride. She felt a twinge of envy. She was forever tormented by her good fortune. Loving, caring, wealthy parents made her feel uneasy, practically cheated of the privilege to suffer. But lately she had had enough suffering. Was her marriage a deliberate act of self-destruction?

Shirin returned to the kitchen. "We'll have to wait a few minutes. I can't find the housekeeper. She must be helping the concierge."

"How is he? I heard he was hurt."

"He almost didn't make it. He was in the hospital for four days. Our driver brought him home yesterday afternoon."

"What happened?"

"He was surprised by a burglar while praying. He was hit on the head by a tool box. I heard the police caught the man early this morning running out of our building. It scares me to death."

"It's awful. Does he have a family?"

"He has no one. He's been working for my father for the past eight years. He comes from a village in the south. I forget which."

The housekeeper came in. Shirin told her she needed the car. The housekeeper placed a tray she was carrying on the counter and left.

After a few moments, Shirin said, "Let's go. The driver should be here soon."

Andrea glanced in the direction of the concierge's apartment. It was in total darkness. There was no sign of life.

"The place is in total darkness Shirin. Are you sure he's all right?"

"He has photophobia. He wants the curtains drawn. Other than that, he's all right."

Andrea saw her chance and quickly took advantage of it. "Do you think he'd mind if I pop in to say hello? He's been awfully kind to me. He helps me carry the groceries upstairs and occasionally calls a cab for me."

"Go ahead. I'm sure he'd appreciate it."

Andrea had to force herself to appear calm. She walked quickly into the apartment.

Mohammed was in bed, propped on an elbow, smoking a cigarette.

"How do you feel?"

"Fine. I'm an old horse. Nothing short of a bullet in the right spot will do the trick."

"Shirin said you have photophobia."

"That's by special order. I don't want your visitors to know I'm back. They will eventually. But the later the better."

Andrea gave him a quick rundown of the past three days events.

"Good job," he said.

"Why didn't they apprehend the rest of the men? Surely they knew about them."

"They need more info. Apprehending them doesn't work. They don't talk. Several of their colleagues died under interrogation without divulging a single secret. We're not dealing with amateurs anymore."

"They want me to go to Ahwaz. They're planning another slow down strike. The targets are the power and water company. The meeting is to take place in the home of Mullah Hamid's sister."

"Date?"

"This Friday."

"They're not wasting much time."

"There's something going on practically every night they're in town."

"When do they want you to leave?"

"They didn't say. I told them I wouldn't do it."

"You must."

"I was stalling until I could contact you or Phil."

"Phil is out of town. I take over when he's absent. Play hard to get and insist on getting something in return."

"What?"

"Permission to leave the country."

"Mani will never agree. Not after he discovers I can be useful."

"Ask for a short vacation with a promise to come back."

"What if he refuses?"

"He won't. He can't afford to. They won't keep him much longer if he's not nice to you."

"When will Phil return?"

"I'll know by the weekend. What's on you mind?"

"They mentioned the word hawk several times. I think they are referring to General Cyrus. They're going all the way. Phil should know."

"He knows. We've had a dozen similar reports. But I will tell him."

"I better go."

"Sayid was here an hour ago."

Andrea stopped. "How is he?"

"The bruises still show but other than that he looked fine."

"I guess he told you what happened."

"He did. Your husband is lucky you're his wife."

"I don't get it."

"Had it not been for his love for you, Sayid would have had him eliminated long ago."

"You're being dramatic."

"Hell, no. You don't know him like I do."

"I guess not."

"Well, I have news for you. You're his sole raison d'e-tre."

"Andrea, are ready to go?" Shirin entered the apartment. "Does he look all right to you?"

"He seems fine. But we're having trouble communicating. I think he was trying to explain why the place is dark."

Mohammed turned to Shirin. He spoke Farsi with the dialect of an ordinary peasant from the south of the country. "Please tell this nice lady not to worry about me. Americans are such soft hearted people."

Chapter 38

A uniformed driver drove Andrea and Shirin to the Imperial Country Club in a Mercedes coupe. Shirin seemed happy, carefree. Andrea found herself relaxing. The guards at the entrance to the club checked the occupants of the car then opened the gates and waved them through.

The club was far more luxurious than Andrea had imagined. The place was crowded with well dressed men who moved and talked with a confident manner. There were no women.

"Let's go for a walk. Then we'll have lunch and later go riding. Can you ride?"

"I sure can."

They walked through the vast grounds. The place was impeccably clean and well kept. It was noon when they returned.

"How about lunch?" Shirin asked.

Andrea had lived on coffee and sandwiches for months. "Let's," she said.

As they walked toward the dining room, a Mercedes

sedan pulled up and two men stepped out. One of them was Dr. Hedayat.

Shirin seemed to know both men. She smiled and walked toward them. "Congratulations," she said to Dr. Hedayat. "How does it feel to be a minister?"

"I'm still getting used to it."

The other man greeted them then walked to the back of the car. He took a bag of golf clubs out. Shirin went to talk to him.

"That's wonderful news," Andrea said to Dr. Hedayat. "When did it happen?"

"A few days ago."

"Irene must be very happy. Is she back?"

"She returned last week. She wanted to call you . . . I asked her not to."

Andrea thought she heard wrong. Perhaps not. Dr. Hedayat had a sullen expression on his face. "Oh, really?"

"Orders . . . Savak . . . You understand. In my present post it's not advisable. Security warned us against associating with your husband . . . I'm sorry."

Andrea was shaking. "I'm not my husband."

"I know. I'm sorry."

Shirin returned. "I'm famished. Shall we?"

Andrea felt like she'd been hit on the head by a huge rock. It was difficult enough to live with her husband. She did not need to be reminded of it, nor could she accept the stigma attached to being the wife of a terrorist. But she had to live with it. There was too much at stake.

They entered the dining room and were seated.

Andrea struggled to pull herself together. Given the atmosphere in the country, it should not have surprised her. But it did. She did not want Shirin to notice her discomfort. So she put on a brave smile and ordered steak. Shirin ordered the same.

Soon their order arrived. Andrea forced herself to eat. Although she had not had beef since she left the States and it tasted good, she had lost her appetite.

"You can return it if you don't like it," Shirin said.

"Oh, no. It's delicious."

"Then why are you picking at it?"

"It's too good to be eaten quickly." Andrea was amazed at her recently acquired talent to tell white lies.

After lunch, they were served coffee and desert.

Shirin was telling Andrea about her four years of schooling in England and the mischief she and her friends had gotten themselves into, when she stopped in mid sentence.

Andrea turned around slowly.

A young man stood facing them.

"Hello, Shirin," he said. "Where have you been hiding yourself. We haven't seen you for a while."

Andrea knew instantly she'd seen him before and where. He was the man who had interrogated her at Savak headquarters in Pahlavi.

"I got married you know."

"I know. I was there."

Shirin stiffened but said nothing.

"Who's your new friend? Aren't you going to introduce us?" He had an arrogant, imposing air about him which seemed to rub Shirin the wrong way.

"Andrea this is Taha. Taha this is Andrea."

"Pleased to meet you."

Andrea raised her head slightly, murmured the same, then continued sipping her coffee.

"May I join you?"

"We were about to leave." Shirin rose. "I have to check the horses."

Andrea followed Shirin to the cashier. They paid and left the dining room.

Shirin walked fast. She looked angry.

At the stalls, where her horses were kept, Shirin told the groom to prepare two horses. "Let's go to my locker. Maybe one of my outfits will fit you."

Andrea was puzzled by Shirin's abrupt behavior but decided not to prod.

They were about the same size. The first outfit she tried on, fit.

"Let's check the pro shop," Shirin said. "You need boots. I don't have an extra pair."

"I'm wearing walking shoes. I can ride in those."

Shirin first looked astonished, then laughed so hard she doubled over. Andrea had never met a person whose moods fluctuated as often and to such extreme. "Do you want to create a scandal? This is the famous Imperial Club. Members come here to show off their latest acquisitions from abroad and you want to ride in those shoes?"

"Would it bother you?"

Shirin became quiet, almost sullen. "No. I guess not."

"You look upset," Andrea said. "I should leave. I'll call a cab."

"No. It's got nothing to do with you. I hate that Taha fellow. I swear one day I'm going to do something very unladylike to him."

"He was probably just being polite."

"Polite? That man's a beast. His only pleasure in life is to inflict pain. His victims invariably develop a sudden deterioration of health or disappear without a trace. It's men like him that give a bad reputation to the government. They'll be our downfall. You wait and see."

Andrea couldn't agree more but said nothing.

Shirin spun around. "To hell with him. Let's get you a pair of boots."

Andrea chose a pair. She tried to pay. A nod from Shirin made the man draw his hand away. The boots were wrapped and presented to her.

"I can't take it. You must let me pay."

"Be so good as not to argue. It's a treat to have someone ride with me. Iranian women are not into such things and for a married woman to ride with a man other than her husband, is not advisable. Unless of course she has a death wish."

"You're much too kind and overly generous."

"I'll tell you what. I'll let you do the same for me when I come to the States."

"When?"

"Name the time."

"What about your husband?"

"My husband is a pilot. He's gone most of the time. We have an understanding. I go where I want so long as I let him know."

"How I envy you," Andrea said and immediately regretted it.

The groom approached with two horses, saddled, ready to go. They got on the horses and trotted off to the trails.

They rode for hours. Shirin seemed herself again. She told Andrea she'd been riding since she was three. She loved the huge animals, the wind in her hair and the pleasure of being alone and together with nature.

"I feel the same way," Andrea said. "I can't think of anything I enjoy more."

"I'm so happy I got to know you," Shirin exclaimed. "We seem to have the same interests. Few women here like the activities I do."

"I like you too."

"Do you have other Iranian friends?"

"A few. One very good friend. Her name is Layla. I went to Pahlavi for two weeks in March. When I returned, she had disappeared. No one seems to know where she is."

"I wouldn't worry about that if I were you. She's probably vacationing somewhere. Chances are she can't get to a phone."

Shirin pulled on the reigns. The horse stopped. Andrea slowed her pace.

"Look over there," Shirin pointed across the flat terrain to a hill. "Can you see a half-finished structure on top of the hill?"

Andrea strained to look. There was construction everywhere. "Which one?"

Shirin laughed. "It's the one next to that monstrous mansion. On the way home we'll swing by and I'll show you our house."

They continued riding. Andrea was lost in thought. Too many conflicting events were taking place in the country at the same time. Unrest, assassinations, random bombings occurred with numbing regularity. In such an atmosphere why would Shirin want to build a home here? It seemed like a matter of time before the smoldering volcano erupted. Not a question of if, but when. She knew. She listened to the voices of dissent often enough. The total commitment of anti-government activists to the violent overthrow of the regime could not be ascribed to temporary discontent. She'd witnessed an oath taking meeting the day after she moved to the apartment. There were twenty two men in all. A mullah asked each member to swear by the Koran to dedicate his life to rid the country of the Pahlavi Dynasty. Included in the pact were suicide missions. Andrea remembered well. She could not figure out the word suicide. She had to look it up in her dictionary. "We must live and die by the sword," the mullah stressed. "You cannot be a revolutionary and have a conscience. We must destroy the past in order to build the future."

Twenty-two men had shouted "Allah-u-Akbar" in unison.

"You're awfully quiet," Shirin commented. "Is something bothering you."

"I was wondering why you would want to build a house here with all the turmoil that's going on."

"We're Jews. Life in Israel is not easy and the Shah is awfully good to us."

"If something were to happen to the Shah, then what?"

"Nothing will happen to him. The American government cannot allow it to happen. It will not be to their advantage or to the advantage of Iranians."

"I'm glad you're not bothered by it."

"Oh, but I am. We can't have this lifestyle if there is a change in government. That's why that Taha fellow got on my nerves. Power has gone to their heads. Who knows how much longer the public will tolerate it."

"Who is he?" Andrea asked.

"A pain. His surname is Diba. He claims to be the Queen's cousin, probably seven times removed. I did not mention his surname deliberately. You did not see the look on his face. It's his only claim to fame and stupid me neglected to mention it."

"How could you possibly be so callous?"

Both women burst into laughter.

To their left there was a small wooded area. Shirin jumped off her horse. "Let's take a break."

They lay on the grass, on their backs and let the spring sun bathe their faces. Soon Shirin propped herself on an elbow. "Would you like to do something tomorrow? We could drive to Dizzin, see the snowcapped mountains. Have you been there?"

Andrea tensed. Mohammed said she should go to Ahwaz.

"I'll have to check with my husband. I'll let you know."

"Do you like shopping?"

"No. I like bookstores. I can spend hours in one."

"Do you like to read."

"I always have but lately that's all I've been doing."

"Don't you have any friends besides Layla?"

"I do. She's in Switzerland, visiting."

"Is she Iranian?"

"She's German. Her name is Helga. Helga Naini."

"General Naini's wife?"

"Do you know her?"

"Not really. I've met her at social functions. I remember her because she's German and she always stands a few yards away from the crowd. You can tell she's not there because she wants to, but because she has to."

"I hope you get to know her better. She's a wonderful person."

"I know her husband well."

"Oh?"

"Wipe that impish smile off your face, Andrea. It's nothing like that. I know he's famous as a lady's man. It's not true. People are jealous. That's all."

"Jealous of what?"

"Well, let's see. He's got the King's ear. The King trusts him as much as an Iranian can trust another. He's scrupulously honest. They've been trying for years, but no one has been able to accuse him of any wrong doing."

"Then what puts that gleam in your eyes when you talk about him."

"You're a terrible tease."

"When Helga gets back, I'd like you to meet her."

"We'll meet, I'm sure. My father is building their house. It's that huge structure on top of the hill next to our house. My father had to move his office to the site. Occasionally I help with the paper work. The General comes often but I have not seen his wife there."

"That's strange. If we were building a house I'd probably spend most of my time hanging around just to make sure."

"This is no ordinary house. It's been under construction for five years and is no where near finished."

"Five years?" Was it the mansion her husband had mentioned to his colleagues? "What's he building, a monument?"

"Worse. I'll take you on a grand tour when we stop to see our house."

If it was the mansion Mani had referred to, then she'd have to get the word to Phil fast.

A soft breeze whistled through the trees. The sun turned into a huge orange ball and sank slowly behind the horizon. The women looked sated, happy. Andrea could sense the beginnings of a beautiful friendship taking seed. A warm feeling swept through her. She liked Shirin almost immediately, something she rarely did lately. Her marriage to Mani had cured her of any illusions she may have had about her ability to judge people. Somehow, with Shirin she was sure. She'd never met a more direct person.

"Let's go back," Shirin said. "I want you to see our house before it gets dark."

They steered their horses to the pathway. A trainer riding an Arabian, came galloping down the path. He struggled to restrain his horse. Andrea's horse reared. She lost her footing and fell.

The trainer jumped off the horse, rushed to Andrea's side and helped her lift herself off the ground apologizing profusely.

"It was not your fault," Andrea said. "I should have looked."

"That's what you get for hiding in the woods." Both women spun around. It was Taha.

"Don't you have anything better to do than follow two married women?" Shirin said half-jokingly.

"Is there a law against riding on this trail?"

Shirin moved close to Andrea. Taha was about ten feet away ostensibly waiting for the women to move their horses so he could pass. Shirin whispered to Andrea, "Go to the stables. I've got to set the score straight with this pest."

Andrea got back on her horse and trotted to the stables.

It was not long before Shirin rode in, her face taut, her lips curled downward pulling furiously on the reigns.

"We'll shower at home. Let's go."

She turned to the driver who waited near the stable. "Please bring the car. We want to go home."

During the ride home, Shirin did not say a word. She tapped her fingers on the door handle from the moment they got in the car until they arrived.

"Have you got a minute," Shirin asked. "I need to talk to you."

"Sure."

She opened the door to her apartment and they walked in.

"Please, take a seat," she told Andrea.

Andrea sat down.

"I have known you briefly," Shirin said. "I like you very much and I want you to be my friend."

"Thanks. Same here."

"I am an open person. I call what's black, black and what's white, white. Shades of gray I don't fool with. I'm completely honest with my friends and expect the same from them."

"Something is bothering you, Shirin. What is it?"

"Of course something is bothering me."

"You asked me to come in. Do you want to talk about it?"

"You're damn right I do. Do you know why that idiot was following us?"

"No."

"He wanted to warn me about you."

"Me?" Andrea was stunned. First she felt cold, then she felt the blood rush to her cheeks. What was going on? A conspiracy? Twice in one day was too much! She knew exactly what Shirin's next statement would be.

"He says your husband is a known terrorist."

She was too numb to answer.

"Is he?"

Andrea took her time before answering. "You're not my husband's friend."

Shirin's voice rose. "You're not answering my question. Is he or isn't he?"

"If your husband was a terrorist would he go around advertising it? Would he tell you about it?"

Shirin stopped to ponder the question.

Andrea clasped her hands together to stop the shaking.

"It's your contention then that you don't know."

"Does it matter?"

"That's not the point, Andrea. We're Jews. We're always suspect. Even if our great, great grandfathers were born here. We're under constant surveillance. Anybody who is somebody, is. But it is worse for us because my husband is the Shah's pilot. Taha was not invited to our wedding. You heard him say he was there."

Something was wrong somewhere. "I don't get it. How could he have come to your wedding? Didn't you say you got married in Israel?"

"Of course we were married in Israel. But the Iranian government does not recognize marriages performed outside Iran. We had to go through the formalities, a second time, here, to validate our marriage. It's the law."

For a moment Andrea thought her heart would bust out of her chest. She was speechless. With determined effort she forced herself to regain her composure. She tried to speak but no words would come out.

Shirin looked perplexed. She reached for Andrea's.hand and gave it a gentle squeeze. "I'm sorry I upset you? I didn't mean to. I don't care what anyone says. You're my friend."

With great effort Andrea tried to control her shaky voice. "Could . . . could you please repeat what you said."

"What do you mean? What I said about what?"

"What . . . what you said about the la . . . aaw and marri . . . aaage."

"I said the Iranian government does not recognize marriages performed outside of Iran. It's got to be repeated here to make it legal. Everyone knows that."

Andrea jumped, threw her arms around Shirin and embraced her, "Thank you. Thank you my friend. You just saved my life."

She rushed out the door.

Chapter 39

Nine men sat quietly on piles of folded carpets, in a warehouse, in downtown Tehran. The tenth man, in his early thirties, of middle height and dark complexion, paced the room, his hands clasped behind his back. He was perspiring profusely. The air in the room was thick, full of cigarette smoke and the smell of perspiration. They had been there since early morning.

The warehouse belonged to Majid's uncle. It was located at the end of a narrow alley, accessible only by foot. Two men stood guard at the entrance of the warehouse and another two men kept watch at the point where the alley joined the main bazaar. To ward off suspicion, a small tea stand was set up for the two men facing the bazaar to sell tea to the merchants and customers. Their stand was in full view of the other two men who were posted to guard the entrance to the warehouse. In an emergency, which meant Savak, one of the men was to drop a tea cup alerting his comrades to flee.

It was an ideal place, with an escape route which had been cleverly camouflaged with a pile of carpets hiding it from view.

Lately, the merchants in the bazaar, who controlled the economy of the country with their wealth and influence, were becoming vocal in their disgruntlements. Their freedom to import and export was eroded daily by new laws imposed by the government. Inflation soared unchecked for years. The Royal Family and its entourage had to be paid regularly. The country was becoming too westernized, too fast, trampling in its path indiscriminately on revered Muslim traditions. The merchants were wealthy, disillusioned men. By 1976, disillusionment had turned into hatred.

Ordinarily, reprisal by Savak would have intimidated the public enough to prevent them from cooperating with the rebels. The assassination of the Americans in broad daylight changed all that.

Majid's uncle had more reason than most merchants in the bazaar to help the rebels. Two of his sons were tortured and brutally murdered by the Secret Service. A month after his sons disappeared, the uncle was asked to go to the morgue and identify the bodies; what was left of them. Ever since that day, he lived for one reason only, to avenge the death of his sons.

He was also a Hadji, a man who had gone to Mecca and worshipped at the most sacred Muslim shrine. The secularization of the country was in his view, an unforgivable sin which should not be left unpunished. He provided the rebels with accommodation, food and funds. Through his nephew, he kept up with their progress.

Lately though, their progress was marred by an inexplicable sequence of events. They were thwarted in carrying out most of their meticulously planned anti-government activities. Invariably, Savak obtained advance information and apprehended the participants.

The group called itself The Revolutionary Council.

This was not a scheduled meeting. Mani and Farhad came directly from Mani's apartment to the meeting, after being up all night. The emergency meeting was called to discuss the capture of Ali and his subsequent disappearance. Ali was Majid's cousin.

Nine grim faced men listened as the enraged leader spoke. "Let's go over every detail again." He turned to Mejid. "The concierge's apartment was dark."

"Right."

"You're sure he was not there."

"Positive. We called the hospital. They assured us his condition was serious. He'll probably be there another week."

"The American did not open the door for you."

"She was asleep. She couldn't have heard us knock."

"How do you know she was asleep?"

"She had to be. She did not hear us knock. When we came back, she came out of her room and asked us to be quiet. It was obvious we had awakened her."

"But you don't know for sure that she was asleep."

"No, I don't."

The man resumed pacing the room.

"May I make a comment?" Farhad asked.

"What?"

"Even if she knew who they were and even if she wanted to inform Security, she couldn't have. She was in her room, we assumed asleep. There's no phone in her room."

"Don't be an ass," the leader snapped. "If someone is determined, there's always a way."

"Impossible," Mani said.

"You listen to me, you idiots. She could have signaled with a flashlight if she had to."

"We don't own a flashlight," Mani said bravely. "I check her room regularly. She had a small mirror she used for her make up. I took it away."

"All right then, since you two are so clever, tell me, who do you think is the informer?"

Mani's stomach growled. It was almost noon. He had not

eaten the night before or in the morning. He had a lot of vodka through the night. He was feeling lightheaded.

"I couldn't say," he answered. "I've racked my brains. I can't come up with an answer. But it's not her."

"What makes you so sure. She betrayed you before."

Mani stopped to think and realized that his boss was right. He had endured the worst suffering in the hands of Savak, thanks to her. But she couldn't have. Unless . . .

"Well?" hissed the leader.

"I can't say. Maybe she contacted someone while I took Farhad to the hospital. But who?"

"Your brother?"

"That's easy to verify. I'll call my mother. My brother doesn't answer the phone. If she called, my mother will know."

Majid pulled the phone from a hidden closet and handed it to Mani.

He talked to his mother and put the phone down.

"My brother has not been home for two days. No one has called. Male or female."

"How about that American who comes to see her. How do we know he is a simple employee at the Embassy?"

"We know that for sure," Farhad interjected. "Our informer has made a thorough investigation."

"Never mind your informer. How can we be sure?"

Farhad hesitated but only for a moment. "I'll call the Embassy and ask to speak to him. I'll say I'm a friend from the U. S. with a message for him."

The leader studied Farhad with cold eyes. "Okay, try."

Farhad dialed the number.

"Mr. Conrad is out town," the secretary at the Embassy informed him.

"I have an important message for him. When did he leave?"

"He's been gone for a while. We don't know when he'll be back. Please give me your name and number. He'll return your call when he gets back."

"I don't have a phone. I'll call next week."

The grim faces stared at each other.

The growling in Mani's stomach got louder. He felt relieved that his wife was not the informer. It would have complicated matters for him. He was hungry, irritable. He wanted the meeting to end. They were getting nowhere. They'd been over the same questions so many times that by now even he guessed what answer would follow what question. But, he was not ready for what Farhad said next.

"For the past four hours we have investigated every possibility thoroughly to no avail. With all due respect to those present in this room, I suggest each of us swear by the Holy Koran. Only then can we be sure our problem involves someone outside the group."

Looking surprised, the leader stopped pacing. No one spoke. He went to a desk in the corner of the room and took out a Koran from the drawer. He was the first to swear by it.

The men lined up and swore without hesitation.

Mani cast a quick glance in Farhad's direction. His friend's brilliance was a source of inspiration for him, always. The Koran meant nothing to Farhad. His hatred of all matters religious was a secret strictly kept between them.

Why was he putting on such a show. Was he the informer?

Mani was horrified by the thought. He watched Farhad walk to the desk, kiss the Koran dutifully, swear and return to his corner on the pile of carpets. Mani followed suit.

The leader sighed. He propped himself on the desk. "What now? That includes everybody."

"Everybody except one," Farhad said calmly.

All eyes focused on Farhad. The leader's voice rose. "You know something we don't?"

"Not really."

"Then speak up or stop making idiotic remarks."

Mani concentrated on the design of the carpet he was sitting on.

"What I am about to say will most certainly shock you," Farhad said. "And I wouldn't have mentioned it any other time. But, the situation is critical. We must investigate every possibility no matter how remote. When we worked on our plans for Ahwaz there were eleven of us, not ten."

Mani dug his nails in the carpet. Farhad's folly could be very costly.

"You're insane," yelled Majid and hurled himself at Farhad, his fists clenched. "Mullah Hamid was the only other person present. He's my uncle. You think he would betray his own nephew?"

Farhad cringed but pressed on. "I'm sorry. In this business we cannot afford to overlook any possibility. If he was my uncle I would welcome an investigation."

"He's not your uncle," snapped Mejid.

Mani understood what Farhad had in mind. The seeds of doubt were sown. Majid's wrath was a minor price to pay.

"Disperse," the leader instructed. "We shall meet tonight at Mani's apartment at eight."

Andrea's day had been unexpected and ended on a positive note. She was invigorated with the outdoor activities and Shirin's casual remark about Iranian law regarding marriages outside Iran gave her an optimism she sorely needed. To obtain an Iranian divorce in a country where women had precious few rights, especially foreigners, was a matter which had caused her many sleepless nights, pain and worry.

She was on her way to the apartment when she thought of checking on Mohammed. The door was locked and the place was in total darkness as Mohammed told her it would be. Darkness provided him with the cover he needed to observe those who went to the fifth floor apartment. It was also his way of letting Andrea know she'd have visitors soon.

Tired, but happily so, she took a shower, put on her sweat suit and curled on the living room sofa with the *Time* magazine as her companion. An article about the Shah caught her eyes. She read it eagerly and was amazed at the contents. For the first time, she was able to read an article critical of the Shah uncensored. Her interest in the complex and often mind boggling politics of the Middle East, and particularly that of Iran had been aroused years ago. In the U.S. she had no trouble keeping herself informed. In Iran it was almost impossible. The local news media praised the King and his great accomplishments. The infallible one, guided by divine vision and the best interest of his country, never made mistakes. Lucky indeed were Iranians blessed with such a monarch.

The front door opened. Mani, Farhad and a third man walked in. Andrea rose and went to the kitchen. She did not recognize the third man.

Someone followed her to the kitchen.

She rinsed the coffee pot and started a fresh pot of coffee.

"Is that American coffee you're making," asked a strange voice.

She turned around. "Yes, would you like some?"

"I'd love some. Where did you find American coffee?"

"On Naderi Avenue. It's fresher. They grind imported Brazilian coffee beans anyway the customer wants."

"That's good to know. I love American coffee. I haven't had any in months."

Andrea placed two mugs on the kitchen table.

"The coffee smelled so good I forgot to introduce myself. My name is Abbas. You must be Andrea."

"Glad to meet you."

He sat across the table from her. Soon the coffee was ready. Andrea poured coffee for both of them. She took her cup. "There's more in the pot if you like." She walked out.

He followed her. "Please, don't go. Is my company annoying you?"

"Not at all. I love talking to people. Unfortunately, I don't get to meet too many. Mani does not want me to mix with his friends."

"We must correct that. Mani has forgotten his manners. Please join us. More friends are coming. You might be able to help."

"Help ? How?"

"What time is it?"

Andrea checked her watch. "Almost eight."

"They should be here pretty soon. There's a matter we have to discuss. We'd appreciate your input."

Farhad and Mani were in the dining room. Neither man spoke.

He's quite a smooth operator, Andrea thought. I'm sure he is high up in the hierarchy. Probably here to take up where Farhad and Mani left off this morning. This is one man whose picture Phil did not show me.

She drifted to the sofa and settled down, hesitantly, not quite sure she was ready for the attention lavished on her. He came and sat near her. "I live in the States. I've been there for seventeen years. I love it."

"Where do you live?"

"In Baltimore. I studied medicine at Johns Hopkins."

"What's your specialty?"

"Pediatrics."

She remained silent. Pediatrics. Children. Painful memories surfaced, sending a chilling sensation throughout her being.

He must have noticed the change in her. "I'm sorry about your daughter. It must be terrible for you to go through such an experience and in a strange country."

While they were talking, one by one the group arrived. There were ten of them. The doctor did not move. He remained seated next to her.

At eight thirty, the square figure of Mullah Hamid made its presence noted by his heavy breathing. Five flights of stairs had left him breathless.

The doctor got up and offered his seat to the cleric. Sitting on one of the dining room chairs was out of the question. He could not fit in one.

"Madame, we meet under better circumstances," the mullah said with a twisted smile. "How very beautiful you are."

Where did he learn such good English and what's he doing here?

Mani came around with glasses of vodka and ice. He served Mullah Hamid first. The mullah took a sip, tried to reach the coffee table to put his glass down, missed and spilled his drink over the carpet.

Andrea did not move. Mani gave her a mean look, went to the kitchen, came back with a rag, picked the ice cubes and returned to the kitchen to fix the mullah another drink.

The doctor called the group to attention. "Let's go over everyone's responsibility one more time."

Andrea rose. The doctor looked up, the mullah's eyes followed her, and Farhad and Mani exchanged knowing glances.

She went to her room, closed the door and settled in bed to read. Mani had taken the only chair in her room and offered it to one of the guests.

She had not been there more than five minutes, when the door was suddenly flung open. Mani and the doctor stepped in.

Speechless, Andrea stared at them. Then it dawned on her. They were checking to make sure she was not making contact with someone outside.

Enraged, but well in control of herself she said, "Did you want something?"

"We're terribly sorry," the doctor said with disarming friendliness. He motioned for Mani to get out.

They left the room leaving the door open.

She got out of bed, shut the door and returned to bed.

She could hear several men arguing outside and a lot of movement, then, there was quiet.

She tried to read but found herself too tense to do so. She

pulled the blanket over her head and plunged into thinking.

There was a knock.

She ignored it. If only she could lock her door. There was a lock when they'd first moved in. It was gone the second day.

The knock was repeated with more urgency.

She ignored it.

"Andrea, please," Mani pleaded with a soft voice. "It's important. We have to talk to you."

"I have nothing to say to anyone."

Mani opened the door and approached the bed. "Andrea, please listen to me. Mullah Hamid wants to talk to you. It will only take a few minutes."

"Leave me alone, please."

"It's rude to keep a clergyman waiting."

There was no getting rid of him. She propped herself up. "Rude? Did you say rude? You should talk about rude when you barge into my room with another man without knocking."

The doctor had come in while Mani tried to pacify his wife. "We will leave," he said "as soon as we've talked to you. Mullah Hamid is the only one left. Everyone else has gone. He's waiting for you. Please come join us."

"What for?"

He looked at her with an expression of sadness and pain. "We've lost some of our best men. We don't know who's betraying us. We're checking every possibility. Please, try to understand."

"What would you like me to understand, doctor? If you're worried about me betraying you, I can offer an easy way out. I'm not here by choice. All my husband has to do is give me permission to leave the country. You'll have one less person to worry about."

Mullah Hamid had sank in the sofa. He tried to lift himself up. He crashed right back.

They watched as he tried again and fell again, wheezing,

short of breath.

The doctor turned to Andrea. "Please, Madame. I know how you feel. It won't take long."

"I'm tired. I want to sleep."

"I understand perfectly. Mullah Hamid wants to talk to you, not us."

She looked around bidding for time to pull herself together and plot her strategy. These were fierce men, with short, violent tempers. Their actions and reactions mostly unpredictable. She decided not to push her luck too far. A look at Farhad convinced her. He had a mean grin on his face and seemed to enjoy the scenario.

She went and sat on the sofa.

Mullah Hamid beamed with pleasure. He took Andrea's hand in his hands, caressing it gently. He wore three rings. The one which struck her most was a large ruby, set in an oval gold frame, surrounded by diamonds. Brilliant beams bounced erratically from the ring competing with the glow from the crystal chandelier.

She sat perfectly still, waiting for the inevitable.

A nod from the doctor sent Mani and Farhad scurrying to the kitchen. The rest of the visitors had left. The doctor sat restlessly in an armchair across from Andrea looking at his folded hands.

"Madame," said Mullah Hamid amiably, "I know how you feel and I truly sympathize with you. You've had it rough. Your husband has not been much help. But all that will change if you cooperate."

He waited for her response but none was forthcoming. He furrowed his brow, stroked his beard and continued. "You seem to be a caring person. I'm told you help a lot of children, teaching them English, basic hygiene and telling them about the world outside. It leads us to believe that you are a woman who's quite different from the ordinary."

He had to stop. Whenever he spoke a few sentences in succession, he got short of breath. He blinked constantly.

A minute passed. Andrea raised her eyes and looked at the doctor hoping he would have a suggestion for the clergyman's breathing problem. The doctor kept his head down, his eyes resting on his folded hands.

The mullah struggled some more. Eventually, his breathing became regular and he stopped blinking. "Have Mani bring tea," he told the doctor.

Andrea wanted to draw her hand away from the mullah's hands without attracting attention. "Excuse me, I need a glass of water," she said and rose.

She returned with the water, settled back on the sofa as far away from him as she could, waiting for the predictable monologue which was bound to follow. She did not have to wait long.

"We have also learned that you spend a considerable amount of time with your cleaning woman who's sick. You have taken her to the doctor, bought her medications, and bought food for her children. Would you say such a person is a caring person madame?"

Although stunned with the extent of his knowledge about her activities, Andrea managed to remain calm.

"Madame, I ask you again what do you think of such a person?"

"I think that for reasons unknown to me I've been under constant surveillance. Why are such measures necessary? Is it too much to ask to be left alone?"

He eyed her sullenly. "Forgive us. We had to be sure. It involves my sister. I could not take a chance."

"What do you mean?"

"I'm not at liberty to give you details but I beg you to help us. We are losing our best trained men, daily. We're literally fighting for our lives. Can't you see?"

"See what? I don't understand. How does it involve me?"

She watched him listening to her with total concentration. His English was perfect. The more educated, the more radical their views seemed to be.

"But you are involved my dear, whether you like it or not. If you have any compassion for your fellow men, you are involved. How can you not be?"

"I still don't understand. Could you please be more explicit."

The doctor stiffened, unclasped his hands and looked apprehensively at the cleric. Clerics were not in the habit of being questioned by anyone except their superiors. And much less women.

Mullah Hamid tried to shift his position but failed. The sofa creaked under his weight.

Mani cautiously approached the coffee table with a tray of tea. There were two cups of tea on the tray. He offered one to the cleric and the other to the doctor. He left the sugar cubes, which Iranians put in their mouths while sipping their tea, on the coffee table, and went back to the kitchen.

Mullah Hamid's dark eyes darted from the doctor's face to Mani's back. He pointed to the tray. "It's dumb things like this which give her the impression that we are a bunch of barbarians."

The doctor rose and went to the kitchen. A few minutes later, Mani returned with a cup of tea for his wife. He seemed ready to explode. A man like him did not go around serving women, much less his wife. A bloodcurdling look from the mullah sent Mani to the kitchen in a hurry.

They drank their tea in silence.

When the mullah finished his tea he did not attempt to put the empty teacup on the table. The doctor darted, took it, and placed it on the table. The doctor had black circles under his eyes and his shoulders sagged. He looked older than his years.

The mullah stroked his beard and blinked. "I beg you not to think of all of us to be the same as your husband. Somewhere along the way, he must have lost the little bit of decency I thought he had. We are men of great compassion. The fact that we're here is proof enough. We're here because we care for the poor and the sick. The ones who are tortured and the ones who are brutalized. We face death daily. Across from you is a man who could be making thousands of dollars a month practicing medicine. He has chosen to devote his life to rid this country of the Pahlavi curse. I, as a clergyman am at the greatest risk. The government hates clerics. They persecute and banish us from the country with the least excuse. Many have disappeared without a trace. But, the struggle must go on. We have no choice."

Andrea waited for him to get over a paroxysm of coughing and gagging. She put her head back and pondered. Was it the man's gross appearance or the perfect performance he was giving which left her ill-at-ease? The intensity with which he was attacking the problem signaled a lack of conviction. He did not impress her as a man who would put his life on the line for any cause but his own. Why had Phil not mentioned him?

Perturbed, she sat upright a dozen questions crowding her thoughts. What was she doing in this gaudily furnished apartment listening to a foxy cleric and a morose doctor? Why was her life so different from everyone else's. She wished she could find someone to blame, someone other than herself, but her mind's finger would point only in one direction, at her.

She heard him say, "Do you understand what I'm telling you my dear?"

"I understand but I don't see what all this has to do with me. I'd like to make it clear that I don't want to be involved."

"You won't be. I promise. This will be the first and the last time."

"What will? Why do you need me? What can I do that anyone else can't?"

"You're a foreigner. You won't be suspect. This is one of our biggest projects. No violence mind you. A sit down strike. We want to paralyze the power and water supply system for a couple of days to let the public here and the rest of the world know that although we are oppressed, we are not helpless."

"I see."

"I don't think you do. It's not as simple as it sounds. A lot of convincing and planning is involved. We have to send an advance team to work with the employees of both facilities. That's where you come in."

"How?"

"My sister has graciously accepted to let us use her home for a weekend. She doesn't know why nor does she need to know, but she has to be informed which weekend. She does not want to be there."

"Why don't you write her a letter?"

"It takes too long to get there and it's not safe to have anything in writing."

"Don't you think it would look kind of suspicious if someone were to see an American woman, a total stranger knocking on your sister's door?"

The mullah blinked, stared at her in disbelief, then asked slowly, like a hunter who had caught his prey unawares, "How did you know that's what we wanted you to do?"

Andrea smiled. "Of course I know. Farhad and Mani spent quite some time trying to convince me this morning."

The mullah sighed, stroked his beard again and again. "And what was your answer?"

"Didn't they tell you?"

"We didn't have time. They spent the whole day searching for clues as to who the informer could be. I was only told that Mani and Farhad had talked to you."

"I find the whole idea of me acting as a messenger ridiculous. Why I'd be so obvious I'd be an instant suspect."

"Not if you wear sunglasses and a chaddor."

"I doubt that will be enough."

The doctor moved in his chair restlessly. The mullah cast a glance in his direction and nodded. Andrea pretended not to see.

The doctor cleared his throat. "We have reason to believe the messenger we sent to Abadan betrayed us. He has disappeared."

"Maybe Savak got him."

"Not maybe. Definitely."

"There's your answer. They made him talk."

"Our members take an oath of silence. No matter how brutally they're treated, they don't talk. He had to be an informer. Otherwise he would not have talked."

Of all the members of the Revolutionary Council, the doctor's involvement made least sense to Andrea. He acted reasonably, was painfully polite and well mannered. The other members were highly charged with emotion in everything they did and said. But not the doctor. He seemed like a man in control, a man who knew what he wanted and knew how to get it.

It bothered her. She decided to ask him. "Are you in charge of the sit-down strike in Ahwaz?"

She regretted it the minute she said it. He looked so shocked he couldn't speak.

"Sorry. I don't want to know. I'm trying to find out how you can be sure that I will escape detection by Savak?"

"That's why we want you to wear a chaddor."

"I don't believe a chaddor will deter them."

The doctor could not help but stare at her. It was evident no one had expected such resistance from a so called 'simple American.' "There are lots of Americans living in Ahwaz. Several American oil companies operate there. You won't be singled out."

"I will be if I wear a chaddor."

The doctor threw a quizzical look in Mullah Hamid's direction.

The mullah blinked. "She's got a point."

"It's worse if she goes without a chaddor," the doctor insisted. "They will wonder what a young American woman is doing in Ahwaz alone. It's not exactly a tourist town you know."

Farhad entered the room. "May I make a suggestion?"

"What is it?" quipped the mullah. "What's so urgent that it can't wait?"

"We overheard you discussing her wearing a chaddor. All she has to do if she is questioned is tell them she's married to a Muslim and that her husband insists that she wear a chaddor."

The doctor and Mullah Hamid exchanged glances. "Very good," said the mullah. "I'm glad to see your mouth is good for something else besides pouring vodka in it."

Farhad's wrath registered on his face instantly. He withdrew to the kitchen.

The doctor and Mullah Hamid looked expectantly at Andrea. She was astonished. Their analysis of some matters was complex and involved but the most basic questions eluded them.

Andrea did not offer an opinion. It was their problem.

"Don't you agree?" the mullah asked.

"Let me ask you a question. Supposing I tell them what Farhad suggested. What should I say if they ask me who my husband is?"

There was silence except for the mullah's wheezing. The doctor resorted to examining his knuckles.

"That idiot," Mullah Hamid's voice rose. "He never thinks before he talks."

"It really doesn't matter. I can't do it."

The doctor looked crushed. He pressed his hands harder against each other and continued staring at them. "I guess it's a waste of time," he said. "We better leave."

Mullah Hamid looked like he'd been slapped.

Andrea rose. "It was nice meeting you doctor." She turned to the mullah. "It was a pleasure talking to you. If you will excuse me I'd like to go to bed."

First, the mullah acted stunned, then he attempted to move. A sudden, severe spell of coughing forced Andrea to turn back and look. It sounded like the man was choking. But the doctor did not seem bothered by it.

"Can't you give him something?" she asked the doctor.

"Why should someone's cough concern you when you don't care if people live or die?"

"What makes you think I don't care? Are you implying that I don't care because I won't go to Ahwaz?"

"No, I'm not implying. I'm making a statement of fact."

"I'm sorry you feel that way," she said astonished at his sudden outburst.

"Don't be a hypocrite. What does it matter to you if a few thousand Iranians get tortured or killed. Like you say in America, it's no skin off your nose."

"You're free to believe what you like. I'm sure you have your reasons for doing what you're doing. I might have trouble understanding them but that's my problem."

There was silence. Miraculously, even the mullah's uncontrollable coughing and blinking stopped.

Mullah Hamid said solemnly, "My dear friend. The doctor has more reason than all of us to get involved. You're not aware of what's going on in this country even though you live in our midst. The doctor is here because it is his duty to be here. He has a very good practice in America. Unfortunately, he had to leave his practice in the care of his partners. He had to come here. Do you read the paper regularly Madame?"

Exhausted, Andrea was ready to scream. She did not. "Are you referring to a particular article? If it's something that can wait I'd prefer to discuss it some other time. I'd like to get some rest."

The doctor looked horrified and so did the mullah. A host in Iran would never tell a guest he's tired. Regardless of how they felt, they waited till the guest left. Andrea was aware of the custom. She was also convinced that if she did not nudge them it could go on much longer.

The mullah disregarded her last remark. "Two months

ago there was an article in the Iranian and English papers about the King pardoning political prisoners. Do you remember reading that article? It was headline news for over a week."

"Yes, I remember reading something to that effect. It was something like two hundred fifty prisoners, if I recall correctly."

"That's exactly right. What they did not write about was the rest of the story."

Andrea waited. Iranians took their time in approaching and solving any problem. It was useless to try and change people's habits. And who could say they were wrong and she was right. At least that's how she talked herself into accepting any concept she found hard to reconcile with.

Mullah Hamid continued, "The doctor's brother was one of those prisoners. Each prisoner was asked to sign a statement that he would never again participate in any political activity in return for his freedom. Everyone did including the doctor's brother. He was in jail for seven years. He was in for life, accused of being a communist, the top leader."

"Was he?" Andrea asked the doctor.

"I really couldn't say for sure. I was in the States."

"That's not important," interrupted Mullah Hamid. "What's important is what they did with those prisoners."

"I saw pictures of them in the newspaper embracing their families," Andrea said.

Sure you did. The old and the infirm. Pictures taken for the public to see how great their King is. The truth of the matter is they let a few go to pacify the human rights people. The rest were shot and killed. Those considered dangerous, by the government's interpretation of the word dangerous, were disposed of conveniently. They shot them after promising them freedom. They shot them in the back. The doctor's brother was the first one killed. Three weeks later, his mother was taken to the morgue to identify the body."

Mullah Hamid seemed absolutely drained. That was the

longest speech he completed without stopping to catch his breath.

"I'm terribly sorry," Andrea said. "I didn't know."

"There is a lot you don't know," the doctor said tonelessly. "I returned to Iran soon after I heard. I'm a U.S. citizen. The government does not dare touch me. So I started my own investigation. They said he tried to escape. They had to shoot him." The doctor's eyes filled with tears. "Can you tell me why a man who's been pardoned and supposedly granted freedom would try to escape?"

The doctor sobbed quietly, uncontrollably.

Andrea was terribly disturbed watching a grown man cry.

He pulled a handkerchief from his pocket and wiped his eyes. "He was my kid brother. He was only twenty nine."

Andrea's eyes drifted to the mullah. Even he seemed shook. "All right. If my going to Ahwaz is the solution to your problems, then so be it." She was certain she was looking at a genuinely tortured man. If he was acting, then medicine was the wrong profession for him.

Both men sighed. The mullah reached over and took her hand in his again. "Thank you. Thank you my dear. I cannot find the right words to express my feelings. I'm very grateful to you and so is everyone else who's involved, I'm sure."

There was silence in the living room but she could hear mumbled words coming from the kitchen.

The doctor was almost smiling. "Your decision makes me very happy. I'll consider it as a personal favor."

"How about a favor in return?" Andrea asked.

"Certainly. What can we do for you?"

"I'd like a short vacation. So much has happened in the last few months that I can hardly think straight. I want to go for a week or two, some place in Europe, doesn't really matter where, to relax, to find myself."

"What's the problem?" asked the doctor perplexed. "Is it money? I can loan you whatever amount you need."

"I don't need money. I need my passport. I also need my

husband's permission without which I'm informed I cannot leave the country."

"Mani," shouted Mullah Hamid, "come here."

Mani approached the sofa slowly, like a man following a funeral procession.

"You take your wife to the police station tomorrow morning before she leaves and sign the permit."

Mani did not answer.

"Is something bothering you?" the mullah growled.

"She should wait till I can go with her. What's she doing to do alone in Europe?"

"Get away from you," said Farhad grinning.

"Do as you're told," Mullah Hamid ordered.

Andrea watched Mani get ready to explode. "She won't come back."

"Why shouldn't she?" the doctor asked sounding surprised.

"Because she hates my guts. She's manipulating you to find a way to leave the country."

"You have the most distorted mind I've ever had the misfortune of knowing," Mullah Hamid quipped. "If she wanted to escape, there are many options available to her. Why would she put up with you for as long as she has?"

Mani remained silent.

"It's settled then," the mullah said. "You leave at ten twenty in the morning for Ahwaz. Your ticket will be ready for you at the Iran Air counter. I'll personally see to it that Mani has your travel documents ready when you return."

"Good night," Andrea said and went to her room.

Chapter 40

The Intercontinental Hotel, the best known landmark in Tehran, was a favorite meeting place for visitors to the country, regardless of the purpose of their visit. Businessmen, intelligence officers, diplomats, and the occasional tourist, filled its rooms, lounges and dining halls, day and night. The place looked like a permanent convention center.

The hotel's attraction did not lie solely in its plush surroundings, exquisite cuisine and impeccable service, but rather the type of customers who used it as headquarters for all kinds of operations.

The establishment did not escape Savak's scrutiny. Its members were strategically located as employees in every department, around the clock.

At ten that night, Sayid joined his friends in a back room of the hotel, a room reserved exclusively for members of the intelligence network. Drinks were served and fresh decks of cards provided. For the four men in the room the day had just begun. They were there ostensibly to gamble, but the real purpose for their meeting was to study the tape provided by

Mullah Hamid of his visit with the rebels the night before.

They were preparing to hear the tape when the guard knocked on the door with an urgent message for Sayid. Sayid stepped out. The two men conferred. Sayid returned to the room, excused himself and took the elevator to the underground parking garage.

Mohammed was waiting for him in his car.

"Have you been briefed?" Mohammed asked, his voice quivering.

"No, I just got here."

"There was trouble in Ahwaz, bad trouble. The main street downtown and several side streets were attacked by mobs. Shops were looted and burned. Cars were set on fire. So far two persons are known dead and scores injured."

"Is the situation under control now?"

"It is. I talked to our contact. After the noon prayers at the mosque downtown, apparently the crowd, inflamed by a speech given by the mullah, surged through the streets with sticks, shouting slogans, demanding reforms. They then attacked stores owned by pro Shah merchants, burned and looted them. By the time the police arrived, they had dispersed. They've made few arrests."

"If the situation is under control why did you want to see me urgently."

Mohammed wanted to say something but the words would not come out.

Sayid waited.

Mohammed could not make himself say what he had come to say.

"There's more, right?"

"There is."

"What is it? Pull yourself together. What can be so bad that you can't talk about it?"

"Andrea is in Ahwaz."

Sayid stiffened. For a moment he felt light headed, the blood suddenly deserting his brain cells. He pulled himself together quickly.

"What's she doing in Ahwaz?"

"They asked her to take a message. She consulted me. I told her to go."

Like a man demented, Sayid lifted his arm and slapped Mohammed across the face. "You idiot. How dare you make such a decision without consulting Phil or me."

"I'm sorry. I should have known it was no simple job they were asking her to do. All our reports indicated it would be a sit-down strike. No violence."

Sayid shook his head in bafflement. "Your intelligence stinks. Those in charge of the sit-down strike were caught and put in jail two days ago. I can't believe that with all the experience you've had in intelligence work, you would send an untrained, foreign woman on a job like that."

Mohammed looked confused. "If the sit-down strike was cancelled, then why did they want her to go to Ahwaz?"

"To test her. She's the only nonmember around when they meet. They've been searching desperately for a clue to the identity of the informer. What made you think they'd be so naive as to overlook such an obvious possibility?"

"They may have suspected her, but they didn't have proof."

"That blow on your head must have really clouded your thinking. They had all the proof they needed. The doctor was not convinced you were still in the hospital. They called. As instructed, the clerk in charge told them you were in the hospital. He checked. He's a doctor. He had no problem getting the information he was looking for. Their lives are at stake. They're not going to sit back and wait to be caught."

"It doesn't make sense. Why her?"

"Because after they verified that you were not in the hospital, they talked to Shirin's maid. She told them you were back and that her mistress and the American from the fifth floor had been in to see you."

"What does that prove? Even if they suspected her, why

would they want her to go to Ahwaz? It still doesn't make sense."

"It makes a lot of sense. Here she has friends she can turn to in case of trouble. In Ahwaz she'd be on her own. It's easier for them to make her talk."

Mohammed remained quiet, apparently stumped for an answer. His cheek was sore. He rubbed it and waited.

Exasperated, Sayid yelled, "Answer me. Why did you tell her to go?"

"She wanted to go to Europe. She thinks they're after General Cyrus. We figured this way she could get her husband to give her permission to leave the country in return for her help. I thought it was a good idea. She could leave without arousing suspicion."

"Where is she now?"

"In jail."

"What did you say?"

"I said in jail. Apparently she got caught in the crowd. I don't know how, but she did."

"There's more, right?"

"Yes."

"Speak or it will be the last time you do so."

"Our contact said she was beaten. I told him to go immediately and get her released."

"Well?"

"The police chief would not let her go. He will not release her unless he's ordered to do so by the authorities in Tehran."

Sayid remained motionless, the anger in him mounting by the second.

"I'll leave for Ahwaz right away if you think I can help," Mohammed offered.

"How?"

"I'll drive. There are no flights till morning."

"It's a ten hour drive. Probably longer at night. Did anyone tell you how kindly prisoners are treated in this country, especially foreigners?"

"What choice do we have?"

"Go back to your apartment. I'll be in touch."

Sayid stepped out.

Upstairs, in the gambling room, Sayid's friends waited impatiently for his return, sipped their drinks and chain smoked. He returned forty minutes later, his face white, barely capable of controlling the tremors coursing through his body. He sat in his chair without saying a word.

"What did he do now?" asked the Assistant Security Chief.

"It's not my brother."

"What is it?" the man persisted. "You look like you just saw a ghost."

"It's his wife. She's in jail, in Ahwaz."

The three men exchanged horrified looks.

The Assistant Chief threw the cassette he was holding on the table. "You want to go to Ahwaz, right?"

"I can't. There are no flights till morning. It takes ten hours to get there when the roads are in fair condition. But they're repairing a long stretch. There are detours. It will probably be more like twelve hours and by then it will be morning. Who knows what they'll do to her by the time I get there."

"You should have been married to her instead of that son of a dog," said one of the men.

Sayid raised his head, gave the man an impassive look, then lowered it, lost in thought.

"I'll be right back." The Assistant Chief left.

His name was Manucheir Khorassani. His friends called him Khorassani.

No one in the room spoke. Sayid's love for Andrea was no secret to his friends. He never mentioned her name or spoke about her. But, Tehran was a big small town, inhabited by shrewd men who made it their business to know all they could about anyone that mattered.

Khorassani returned shortly. "We can leave right away. I got permission from the department. The plane is kept ready for emergencies and I've given instructions to the driver. Let's go."

Sayid rose, took his cigarettes and walked out with Khorassani. They rode the elevator to a level below the ground floor, to a parking lot reserved for use by Security. They drove to the airport in silence. Sayid's pain-racked face made any manner of conversation impossible.

The flight to Ahwaz was uneventful. Khorassani passed the time drinking Scotch. Sayid refused alcohol. The problem plaguing him demanded his undivided attention. He drank tea.

They drove directly to the police station on Pahlavi Avenue. Sayid told the driver to wait. They walked in. There was a guard, a young man, asleep behind the desk.

Khorassani poked the guard in the ribs. The guard jumped, looked around, then demanded to know who they were and what they wanted.

Khorassani told him who they were and ordered him to telephone the police chief and tell him to come to the station immediately.

The guard did what he was told to do, shaking with fear, expecting the worst.

"Where's the American woman?" Sayid asked.

"I know nothing about an American woman. There's an Italian man in the cell on the left."

"How many cells are there?" Sayid asked.

"Six. I don't know who's in the other cells. The Italian speaks Farsi. He's been hollering all night. Maybe he finally got tired and slept. I don't know."

The police chief walked in.

Sayid did not wait for the lengthy greetings which preceded meetings between Iranians. "Do you have an American woman here?"

The police chief remained glued to the spot, scared witless, his eyes searching the intruders for an explanation.

Khorassani took out his wallet and flashed a badge in the man's face. "Where is she?"

The police chief looked dazed. He took the keys from the terrified guard, turned and walked down a narrow passageway toward the back of the building.

The guard turned on the lights from the control panel behind the desk.

They were about to turn the corner when they came face to face with the Italian. He was not asleep. He paced the small cell like a lion in heat. The moment he saw them he stopped. "Hey you," he yelled in Farsi. "Stop."

"We'll talk to you in a moment," Khorassani replied. "We're busy right now."

The Italian banged his fists on the iron bars. "What are you, animals? There's a woman dying in there. Doesn't anyone in this place have a breath of humanity left in him?"

Sayid stopped instantly. "Did you say a woman dying?"

"I've been saying it for ten hours," the Italian shot back. "I can't get one of these bastards to move a finger to help."

"Open the door," Sayid ordered the police chief.

The police chief rushed to the door, key in hand. The Italian marched out with a huff.

The police chief continued to walk down the narrow, dimly-lit, filthy corridor, followed by the men.

Neither Khorassani, nor Sayid were prepared for what they saw when they reached the cell. For Sayid it was the culmination of years of agony which had racked his being from the moment he'd found out the relationship between his brother and the woman he loved.

Andrea lay unconscious, in a pool of blood, on a filthy mattress on the dirt floor, curled up into a ball. Her dress was in shreds, her face swollen beyond recognition, her hair in tangles partially covering her bare shoulders.

Sayid turned to the Italian. "Do you know how it happened?"

"Of course I do. I was there. Don't worry. It will be my pleasure to take care of them."

"Would you recognize them if you saw them?"

"Open the door," Khorassani ordered.

"Get a blanket," Sayid told the police chief without waiting for an answer from the Italian. And then it hit him. The man who was known as the ice block for never losing his temper or changing the permanently blank expression on his face, suddenly turned white and wobbled. He was about to hit the ground, when Khorassani grabbed him and clung to him until the Italian rushed to help. They lay him on the floor. The Italian ran to the front desk, shoved a startled guard off the only chair, grabbed it, and dashed back to the cell. They lifted Sayid and placed him on the chair. Khorassani shook his head. "He has finally reached the limit of his endurance."

"Is he the husband?" asked the Italian.

"No, the brother-in-law."

"My name is Dino. Sorry I did not introduce myself before. This has been one hell of a day."

"Khorassani. Pleased to meet you."

A few minutes later, Sayid pulled himself together, looked around, leaped up, grabbed the blanket from the policeman's hand, wrapped Andrea in the blanket and marched out carrying his precious bundle like a China doll.

Khorassani and Dino followed him to the car. Khorassani told the driver to take them to the Royal Astoria Hotel on the banks of Karoun river.

"Call Doctor Ganji," Khorassani shouted at a sleepy clerk manning the front desk of the hotel, "immediately."

Upstairs, in a room meticulously decorated in Persian motifs, Sayid settled Andrea's unconscious form in bed. Except for her regular, deep breathing, there was no sign of life. He pulled a chair, sat next to the bed and clung to her arm, his fingers on her pulse. Breathing alone was not enough to reassure him she was alive. He seemed to derive extraordinary relief by feeling her pulse beat against his fingers.

The doctor arrived shortly. He was ready with his verdict after examining her. "Shock," he said. "She is in shock. It will take two to three days before she shows any sign of life. Some patients never recover from a traumatic experience like this preferring to shut out the world which they feel incapable of coping with. We'll have to wait and see. I'll be back in the morning, or rather at noon. It's almost morning now."

Stunned, Sayid looked to the doctor for an encouraging sign. "I don't want to give you false hope," the doctor said. "I work for Savak." He cast a reproachful glance in Khorassani's direction. "Despite myself, if I may say so. I see many cases like her. Some recover, some don't. She's been raped repeatedly and beaten badly. Something has to give. More often than not it's their sanity."

The doctor left.

His worst fears confirmed, Sayid slumped in the chair, the blank mask giving way to undeniable grief and pain.

Khorassani considered himself to be Sayid's best friend, the only person who could occasionally get Sayid to say a few words beyond the absolute minimum. Try as he would, Sayid remained withdrawn, lost in thought, answering questions directed to him in monosyllables.

Khorassani turned to Dino. "You say you were there?"

"Everyone was. I think the whole town was there."

"Tell me what you saw."

"I am in charge of an Italian construction firm here. It's called Puerta. We are building residential units for employees of Sedco, the oil company. The workers get a break for an hour at noon for lunch from twelve to one. Usually they go to the mosque on Pahlavi Avenue and pray then eat their lunch and come back to work. They know they have to be back on time or I dock their pay. But today, I mean yesterday, they did not return. No one did. I waited till ten minutes to two then went looking for them. I reached Pahlavi Avenue and stopped. There was a full scale riot going on. Cars were set on fire, shops were burned and looted. It was pandemonium. I rushed back to my car. I wanted to park it at a distance in a side street. While running, I saw a woman wearing a chaddor cautiously make her way, past the demonstrators. She had a piece of paper in her hand. It looked like she was trying to locate an address. She approached a door. It was the door to the mosque. She looked puzzled. Several men stood near by. She talked to one of them. Just then, from the corner of my eye I saw a bunch of hoodlums attack my car. So I ran, fought them off, got in my car and drove off."

"Did you come back?"

"I did. That's when I practically fell on my face. The woman I had assumed to be an Iranian was Andrea."

Sayid shot up from his chair. "How did you know what her name was?"

"I knew her from the International Hotel when her daughter was sick. They gave me her room while she was in the hospital with her daughter. Then they managed to lose her suitcase. Interpret the word lose as you like. I tried to find it for her but couldn't."

"Go on."

"The men who were gathered near the door of the mosque waited till she took a few steps. There were five or six of them. I saw one of them, a tall man, with a curved neck, and a bulging eye, nod. Suddenly, the group jumped on her and dragged her around the corner."

"Were there any police around?" Khorassani asked.

"No, none. They took their time getting there, believe me. The whole town was there but not the police even though the station is only a couple of blocks east of where the rioting took place."

"Do you think you'd recognize the man who nodded?" Khorassani asked.

"I would recognize him anytime, anywhere. He is

unique, trust me. In all my life I have never seen anyone quite so different from the human species and still qualify as a human being."

Sayid reached for a cigarette. "Tell me every detail. Everything you saw. Leave nothing out. I'll take care of the interpretation."

There was a knock on the door. Khorassani had ordered drinks. The waiter came in, placed the drinks on the coffee table and asked if they wanted anything else.

"Tea, please," Sayid said.

"You need a drink, not tea. You look like a man ready for the grave. A drink will do you good."

Sayid nodded.

Dino was thirsty and in an agitated state of mind and body. He gulped his vodka down in one swallow and poured another. "I have never been so frustrated in my life. I see these men drag her. So I throw myself at them. I bloodied a few noses but there were half a dozen. They overpowered me, threw me on the ground and stomped on me. Suddenly flames shot up from a car overturned and set on fire. Then there was an explosion. The flames spread to shops. Shoppers, pedestrians, screamed, pushed, shoved and ran. It was hell. As soon as I could, I rushed to the corner to look for Andrea. There was no sign of her or the men anywhere. The explosion was either deliberate or God sent for those bastards. I searched everywhere. Nothing. The street was totally deserted."

Dino stopped to catch his breath and pour himself a drink.

Sayid rubbed his face with his hands. He looked drained, exhausted, like a man who expected harsh blows from life and was never disappointed.

Khorassani walked to the window, walked back, walked to the window again. He banged his right fist in his left palm repeatedly. He stopped. "How did you find her?"

"Give the man a chance to catch his breath," Sayid

admonished. "We're not at Savak headquarters."

"It's all right," Dino said. "You probably should have the facts before those maniacs escape. Maybe they already have."

"Don't worry about that," Khorassani quipped. "We'll get them. If you can identify them, we can get them. I will call the office and have someone bring us the book of suspects."

He called the Bureau and gave instructions for the book to be delivered immediately.

"I searched everywhere," Dino said. "I knocked on doors and had angry women slam their doors in my face. What American woman? they asked. I was about to lose my mind. How could they have disappeared without a trace? The sight of those men dragging her around the corner, curdled my blood. I had to find her."

Dino chain smoked, ran his fingers through his hair and cussed in Italian. "There's a big, stone house behind the mosque. I was sure it was the mullah's house. I sat on the sidewalk across the street and waited. For what I don't know. I was disgusted with myself for not having acted faster. Then an old woman, I think the maid, came out the back door of the house with a shopping bag in her hand. I followed her. I stuck a thousand rial note in her hand and asked her if she had seen an American woman. She did not make a sound. She turned her head in the direction of the big house behind the mosque and resumed her walk."

Dino's feet hurt. He stopped pacing and collapsed in a chair. A moment later, in a spasm of fury he jumped. "What the hell was she doing here anyway?" He rushed toward Sayid and grabbed him by the collar. "Did you send her here? Did you send her to do your dirty work for you?"

He clenched his fist and was ready to punch Sayid when Khorassani grabbed his arm.

Sayid did not move.

"He had nothing to do with it," Khorassani said.

"Don't tell me she came to vacation in Ahwaz. Only a fool would do that. And she's no fool."

"The perpetrators of this crime will receive their due punishment," Khorassani promised. "Have no fear."

Dino's eyes shifted from Sayid to Khorassani then back to Sayid. "Sorry. I guess I lost my head."

Sayid did not reply.

There was a knock on the door.

It was the messenger from Savak headquarters with the book. Khorassani asked Dino to look through it.

He tried. "I can't see well. My eyes are blurred."

"Rest a while," Sayid suggested.

"How can I rest?" Dino shot back. "How can I do anything until those criminals are behind bars. You think it's easy to break into a room and come face to face with a barbarian who has just finished raping a helpless woman? He was buttoning his pants when I broke the door down and crashed in. He grinned contentedly under the approving glare of his comrades. No, barbarian is too kind a word for that poor excuse of a man. Not only did he look like an animal, he behaved like one. The others escaped through the window when they saw me. But not this one. He stood nonchalantly staring at me. So I let him have it. He was not smiling when I was through with him. I would have killed him had it not been for his accomplices. They came back. I could hear them. They talked loud, shouted obscenities and cursed the American traitor. They congratulated each other for teaching her a lesson and wondered why Mehdi, was taking so long getting rid of the foreign man. I guessed Mehdi was the man's name still in the room. Maybe he needs help, one of them said. He was told not to worry. Mehdi was armed."

"I knew I had to get out fast. I removed the gag from Andrea's mouth, grabbed her and ran to my car. The men saw us and chased us. I threw Andrea in the back seat, locked the car and punched the hell out of the first two who attacked. Finally the police arrived. Was I ever happy to see them! I was sure they'd go after the bastards. They did not. They just stood and stared at us. The men ran down the street, straight into the mosque. I tried to drive off. The police decided to act. They surrounded the car pointing their machine guns at me. I tried to explain. They were not interested. They grabbed us and threw us in jail. No questions asked. Not even our names. They dumped us, like two sacks of potatoes in those dingy cells and locked the doors."

Dino threw himself in a chair exhausted.

"When you feel better," Khorassani said, "look through the book again. Let me know if you see anyone you recognize."

Dino went to the bathroom, washed his face with cold water and returned. Within minutes he located the picture of Mehdi, Kurosh and Mejid. The other two were not in the book.

Andrea stirred, opened her eyes for a second and instantaneously went back to sleep.

The three men jumped. Sayid was on his knees next to her pleading for her to say something.

"Give her time," Khorassani urged. "I've seen many cases like her. She's a strong woman. She'll pull through."

"If you had better intelligence, she wouldn't be in this shape."

"You're right. We're doing the best we can, but lately, with problems plaguing us all over the country, we don't know where to look first."

"Maybe you don't. But I do. Your methods are counterproductive. I'll show you how to deal with criminals. You will not have to wait long either."

Khorassani threw a worried look in Sayid's direction.

"I want those policemen punished," Dino said angrily.

Sayid rose. "It's not the fault of the police. Most are uneducated peasants. The fault is with the system. You are guilty until proven innocent. We have a history of thousands of years, yet it has taught us little. We have barbaric customs adopted over centuries from conquerors and colonizers. Some day we'll change them, maybe. For now, we simply pass it on to the next generation."

"It stinks," Dino growled.

Khorassani fidgeted. "I better go to headquarters. This might be a good time to surprise the culprits. I'll probably do them a favor by apprehending them. No matter what their sentences are, they'll be better off with us than with Sayid."

Sayid said nothing. He pulled the chair closer, reached for Andrea's wrist, and planted his fingers on her pulse.

Khorassani left.

Dino stood a few feet away, his fingers in his hair, his eyes blood red. Then he moved closer. He put his hand on Sayid's shoulder. "I have known you briefly but it's easy to see why you're here. If my guess is correct, you are a man of action not of words, a man who does not shirk his responsibilities. Khorassani's version of justice is not for you and me. Mine is simple, Mafia style. Yours is for you to decide. Perhaps you already have."

Sayid listened without changing expression.

Dino stepped back. "Go. You have a job to do."

Sayid cast an anxious look on the form lying helpless across from him.

"Go." Dino's voice rose a pitch. "I'll take care of her until you return."

Sayid rose, walked to the door, stopped, turned back as though he wanted to say something, but didn't.

He walked out.

Chapter 41

Sayid returned to the hotel at three in the morning, dozed on a chair for a couple of hours then left. Dino urged him to leave. It made no sense for both men to stay with Andrea. Someone had to do the job. Since Dino was not Iranian and his knowledge of how to go about apprehending the rapists limited, he agreed reluctantly to allow Sayid to take over while he took care of Andrea. Sayid launched a massive manhunt, discreetly, in cooperation with friends he could trust.

The doctor came with Khorassani at noon. Khorassani had dark circles under his eyes, he needed a shave and his suit needed to be at the cleaners instead of his back. He had not slept since he left Tehran. Ahwaz was in turmoil, the clergy hidden behind closed mosques, the public hostile, defiant. Khorassani's investigations gave him severe stomach cramps and no leads. No one had heard or seen the incident.

Dino snored in a chair next to Andrea's bed. Andrea sat in bed with a sheet wrapped around her shoulders. Except for two trips to the bathroom, she had not left her bed, nor had she eaten or spoken.

"You look better," the doctor remarked. "Do you feel better?"

Dino awoke with a start.

"I'm all right," Andrea said. "Thank you."

She saw a gleam in the doctor's eyes. He sat next to her, on her bed. "You're dehydrated. You should have been on intravenous fluids but your brother-in-law would not let me take you to the hospital."

What was a gentle, warm person like him doing working for Savak. Nothing made sense.

Meanwhile Khorassani dashed into the adjacent room and then the bathroom.

"Where's Sayid?" he asked Dino.

"He went out."

"When?"

"In the morning."

"Oh, no." Khorassani collapsed in a chair.

"What's the matter?"

"I should have known."

The doctor removed the stethoscope from his ears. "I'm delighted. Except for the bumps on your head and the bruises on your body, your recovery is definitely miraculous."

"Thank you," Andrea replied. "I feel better but I'm filthy. I'm told there's no water."

"There was a report on the radio this morning. Last night an emergency crew flew in from Tehran. We are supposed to have water and power today. Have Dino call the desk to make sure."

Khorassani rose, paced the room and repeatedly banged his right fist in his left palm. He seemed concerned about Sayid's whereabouts. Andrea studied the man, her anxiety climbing to new heights. Sayid's behavior was unpredictable at best. What he would do when someone innocent was victimized, someone he cared about, was too horrible to contemplate.

The doctor indicated he wanted to leave.

"Tell the driver to take you wherever you want to go," Khorassani said impatiently. "Send him back when you're done with him."

The doctor gave Andrea his card. "Call me if you need me, any time day or night. It's worth it if one patient recovers like you did."

Andrea observed the pain in the doctor's eyes, pain such as she had rarely seen. They exchanged looks. His prematurely gray hair added years to his appearance. He bent down and held her hand. "It's a cruel world. We make it so by inflicting pain and suffering on each other. There are a few though, with strength, strength in their souls, strength which cannot be snuffed out in spite of the worst physical, emotional and mental abuse. You are unquestionably one of the very few. Don't ever let anyone break that spirit in you."

Tears welled in Andrea's eyes. Unexpected kindness always had an adverse effect on her. She watched him force his stooping shoulders back, reach for his medical bag, hesitate, then turn to Khorassani. "What are your plans for her?"

Khorassani gave the doctor a stern look. "Why do you ask?"

"I have an idea. I'd like to call my wife and check with her. I have no doubt she'll agree. I'd like to take Andrea to our house to recuperate. There's no sense in keeping her here."

"You should have been a missionary in the Congo," Khorassani quipped. "I can't make that decision. You have to ask Sayid."

"Anyone know where he is?"

"He went out," Dino said.

Khorassani resumed his pacing and banging his fist. "I should have known, damn it, I should have. I did not think he'd leave her." He turned to Dino. "Don't you have to be at work?"

"My assistant will do the job until I get there."

"Please go, Dino," Andrea pleaded. "There's no need for anyone to stay with me."

"Sayid will kill me."

"He won't. I promise."

"Are you sure?"

"Positive. Go."

"Leave a number where you can be reached." Khorassani lit a cigarette, realized he had one already in the ashtray, crushed it and resumed his pacing.

Dino scribbled the number on a piece of paper, gave it to Khorassani, said goodbye and left.

"I have to be at my office. I'm late already. My wife will come for her."

"How can she go anywhere? She has no clothes to wear."

"I'll have my wife bring her whatever she needs. I have two daughters. I'm sure between my wife and the girls they'll manage to find enough clothes to last a year."

The doctor cast a quick glance at Andrea. She listened impassively, wondering why decisions about her were taken without consulting her. Realizing his mistake, the doctor approached her. "I'm sorry. I should have asked you first. We would be delighted to have you stay with us. Would you like to come?"

Andrea smiled. "I'd love to if your wife won't mind."

"She'll love it. I'll call her right now and have her come over."

"I won't be able to leave until Sayid returns."

"That's all right. She'll keep you company."

The doctor called his home, talked to his wife, then turned to Andrea. "My wife was delighted. She'll be here as soon as she puts a few things together for you. My eighteen year old is about your build. It should work out fine. She's been very lonely since the girls left for school in England. You'll keep each other company. Remember what I told you. Drink lots of fluids, rest and keep that spirit up. Goodbye."

"Bye doctor and many thanks."

Khorassani slowed his steps. He approached the bed. "You're probably wondering why I'm so upset. I've known Sayid ever since he was a boy. He loves fiercely and hates destructively. There's no telling what he'll do to your attackers when he gets hold of them. It's not a question of if. He'll get them if it takes him the rest of his life."

"I don't know Sayid as well as you do but I think he'll use violence only if he has no other alternative. He hates violence." After she said it, she realized she didn't sound convincing. Not even to herself.

"Not when it involves someone he's crazy about." Khorassani fixed his gaze on her.

"Rumors like that can be very detrimental. He's my brother-in-law. That's all."

"Are you trying to convince me or yourself?"

"I'm sure you'd feel much better if you were out there looking for him. Why don't you go?"

"I can't. Someone should be here with you."

"I'll bolt the door. Please go."

Khorassani studied her for a moment. "I'll wait. Hopefully he'll be back soon."

"Is it me you're worried about or uninvited visitors?"

"You. We have two men guarding this room and four more at the entrance. They're our people." Khorassani sighed. "But these days we can trust no one."

Andrea cringed. The idea of strangers lurking outside her door did not appeal to her but she chose not to press the issue. "I'm well enough to take care of myself. Please go."

"All right, if you insist. Call this number if you need anything."

"I'll call if necessary."

The phone rang.

Khorassani answered it. He turned to Andrea. "There's hot water if you want to shower."

"Do I ever!"

"Make sure you bolt and chain the door."

"I will."

Khorassani left.

Andrea got up, wobbled unsteadily on her feet, felt giddy and collapsed in a chair. The room whirled around her, her head throbbed, her knees knocked against each other. She held her face in her hands, broke down and cried.

She thought of revenge, of the pain she'd like to inflict on her attackers, her husband, his friend Farhad. Why had they stooped so low? How could a man she believed to be decent, honest, an ideal husband and father metamorphose, rather degenerate to such an extent and in such a short time? Was revenge the answer?

Block it out of your mind, a voice within her urged. It never happened.

You have no one to blame but yourself, another voice kept harping. You were warned. You made your choice.

Don't let the culprits go unpunished, yet another voice made itself heard.

Regardless of which thought was nagging at her at a particular moment, she could not erase from her memory the picture of the man she had nicknamed Emu. There he stood, his pants around his ankles, panting like a dog in heat, his neck stretched to the limit, his bulging eye ready to pop out, the anticipation of the prize catch he was about to possess making his demonic features unquestionably unforgettable.

She sat for a long time, her face cupped in her hands, her elbows resting on her knees to stop them from shaking. She needed time to think, time to recuperate, time to learn to forgive.

A knock on the door startled her. She had forgotten to bolt the door. It seemed awfully soon for the doctor's wife to get there. Who else could it be? Terrified, she froze on the spot. She wanted to dash to the door and bolt it but she couldn't move. The door opened slowly. A woman poked her head in. Andrea took a deep breath and leaned back.

"Hi," said a slim, beautifully groomed woman with

intense brown eyes, long, black lashes accenting her naturally attractive look. She had dark brown hair resting on her shoulders in large curls, and wore a simple beige dress. "I'm Guita, the doctor's wife. I frightened you. I'm sorry. My husband said you were expecting me." She was carrying a small suitcase. She placed it on the carpet.

It took Andrea a few moments to regain her composure. "I didn't expect you so soon. Thanks for coming."

"We live near by. Let's see now. I brought shampoo, toothpaste, toothbrush and Badedas for your bath. And three different sizes of clothing. My husband said you're the same size as our eighteen year old. But I think you'll be more comfortable in my clothes."

"It's very kind of you. I'm sorry to have put you through all this trouble."

"Don't give it a thought. It gave me something to do. Since the girls left, I've been doing all kinds of mindless things to keep myself occupied." Guita opened the suitcase, took a dress and held it against her body for Andrea to see. "Put it on. Let's see if it will fit you."

Guita seemed easy going, friendly and good natured. Andrea felt herself relaxing. Most important, she did not ask questions. A rare trait among Iranians who hardly ever had any qualms about asking total strangers the most personal questions. It felt good.

"I'd like to shower first, if you don't mind."

Guita handed her the toiletry bag and a few articles of clothing. "Please do. Luckily, we have water today."

Once in the bathroom, Andrea decided she needed a bath. A hot bath to cleanse herself. She opened the door. "I'll probably be a while. Do you mind?"

"Take as long as you like. I brought a book with me. I'll read. I'd have done the same if I were home."

Andrea filled the tub with hot water and Badedas, and soaked her aching body in it. The warmth of the water, the kindness and generosity of total strangers, gradually dulled the pain. The evildoers, the inhuman, the beastly, were a minority. Best buried and forgotten.

If only she could get through to Sayid. Her brother-in-law's quiet wrath scared her far more than Savak with all the facilities of torture at its disposal. It scared her even more so when he drank. She had not seen him drink the past two days. Would he resort to the bottle again if his efforts at finding the culprits failed?

Forty five minutes later, she dragged her reluctant body out of the tub, washed her hair and got dressed. Guita's dress fit her quite well. Except for the swelling in her face and eyes, it would have been difficult to tell she had been through the worst experience of her life less than two days earlier.

Sayid was waiting for her when she stepped out of the bathroom. For a flitting second there was a faint smile on his lips. A blank expression replaced it immediately.

"The doctor and his wife have invited me to stay with them," Andrea said.

Sayid did not comment.

"Do you mind?"

"Do you want to go?"

"I'd like to."

"I see."

"When do you plan to return to Tehran?"

"There are matters I have to attend to. I don't know how long it will take."

"Then I'll return to Tehran on Monday."

"No."

"Why not?"

"You will not return until we tell you it is safe to do so."

"Who's we?"

"Me."

Guita looked from one to the other seemingly baffled. Andrea figured the doctor had not told her what had happened. She felt relieved. However, Sayid's curt answers succeeded in confirming her fears. She turned to Guita. "Please excuse us. I'd like to talk to my brother-in-law in the other room for a few minutes."

Sayid followed her to the room. She closed the door.

Aloof and morose, he stood waiting for her to talk.

She found it difficult to communicate with a man who was consistently unapproachable. Yet there was too much at stake for her to dismiss it as over reacting on her part. Khorassani could be right. He might react differently if someone he cared about was involved. She wanted to believe that he was incapable of violence, but she wasn't sure. If Sayid took it upon himself to punish those men, there was no telling what he'd do. And what would happen to him? Even if he could escape jail because of all the connections he had, he could be hurt or killed. These were no ordinary criminals. They were men with no qualms about committing any kind of crime. Anything was preferable to revenge. Justice, yes. Revenge, absolutely not. She had to reach him somehow. Otherwise, she'd never forgive herself. Perhaps if he realized how she felt, he might think differently.

"Please, Sayid," she pleaded. "If you're after finding those men and punishing them, please don't."

His reply was a cold stare.

"How can I get you to understand that I'd hate for you to take the law into your hands? Why can't we return to Tehran and let the authorities here take care of the matter?"

He said nothing.

No wonder people call him the Ice Block, Andrea thought. She doubted there was anything she could do to change his mind. But she had to try.

"Sayid, do you want to hurt me?" she blurted in desperation.

The malevolent glare he gave her was enough to burn a hole in her flesh. Still, he said nothing.

"Please listen to me. Forget the whole thing. Let's return to Tehran tonight. I'll go to a hotel, return to the States, do whatever you want me to do. Let's just get out of here. Please."

He stood motionless, his muscular frame relaxed, a man who knew what he wanted and would let no human being or circumstance get in his way. "Your purse was located in a trash can near the mosque."

Andrea felt the blood rush to her cheeks. She hadn't thought about it. Besides money, she had the bracelet hidden in her purse. The bracelet Dariush had given her in Beirut. She took the purse with her every where, even to bed so Mani would not get hold of it. "How do you know it's mine?"

"Your driver's license was in it."

Poor Dariush. He'll be heart broken. I must look for a similar one in Tehran before he gets back.

"How much money did you have in it?" Sayid asked.

"Eight hundred eighty four dollars."

His facial muscles twitched. He studied her for a long moment. "Why were you carrying such a large sum around?"

"I know it sounds foolish but I felt safe having the money with me, call it a security blanket if you wish. I kept it in my purse and took the purse with me every where I went, even to the bathroom. There's not much privacy in that apartment. Your brother checks my room regularly."

"My brother has a name."

"Sorry."

Without hesitation he reached inside his coat pocket, took out a checkbook, wrote a check for the exact amount and handed it to her.

She'd always had trouble figuring him out but lately his actions were more puzzling. "I don't need it," she said softly. "Why should you have to pay for my mistake?"

He smiled, a tense, brief smile. "You can't cash it here. It's in dollars. You have to wait till we get back to Tehran." He reached for his wallet, took out a bunch of Iranian money and gave it to her.

"Thank you. I don't need money."

"Take it. Shop for clothes. I don't appreciate your wearing someone else's clothes."

She was often frustrated and nervous in his presence. His brief, curt replies left her ill-at-ease. She had worked hard to prepare herself to face a different culture with different values and diametrically opposed approaches to solving problems, yet she felt lost when it came to coping with a man whose values were like no one else's. She feared he could be beastly when provoked but overgenerous and caring with those he loved. "You're very clever," she said nervously.

He was tired of stretching his hand out, holding the money. He placed it on the coffee table. "You're wrong. I'm not clever at all. If I were, you wouldn't be here."

"My being here has nothing to do with you. I came here of my own free will."

"Precisely."

"You've managed to confuse me again. What do you mean, precisely?"

"That's for you to figure out."

"You give me far more credit than I deserve. I don't understand."

He walked about the room restlessly, stopped, walked again, then looked her straight in the eye. "Who was it who said, 'For those who understand no explanation is necessary. For those who don't, no explanation is possible.'"

She was losing control. "Sayid, please listen to me. If it makes you happy, I'll borrow the money to buy clothes but I will not take the check."

Unperturbed and in the same monotonous tone, he said, "It's not charity. I intend to retrieve every single penny taken from you."

"That's exactly what I'm afraid of. I don't want the money and I don't want you to go looking for those men. I'd much rather you didn't get involved."

"I don't recall asking your permission."

She was at her wit's end. Nothing seemed to faze the 'Ice Block.' "Is there anything I can say or do to make you change your mind?"

He walked to the door. "The doctor's wife is waiting. You'd better go."

Andrea did not move. She was silent, her eyes downcast. She raised her head slowly. "Sayid, I beg you not to take matters into your hands."

He stopped and glared at her. "Never beg anyone for anything."

He opened the door and walked out.

Chapter 42

The doctor's house was located in an exclusive suburb of the city. It was an old, stone house, built around a courtyard with a fountain in the center. The design was typically Persian with arches over every door and huge windows to allow in sunlight in the winter and fresh air in the summer. The main building stood apart from the servants' quarters. A small, covered space in front of the main entrance was reserved for removing shoes before entering the house. A cement wall, over five feet high surrounded the building. The only way in was through an iron gate.

Guita stopped her Porsche in front of the iron gate and honked the horn. The gate was quickly opened by the house boy. When he stepped back to allow the Porsche to be driven in, he knocked over a large pot of flowers. The pot shattered.

Guita turned to Andrea, a look of resignation on her face. "He's new. He's been with us since yesterday. He works real hard but is a very nervous person."

Andrea took a quick look at the young man and her stomach did a flip flop. She recognized him. He was the man who had come to see Farhad and Mani after their encounter with Savak to give them instructions to contact Mullah Hamid, the man who had been surprised by Sayid. Andrea had gone back to the house to pick up a few personal belongings after her suitcase was lost in the International Hotel, and had witnessed the incident between Mani, Farhad and the man who said to call him Bahram. And then Sayid had interrupted the visit.

After throwing Bahram out of the house, Sayid had discovered Andrea hiding behind the door of her room. He had advised her to leave the house immediately. Bahram had not seen her that day but she knew he'd recognize her. She had overheard him tell Mani and Farhad that Sayid was with an American woman at the International Hotel and was told by Mani she was his wife.

Had he recognized her? She couldn't tell. He'd given her a quick look but there was nothing in his manner to indicate that he'd seen her before.

"I really don't need him," Guita said. "With the girls gone, we don't need a house boy. My husband hired him to work in his clinic, to clean the place and water the garden. He hasn't gotten around to taking him to his clinic yet."

Andrea stiffened. Bahram's presence at the doctor's house did not make sense. But if he was hired to work in the clinic, he would have access to the files, know who was being 'interrogated' by Savak, and inform his colleagues. Andrea shuddered.

Another disturbing thought occurred to her. Sayid said he'd come for her when he was ready to return to Tehran. If the house boy was still at the doctor's house, Sayid would undoubtedly recognize him. The doctor and his wife had gone out of their way to help her, a total stranger. Bahram's presence in Ahwaz when the city was experiencing its worst turmoil, had ominous implications. She recalled the authoritative way he talked to Mani and Farhad and how both men accepted his abusive language without protest. He had to have a high post in the revolutionary hierarchy. But maybe he no longer was a member of the Revolutionary Council and needed a job. However, she'd heard otherwise, on several occasions. No member could leave. It was a guarantee for a quick trip to the mortuary.

What was she trying to do? Delude herself? Was her recent experience playing havoc with her mind? She had to warn the doctor or at least tell his wife what she knew.

She didn't need this. Although outwardly calm, the sight of Emu with his pants around his ankles, salivating, trembling, hung like a mobile picture permanently displayed within the range of her vision. It went where she went. She had forced herself to present a brave facade after overhearing a conversation between Sayid and Dino late in the night after the rape. Initially, in her confused state of mind, she was delighted that there were at least two persons who cared enough to go after those animals, but when her mind cleared, she realized the futility of it all. She had to pull herself together, and soon, to minimize the destructive effect it had on Sayid and surprisingly on Dino.

The housekeeper greeted them and offered to bring refreshments.

"Tea or coffee?" Guita asked.

"Makes no difference," Andrea answered absent-mindedly.

"Is something the matter? You look pale. Would you rather have something cold to drink?"

"A glass of water, please."

Guita eyed her suspiciously. "I make it a point not to question my husband about his patients. He wouldn't tell me or anyone else, regardless. Anyway, I'm better off not knowing. But this is a small city. I heard from my housekeeper about what happened downtown. Of course she did not know it was you but there aren't that many American women tourists in Ahwaz. It was not difficult to conclude it was you."

Andrea listened. She neither confirmed nor denied her hostess's allegations.

Guita moved next to her and gave her hand a gentle squeeze. "You are safe here. You have nothing to worry about. Stay as long as you like. There's enough room in this house for six house guests to visit comfortably for months. Half the rooms are closed. It's too big for us but my husband loves this old place and refuses to move. This is where he grew up. The house belonged to his parents."

Tears choked Andrea's words as she tried to express her gratitude. "You're both much too kind. I cannot thank you enough."

"There's time enough for that. Let's have our tea then go for a walk. Would you like to?"

"I look a sight. Especially my eyes. I should probably buy a pair of sunglasses."

"There are no stores open on Friday. There must be at least half a dozen pairs lying around here someplace. Fatima will get you a pair."

She rang the bell. The housekeeper appeared in the doorway. Guita told her to bring a couple of sunglasses. She turned to Andrea. "Fatima is the best housekeeper. She has worked for my family ever since I was born thirty years ago. Where I go, she goes. I don't worry about a thing. She runs this house far more efficiently than I ever could."

"You're lucky to have someone you can trust. The Iranians I've talked to complain about the poor quality of help since Americans arrived here. They claim we spoil the help because we're not used to having any."

"Probably by treating them like human beings," Guita interjected. "By refusing to admit that we've got to change our ways, we only hurt ourselves. The time has passed when we could treat servants like slaves. But few are willing to admit or accept the idea."

Fatima came in with three pairs of sunglasses. Andrea chose one and returned the other two.

Fatima did not look happy. Her mistress sensed it and questioned her. "It's that nosey young man the doctor hired," the housekeeper said in whispers. "This morning, I caught him looking through the doctor's chest of drawers. I asked him what he was doing. He said he was tidying it. Have you ever heard anything more absurd? Everything in this house is always neat and in place. Why of all the places does he want to tidy the doctor's chest of drawers? I don't like him. Let the doctor have him if he wants to. I don't want him in this house."

"Fatima, you shouldn't let him upset you. I'll tell the doctor to take him to his clinic. He came very highly recommended you know."

"I don't care who recommended him, Madame. I don't want him. I don't know what. But something about him is not right." She cocked her head and thought for a moment. "His eyes. Yes, that's it. His eyes. The way he looks. He sends shivers through my spine."

Andrea's suspicions were confirmed, heightening her fears and overwhelming her with guilt. What if he was planted to do more than check the files? If he had a high post, which he probably did, he would be assigned more serious jobs. Checking files would be more like a job for her husband, Mani.

Bahram's presence had one positive result. Andrea forgot her own problems, at least for the time being.

"Let's go for a walk," Guita said when they finished their drinks. "Hopefully, when we return Fatima will be in a better mood."

They walked by the banks of the River Karoun. Andrea was tense and restless. Guita cast an occasional worried glance in her direction but did not pry. "How about we stop at a tea house?"

Andrea checked her watch. "It's almost eight o'clock. When do you expect the doctor home?"

"That's one question I can't answer. He comes when he's

through with his work." Then as though the thought suddenly struck her, Guita said, "Let's go to the clinic. Maybe we can persuade him to take us out to dinner."

Andrea was surprised by the suggestion. "Wouldn't he mind?"

"Of course he will. But we will ignore his protests. I have a very good excuse. You. He can hardly refuse."

"Is it within walking distance?"

"No. We've made a full circle. We're only a couple of blocks from home. Stay here. I'll get the car."

Andrea walked slowly while Guita went ahead and returned with her car. She pushed the door open and Andrea got in. Guita drove cautiously through narrow, cobblestone streets but did not speak for a while. Then she half turned. "Strange," she said, shaking her head, "When I went to get the car, Fatima came running to the door. She said the house boy left soon after we did. He didn't say where he was going or when he'd be back. Do you think he overheard Fatima complain about him?"

"I don't think so. Wasn't he outside gathering the pieces of the shattered pot?"

"I don't know. I didn't look. Let's forget him. He probably went to buy a pack of cigarettes or something. Let's think of a place to go."

Andrea's thoughts slipped into high gear. Did he leave to pass the news on to his colleagues about her presence in the doctor's house? If he went to get a pack of cigarettes, like Guita assumed he probably did, why not tell the housekeeper?

"Ahwaz is a drab city," Guita said. "There's little in the form of entertainment. There are a number of good restaurants which serve Iranian food, a few movie theaters and a recently opened nightclub at the Astoria Hotel which draws big crowds. Where would you like to go?"

Andrea was on a different wavelength altogether. "I'm sorry. I heard you but it did not register. I was thinking about something else."

"I asked you where you would like to go."

"Yes. Yes, of course. Wherever you'd like. I'll leave the choice to you."

Guita pulled in front of a four story building and parked the car. "Here we are. Let's hope he doesn't have an emergency."

The doctor's spacious clinic was on the first floor. The receptionist, a middle-aged woman, greeted Guita profusely and with great respect. She informed them there were two more patients in the waiting room.

"That will take him another hour," Guita complained.

"At least," the receptionist confirmed.

"Well, I tried. Let's go, Andrea."

"Let me talk to the doctor," the receptionist offered. "They're here for follow up. It's nothing that can't be done tomorrow."

She returned shortly, talked to the patients and smiling triumphantly informed Guita the doctor would join them in a few minutes.

The two patients left.

Ten minutes later, the doctor said goodbye to the last patient, stepped out and greeted the women. "What a pleasant surprise," he said amiably. "You must have read my mind. How about something to eat and some music perhaps. Any suggestions?"

"If you want music," Guita said, "we should go to the Astoria."

"Would that be all right with you?" the doctor asked Andrea.

Andrea was having trouble concentrating again. "Anywhere you'd like to go is fine with me."

"The Astoria it shall be," The doctor said. "Give me a minute to make reservations and call the house. I have to let Fatima know where I can be reached."

He returned in a few minutes. He turned to his wife.

"Fatima said to tell you the house boy came back."

"Good."

The night club was in semidarkness. They were ushered in. The decor was similar to the Cave du Roix in Beirut but not as rich. Most of the customers looked like foreigners. There were only two tables which were not occupied. The head waiter recognized the doctor. He removed the reserved sign and seated them at one of the two tables. Soon after they were seated, another group walked in and the last table was taken. The live band played soft, dinner music. Andrea made a conscious effort to relax.

"We live in strange times," the doctor said. "A couple of days ago, I spent eighteen hours suturing wounds and treating burns. But sitting here and listening to this music makes me feel like the looting and the burning downtown never happened. It's so deceptive."

"I hope we've seen the end of it," Guita said.

They were halfway through their dinner, when Andrea spotted a familiar figure standing in the doorway. It was Sayid. He looked around, talked to a waiter, lingered briefly then walked out. Andrea's eyes followed him.

The doctor must have seen him as well. "Was that Sayid?"

"I think so," Andrea replied.

The doctor put his napkin on the table and quickly made his way out. He returned with Sayid. The waiter brought a chair and Sayid joined them.

"I did not expect this place to be so crowded this early at night," Sayid remarked.

"It's the place to be so everyone comes early to assure themselves a spot," the doctor said.

"Thank you for inviting me."

"Please give your order to the waiter. He's behind you, waiting. The show starts soon. They dim the lights. It will be difficult for you to see your food."

Sayid gave his order.

At nine the show was announced, followed by an orchestra blasting music at maximum volume, drowning the sounds of conversation by the audience. The customers were left with little choice. They had to watch the show.

Sayid sat between the doctor and Andrea. Sayid's presence was a big relief for Andrea. She tugged at his coat sleeve gently, with urgency. He leaned closer.

"I have to talk to you," she said. "It's important."

"If it's the same subject you talked to me about earlier, forget it."

"No."

"I heard there is dancing after the show. I'll ask you for a dance."

"Thank you."

It was a two hour show with a twenty minute break after the first hour. The customers had to buy a bottle of Scotch for each table for the privilege of watching the show. The doctor and Sayid drank Scotch with Sayid doing most of the drinking. Guita and Andrea had wine.

Sayid left the table when the show host announced the break. He found the head waiter. They moved behind the bar, talked, then Sayid returned. Presently, a waiter brought another bottle of Scotch and placed it on the table. Andrea's stomach churned. Sayid was drinking again, heavily. Translated, it meant, he had no luck in his search for the culprits. Should she be relieved? Not so fast. Sayid was not a man who gave up. And when he drank . . . What boggled her mind though was the amount of alcohol he could drink without it having any apparent affect on him whatsoever. The doctor was watching the show when the waiter brought the Scotch. When he turned, he saw it, cast a quick glance at Sayid but made no comment.

"Last week Hushang bought the most handsome Arabian stallion," Guita said. "My husband loves horses. Do you ride, Andrea?"

"I do. I love horses too."

"How about you, Sayid? Would you like to go riding with us tomorrow?"

"It depends. I have an urgent business to attend to. If I finish early, I might."

Did Sayid have a lead? Andrea wondered if Emu and company were still in Ahwaz or some other city savoring their conquest, plotting more death and destruction. Which way would their poisonous arrows dart next? Would Sayid leave her in Ahwaz to pursue them? Her dilemma was compounded knowing Bahram was in the doctor's house. Now that he'd seen her, and undoubtedly knew about the rape, what would stop him from silencing her? Despite her fear that Sayid might do something rash, she had to tell him.

The second portion of the show was announced with yet another blast from the loudspeakers. A magician performed tricks that amazed some and bored others. Andrea waited impatiently until it was over.

The stage was cleared and the band returned. They played dance music. The doctor asked his wife to dance. They walked hand in hand to the dance floor.

"They look beautiful together," Andrea said.

"She's quite an attractive woman," Sayid said, "at least twenty years younger than he is."

"I think he looks older than he is." Then she whispered in his ear. "How come a nice man like him works for Savak?"

"Are you implying that only men who are not nice work for Savak?"

"I'm not implying. I believe it's true."

"Not everyone works for Savak by choice. Some do because they're power crazy. The doctor has to because he has no choice. It was the price he agreed to pay in return for his brother's freedom. His brother was sentenced to death for trying to kill the King. He was caught red-handed."

"That's a steep price to pay."

"Our society does not discriminate who pays what price for whom, especially when it involves family members."

How true, Andrea thought. He should know. He has had his share of brother trouble.

"We'll dance when they return."

The first bottle of Scotch was empty. Sayid put it aside and opened the second bottle. Presently the doctor and his wife returned.

Sayid turned to the doctor. "I drank most of the first bottle. Please help yourself."

The doctor was in a happy mood. "I think I'll do that." He poured himself another drink.

Sayid took Andrea's hand and led her to the dance floor. This was the first time she was in his arms and their bodies touched. He danced like a pro, his muscular body moving lightly, effortlessly. The second he took her in his arms, she was overcome by a bewildering sensation, a feeling she'd never had before; total abandonment coupled with a surge of heat coursing through her body, then a wave of cold perspiration.

"What did you want to talk to me about?" he whispered.

"What?"

He repeated the question.

"Oh, that?" A trip to dream land, a brief respite. But brief as it was, it revealed more than months of contemplation and soul searching. If she could stop the hot and cold flashes and the shaking, she could finish the dance without making a fool of herself. But it wasn't to be.

"Are you drunk?"

"On one glass of wine? Hardly."

"Your hands are wet and you seem unsteady on your feet. Aren't you feeling well?"

"I'm all right."

They continued dancing. She cast a quick glance at their table. The doctor held his wife's hands in his and their eyes spoke their love for each other. How can anyone hurt such a gentle, generous, kind man. She was concerned more for the doctor than for herself. She had to tell Sayid. There was no one else to turn to.

"Remember the night I returned to the house from the hospital to pick up my clothes?"

"You mean the night you were hiding behind the door?"

"Yes. Do you remember the young man who had come to talk to Mani and Farhad?"

"Yes, I know him well. Why do you ask?"

"He's working as a house boy at the doctor's house."

Sayid stopped dancing and stared at her. "Are you sure?"

"I never forget a face."

He resumed dancing, going through the motions like a robot now. Guita and the doctor watched, still holding hands. "They're watching us," Andrea whispered. "We should either dance or sit down."

"Sorry," he said pulling himself together. "It's too crowded and too noisy. Let's sit down."

They returned to their seats.

"The music in this place leaves a lot to be desired," the doctor remarked.

"It's much too loud for such a small place," Guita said.

"Let's go to the Ahwaz Hotel," Sayid suggested. "They have a nice cocktail lounge. It's not as noisy as this place."

"It's late." The doctor motioned for the waiter to bring the bill. "Maybe some other time."

Sayid shifted his weight about nervously.

The waiter returned momentarily. "Your bill has been settled."

"Did you do that?" the doctor asked Sayid, smiling. "Well then, we must go to Ahwaz Hotel for a night cap, but on one condition. This time, I pay. Agreed?"

"Agreed," Sayid replied.

They walked out to the crisp, fresh, night air. It was a welcome relief after the smoke-filled, thick air of the night club. Although the temperature during the day reached the eighties at the end of May, the nights were almost always cool. Doctor Ganji instructed the valet to bring his car around.

When the valet returned with the car, Sayid opened the door for the women and helped them in. Guita insisted on sharing the back seat with Andrea. The doctor got behind the wheel and Sayid opened the front door to get in. Just then, a Peykan, an Iranian made car, wheezed by, its lights turned off. Sayid saw what the others missed; the tip of a sawed off machine gun. It was pointed at the doctor's car then suddenly retracted. The car slowed down ever so slightly at the entrance to the hotel, then raced down the road like a missile.

Unaware of anything unusual, Dr. Ganji maneuvered the Mercedes carefully and made small talk.

The lounge at Ahwaz Hotel was vacant. The waiters looked dismayed at the sight of the newcomers. "Only one drink," The doctor assured them, "and then we're on our way. Tomorrow is a working day."

They ordered drinks and the waiter left. Sayid did not waste words. He faced the doctor. "I hear you have a new house boy. Do you know who he is?"

The doctor was surprised with the abruptness of the question and looked at Sayid askance. "I'd forgotten all about him until tonight when Fatima, our housekeeper mentioned him. Why do you ask?"

"Please answer my question."

"A mullah called me from the mosque. I don't remember his name. He said Mustafa had worked for foreigners and that he had excellent recommendations. My office boy had to return to his village because his father died. I needed someone to replace him. I told the mullah to send the young man over."

"When did he call you?"

"Thursday afternoon."

"Did Mustafa bring his recommendations with him?"

"I was at the hospital when he came. I haven't had time to talk to him. I'll check tomorrow."

Guita listened. She looked flustered. "The secretary

called me and asked me what to do. I told her to send him to our house. He did not bring any recommendation with him. But it was my understanding that he came highly recommended."

"You're repeating what I told you about him," Dr. Ganji interrupted impatiently. "Obviously there is more to it than we're aware of."

Sayid studied his guests with sad, all-seeing eyes. "The man is a trained killer. He returned from Lebanon recently. He's in charge of cleaning house. Do you know what that means doctor?"

Andrea held her breath. She'd been struggling to break the habit ever since she was a child but it popped up, occasionally leaving her at war with herself.

"Cleaning house?" the doctor asked astonished. "No, I can't say that I do."

"Our clergymen have been busy lately putting together a list of Iranians they feel the country would be better off without. Last night, we raided one of their hideouts. We had a rude awakening. They're far better organized and determined than we've been giving them credit for. We also discovered a long list of Iranians targeted for liquidation. Your name was on the list."

Andrea forced herself to breathe. She had made the right decision. Sayid's cool, composed approach helped allay her fears that he might act irrationally.

Guita's half smile froze on her face. Stunned, the doctor examined Sayid's face in disbelief. It took a while before he could speak. "How . . . how did you learn about him?"

"Andrea recognized him. We had the misfortune of meeting him in Tehran under circumstances over which we had no control."

Dr. Ganji turned to Andrea, his expression full of gratitude and pain. "We're very grateful to you. These are indeed very difficult times for our country. It's impossible to know who to trust."

"When we knew him," Sayid said, "his name was Bahram, not Mustafa but that's not important. You're a prime target. You need around the clock protection. I will see to it that you get it. So does Andrea. He must have known she recognized him. They were out to get us when we left the hotel. They'll be back."

Guita's warm eyes turned cold. Her voice quivered. "What do they want from Hushang? He's a doctor. Everybody knows he works for Savak not because he wants to but because he has to."

"Terrorists have a way of overlooking such minor details," Sayid commented dryly. "They're professional killers. They're given a list and told to do the job. They don't discriminate."

Guita sank back in her chair distraught. The doctor seemed to have aged years in front of their eyes. His shoulders drooped more and the lines on his face took on renewed intensity.

"I'll call headquarters for cover," Sayid said. "I'm sure they're waiting outside. They must have followed us. Unless you want me to make arrangements for you to spend the night here."

"I prefer going home if at all possible," Dr. Ganji said. "Fatima is alone in the house with the house boy and the hospital has my home phone number. If we stay here, I have to let Fatima know we're spending the night in a hotel and I have to give the hospital the number of the hotel."

Sayid rose, inspected the lobby and returned. "There are no pay phones," he said. "Stay where you are. I'll be right back." He approached the desk and talked to the clerk. The clerk fetched a bunch of keys from a locked drawer, walked past the desk to a back room and unlocked the door. Sayid went in and closed the door.

Soon after, he returned to the lounge. "We have to be ready to leave in eight minutes," he said. "The valet will have the car ready."

Instinctively they checked their watches. It was the longest eight minutes Andrea could remember. Sayid sat passively in a chair betraying no emotions. The doctor, Guita and Andrea were not so lucky. They turned and twisted every few seconds. Finally, it was over.

"Time to go," Sayid said. "I'll step out first. You three follow about a yard behind me. If I sense trouble, I'll throw myself on the pavement between your car and the entrance. You throw yourselves down behind the door. Do not come out. I repeat. Do not come out. Do I make myself clear?"

"I can't allow you to do that," Dr. Ganji objected pathetically.

"There's no time for arguments." He faced Andrea. "That applies to you as well. Don't do anything foolish. Stay behind the door. The minute I throw myself on the ground, you do the same. Let's go."

Sayid had barely put one foot out the door when a volley of shots rang through the air.

Chapter 43

For twenty-nine days the doctor, his wife and Andrea lived in a safe house on the outskirts of Ahwaz. For Andrea, it was an excruciating period of painful memories, soul searching, battling with herself endlessly to snuff out a burning desire to have the guilty behind bars. It was no longer a question of what they had done to her but what they had attempted to do to a gentle, compassionate physician who spent his life treating the pain inflicted by men on other men and women. There were moments, when unable to tolerate the constant bombardment of horror she would seriously consider ending it all. Gradually, she would talk herself out of it, block the recent past deliberately and dream about the wheat fields, her father, his arms, and Kelly. Kelly, innocent, beautiful, helpless. Then invariably, her blood would boil and she would once again determine to do her utmost to see the criminals get their just reward.

As the days dragged on, she vacillated between her desire for revenge, the possibility of leaving it all behind and getting out, or, resorting to a wait and see attitude. What puzzled her though was the doctor. Despite the attempt on his life, his loss of freedom and the loss of his patients, he never said an unkind word about any one. Neither did his wife. It was as though people in that part of the world expected harsh blows, were not disappointed when the blows came and accepted them as part of life. And when she questioned them about it, they both smiled. "Hope," the doctor said. "Hope is what keeps us going. To you it may seem like disappointment deferred but to us . . . Well, that's all we have."

She thought about it. She thought about it a lot because it was the truth, a truth she did not want to acknowledge but had no choice. Eventually, his calm understanding and the love he and his wife had for her, enabled her to accept life as it chanced to blow her way, the good mixed with the ugly and the bad. She was not yet at peace but she was getting there.

But the doctor's words had little impact on Sayid and Dino. Disguised as Arabs, they combed the city looking for the men who had raped Andrea and the men who had made an attempt presumably on the doctor's life. Sayid was convinced both acts were committed by the same group and he was determined to apprehend them regardless of how long it took. Dino took his summer vacation early. He didn't want to miss the opportunity of tracking down the criminals. He had one more day left and then he had to return to his job. Dino was frustrated and very vocal about it.

"Damn it," he said, like he'd done after every day of futile search. "It's the same every day. Nothing. They could not have escaped. Every possible exit from this city is blocked. I say they're hiding in the mosque. Let's storm the place and flush those bastards out. Sayid says it can't be done."

They were sitting in the garden of the safe house guarded around the clock by security agents. It was close to midnight.

The possibility that the men could be hiding in a mosque bothered Andrea. If Sayid and Dino were sure the men had the protection of the clergy then why were they wasting countless days searching throughout the city? Would inquiring about it be construed as meddling in matters she knew little about? She decided to take a chance.

"What makes you think they're hiding in the mosque?" she asked.

Dino smiled mischievously. "I have my ways. Remember the old woman who let me know where to find you the day of the rioting? I followed her to the bazaar today. She told me."

Andrea turned to Sayid. "Do you think she's telling the truth?"

"I'm sure she is."

Dino got up, took a few nervous steps, stopped, then pounding his fist on the table said angrily, "Give me one good reason why we can't flush those bastards out of there."

"Dino, you're a hotheaded Italian," Sayid replied. "We have strict orders from the Shah to avoid any confrontation with the clergy. I explained that to you."

"Why don't I believe you?" Dino snapped.

Sayid sat impassively watching Dino work himself into a frenzy.

"I'll tell you why I don't believe you," Dino persisted. "I don't think you give a damn about orders from the Shah or anybody else. You and I broke quite a few this past month. Why weren't you concerned then?"

"We'll get them. Don't worry."

"I want to catch those bastards before I start work day after tomorrow. But you sit there cool and composed like we're here for a picnic. What's the matter with you? Do you have ice in your veins?"

"Here, have a drink. Relax." Sayid poured half a glass of Vodka and handed it to Dino.

"I don't need a pacifier. I need you to act. Khorassani told me you're the only person in this country who has carte blanche from the Shah and can do just about whatever you want. You're not worried about orders. You're worried about others who might be at the mosque when we attack. Workers, or innocent bystanders. Isn't that what's bothering you?"

Everyone focused their attention on Sayid. He shifted his position, looked around, but said nothing.

Dino chuckled nervously. "I can't believe it!" He walked back and forth, ready to blow up. "I can't believe that a man of your power can allow the perpetrators of such crimes to go unpunished."

"Take it easy, Dino," the doctor counseled. "Sayid is no fool. He'll make sure those men pay for their crimes in due time. There are too many people taking the law in their hands as it is. We need more people who think before they act, not vice versa."

"Nonsense," quipped Dino. "You did not see what I saw. I will not leave this place until those men are brought to justice with or without Sayid."

Andrea cringed. She had worried unnecessarily about what Sayid might do not realizing how strongly he opposed violence. Her concern shifted to Dino, her self appointed guardian. She rose and walked toward him. "I have given the matter a lot of thought, Dino. I don't hold a grudge against those men. They were tools in the hands of others who put them up to it. And I think I know why. Let's leave it at that, please."

Dino stared at her as though she'd just slapped him across the face. "You're crazy," hc yelled. "You're all crazy. In my country this sort of thing would be pursued if it took a lifetime. How can you sit there and tell me in such a matter of fact manner that you don't hold a grudge against them? Who gives a damn who put them up to it. They did it, didn't they? What's the matter with you all?"

Sayid rose and walked over to where Dino stood. He put his hand on Dino's shoulder. "Nobody is taking the matter lightly. Otherwise we would have returned to Tehran weeks ago. No one who took part in attacking Andrea or the doctor will go unpunished. You have my word of honor. But I have to do it my way. Can you accept that?"

Dino cocked his head to one side, looked at the man with whom he had spent every hour for the past month and smiled. "Yes, Sayid, I can accept that. But only because it came from you."

Sayid returned to his seat, lifted the empty bottle of Scotch, looked at it, then sat it back on the table. "Do we have another bottle?" he asked Dino.

"There's a whole case in the trunk of the car. We bought it yesterday. Did you forget?"

"I guess I did. Do we have ice Andrea?"

"I doubt it. I'll check. We had no power or water for three days until today noon. A few more days of these paralyzing strikes and the country will come to a standstill."

"It's unbearable," Guita added. "It's so hot and humid. We've been quenching our thirst with Coke. There's nothing else to drink. Not even beer. The factory had to shut down for lack of water. I'm afraid it will be the Coke factory next. Oh, God, it's such a mess with no end in sight, and it seems to be getting worse by the hour."

The doctor turned to Sayid. "It's almost a month. If we wait much longer, I think I'll lose my mind. I can't remember when I last took a vacation. My wife and I would like to visit the girls in England until the situation here calms down. I'm no good to anyone here anyway. Andrea can come with us if she wants to. Do you have any objections?"

Andrea studied Sayid as he stared into space. His eyes were swollen from lack of sleep, his face drawn.

"I'll make the necessary arrangements for you and Guita to leave in the morning," he said. "There's no need for you to stay. Savak has hired another doctor to replace you temporarily."

"What about Andrea?" the doctor whispered in Sayid's ear. "She can't stay here alone. I don't trust the security men guarding this house."

Sayid straightened his sagging body slowly and gave the doctor a quizzical look. "Do you mind explaining your last statement?"

The doctor motioned for Sayid to follow him inside. Although outdoors was often used to discuss matters of importance, there was a remote possibility that the guards outside could hear them.

Once inside, the doctor wrote quickly on a piece of paper and handed it to Sayid.

Sayid read it. "When?"

The doctor scribbled his answer on another piece of paper and gave it to him.

Sayid wrote a couple of lines then went out of the room and motioned for Dino to join them. He gave Dino the note.

Dino left. The rest gathered around the table in the garden. No one spoke.

In less than ten minutes a military jeep raced up the street and came to a halt in front of the house. They watched as the guards got in and the jeep drove away.

Dino opened the gate and entered the garden.

"Tell me exactly what happened," Sayid said to the doctor.

"Andrea spotted them."

Sayid turned to Andrea. "Don't overlook anything. Tell me in detail exactly what you saw."

"Last night, I could not fall asleep. For about an hour I stared at the ceiling then got up and walked to the window. I was about to go downstairs to find something to read, when I noticed a car approach the house. The only cars we've seen since we came were the jeeps bringing guards for the shift changes. They come at eight in the morning and eight at night. And, of course, the Security car which brings you and Dino. I checked my watch. It was exactly one in the morning."

"Go on."

"I was surprised to see a mullah stick his head out of the

car window. He gave a package to one of the guards and drove slowly down the hill."

"Could you see anyone else in the car?"

"I could be wrong but I think the driver of the car was also a mullah."

"What did the package look like?"

"It was small. That's what worried me. I was afraid it might contain a bomb."

"Was it wrapped?"

"I think so. I couldn't say for sure. I was scared so I woke the doctor. We didn't put any lights on. We watched."

"Go on," Sayid urged.

"The other three guards came around quietly. One of them took a small cassette player from his coat pocket and handed it to the guard who had the package. The guard opened the package and took out a cassette. I could see clearly. They stood under the street light. They inserted the cassette and although they kept the volume low, we had no trouble hearing through the open window of my room."

The doctor pulled his chair close to Sayid's. "I listened very carefully. It was a message from Ayatollah Khomeini, from his exile in Iraq, for all believers of Islam to rise against the Pahlavi regime and wipe it off the face of the earth. It was the most virulent attack against the Shah I have ever heard."

"Now I understand," Dino exclaimed excitedly. "Lately, a number of our local employees who own cassette players have become very popular. During lunch break the laborers gather around and listen to what sounded to me like a sermon. But when you mentioned Khomeini, I realized the oratory always started by mentioning that name. Who is he?"

"An exiled religious leader who has a personal grudge against the Shah," Sayid explained.

The doctor shook his head. "Swaying the minds of illiterate construction workers is easy enough but these men were supposed to be here to protect us against the enemies of the regime. They are trained and employed by Savak. That's what's so scary." The doctor rubbed his hands together nervously.

Andrea eased herself slowly into a chair. How long could she hope for miracles to keep her going? How long could she watch death and destruction before becoming permanently scared? Did her presence in the country really make a difference or had she chosen to stay to pacify her guilt for indirectly causing the death of her daughter? Had the time come for her to leave this crazy life behind and move on?

Dino said to the doctor, "Khorassani said to tell you he'll be here in the morning to talk to you about arrangements for your departure."

"We want to leave as soon as possible," Guita said. "But not until we make sure Andrea has a safe place to stay or can go with us."

"That won't be necessary," Andrea said. "I'm returning to Tehran in the morning."

Sayid glanced in her direction but said nothing.

"What makes you think you'll be safe in Tehran?" Guita asked.

"Please, don't worry about me," Andrea said.

"Hopefully, it will only be long enough to arrange for my departure home."

"Oh, Andrea." Guita rushed and embraced her. "I'm so glad you've made up your mind. May God go with you."

"Thanks, Guita. I appreciate all that you've done for me. I hope to repay you soon. Remember your promise. I'll be expecting you."

"It looks like we have to stay here tonight," Sayid said to Dino. "Khorassani must be having trouble replacing the guards. We can't leave the doctor alone with the women here. Did Khorassani tell you what he planned to do?"

Just then the front door opened and Khorassani let himself in.

"Sorry about the intrusion," Khorassani said. "I was

planning to come in the morning but I had to come now. There are new developments. I've been on the phone to Tehran the past hour. There are rumors that the employees, and I mean all the employees of Iran Air are planning to go on strike tomorrow morning. Sayid, you and I have to return to Tehran immediately."

"If that's the case," Sayid said, "then make arrangements for all of us to leave. The doctor and his wife want to fly to London, Andrea will come with us. I don't know what Dino wants to do."

"I have unfinished business here," Dino replied.

"You come with us," Khorassani said. "I don't trust you here alone. I like to have you where I can keep an eye on you."

"What makes you say something like that?" Dino had an impish grin on his face.

"Never mind," Khorassani said. "There's no reason for you to stay. Your workers are on strike just like everybody else."

Dino jumped out of his chair. "When? When did it happen?"

"Yesterday."

"Oh, my God, I'm finished." He slumped back into the chair.

"Don't worry," Khorassani said soothingly. "I notified your office in Tehran. They realize it's a problem affecting the whole country and I told them you were in protective custody so there will be no repercussions against you."

Dino studied Khorassani for a moment, then burst out laughing. "And they say Savak agents are a bunch of murderers. What are you trying to do? Destroy your reputation?"

"Don't get carried away," Khorassani replied impatiently. "I only did it because Sayid would scalp me if you got in trouble for helping him."

"Oh, well, have it your way."

"We must leave for Tehran immediately," Khorassani

said. "The mullahs who delivered the cassettes are in our custody. They're doing a lot of talking. When news of their apprehension reaches the rebels, they might change their plans. But for now, we have to assume that the strike will take place. If the doctor and his wife want to go to England, we must hurry. They could catch an early flight before the strike begins. It's planned for eight in the morning. But we got the names of the leaders from the mullahs. Hopefully they'll be in our custody before the night is over and there will be no strike."

"Is there a chance we can stop by our house," Guita asked. "We need a few personal items to take with us and we should tell Fatima we're leaving."

Khorassani fidgeted, banged his right fist in his left palm, eyed Sayid, then banged his fist again. "I don't advise you to."

"We can't leave with only the clothes on our backs," the doctor protested. "And we've got to let Fatima know we're leaving. We don't even have our passports with us for God's sake."

Khorassani ran his fingers through his hair, lit a cigarette and paced.

"What's the problem?" Guita asked. "It'll probably take us half an hour. Can't you provide security for half an hour?"

"Security is not the problem. Doctor Ganji, did you have anything in your house, anything at all that might be of interest to the terrorists? I know we've gone over it a dozen times, but I want you to tell me again the events of the evening you took your wife and Andrea to the Astoria. We have overlooked something."

Dr. Ganji thought for a while then shook his head. "No. There was absolutely nothing in the house, not even a scrap of paper with a phone number on it."

"How about you Guita? Can you think of anything? Did you talk about your house boy to anyone on the phone?"

"No. I told Andrea he seemed rather nervous."

"Besides knocking the pot over and searching the doctor's chest of drawers, did he do or say anything unusual?"

Guita shook her head.

Just then, it hit Andrea like someone suddenly waking from a dream with the memory of the dream still fresh. "Mr. Khorassani. I don't know if this is important or not. That day, when we went for a walk, we were a few blocks from the house when Guita suggested we ask the doctor to take us to dinner. It was on the spur of the moment decision. Guita went to get the car. When she returned, she looked perturbed. Fatima told her Mustafa left the house without telling her where he was going or when he'd be back."

For a moment Khorassani looked like a frog, his eyes protruding, his body ready to attack. "Why wasn't I told about this?"

Guita looked confused. "I figured he went to buy cigarettes or something. He wasn't gone very long. Before we left Hushang's office, Hushang talked to Fatima. Fatima said to tell me Mustafa was back. That's all there was to it."

"Damn!" Khorassani yelled. "Damn! How could you overlook something so important. That gave him enough time to inform his colleagues about Andrea being in the doctor's house. And enough time to prepare an attack."

"That's crazy," Dino interjected. "He could have phoned. Why did he have to leave the house."

"The doctor works for Savak, Dino," Sayid laughed a nervous laugh. "Mustafa or Bahram or whatever his name is would know the doctor's phone is tapped."

"Damn it." Khorassani's yelled. "He must have gotten hold of the conversation the doctor had with Fatima. That explains it."

"Explains what?" The doctor put his chin in his palm waiting for an answer.

Khorassani stopped pacing and banging his fist. He threw his head back, brought it forward but avoided eye contact. "Your house was demolished last night by two powerful bombs. There's nothing left of it."

Guita stared in disbelief at the man who had wiped out her past with two brief sentences. She remained on her feet for a few seconds, then her eyes rolled back and her body went limp. She would have hit the floor had it not been for Andrea. Andrea sensed the effect Khorassani's words had on her. She grabbed Guita, clung to her, until Sayid rushed over.

They eased her into a chair, Andrea's arms around her shoulders. Dino ran to the kitchen and dashed back with a glass of water. The doctor seemed paralyzed, unable to move to help his wife or himself.

Sayid knelt next to Guita's chair, took her hand in his and rubbed it gently. "Please, pull yourself together. You must, for your sake and your husband's."

Guita tried to say something but couldn't.

Sayid raised his eyes and saw tears flowing down Andrea's cheeks. He looked like a man with a painful stab wound, a man lost in a world of violence, senseless, indiscriminate, destructive. He urged Guita to drink a sip of water. "Please try. I'll help you all I can."

Guita opened her mouth to say something between sobs but she heaved so badly no one could understand her.

Looking distraught Sayid pulled his handkerchief from his pocket, stuck it in the glass of water, then placed it on Guita's head. "I . . . I can't tell you how sorry I am. If there's anything I can do. Anything at all. Tell me."

The Ice Block was anything but. Andrea watched his broad shoulders sag, his eyes well with tears and listened to his voice crack. What a misunderstood, unfortunate man. To have so much love to give, yet be forced to spend his life fighting pain and suffering.

Guita's head shook uncontrollably as though propped up on a spring. She forced herself to get a message across. Couldn't. Then she lost consciousness.

Sayid dashed to get the doctor. The doctor had his head down, his face covered with his hands. He rose and followed

Sayid.

Crushed by the sight of the woman whose kindness and generosity had been crucial in her recovery from her ordeal, Andrea felt helpless, forlorn. But only momentarily. She pulled herself together and concentrated on what Guita had struggled to convey. "Oh, my God," Andrea cried. "It's Fatima. She's worried about Fatima."

The doctor had his wife's head in his lap. He talked to her hoping to comfort her. He stopped, looked up, his eyes full of pain and sorrow, speechless. Sayid was on the floor, next to the doctor. He rose, took a couple of steps, planted his feet apart and focused on Khorassani. "Did you check the area for casualties?"

"We haven't had time." Khorassani's voice pleaded for understanding.

Sayid reached for the man's collar, grabbed it and shook him. "Find her. I don't care how you do it. I want it done now. Take as many men as you need. But find her."

Chapter 44

They arrived at Mehrabad International Airport two days later, after Fatima's dismembered body was buried next to Guita's parents. The doctor and his wife were whisked to the VIP lounge from where they departed for London with the first flight out of the country. There was nothing unusual going on at the airport. Flights landed and took off as scheduled. Dino remarked, with his usual openness, that most probably Khorassani's information about the airport employees going on strike was incorrect or exaggerated at best. Khorassani replied half-jokingly that if Dino did not stop meddling in Security matters, he, Khorassani, would personally see to it that his next trip would be a flight out of the country.

Phil waited for them at the Hilton Hotel in the special room reserved for intelligence activities.

He seemed surprised to see Dino enter the room with the group.

"He's working for me," Sayid said.

Phil introduced himself, shook hands, then invited everyone to take a seat around the table. He approached Andrea. "I'm terribly sorry about what happened in Ahwaz. But I have to admit. Had I been here, I would have advised you to go."

Sayid cast a disapproving glance in Phil's direction. "I assume you are here because you have something to tell us. Let's get on with it."

"The news is very distressing. This so-called discontent is out of control. It's no more a matter of small, disorganized groups fighting the Monarchy. We have reason to believe that the National Front Party, the Tudeh Party, the Mujahedin and the Fedayin have joined forces to fight what they consider to be their common enemy, the Shah. We need a well planned strategy to deal with the situation. The Shah asked me to talk to you about it."

"I will help on one condition," Sayid said. "No, make that two. Andrea should leave the country immediately and violence must be avoided at all cost."

"I had a feeling you'd say that," Phil replied. "Yet, somehow I had hoped that with the situation deteriorating faster than we expected, you'd understand it would be almost impossible to work under those terms."

"You don't have to worry about me," Andrea said. "I have decided to return to the States. Phil, you mentioned earlier that you'd provide me with the necessary documents if I decided to leave. How long do you think it will take?"

All eyes focused on her.

"A couple of days."

"It's not that urgent. I want to visit Kelly's grave before I go. But I'm not quite sure how to go about it."

"I can't say that I blame you," Phil said sadly. "Your contributions have been invaluable. We'll miss you. But if you feel you can't handle the job, then there's not much I can do to persuade you to stay."

"I can handle the job. That's not the problem. I'm afraid my usefulness is over. I'm a marked woman. There's no way they'll trust me again."

Phil shook his head in disagreement. "The mere fact that you accepted to go to Ahwaz was proof enough to them that you sympathized with their cause."

"That doesn't make sense."

"Sure it does. We have information which leads us to believe that they've concluded you're a harmless person, caught in the middle with no way out."

"Leave her alone," Sayid snapped.

"We have a brewing revolution on our hands. We've got to have intelligence. We'll do our best to protect her."

"Your best is not good enough."

Andrea turned to Sayid. "I appreciate your concern. But I promised Phil to work for him. If he feels he needs me, I'll stay. The way I see it, if I can help save one life, it's well worth it."

Dino smiled broadly. "I love it. I love it! Here's a woman with guts. She's fantastic. I'll work with you anytime."

Sayid looked forlorn. "I must insist. You must leave for the same reasons that Phil wants you to stay. You said you had made up your mind, remember?"

"I know I did. I could not see what my presence here could accomplish. Perhaps I was hasty in my decision because I believed differently then. Also Guita and Hushang would not have left had I not assured them that I would be leaving as well."

"Phil can recruit someone else."

"I'm sure he can. I have other considerations to take into account."

"If it's Mani you're thinking of," Sayid replied tonelessly, "forget it. He's gone into hiding together with his friend, Farhad."

"It seems to me I'm always the last one to know. Why wasn't I told?"

"They're not hiding from Security," Khorassani said. "They're hiding from Sayid. Promise or no promise. This time Mani went too far and he knows his brother will see to it that he is amply rewarded for sending his wife to be raped."

"Shut up, Khorassani," Sayid grumped.

"That complicates matters," Phil said. "We were hoping to keep track of their activities through Andrea. We must find a way to lure them to come out of hiding."

"We'll wait," Khorassani said. "They're bound to surface sooner or later. In the meantime, Andrea can go on vacation. We'll ask her to return when we feel we can use her."

Dino jumped. "How about going to Rome with me. You will see Rome like no one has seen it before."

Dino's exuberance was infectious. Andrea smiled. "Thanks, Dino. I'd love to. But first I want to find a place to stay, visit Kelly's grave, and hope my husband shows up. If he doesn't, then I'll think about traveling."

"You can use the apartment," Phil said. "There's no one there. I could be wrong but if your husband and his friend decide to return, they'll most probably come back to the apartment."

"There are two things which will make them come out of hiding," Khorassani said. "If Sayid leaves the country and the lure of money. With the activities of the opposition gaining momentum fast, they can't afford to hide for long and we can't afford for Sayid to leave the country. We'll wait a while and if they still remain in hiding, we can arrange for a large sum to be deposited in Andrea's account in a bank where the opposition has contacts. They'll be there in no time. Trust me."

"What do I do in the meantime?" Andrea asked.

"You could be of great help to us in another matter," Khorassani said, "but I know Sayid will object."

"Leave her out of it," Sayid said.

"What did you have in mind?" Phil asked surprised.

"Maybe I'm paranoid," Khorassani said. "But I've been in this business too long to dismiss details which seem harmless initially. Last night, we took four of our own security agents into custody. They were caught red-handed listening to cassettes smuggled in from Iraq, cassettes recorded by Khomeini and distributed by the clergy. The mullahs who provided the cassettes confessed their supply came from Tehran, from Mullah Hamid. I'd like to know how he receives them."

"That's not a job for her," Sayid snapped.

Khorassani sighed resignedly. "I knew you'd say that. But the clergy have waited for decades to get even with the Shah for stripping them of their power and taking vast chunks of their land. Mullah Hamid might have the Americans convinced that he's working for them but he's a slimy character who shifts allegiance to whomever serves his interest best. If there is a chance for the clergy to win, you know he'll do everything in his power to help them succeed."

"Please, Sayid," Andrea said before Sayid had a chance to object. "I want to do it. Mullah Hamid owes me one. He and that doctor friend of his. What an actor he was! Does anyone know the doctor's whereabouts?"

"The doctor is in the States," Phil said. "He escaped after the riots in Ahwaz. Mohammed kept me informed. I made it a point to meet him. He was in a mental hospital suffering from a nervous breakdown. He assured me he was duped into believing that you were being sent on a legitimate mission. He believes someone in the group, a traitor, set those men up. He suspects Farhad but has no proof."

"That's a shame," Andrea said, genuinely upset. "He seemed like the only rational person in the group. He actually collapsed and sobbed when I said I wouldn't go."

"Yes," Phil said. "A brilliant mind gone to waste. He was so consumed with avenging his brother's death that he had lost all sense of reality."

"How do you propose for her to contact Mullah Hamid?" Sayid asked tersely.

"That's easy," Andrea replied. "I want to visit Kelly's grave. The last time I talked to him about it he gave me his private number where he could be reached. He said special arrangements had to be made because I'm Christian and he said he'd do it for me."

"You must be very naive to think that he'd have anything to do with you after what happened," Sayid said wearily. "My guess is that he'd avoid you like the Black Death."

"I'll assure him I'm convinced it wasn't his fault."

"You have to find him first," Khorassani said. "Our understanding is that he has not left the mosque since news of the discovery of the cassettes reached him."

"How did he find out?" Phil asked.

"Come on, Phil," Khorassani replied. "The mullahs who provided the cassettes are in our custody. How long do you think it will take him to figure out what happened even if his informers did not notify him immediately?"

"You're right. News travels much faster nowadays, especially bad news."

"Despite it all," Sayid said, "You want to involve an inexperienced, young, college graduate to do your dirty work for you."

"Please, stop worrying about me. I'll be careful. I promise."

"There are fifty thousand Americans in this country. Let him find someone else."

"It's my choice, Sayid. Please, try to understand."

"There's nothing to understand. Obviously you've made up your mind."

"Why are you in it then?"

"You're not me."

"That's true. But I suspect you're in it for the same reason I am. To avoid bloodshed."

Sayid looked at her with a pained expression. "If you are sure that revenge is not your motive then I will welcome any assistance you give us to help restore tranquility in our country. Revenge does not appeal to me. It's consuming and destructive for all concerned. Justice is what I'm after."

Andrea pondered the remark for a few seconds. "I have to admit I entertained the idea of revenge for quite a while and I thought you did too. I don't like it for the same reasons you don't. I prefer to do what I can to help resolve the differences between the government and the people by peaceful means. It's probably presumptuous of me to think that any one person can make a difference. But I do. And I hope I'm proven right."

Phil heaved a sigh of relief. "Great. Now that that's settled, let's work on an arrangement so Andrea can have a dependable channel of communication with Sayid and me."

"I'm at your service," Dino said with an exaggerated bow.

The special phone rang.

"It's probably for you," Phil said to Sayid. "Do you want to answer it or do you want me to?"

"I'll answer it."

The conversation lasted over three minutes. Sayid said little. Gradually his face became ashen and he almost dropped the receiver. He pulled a chair and lowered himself slowly into it. He covered his face with his hands and listened.

When he put the receiver in the cradle, all eyes were focused on him.

"What happened?" Khorassani asked.

"It was the Shah. General Naini and his wife barely escaped death. A bomb was discovered in their airplane timed to go off two hours after take off. They were preparing for take off when the call came through."

Andrea collapsed in a chair.

"How did they find out?" Khorassani asked.

"It was not thanks to your intelligence. An anonymous caller, a woman, tipped the authorities. They think the woman was Iranian. Apparently she spoke fluent English with an Iranian accent."

"Where are they now?"

"Somewhere in Europe, recovering from shock."

"That's incredible," Phil said. "Cyrus never plans his flight schedule except a couple of hours in advance. That's the way he's always been. He travels on impulse."

"That's what's bothering me," Sayid said. "The information had to be passed on by an insider, very probably a close friend or relative. Someone he trusted."

"It can't be!" Andrea had spoken out loud without meaning to.

"You're thinking of Dariush, aren't you?" Phil asked.

"You're right. But I know my thinking is all wrong."

"Why?" Sayid asked.

"Because Dariush would never do something like that. He wasn't crazy about his uncle, but he adored Helga."

"You got to know him quite well in Pahlavi and in Lebanon, didn't you?" Sayid asked.

Did she detect a touch of cynicism or envy in his voice? She wasn't sure. "We were friends. That's all."

"Then your job is cut out for you. When he returns to Iran you must renew your friendship and keep a close eye on him."

Was Sayid being sarcastic or was he trying to determine the extend of her involvement. Did he think she was in love with Dariush? Was that why he always behaved in a cautious, calibrated manner in matters involving her? Perhaps he had wanted her to leave for the States knowing Dariush eventually would return to Iran defying the General's orders. Should she relieve him of such misconceptions? Perhaps later. "Dariush spends summers in Pahlavi," she said. "If I am to be of any use to you, I should remain in the country."

Sayid had a faraway look in his eyes but made no comment. He turned to Khorassani. "Where did you say Mani and Farhad are hiding?"

"I didn't."

"What's that supposed to mean?"

"It means we know they're hiding but we don't know where."

"You're slipping badly. I think you should retire."

"Don't be so hard on him," Phil said. "He's had plenty to keep him busy lately. The latest report indicates they're headed for Zurich from Milan."

"You mean they're out of the country?" Andrea asked surprised.

"They left . . . let me see," Phil checked a small notebook he carried in his coat pocket, "thirteen days ago. They were in Milan for a week then traveled by car to Geneva."

Her husband and Farhad in Europe, the General and Helga barely miss being blown up, an anonymous phone call. Coincidence? Stop, she warned herself. It's too horrible to contemplate.

"The picture is far from complete," Phil continued. "This is the second time disaster was averted because someone bothered to inform us. I suspect in both instances it was the same woman. Any ideas?"

For a few moments no one spoke.

Andrea shuddered. Could it be Layla? Where was she? Of all her friends, Layla's sudden, unexplained disappearance dismayed her most and was on her mind constantly.

Sayid kept his gaze focused on her. When no response was forthcoming, he turned to Khorassani. "Do you remember I came to your headquarters a few months ago to release a woman called Layla?"

Instantly, Andrea's senses went on full alert. Sayid suspected Layla just as she did. But how could Layla be in Europe? She had no money and three young children to take care of. Andrea felt the blood rush to her cheeks. God, I hope she wasn't foolish enough to join the Mujaheds. But what other explanation was there?

Khorassani asked, "The woman whose children you had trouble locating?"

"Right."

"Yes, I remember her well."

"Did you keep her under surveillance after her release?"

"Your memory fails you. When you ordered her release, you insisted that we leave her alone. Remember?"

"I want a complete report on her whereabouts the past two months as soon as possible. I will drive Andrea to the apartment. Assign two agents, agents whose integrity you can vouch for, to keep the apartment under surveillance around the clock. If you slip this time, you'll be delegated to shining shoes in the bazaar. Do I make myself clear?"

Chapter 45

Finding Mullah Hamid turned out to be far more complex than Andrea had imagined. The private number he gave her happened to belong to the owner of an apartment complex. The single line was shared by six families. Each time she tried the numbcr a different person assured her no such person lived in that building.

Alone and frustrated, she found herself anxiously waiting for Sayid's visits.

He came every night, at different times, stayed for a while, then left. He told her the reason for his visits was to make sure she was all right and to collect any information she may have gathered during the day.

He smiled rarely and spoke little. The sad look was always there as though it was a natural part of him. She felt it would be hard to recognize him without it.

He arrived early on a Wednesday afternoon, mumbled a curt hello, lit a cigarette, examined it, walked to the sink, held it under running water then threw it in the trash can.

"Dariush has returned to Iran," he said casually. "He's in

Pahlavi. You should arrange to go there. Phil thinks you should call Helga tonight or early tomorrow morning. She'll be leaving for Pahlavi tomorrow afternoon."

They were in the kitchen. Sayid seemed on the verge of collapse. He is like a Vietnam vet, Andrea thought, defeated and with no one to share his pain with.

"I'll call her. I must first figure out a way to reach Mullah Hamid. I'm at my wit's end. Could he have left the country?"

"No, he's here. You can hear his fiery speeches every Friday from the mosque. All you have to do is tune in."

"What does he have to say?"

"Plenty. He's urging the people to rise against tyranny and oppression. The message is very subtle. He never mentions the Monarch by name. It's those foreigners and people in government in the pay of foreigners he wants the public to rid themselves of."

"What's he up to? Do you know?"

"It can mean only one thing. He knows something we don't. Something that more or less guarantees the restoration of clerical authority."

"Do you think they have a chance?"

"I really don't know what to think. A clergyman who works for me tried to convince me this afternoon that the U.S. Ambassador himself was involved with the efforts of the clergy and with bringing the opposition factions to work together."

"That's crazy."

"Here, everything is crazy."

"Do you know if the mosque has a phone?"

"I have the number with me but it's useless for you to call. He won't come to the phone. We've tried."

"But I must talk to him. He has put off my requests to visit Kelly's grave repeatedly. There's got to be a way."

"I'll see what I can do."

"Please don't. I want to take care of my problems myself. You've done more than enough already."

He looked at her with blank, uncomprehending eyes. "How?"

"I don't know. I'll think of something."

"That's what I am afraid of."

He collapsed in a chair.

"You're waging a one man crusade against all that's wrong in this country," Andrea said. "Let's face it. It's an impossible task. Even for you."

He shook his head despondently. "Summer is almost over and we have accomplished nothing. There's no news of Mani, Farhad or Layla. We have dozens of agents working around the clock but they've come up with nothing. Absolutely nothing."

"Maybe they're taking the summer off and maybe you should do the same. You look exhausted."

He went to the bar, poured each of them a Scotch, then sat on the sofa in the living room and sipped his drink.

"Is the lack of progress bothering you or is there something else?" Andrea's feelings for him had changed, gradually, over time. She could not explain it even to herself. She was determined not to get involved, at least not with someone from a different culture. Yet seeing his pain-racked face, sent sensations through her she had never experienced before.

He raised his eyes, studied her for a moment, then said, "I better go. You must be quite tired of my frequent visits."

She walked over and sat next to him. "I love your visits." She placed her hand on his.

He stared at her in disbelief. She saw a flicker of a smile cross his face. It disappeared instantly.

"I better go," he repeated as though afraid of what might follow.

"Must you? I thought perhaps you could stay a while. Is there something urgent you have to attend to?"

He lowered his head and concentrated on examining her hand resting gently on his.

"What are you running from?"

He didn't answer.

"It's me, isn't it?"

He still didn't answer.

"Please talk to me. I care about you. A lot."

He took her hand and moved it away gently. Then he rose, stuck his cigarettes in his pocket and prepared to leave. "That's very generous of you. You care about the poor, the sick, children and me. Probably in that order. I guess I should consider myself privileged to be on your list."

Puzzled, she searched her mind for a clue to his negative reaction. Then she realized he had every reason to be cautious. He was always there when she needed him, but she had never given him reason to believe that there was any more to their relationship than an association through her marriage to his brother. She had to change all that. She jumped and embraced him. "I had to be sure, Sayid. I did not want to hurt you a second time. I love you very much."

For a few seconds, he stood transfixed, unable to move or speak. Then slowly, like a man waking from a dream, he cupped her face in his hands his eyes probing hers apprehensively, craving for reassurance. She could feel his reserve, his fear that he might have heard wrong or assumed he'd heard what he had wanted to hear for years. The gleam in her eyes and the joyful smile on her face must have reassured him. Hesitantly, he put his arms around her and embraced her for the first time, tenderly, cautiously, afraid to hold her too tight lest something happened to her and his dream shattered. They remained in each others arms, spent by the ordeal of suppressing their true feelings for each other. Soon he recovered from the initial shock, tightened his embrace and covered her face, neck and shoulders with kisses with an intensity which seemed to be beyond his control. She trembled. He lowered her on to the sofa, cuddled her in his arms and pressed her against his chest. "I have loved you from the moment I set eyes on you. I never believed this day would come. You've made my life worth living once more."

Had she not witnessed the instant transformation which took place in front of her eyes, she would have dismissed it as a figment of her imagination. He stood and lifted her gently as he did so. He looked tall, powerful, strikingly handsome, his manner that of a man ready to conquer the world, the sorrowful expression replaced by love of life.

"Now everything is possible," he said in between kisses.

"I love you."

"I love you too. Too, too much." He lifted her and carried her back to the sofa.

She snuggled close to him. "Do you have any commitments tonight?"

"Why? Why do you ask? Did you have something in mind?"

"I thought maybe we could go out to dinner or something."

"I'm sorry darling. I have to meet Phil at ten. Savak has confiscated a large cache of weapons, tapes, cassettes and leaflets all smuggled into the country by the followers of Khomeini. Khomeini's using a weapon never tried before, psychological warfare. It scares me. The public is too vulnerable."

"Don't worry about it. It was just an idea. We can do it some other time."

"Let's see. Tomorrow is Thursday. I have to go to Qom to talk to a clergyman there. I don't know when I'll be back. Friday, I'm free. I'll take you anywhere you like. Please tell me you're not upset."

"Of course not. Friday is fine."

He checked his watch. "It's ten minutes to ten. I better go."

Thursday morning she called Helga.

"I'm leaving for the airport in fifteen minutes," Helga said. "I got a call this morning from Germany. My father has had another stroke. The doctors fear he might not pull through this time."

"I'm terribly sorry. Is there anything I can do to help?"

"Call Dariush, please. He's in Pahlavi. Since the bomb incident, he's become extremely depressed. The persistent rumors about his involvement have made matters worse. I'm worried about him."

"I'll do my best to reach him."

"There's one other thing I'd like you to talk to him about. We've learned that he has made arrangements to dispose of all his property and money. He wants it distributed to the poor villagers in Pahlavi. Cyrus thinks he's gone crazy. He wanted me to go to Pahlavi to talk to him. I planned to, but then I got the call about my father. Maybe you could talk to him. He'll probably listen to you more than he would me."

"I'll try. I don't know if you had noticed it. But he did give a lot of money away when I was with him last summer."

"We're talking millions, Andrea. In Swiss Francs. His entire inheritance. He has willed his house to his nanny, his orchards to the owner of the restaurant whose son drowned and the rest to the Kurds. Something is wrong. I'm worried sick. Please talk to him."

"I'll try. I did earlier. He didn't like it."

"He feels guilty because he has so much and there are so many who have so little. He is out to change the world. He needs help."

"How? Can his decision be reversed?"

"Here, with money, anything can be reversed except death."

"I'll talk to him."

"He suffers from terrible mood swings. When he gets over his depression, he's sure to regret it. By then, it might be too late. I think you're the only person who can help him."

"I hope you're right."

"I know I am. He's crazy about you. That's why his giving away everything makes no sense. No sense at all."

"There has to be a reason. He is not an overprivileged air head."

"Depression can play havoc with a person's thinking. Especially someone as sensitive as Dariush. Please stay in touch with him until I return. I plan to be back soon after I admit my father to a nursing home. Probably a week."

"I will."

"I've got to go. Bye."

Andrea tried until noon to reach Dariush. No one answered the phone.

She dressed and went to Furushgahe Bozorg, a department store downtown, bought herself a chaddor and returned home. The rest of the afternoon and evening she tried to reach Dariush. There was no answer. He could be out sailing or might have unplugged his phone she thought, and decided to wait a while before she called again.

She tried again all morning Friday but failed to reach him. Soon it would be time for Friday noon prayers. Vartan waited for her in his cab in front of the house. She took the chaddor and her sunglasses, walked down the stairs, got into the cab and asked Vartan to take her to the mosque in Ekhtiaryeh.

There were a few women and children in the courtyard. She approached the open door to the hall. The congregation, all men, in their stockinged feet, knelt and listened to a speech coming from loud speakers strategically located on top of the four corners of the building.

The speaker was Mullah Hamid.

He spoke, or rather screamed, into the microphone as vigorously as his lungs would permit. Taking time out to catch his breath. When the service was over, the crowd rose as the speaker carefully lifted his robe above his ankles and stepped down from the podium.

Andrea covered her face with her chaddor to the bridge of her nose and walked down the hall in hurried steps toward Mullah Hamid.

She caught up with him before he could descend the stairs in the back of the hall.

"Hi, remember me?" she asked, a broad smile on her face.

He looked flabbergasted at first but recovered quickly. "What brings you here, my dear?"

"I'd like to talk to you."

"I'm sorry. You have to believe me. I had nothing to do with it."

"I don't believe you did. That's not what I came to talk to you about. I want to visit Kelly's grave. Can you make the necessary arrangements?"

He cocked his head to one said, stretched his short neck as far as it would go, then said, "It will cost you. A donation is in order."

"Naturally."

"This is not a place to discuss such delicate matters."

"Would you prefer to come to the apartment tonight? I can have the check ready for you if you like."

"I would indeed," he replied gleefully. "I'll be there at eight o'clock."

She thanked him, said goodbye and left.

Pleased that she had finally been able to talk him, she hurried home.

Sayid was in the apartment and the apartment was full of baskets of flowers. He took her in his arms, hugged and kissed her passionately. However, he could not fool her. Instinctively, she sensed something was wrong. Something was terribly wrong.

She went to the kitchen, prepared coffee and waited for it to brew.

He followed her, sat across from her but said nothing.

She thanked him for the flowers and told him about her visit to the mosque and the look on Mullah Hamid's face when he recognized the face behind the chaddor. He listened but did not seem to hear.

"Okay. Let's have it."

"I'm sorry. What did you say?"

"You've got something on your mind. What is it?"

He studied her for a moment, hesitated, bent his head low and with his voice barely audible, said, "The police found Dariush's body hanging from a rope in his bedroom."

Andrea felt her body go limp, her nerves tingle, then a cold clammy perspiration crawl on her skin. Impossible. It was a cruel joke. No one so full of life, young and so much to live for could possibly do such a thing. "It . . . it . . . it's not true. It can't be."

He moved closer, put his arm around her shoulder and pressed it gently. "I'm so very sorry. You've suffered so much. I . . . I . . . feel so useless. The more I try to protect you the harsher the blows get. I . . . I don't know what to do."

Andrea sobbed uncontrollably. She wanted to stop sensing the pain it caused him, but couldn't. "Did he . . . did . . . he . . ."

"He left a note. He said he wanted the world to know that he had nothing to do with the bomb in his uncle's airplane and that he wished he did. He holds his uncle responsible for perpetuating a regime despised by all but a privileged few. He said he decided to end his life because he could no longer endure the injustice inflicted on the people of Iran by those in power. His last words were for you."

Sayid looked devastated.

"Please, don't," Andrea pleaded. "I don't want to hear it." She pulled herself together. She could not bear to watch the man she loved suffer any longer.

It was almost as if he was reborn. He smiled, heaved a sigh of relief and spread his arms. She fell into them. He embraced her, held her so tight she could hardly breathe. She raised her tearful eyes and met his. "I want to hear those words from you and only you."

He cupped his hands around her face, his eyes probing

hers. “You will my love. The rest of our lives. I love you. Always have, always will.”

She clung to him, rested her head on his shoulder and despite her best efforts, tears coursed down her cheeks.

Chapter 46

At eight that night she heard the heavy footsteps and the labored breathing of Mullah Hamid announce his arrival. Andrea hurried to open the door. As she did so, she heard a loud crash, followed by repeated poundings. She opened the door and rushed out.

Mullah Hamid lay on the landing of the fourth floor, bleeding from his nose and mouth. He looked unconscious.

She sorted her options quickly. She could not move him. He was too heavy. Calling an ambulance would take time and was often unproductive. Sayid had left a few minutes earlier and was probably still on his way to the Hilton. She'd asked him to leave because she did not want him in the apartment when Mullah Hamid came. Mohammed was transferred to another assignment as his presence there had become a liability. Shirin had moved to her new house and was instructed by her father to put an end to her relationship with Andrea because Andrea was the wife of a terrorist. She decided to call a number she was given by Sayid and Phil to be used only in the direst circumstance. What could be more calamitous than an unconscious mullah on the way to her apartment?

A woman's voice answered. She instructed Andrea to go back to the apartment and stay there. The matter would be taken care of.

Andrea rushed back to the apartment and called Sayid's private number. He had not yet arrived but they were expecting him. She left a message for him to call her and returned to check on Mullah Hamid. Despite what the woman said, she felt she had to do whatever she could to help. The mullah's breathing was shallow, labored, his pulse weak, irregular. His lips and finger tips were blue. She put her ear on his chest but could not hear any heart sounds. She called his name several times. There was no response. Then she heard the ambulance siren followed by footsteps. She dashed back to the apartment and watched from behind the partially open front door. Six men rushed to the fourth floor, carried the mullah down the stairs, placed him in an ambulance and drove away.

Within minutes, the phone rang. It was Sayid. She was so shook up she couldn't talk. He was there within fifteen minutes. He sat next to her on the sofa, hugged her and caressed her hair. Eventually, she regained her composure and told him what had happened.

"Could we go to the hospital, please," Andrea asked. "I feel awful. I shouldn't have asked him to come to the apartment."

"You must stop blaming yourself. It sounds like a heart attack. I'm not a doctor, but I imagine in his case it was bound to happen."

"He looked strong, his voice loud, his fury louder when he gave the sermon at the mosque. But when I checked him, before they took him away, he was ashen, almost dead. God, I hope they make it to the hospital on time."

"Let's go," Sayid said. "You won't rest until you make sure. I told the nurse to call me here. But I think you'll feel better if we go there."

Astonished, Andrea searched his face. "Did you know what happened before you came?"

"The guards notified me immediately."

"Oh, yes. I'd forgotten all about the guards. I hardly ever see them."

"They're here. Not to worry."

Andrea grabbed her purse. "Shall we go?"

They were in the waiting room for over an hour before the cardiologist came to talk to them. "He's in a coma. He suffered a massive heart attack. We suspect the fall and tumble down the stairs added to his problems. Most likely he is bleeding internally. We're not sure."

Fall, internal bleeding, hospital waiting room, Kelly, excruciating memories. She wanted to scream, bang her head against the wall, do something so crazy she'd never forget.

Instead, she walked to the window and stared at the street lights below. Sayid watched, smoked but said nothing.

Hours later, the head nurse entered the waiting room. "There's a good chance he'll remain in a coma for days. You should go home."

Dawn was breaking when they reached the apartment. Andrea thanked Sayid and collapsed on the living room sofa. Exhausted, she fell asleep immediately. When she opened her eyes, it was late Saturday afternoon. Sayid was still there, in an armchair across from her.

"How is he?" she asked.

"The same."

"Has his family been notified?"

"Yes. I wanted to talk to you about that. It's not advisable for you to go to the hospital."

"Why?"

"His family will not like it. They will blame you for what happened."

She knew he was right. "I understand."

"Cheer up. He's only thirty two. He'll pull through.

Actually, he has no one to blame but himself. But you can't tell that to his family. He was warned years ago to stop eating so much. He chose to ignore the warning. It was bound to happen and it did. A lot sooner than they expected."

"I didn't realize he was that young. He looked over forty."

"He's in good hands. I requested the services of the best cardiologist in the country. The cardiologist is with him now."

"Thanks." Andrea planted a kiss on his cheek. "You're always so thoughtful. When will the doctor let us know?"

"Probably late tomorrow. He wasn't sure."

"Coffee? Sandwich?"

"No. Let's get out of here. We'll grab a bite to eat at the Intercontinental Rotisserie. The change will do us both good."

"Give me half an hour."

She showered, put on a simple black dress, a touch of makeup and was ready to go.

"I doubt I've ever seen a more beautiful woman." He put his arm through hers. "I love the bounce in your hair, the naughty twinkle in your eyes, and that gorgeous body. God, how I love you!"

"You're spoiling me rotten."

"I have yet to begin."

"Oh?"

"Are you very hungry?"

"No, not really."

"I bought something yesterday. I want you to see it."

"I thought you said you had to go to Qom to talk to a clergyman."

"I did. He wouldn't talk to me. Times have changed. When I returned to Tehran I called you but you were not home. I had nothing better to do so I went to see an old friend."

"And?"

He chuckled. "It's a surprise. You're not going to con me into telling you."

They drove through downtown Tehran to an area south of the city to the poorest neighborhood. Places she'd never seen before. About a mile off the main road he stopped in front of a large, one story building.

They got out of the car. He asked her to follow him, reached in his pocket, took out a key and opened the front door.

It was a huge, empty building.

"What is it?" she asked.

"I bought it for you."

"For me? It looks like a school. What would I do with it?"

"I thought you could use it as an orphanage."

She stopped and looked at him quietly for a few seconds. Kelly's death had left a gap in her life, an emptiness which gnawed at her. She spent a lot of time with the neighborhood children and the children of an orphanage located on the outskirts of the city. She taught them English and whatever else she knew and could. But the pain was always there, the memory vivid. Kelly's wide-eyed gaze followed her everywhere. There was no escape. "Have you been following me?"

"Would I do such a thing?" He laughed.

"Yes, you would."

"No, my love. I didn't follow you. But I must admit Vartan's frequent presence in front of the apartment did arouse my curiosity."

"I don't know what to say."

"Don't. The children will keep you busy until we learn Mani's whereabouts. Once you get your divorce, we can live wherever you chose and do whatever you want."

"I don't need a divorce. We were never married here."

"That's one less complication. A major one. But you were married in the States and you will need legal documents proving you're divorced. If you want to remarry that is."

"Remarry?" she teased. "How can I remarry. No one has asked me."

He laughed, fell on knees, brought his hands together and raised his head. "Darling, will you marry me?"

She burst out laughing.

He rose, took her in his arms, his lips hungrily devouring hers. "I can't wait to tell the whole world about it!"

"Neither can I."

They continued walking, hand in hand, two lovers without a worry in the world. Or so it would seem.

They entered a room which was used as an office by the principle of the school. "This room is quite large and centrally located," Sayid said. "You could use it as an office."

With the word office, Andrea's mind drifted to Mani. "This is all very nice. But what about Mani?"

"Don't worry. He won't be a problem. Not unless he finds out about us. He hates my guts. Then even money will not do the trick. That's why we have to guard against publicizing our relationship."

"That's all right with me. But how come it's taking so long to locate them? It's been over two months."

"Several reasons. Security agents are busy with disturbances all over the country. There simply aren't enough trained agents. And as long they're not around to cause problems, Security agents have that much less to worry about."

"Something has been bothering me for a long time. Do you mind if I ask you about it?"

"Go ahead."

"It's about your father. One day we received a letter notifying us that he was coming to the States. Ten days later we heard he died. I've heard all kinds of rumors. What happened?"

The old, sad expression returned to Sayid's face. "It's a subject I never discuss but I think you have a right to know. I was studying in England at the time. I received a phone call from my sister asking me to return home immediately. I saw my father about half an hour before he died."

"That story about him having had a stroke or a heart attack was not true, right?"

"It was partially true. Apparently, as he got ready to board the plane, a young man came running toward him and gave him a small package to give to Mani. My father took the package and stuck it in his coat pocket. Just before take off, Security agents seized him and demanded he hand the package over. He did. It contained heroin. The penalty for possession of heroin in this country is the firing squad. After interrogation by Savak. And you know what interrogation by Savak means. When my father could not provide them with the identity of the man who gave him the package, they beat him until he had a heart attack and was on the verge of death."

"Oh, I'm so sorry. Please forgive me. I shouldn't have asked."

"You have a right to know. It involved your husband."

"That may be so but I can see how it upsets you to talk about it. Let's talk about something else."

"Let me finish. They caught the man while my father was still in their custody. He confessed. The profit from the sale of the heroin was to be used for demonstrations in the U.S. against the Shah. The Shah was scheduled to visit the States in about two months."

"Did Mani know?"

"Of course he did. He was not dying to see his father. He invited his father to come so he could bring the package. They figured no one would suspect an old man. But Security agents had advance information and were waiting for it to happen."

"Did your father know that Mani was involved?"

"He did. That's why he made me promise before his death, not to do anything to hurt Mani. He always said, violence begets violence. We have to be above all that or face extinction."

"You must have loved him a lot."

"I did. He had the best philosophy of life."

"You have it too." Andrea gave his arm a gentle squeeze.

The Gentle Giant, for so she thought of him, smiled the type of smile she had not seen since her father passed away. Strangely, the agony, the suffering, the ordeal of being the wife of a despicable man, did not seem to matter any more. It was worth it to meet a man like Sayid.

As they walked hand in hand through the rest of the building, Andrea's excitement rose. The building had a solid structure and would scrve well as an orphanage. It could easily accommodate sixty to a hundred children. She went from to room to room, drawing mental pictures of where she would put what. How she would decorate the place, fix the yard, the kind of toys, books and musical instruments she would buy. It all seemed like a dream come true. She was overjoyed and told him so.

He just smiled.

The tour over, they returned to the car. "You have a lot of work to do," he said. "I have opened an account in your name in Bank Melli. Buy whatever you feel is necessary. Furniture, toys, swings, everything. Whatever makes you happy."

"Do I detect something sinister in your words?"

He threw his head back and laughed. "You read me like an open book. Yes, you could call it a bribe. I have to go on a trip."

"Oh?"

He opened the door and helped her in.

"I'm not going to sit around and wait for Savak to find Mani and his friend. They've got more pressing matters to attend to and are happier if the pair is not around to cause more problems. But wherever they are, and however long it takes, I'll find them."

"Do you really think you should? They're bound to surface when they run out of money. Why not wait?"

"They won't run out of money. According to intelligence reports, the opposition is receiving financial support from the clergy. They have all the money they need."

"Do you trust those reports?"

"No, that's why I deposited a quarter million dollars in your name, in Bank Melli soon after we returned from Ahwaz. We know a number of employees there belong to different opposition groups. Two who belong to the same organization Mani and Farhad do. The money hasn't been touched."

"Maybe they feel it's a trap."

"It's possible. But I know my brother. He could never resist the smell of money."

"Khorassani said they were hiding from you. I'm afraid as soon as you leave, they'll show up. I've been so happy with him gone, I dread to think of living with him again, especially with you gone."

"I've given that matter a lot of thought. I have a gut feeling he won't dare come back. You'll have a number to call for emergencies and around thc clock guards, guards paid by me. Koreans instructed not to allow anyone they don't recognize to enter the building."

"But they'll have to allow Mani and Farhad. The apartment was rented in their name."

"Sure. I hope they come back. If they do, I'll be notified immediately."

"When are you planning to leave?"

"I will know tonight. After dinner I have a meeting with Phil and the Security Chief. If they have nothing positive to report, then I'll probably leave tomorrow or day after."

They reached the hotel. They took the elevator to the restaurant. Despite Sayid's repeated efforts to cheer her up, news of his departure distressed her. She felt the emptiness already. He'd always been there when she needed him.

Always.

The dinner was excellent and so was the wine. Nevertheless, Andrea could not eat. She picked at her food, barely touched her wine, and refused dessert.

Throughout the meal, Sayid tried to make light conversation to cheer her up, coaxing her to share in his joy of their being together. But for some reason, which she herself could not understand, she felt unusually depressed and could not shake it off. Incidents which she fought to forget and had consciously forced into her subconscious, kept popping into her mind. For she knew that given the circumstances, she could not have survived in that country without him.

The waiter brought two brandies.

"If it bothers you that much, I won't go."

It was as though someone had awakened her from a reverie. "Please forgive me. I'm being terribly selfish. You do what you feel is right."

"You're not selfish. I am. I can't wait much longer. I want you so bad, it hurts."

Andrea sipped her brandy slowly, her hands cupped the large glass, her mind in turmoil. "Will your meeting take long?"

"Not unless they've come up with something."

"I'll wait for you."

"I'll be there."

Chapter 47

Andrea awoke the next morning to the delicious aroma of coffee brewing. She put her robe on and went to the kitchen. Sayid had breakfast ready.

"Hey," Andrea teased, "You can't do that. That's a woman's job."

He rushed over and embraced her. "No, my love. It's a job for servants. And you shall have as many as you like."

"You keep this up and we'll both be in trouble."

The door bell rang.

Andrea was surprised. "Who can that be?"

"Relax. I told Dino to come at nine. It must be him."

Dino marched in. He gave Andrea a big hug. "Mama Mia, have I got news for you!"

"Sit," Sayid pulled a chair for Dino. "Help yourself to breakfast."

Dino sat but he couldn't contain himself. "I talk first, then eat."

Phil had advised Sayid to send Dino back to Ahwaz. There was a strong possibility that the men who attacked

Andrea and the doctor were still in Ahwaz. Dino had a legitimate reason to be there. The strike was over two days after the riots and the construction workers had returned to their jobs. Dino resumed his post as supervisor of the construction company during the day and spent most nights searching for clues.

"I know where your husband is." He grabbed a chunk of Barbari bread.

His exuberance was infectious. Andrea smiled. "Really? Where?"

"He and his friend . . . what's his name, are in Iraq."

"Iraq? What are they doing in Iraq?"

Sayid placed a plate of scrambled eggs in front of Dino.

"We'll soon find out. I heard about it two weeks ago. We're doing construction work in Iraq as well. I heard this fellow Khomeini lives there and receives a stream of visitors daily. So I asked a couple of my friends to investigate, discreetly mind you, and let me know who the old man's visitors were. They did."

"How can you be sure it's them?"

"That's why it took two weeks. I asked my friends to send me pictures of everyone who went in and out of Khomeini's house. I have the pictures with me. Do you want to see them?"

Dino did not wait for an answer. He took a bunch of pictures out of his coat pocket, selected two, and gave them to her.

"That's them all right," Andrea said.

"You've been a big help, Dino," Sayid said. He turned to Andrea. "It will probably take a week, perhaps less to bring them back. We have good contacts in Iraq. We should have no trouble."

Andrea felt relieved. "It sounds a lot better than the wild goose chase you had in mind."

"We must leave right away."

"We?"

"I promised Dino I'd take him with me."

"I insist." Dino wiped his plate clean with a piece of bread.

"What about your job?" Andrea asked.

"I like this one better."

"Dino, you're incorrigible."

"Incorrigible? What's that?" He laughed.

"Never mind. Let's go," Sayid said. "We've got a plane to catch."

Andrea had mixed feelings about the news. She was pleased that her husband was finally located but saddened at the thought of Sayid's departure. "You knew about it last night but you didn't tell me. You devil."

Sayid chuckled. "I wanted to surprise you."

"When we return, I want to teach you belly dancing," Dino said as Sayid nudged him toward the front door. "A beautiful Arab woman taught me. Like this." He shook his chest and rotated his abdomen on his way out.

Andrea burst out laughing. Dino always made her feel good. "I'll be waiting."

Sayid placed a light kiss on her forehead as Dino made his exit and they were gone.

A week later, Sayid called from Baghdad.

"It's hot and humid here." That was the code Andrea and Sayid had agreed upon. It meant they had not succeeded in finding the men.

Soon it became a ritual. He called every Saturday, at the same time, from different countries and repeated the same sentence.

The days stretched into weeks, then into months.

She kept her sanity by staying busy. Helga was back, devastated by Dariush's death and eager to immerse herself in work to forget the pain. Together, they put in sixteen to eighteen hour days getting the orphanage ready. Within a month, they had seventy-three children, from newborn infants to teenagers from all over the country. Andrea hired the necessary personnel to run the place and succeeded in involving a group of American women who volunteered their services on a regular basis. She was pleased with the progress they made and felt fulfilled when she saw the tremendous change which took place in the children's health and outlook on life. But, try as she would, she could not interest a single well-to-do Iranian woman to volunteer her services. That bothered her a lot. Hopefully, in due time, their perspective on such matters would change.

Calm had returned to Iran. There were few disturbances to speak of throughout the summer and late 1977. People relaxed, hoped it was all over and went about their business.

Sayid had given her his car and hired Vartan to work for her full time.

Vartan appointed himself as her guardian and saw to it that her smallest whim was satisfied. He brought her a hot meal everyday, prepared by his wife and waited by her side until she ate.

In late 1977, Khomeini's son Mustafa, died under mysterious circumstances. Andrea heard about it from Helga and later it was broadcast by Radio Israel. There was no mention of the incident in the local news media but it was not long before the news spread rapidly. Once again the country braced for trouble as it became evident that Khomeini held the Shah responsible for his son's death as well as his father's death earlier in the century. Those who knew Khomeini knew the deaths would be avenged.

On December 24, Sayid and Dino returned to Iran unexpectedly.

"I did not want you to spend Christmas alone," Sayid said.

"What's the latest?" Andrea asked.

"They're in Lebanon, training in terrorist tactics."

"There hasn't been too much trouble here since you left. I was hoping it would stay that way."

"It won't. There are many powerful undercurrents and

anti Shah sentiment is stronger than ever. My guess is that they're regrouping, organizing, looking for an approach which will help them achieve their goal. You can be sure there will be trouble from Khomeini, and soon. You must have heard about his son's death. He's not the type who forgives or forgets."

"Do you know when Mani and Farhad will be coming back?"

"Most probably in February. The normal training period is six months. Dino will leave for Lebanon in January to gather what information he can, and we wait."

"That's not so bad." Andrea reached for his hand. "It'll be February before you know it. Time flies, especially when you enjoy what you're doing. Did I ever tell you how much I appreciate the gift you gave me?"

"A thousand times."

"Come on, Sayid, cheer up. You've done more than your share to prevent violence. Don't be so hard on yourself."

"It's my country I'm worried about, not myself. When we were in Iraq, we heard a lot of talk about using religion as a weapon to rid the country of the Pahlavi Dynasty. Psychological warfare they call it. Anti-American sentiment among the followers of Khomeini had reached the point of hysteria. I'm afraid those who are in a position to do something about it will underestimate the potential danger this sort of fanaticism is bound to harbor."

"We'll wait and see. We have no choice."

It was not a long wait. Soon there were frequent reports of disturbances in the provinces, strikes, shortages of water, power and oil due to the strikes. The mosques overflowed with worshippers suddenly turned religious. Cassette players gained unprecedented popularity and anti Shah slogans were broadcast with bullhorns.

Alarmed, Sayid spent hours every night trying to convince Andrea to leave the country, at least until the situation could be brought under control.

Then on June 18, 1978, Khomeini openly called on the people of Iran to overthrow the Shah. Sayid quickly wrapped up a meeting he was having with the Security Chief and headed for the apartment. He found Andrea immersed in paperwork.

He came right to the point. "Andrea, this call by Khomeini is sure to incite the opposition forces to a frenzy. It's what they've been waiting for. Take a vacation, go someplace, any place, please."

"I can't Sayid. I've got a zillion things to do. I have seventy three children to take care of."

Three weeks later, Sayid was back at it again. "Just as I predicted, major clashes have erupted in Isfahan. The government was forced to impose Martial Law. Riots have broken out in Mashad and Shiraz. A movie house in Abadan has been burned to the ground killing hundreds of people. You've got to come to your senses. You've got to leave."

Andrea sighed. "I probably should. But how can I?"

"It will get worse. We have reason to believe that the opposition forces, which have only their hatred of the Shah in common have united in an effort to overthrow the Pahlavi Dynasty. The constant bombardment of vitriolic slogans from Iraq is giving them a backing and a psychological boost they never expected. It will be Tehran next. There's no doubt about it."

"Any news of Mani?"

"Oh, yes. Mani and Farhad have been seen in several cities leading demonstrations, shouting slogans, burning and looting."

"It's amazing," Andrea said. "A few months ago they would have shivered at the sight of Security agents. Isn't there anything that can be done?"

"The Shah asked me the same question last night."

"Well?"

"Not unless you want to kill them all."

On September 8, Andrea left for the orphanage early in

the morning. A couple of hours later, Tehran was gripped with the worst rioting the country had ever experienced. Hundreds were reported killed and many more wounded. Even ambulances were not immune. They were burned together with their occupants, in broad daylight wherever the demonstrators spotted them. The vital supply lines were cut. Life in the capital came to a virtual standstill.

It became known as "Black Friday."

It took place in Jaleh, in the south of the city, less than a hundred yards from the orphanage.

Throughout the day, Vartan insisted on taking Andrea back to the apartment, in the north of the city where she would be safer. She would not leave. Bullets whistled erratically, between the rioters and the military, breaking windows and forcing the children to take refuge under their beds.

By the afternoon, the military blocked all traffic to Jaleh except for military ambulances to remove the dead and the wounded. Andrea spent the night at the orphanage.

Sayid came the next morning with the necessary documents and a plane ticket for her to fly to Paris. "I will not take no for an answer," he said as firmly as he could. "You have to leave."

"Please, try to understand. I'll leave as soon as I find a reliable person to take over the running of this place. I haven't had any luck so far."

"Double the pay."

"That's not the problem. It's the location. They can't get here."

"I should have waited a while before buying this place. An operation like this is much too big a responsibility for any one person."

"Not really. The children are marvelous. They help. We're like one big family."

"Still. You can't leave because of them."

"I love it. The joy I get from working with the children far outweighs the problems. Their welfare is very important to me. I can't just walk away. It would be like leaving part of me behind."

In October, now deported from Iraq and living in France, Khomeini attacked the Shah incessantly and with more virulence, propelling the highly charged masses into hysteria. Shops, banks, tires, cars and homes of sympathizers of the Shah and property belonging to innocent bystanders were burned and looted despite the strict controls decreed by the government and dusk to dawn curfew.

There were daily massive demonstrations. Pent up hatred, suppressed for decades, spread all over the country, in megadoses, like a volcano blowing its top. The clergy increased the number of loud speakers in all the mosques and set the volume at maximum. The country was at war with itself.

Once again, Sayid pleaded with Andrea to leave.

She refused to abandon the orphans. She would stay.

In November, it became impossible to drive to "Friendship House," the name Andrea had chosen for the orphanage. Demonstrators in the south of the city and police everywhere effectively prevented movement within the city. There were roadblocks at most major arteries.

As of early October, all nonessential personnel and dependents of American companies were evacuated. Andrea was disheartened by the news but talked herself into waiting a little longer. By the middle of November, anti-American sentiment had reached such a high pitch that most Americans, including Andrea, who were still in the country were afraid to go out. Neither Andrea, nor Helga, had been to Friendship House in ten days. The military escort which helped them earlier to pass through roadblocks when it was impossible for them to do so on their own, was reassigned to more urgent duty.

Helga had another problem to deal with. Her son, who was a student at M.I.T. had returned home unexpectedly and refused to leave. He was concerned for his father's safety and the rapid deterioration of the country. He came to the orphanage frequently when the roads were still open and spent hours playing ball with the children. He was unusually similar to Dariush both in looks and character. In mid November, after miraculously escaping an attempt on his life, he was whisked to an undisclosed destination.

There were two more attempts to assassinate the General. Both were unsuccessful.

On November 26, Sayid came to the apartment determined to put an end to her stubborn refusal. To his surprise, she did not object. "I managed to get in touch with an Iranian school principal," Andrea said. "She'll take over the running of Friendship House in my absence. Helga knows her well and recommends her highly. I talked to her this afternoon. I offered her free board and lodging. She will move in tomorrow."

"That's the best news I've had in a long time. Any more threatening calls?"

"After the last one I stopped answering the phone."

"When was that?"

"About twenty minutes ago."

"I would think Mani would have more important matters to attend to."

"He probably does. He had his mother call me."

Sayid looked at her askance. "How do you know it was her?"

"I recognized her voice and besides who else would call me 'Jende'?"

"That does it. When do you want to leave?"

"I talked to Vartan. He says it's impossible to find space on any airline. Apparently there are hundreds of people at the airport, mostly supporters of the regime who have swarmed the airport and the parking lots. Many haven't left the place for over a week. They're ready to pay any price for a seat on any plane flying out of the country. They don't care where it goes."

"Vartan is right. I've been to every travel agent in town. They are booked solid for months to come. I could not find a ticket, regardless of how much I offered, even on the black market."

"Then how can I leave?"

"We might still have a chance."

"We?"

"I had a meeting with Phil before I came to see you. He wants the General and me to go to Washington. He's being bombarded with conflicting instructions and his intelligence reports are contradicted by those sent by the U.S. Ambassador. There's friction between Phil and the ambassador. With Mullah Hamid's death we lost a valuable source of information. Phil wants us to present the facts to President Carter as they are."

"When does he want you to go?"

"As soon as arrangements can be made. Most probably tomorrow at dawn. We'll take the General's plane. Phil is working right now on making arrangements for you and Helga to fly with us."

"Has Helga been told?"

"Phil discussed the matter with the General and Helga two days ago. He wanted us to fly to the States right away. Helga refused to leave without her son."

"Can't he be reached?"

"We tried. He's gone hunting near the Pakistani border despite strict instructions from his father not to leave the safe house he was in. A search party has been looking for him for two days but they couldn't locate him. We don't have time. We've already lost two days. The General and Phil are very nervous about it. The longer we delay our departure, the more the chances are for something to go wrong."

"But what about her son? Won't he be upset when he learns his father and mother are both gone?"

"Cyrus will not be gone more than a few days and Phil will see to it that his son leaves soon after he returns from his hunting trip."

"Does Helga know about it? Has she agreed?"

"Reluctantly, yes."

"It's amazing how quickly the situation deteriorated. I would have never believed it had I not been a witness myself."

"The General, Phil and I have to meet again tonight. You can't stay here alone and it's easier if we're all together. I'll take you to the Hilton. We'll find a way to get Helga there too without arousing suspicion and if all goes well, we take off before sunrise."

"Let me throw a few things in my suitcase and I'll be ready."

"Forget everything. Take your purse, your toothpaste and toothbrush. If you walk out of here with a suitcase in your hand we probably won't make it to the hotel."

Andrea stared at him in disbelief. She waited for a moment, hoping, for what she did not know, realized it was useless, reached for her purse, went to the bathroom, put her toothpaste and toothbrush in it, and returned. "I'm ready."

He rose and followed her to the door, his head down, his shoulders stooped.

"You mustn't be so upset," she said. "I'm sure this too shall pass and we will be back doing what we do best, work for a world without violence."

He walked over, took her in his arms, kissed her hungrily, clung to her, unwilling to let her go.

The phone rang.

They waited for it to stop.

It rang and rang.

He took her hand and together they walked out the door.

The phone was still ringing.

Helga and Andrea were given a room with two beds. They did not use them. Helga looked nervous, edgy. Andrea had never seen her like that. She said very little. Mostly, she stared into space.

Sayid came at three in the morning. They took the special elevator to a secret parking area in the basement of the hotel. They drove in two separate cars to the airport, without police escort. The movements of the General and Sayid had to be kept top secret until the plane cleared Iranian airspace.

Sayid and Andrea arrived at the airport without incident. Soon the General and Helga joined them in a small room adjacent to the VIP lounge. The General looked disturbed. "Something is wrong," he said pacing restlessly. "Something is terribly wrong. There is supposed to be dusk to dawn curfew, strict orders for all cars traveling during curfew hours to be stopped, searched and the identities of the occupants checked. I did not see a single guard. We were not stopped once. I don't like it."

"Do you want to cancel the trip?" Sayid asked.

The General darted back and forth in the small room and forced his fingers through his thick, curly hair. "Oh, damn," he said through clenched teeth. "What's the use. Let's get on with it."

A small van, with its lights off, crept slowly to the back of the building. The General suggested Helga and Andrea go first. It would give them a chance to observe if the women were being followed.

The women prepared to leave but the General moved between them and the door. "I want to talk to you before you go. Listen very carefully. If for some reason we get separated, or injured or killed, those who survive must not, I repeat must not under any circumstance turn back. Get yourselves inside the aircraft without delay. My pilot has orders to fly immediately if he senses trouble regardless of who is left behind. We don't want martyrs. Do I make myself clear?"

The women looked at him apprehensively, hesitated, walked out, got in the van and the driver took off.

The eerie stillness of the night sent shivers down Andrea's spine. Helga saw her rub her arms. She removed her jacket, put it around Andrea's shoulders and gave her hand a gentle squeeze. They did not speak.

They reached the plane. The engines were running, ready to go.

Helga stepped out first. She cast a quick glance back. "They're coming," she whispered. "They're right behind us."

She climbed the steps to the airplane and without looking back, quickly entered the cabin.

Andrea followed her in a daze, numbed, confused and hurt by the pain men inflicted on men, the terror, the destruction, the anarchy. Brotherhood of men! How could I possibly be so naive, she admonished herself.

She reached the top of the stairs, considered entering the plane without looking back but couldn't help herself. Just as she turned, she caught a glimpse of half a dozen men with machine guns pointed at the airplane. She froze on the spot. She thought she recognized two of the men. One of the men looked like Mani, the other like Farhad. But she wasn't sure. The airfield was dimly lit. She couldn't see well. At that very moment, a woman guard, appeared suddenly from the cockpit, pounced on her, knocked her down on her face and threw herself over her.

Simultaneously, a volley of shots shattered the still night. It sounded like machine guns.

Andrea could hear but could not see. Her face was against the floor of the landing of the stairs with the guard still lying on top of her. She could not move.

Following the first round of shots at least two dozen more shots were fired in quick succession.

Andrea felt curiously calm, even detached. The situation seemed too surreal, too absurd. It was happening to someone else, somewhere else. Then she felt something warm dribbling down her neck and her body independent of her mind was terrified. She tried to pull herself away from the guard's body pinning her down. Surprisingly, the guard did not resist. Her body fell next to Andrea. Andrea raised her head slightly and saw the woman's face. The eyes looking at her pleaded for understanding. That very instant, Andrea lost control of her senses.

Like in a dream, she heard a voice, a familiar voice. "I'm sorry," Layla whimpered. "I'm so very sorry. I tried to phone you . . . last night . . . to warn you. No answer. I rushed . . . apartment. Nobody. Farhad . . . Mani . . . they want to kill the General . . . Sayid. I found the Italian. Dino . . . He . . . he . . . kno . . ."

Blood was gushing from her neck and abdomen where she was shot. She was dead before she could finish her sentence.

Suddenly, bright lights flooded the airfield. The shooting stopped.

Andrea reached for Layla's shoulders, lifted her body, placed it next to hers, her arms wrapped around her. Close by, on the airfield, the General and Sayid had fallen a few yards short of the steps. Further away, the unmistakable figure of Emu sprawled in a pool of blood, his right hand resting on a machine gun. There were six other men. Andrea recognized them all. Mani, Farhad, Bahram and the men who had raped her. They all looked dead.

She saw soldiers in jeeps, machine guns ready, cautiously approach an Iran Air van parked close to where the shootings took place. She saw two hands raised up, then the familiar figure of Dino emerge from behind the van as the soldiers closed in on him. And Andrea understood what Layla had tried to say before she died. Alerted by Layla, single handedly, Dino had wiped out the terrorists and their leader.

Only it was too late.

Dino's eyes wandered toward the airplane, saw Andrea look at him, then in a voice that could be heard a mile away, shouted, "Go home, beautiful. Go home."

The soldiers grabbed him and shoved him in the back of the open jeep. They rode with him, machine guns ready. As they passed the plane, Dino raised his right hand and pointed at the last traces of the moon in the morning sky and yelled, "Think of me when you see a crescent moon."